THE JOHN HARVARD LIBRARY

Bernard Bailyn
Editor-in-Chief

THE JOHN HARVARD LIBRARY

THE
IMPENDING CRISIS
OF THE SOUTH

HOW TO MEET IT

by HINTON ROWAN HELPER

Edited by George M. Fredrickson

THE BELKNAP PRESS OF
HARVARD UNIVERSITY PRESS

Cambridge, Massachusetts

1968

*John Harvard Library books are edited
at the Charles Warren Center for Studies
in American History, Harvard University.*

Library of Congress Catalog Card Number 68-21973
Printed in the United States of America

CONTENTS

INTRODUCTION

INTRODUCTION

I

The Impending Crisis of the South by Hinton
Rowan Helper is one of those rare works which not
only gave direct and vivid expression to an historical situation, but also had a dramatic influence in
shaping events. Indeed, it would not be difficult to
make a case for *The Impending Crisis* as the most
important single book, in terms of its political impact, that has ever been published in the United
States. Even more perhaps than *Uncle Tom's
Cabin*, it fed the fires of sectional controversy leading up to the Civil War; for it had the distinction
of being the only book in American history to become the center of bitter and prolonged Congressional debate.

The work of an obscure North Carolinian who
had migrated to the North, *The Impending Crisis*
was published in New York in 1857 at the author's
own risk. As an attack on slavery, it said very little that had not been said before. But two things

about the book drew the interest of Horace Greeley, influential antislavery editor of the *New York Tribune*. One was the potential effectiveness of the book as an antislavery polemic. It combined, as Greeley put it in a full-page review on the day the book was published, the "heavy artillery of statistics" with "rolling volleys and dashing charges of argument and rhetoric." [1] Secondly, it was written by a Southerner and attacked slavery by appealing to the interests of the non-slaveholding whites of the South. The core of the Republican assault on the extension of slavery into the Western territories was the claim that the South's "peculiar institution" denied to white farmers and workingmen the opportunities for economic and social advancement which were theirs in a society based on free labor. Hoping to appeal not only to the minority of Northerners who were opposed to slavery for clearly defined moral and ideological reasons but also to a majority with more mundane interests, Republicans were seeking ways of emphasizing the argument that slavery was incompatible with the hopes of many for a better life in the new terri-

---

[1] Quoted in Hugh C. Bailey, *Hinton Rowan Helper: Abolitionist Racist* (University, Ala., 1965), p. 42. Bailey's book, the only full-length study of Helper, is an invaluable source of biographical information despite a certain slipshod quality which is manifested in minor factual errors and mispellings of names.

tories. Greeley welcomed the book as a way of demonstrating exactly how slavery could thwart the hopes of the masses for self-improvement. There was one serious difficulty with the book, however— which Greeley as a member of the radical wing of the party did not fully appreciate—it was an avowedly abolitionist book and seemed to conflict with the professed purpose of the Republican Party to leave slavery alone where it was already established under state law.

After its initial publication, the book was promoted by Greeley, praised by the antislavery press, and attacked violently in the South. On March 20, 1858, it was cited in Senate debate by Senator Henry Wilson of Massachusetts as an accurate picture of Southern society and the harmful effects of slavery.[2] But the book did not reach the mass audience to which it was directed until after Helper, with the assistance of Greeley, had circulated an appeal for financial contributions and endorsements from prominent Republicans, for the purpose of distributing an inexpensive compendium, or digest, of *The Impending Crisis*. In July 1859, the *Compendium* was published, with the endorsement of a number of Republican leaders, and plans were quickly developed to distribute this version as a

[2] *Ibid.*, p. 44.

Republican document during the election campaign of 1860.[3] The *Compendium* was a somewhat watered-down version of the original, with some of the inflammatory passages and personal attacks deleted.[4] But the substance of the argument was untouched: slavery was totally incompatible with economic progress and individual opportunity, and should be abolished in the interest of the oppressed non-slaveholding majority of the South.

By December 1859, the demand for the *Compendium* was enormous; the *New York Tribune*, as the main source of distribution, was sending out five hundred copies a day and hoped to increase the number to one thousand.[5] During the same month, Helper's book took the center of the national political stage, as it became a factor in the bitter controversy over the election of a speaker in the House of Representatives. As a result of the Congressional elections of 1858, the Republicans had won a plurality but not a majority in the House. In order to elect a speaker they needed not only

[3] *Ibid.*, pp. 45–55.

[4] For the important passages which were eliminated in the preparation of the *Compendium*, see notes 1, 9, 11, 13, 14, 15, 16, 17, 18, 19, 21, and 22 of Hinton R. Helper, *The Impending Crisis of the South: How to Meet It* (John Harvard Library edition).

[5] Bailey, *Helper*, p. 56.

solid Republican support but also a few votes from
Northern Democrats or members of the American
Party. The Republican candidate was John Sherman of Ohio, one of the endorsers of the *Compendium,* and his name had no sooner been put in
nomination than a Democratic representative from
Missouri presented the following resolution:

> Whereas certain members of this House now in nom-
> ination for Speaker, did endorse and recommend the
> book hereinafter mentioned, Resolved that the doc-
> trines and sentiments of a certain book, purporting to
> have been called "The Impending Crisis of the South
> —How to meet it," written by one Hinton R. Helper,
> are insurrectionary and hostile to the domestic peace
> and tranquillity of the country, and that no member
> of this House who has endorsed and recommended it,
> or the compendium from it, is fit to be Speaker of
> this House.[6]

Sherman found this situation politically embarras-
sing because, like most Republican leaders, he was
unwilling to go all the way and endorse Helper's
abolitionist philosophy. He read into the record a
letter from Francis P. Blair of Maryland indicating
that Helper had been requested to delete some of
the more "objectionable" passages from the original in his preparation of the *Compendium,* and that

[6] *Cong. Globe,* 36 Cong., 1 Sess. I, 3.

it was only on the understanding that this had been done that the book had received Republican endorsement. But, apparently recognizing that the book, however altered, was still an abolitionist tract, Sherman went on to maintain that he had no recollection of endorsing the *Compendium,* that he had never read it, and that, speaking for himself, he was "opposed to any interference whatever of the people of the free states, with the relation of master and slave in the slave states." [7]

This disavowal did not mollify Sherman's opponents, and an intense debate developed that has been seen by historians as the most important rehearsal for the secession crisis that was to follow within a year. Coming in the wake of John Brown's raid, the speakership contest was the product of a deep-seated distrust of the Republicans, emanating not only from the South but from many Northern Democrats and conservatives. It turned out to be the longest speakership battle in American history, lasting almost two months. During the course of the debate Southern representatives demonstrated such a violent antipathy to Sherman that the belief

[7] See John Sherman, *Recollections of Forty Years in the House, Senate, and Cabinet* (Chicago, 1895), I, 170–171; and Oliver Crenshaw, "The Speakership Contest of 1859–1860," *Mississippi Valley Historical Review,* 29 (December 1942), 325.

developed "in some quarters that dissolution of the union might follow Sherman's election." [8] At times violence almost broke out on the floor of the House, and there were proposals from prominent South Carolinians, both inside Congress and out, for Southern withdrawal or efforts to depose Sherman by force should he be elected.[9] The Republicans, recognizing the deadlock which had developed after Sherman had failed in ballot after ballot to win a majority, finally put up a new candidate— Pennington of New Jersey, a recent convert to Republicanism and a non-endorser of the *Compendium*—who was able to win a narrow majority.

The greatest significance of the struggle in terms of what happened subsequently was that it provided new and important ammunition for Southern secessionists in their effort to persuade their more hesitant compatriots that a Republican electoral victory was in itself adequate justification for dissolution of the Union. Southern extremists had been arguing since the formation of the Republican Party that, despite its protestations that it was a "free soil" and not an abolitionist party, it really harbored definite plans to launch an assault on slavery in the Southern states. Republican endorse-

[8] Crenshaw, "Speakership Contest," p. 331.
[9] *Ibid.*, pp. 332–335.

ment of Helper's book seemed to many Southerners incontrovertible evidence that the Republicans were in reality an abolitionist party in the full sense. By the election of 1860, a majority of Southerners, including a large number who did not feel strongly about the territorial question *per se*, had accepted the view that the Republicans were abolitionists and that the election of a Republican President would be equivalent to the triumph of Hinton Rowan Helper. Nothing Republican leaders could say disavowing abolition, nothing they could propose—such as unamendable amendments to the Constitution protecting slavery where it already existed—could allay the fears of even the more conservative and formerly Unionist Southerners once Helperism had been identified with Republicanism. This reaction was intensified by the fact—which secessionists were quick to seize upon—that the original version, as distinguished from the *Compendium,* had suggested violence and even revolution on the part of non-slaveholders, if the slave-owning South should refuse to abolish slavery voluntarily. Nothing, except the specter of slave rebellion—which was also hinted at in the original —was more calculated to arouse the fears of the moderate, heretofore Unionist, planters, who had long resisted the secessionism of the fire-eaters.

Even the call for class-oriented, antislavery political activity of a more conventional kind, which
was what the *Compendium* ended up advocating,
was deeply disquieting to conservative slaveholders,
who now had the sense of sitting on a powder keg to
which the Republicans would light the match if
they got the chance.

Evidence of the importance of the identification
of Helperism and Republicanism in weakening influential opposition to secession can be found in
Southern editorials immediately before and after
the presidential election. On October 11, 1860,
the *Charleston Mercury* argued that the Republicans, once in power, would be able to appeal to a
latent Helperism among Southerners and organize
"an Abolition Party in the South of Southern men."
Under these circumstances, "the contest for slavery
will no longer be one between the North and the
South. It will be in the South, between the people
of the South." [10] This argument had great impact
on those slaveowners whose social conservatism
and fear of disorder had previously expressed itself through the Whig-Unionist politics of sectional
compromise. On the eve of the election, the *New
Orleans Daily Delta* played even more directly on

[10] Dwight L. Dumond, ed., *Southern Editorials on Secession* (New
York and London, 1931), p. 179.

the fears of the dominant class in the South in advocating secession as the proper response to a Republican victory. Pointing to the political leverage the Republicans would gain from having control of federal patronage in the South, the *Delta* asked a disturbing question: "Does anyone suppose that when this Black Republican party is formed in every Southern State, it will be without followers and sympathizers? . . . Even now the arguments of Helper's infamous book have been reproduced in the South. . . . Let us beware of the day when the struggle shall be transferred to our own land; when the slavery question shall cease to be a sectional question and shall become a domestic question; armies of our enemies shall be recruited from our own forces." [11]

The effects of this appeal to conservative fears of Helperite abolitionism and class struggle in the South can be discerned in an editorial which appeared a few days after the election in another New Orleans paper, the *Crescent*, which had supported Bell, the Constitutional Unionist, in the election and had previously attacked militant sectionalism. In justifying a shift from moderation to strong support of secession the *Crescent* placed great emphasis on the belief that Republican control of

[11] *Ibid.*, pp. 202–203 (November 1, 1860).

federal patronage in the South would "build up an abolition party in our midst." [12]

Helper's book and the controversy to which it gave rise did not by itself cause secession. But as one important factor in converting the South to the view that the Republicans were committed to subverting the slave system in the South, it provides part of the explanation as to why the South found the election of Lincoln intolerable and seceded without allowing the Republicans to take office and show their true character. As it was, there was an important minority in every state of the lower South except South Carolina which opposed single state secession and argued that the South should wait for an overt act or the response of a Republican administration to a Southern ultimatum before dissolving the Union. Without Hinton Rowan Helper's *Impending Crisis* and Republican endorsement of it, that minority might have been a majority.

II

The historical impact of *The Impending Crisis* is somewhat easier to understand than the nature of the intelligence that produced it. What made a

[12] *Ibid.*, p. 240 (November 15, 1860).

native of the South like Hinton Rowan Helper turn
with such vehemence against the dominant thought
of his own section? To attempt to determine how
and why Helper became a dissenter, it is necessary
to turn to a rather meager body of information
about his early life.[13] These data, when combined
with a close reading of Helper's works, can provide some clues to the mind and personality of
the man whose writing agitated a nation.

Hinton Rowan Helper was born in Rowan
County, North Carolina, on December 27, 1829,
the son of a yeoman farmer of German descent.[14]
He came, therefore, from an area and an ethnic
group more likely to produce dissent on the slavery
question than most others in the South. The Germans in North Carolina, as elsewhere in the South,
had not taken readily to slaveholding. In the colonial period, North Carolina Germans had demonstrated a strong "preference for free labor." [15] By

---

[13] There is no known collection of Helper papers and only a few
Helper letters have turned up in the papers of Helper's cor-
respondents.

[14] For information on Helper's early life, see Bailey, *Helper*,
chap. 1; and Hugh T. Lefler, *Hinton Rowan Helper: Advocate
of a White America* (Charlottesville, 1935), pp. 30–34. A short
autobiographical sketch appears in Helper's *Nojoque; A Question for a Continent* (New York, 1867), pp. 11–13.

[15] William Herman Gehrke, "Negro Slavery among the Germans
of North Carolina," *North Carolina Historical Review*, 14
(October 1937), 308.

the early nineteenth century, they had weakened somewhat in their resolve not to hold slaves, but had retained doubts about the institution—doubts which seem to have been rooted in practical, economic considerations. They continued to ask whether or not slavery was compatible with the traditions of diversified agriculture and prosperous self-sufficiency which their German forefathers had brought with them to America.[16] It was thus no accident that Germans played a major role in the diminishing opposition to slavery in ante-bellum North Carolina. In 1840, a North Carolina representative of German extraction, Thomas L. Clingman, was the only representative from the Southern states to vote for repeal of "the gag rule," a restriction which prevented Congress from receiving antislavery petitions. By the 1850's, public opinion had silenced most antislavery sentiment in the state, but of the half-dozen North Carolinians who spoke up publicly and unequivocally against "the peculiar institution," three were Germans.[17]

If Helper derived a bias against slavery from

---

[16] *Ibid.*, pp. 317–318. For information on the agricultural tradition which made the Germans reluctant to adopt slavery and the staple system, see Richard H. Shryock, "British versus German Traditions in Colonial Agriculture," *Mississippi Valley Historical Review*, 26 (1939–1940), 319–324.

[17] Gehrke, "Negro Slavery," p. 308.

his German ancestry, he also came from a part of North Carolina in which slavery had not taken deep root and where attachment to the institution was not as strong as in other areas of the state. As late as 1860 in Rowan County, only one planter in a population of 14,589 owned one hundred slaves or more, and only thirty-seven owned more than twenty. The bulk of the white population were yeomen, and Rowan County was in most respects quite similar to other parts of the Southern back-country which were geographically and socially remote from the great plantation regions. But positive resistance to slavery was stronger in Rowan County than in most similar areas, not only because of the large German population, but also because there were a substantial number of Quakers.[18]

When Helper was nine months old his father died, leaving the family in poverty. Of his childhood, we know almost nothing except the fact that he somehow managed to attend the well-known Mocksville Academy, which was within walking distance of his home. Here he obtained the literary and historical education which enabled him to become a writer. After graduating from Mocksville, Helper

[18] Bailey, *Helper*, p. 4. See also Jethro Rumple, *A History of Rowan County* (Salisbury, N.C., 1881), pp. 251–255.

was apprenticed to a Salisbury, North Carolina, storekeeper. In 1850, at the end of his indenture, Helper migrated to New York City to seek his fortune, taking with him some money that he had stolen from his employer over a period of years but which he went out of his way to repay a few months later, despite the fact that the shortage had never been noticed. This curious mixture of dishonesty and high principle (he had resolved all along to pay the money back) was characteristic of Helper and would be demonstrated in more subtle ways in his later career. Unable to get employment in New York, Helper contracted gold fever and determined to go to California with the hope of making a quick fortune. Having failed as a storekeeper and as a young man making his way in the city, he now failed, inevitably, as a gold prospector, and, after two and one-half years of frustration, returned East.

Even this very sketchy picture of Helper's early career reveals the familiar American pattern of the ambitious young man with grandiose dreams of success whose every effort ends in failure and humiliation. But at this point Helper did the unexpected: instead of trying something entirely new, he decided to capitalize on his failure in the West by writing a sensational book, discouraging migration to California by exposing its promise of wealth and happiness as a fraud. The result was *The Land of Gold* published in 1855. Having failed to get rich as the promoters of California had promised, he became that curious reversal of a prevalent American type, the anti-promoter. Using the same kinds of half-truths—exaggerations characteristic of promotional literature—the anti-promoter seeks to destroy the image the promoters have created. Becoming a professional debunker was Helper's way of relieving his frustrations and of charting a new career for himself as a popular writer. It is possible that his later decision to expose the South as an economic wasteland was a similar action. Believing that the South, like California, denied him the possibility of personal success, he expressed his bitterness by turning against it the same kinds of statistical and rhetorical devices that were being used by promoters of Southern progress to create the illusion of opportunity and prosperity. He became a J.D.B. De Bow in reverse.[19] To some extent, then, Helper was a man who excused personal failure and compensated for it by showing that economic failure was characteristic of an entire region that denied him access to its wealth.

---

[19] See note 3, *Impending Crisis,* for a brief description of the career and significance of J. D. B. De Bow.

This is not to say that his argument was invalid. It is merely to suggest that he may have been less a reformer by instinct than a man whose original ambitions had soured.

Leaving it at that, however, would oversimplify Helper's mentality. He was somehow both a frustrated opportunist and a man who held deep, even fanatical, convictions about some subjects. If he had his eye on the main chance, he also believed that there were certain truths which needed to be asserted regardless of the consequences. These deep and rigid convictions, which were the foundation of Helper's intellectual life, come through strongly in *The Land of Gold* and were to reappear in a variety of forms in all his subsequent writings, including *The Impending Crisis*.

The Land of Gold professes to tell "the truth" about California by exposing "its rottenness and its corruption, its squalor and its misery, its crime and its shame, its gold and its dross." [20] Much of the book is a description of the moral laxity, lawlessness, primitive living conditions, and poverty which Helper found characteristic of California. Playing his role of anti-promoter to the limit, Helper even attacks the climate. It is clear, however, that the single thing that disturbs him most

[20] *The Land of Gold: Reality versus Fiction* (Baltimore, 1855) p. vi.

about California is the racially mixed nature of the population. The crowd on the waterfront in San Francisco strikes him as "one of the most motley and heterogeneous that ever occupied space." He lists the various races present and concludes that one is confronted with "a complete human menagerie." [21] Commenting generally on the racial and cultural heterogeneity of the population he maintains that "its ingredients cannot be compounded into a harmonious, perfect, and complete whole." [22] The Chinese receive a great deal of attention and are labelled "semi-barbarians" whose immigration ought to be resisted.[23] He finds the Mexicans, the Negroes, and the Indians (who are "filthy and abominable") equally objectionable and concludes his discussion of the Chinese with a classic statement of a generalized American racism:

> No inferior race of men can exist in these United States without becoming subordinate to the will of the Anglo-Americans, or foregoing many of the necessaries and comforts of life. They must either be our equals or our dependents. It is so with the negroes in the South; it is so with the Irish in the North, it was so with the Indians of New England, and it will be so with the

[21] *Ibid.*, p. 47.
[22] *Ibid.*, p. 39.
[23] *Ibid.*, pp. 92–94.

Chinese in California. The Indians, it is true would
not submit to be enslaved, but they had to suffer exile,
hunger, and death as a consequence of their intracta-
bility. Certain it is, that the greater the diversity of
colors and qualities of men, the greater will be the
strife and conflict of feeling. One party will gain the
ascendency, and dominate over the other. Our population was already too heterogeneous before the Chinese
came; but now another adventitious element has been
added; and I should not wonder at all, if the copper
of the Pacific yet becomes as great a subject of discord
and dissension as the ebony of the Atlantic.[24]

In this defense of "Anglo-American" supremacy,
Helper revealed the racism that was to be the
ruling passion of his life. And it is apparent in
The Land of Gold that his antipathy to non-white
races had its roots in a feeling of intense discom-
fort when faced with any form of racial and cultural heterogeneity. He was also strongly anti-
Catholic and would probably have limited heaven
itself, had he been given the power, to white Anglo-
Saxon or Teutonic Protestants. That his bigotry
had an economic dimension is indicated in his
suggestions that racial and cultural heterogeneity
is one factor holding back California's economic
development and making it harder for men like
himself to succeed. His prescription for California's

[24] *Ibid.*, p. 96.

ills is restriction of Chinese immigration and the subordination of those already there, along with the building of a transcontinental railroad to expose California more directly to salutary influences.

Because of the antislavery nature of his next book, *The Impending Crisis,* Helper's passing comments on the Negro and slavery in *The Land of Gold* deserve close attention. Observing the Negroes in California, he notes that "like free Negroes everywhere else, they inhabit the worst parts of the towns . . . and live commonly in characteristic filth and degradation." The few slaves who have accompanied their owners to the West are ridiculed for a childlike devotion to their masters which prevents them from responding to the enticements of abolitionists and claiming their freedom in a free state. Some, he indicates, fall victim to abolitionist blandishments and have a try at being free men, "but, disgusted with a freedom that was of no value to them, they have been eager to return again to their masters." He then tells the story of a slave whose master attempted to force freedom upon him as a punishment for running away, but "the negro dropped with despair at his master's feet and wept like a child," at which the master relented and agreed to take him back.[25] Helper's

[25] *Ibid.,* pp. 275–278.

description of the Negro slave in *The Land of Gold* is close to the conventional proslavery image of the contented bondsman. But there is a note of disdain and disgust which is at odds with the sentimentality and condescending affection which characterized most Southern portrayals of the slave as faithful retainer.

At one point in *The Land of Gold*, Helper gives some suggestion of his views on the ultimate destiny of the Negro. In describing Nicaragua, which he visited on his return voyage from California, he maintains that this undeveloped country, in stark distinction to the South of *The Impending Crisis*, "can never fulfill its destiny until it introduces negro slavery. Nothing but slave labor can ever subdue its forests or cultivate its untimbered lands." The heat, he argues, prevents white men from doing the heavy labor that is required.

> The time may come when negro slavery will no longer be profitable in the United States, and it is possible that the sons of Ham may finally work their way beyond the present limits of our country. But if these fated people ever do make their exodus from the hands of their present owners, they will find themselves journeying and toiling under the control of new masters, in the fertile wildernesses and savannas nearer the equator. . . . if negro slavery ever ceases to exist in the United States, Mexico, Central America, and the

countries still further South will have to become its outlets and receptacles.[26]

III

The references to slavery in *The Land of Gold* seem on the surface to conflict with the antislavery doctrine of *The Impending Crisis,* which was published only two years later. Helper subsequently maintained, however, that the original draft of *The Land of Gold* had contained some mildly antislavery passages. On the theory that city life required capital and talent, and the Negro had neither, Helper had argued that slavery should be limited to rural regions. These passages were deleted, he recalled, on the insistence of his proslavery Baltimore publisher.[27] But Helper was responsible for the passages that were included, and they raise the question of how much, if at all, his ideas on race and slavery changed between the writing of *The Land of Gold* and the writing of *The Impending Crisis.*

A close reading of *The Impending Crisis* reveals that there is no essential contradiction between the two books, although there are differences in emphasis. In the later work, as in the earlier, Helper reveals his hostility to the Negro as a racial type.

[26] *Ibid.,* pp. 221–222.
[27] Bailey, *Helper,* pp. 16–17.

As he puts it in *The Impending Crisis,* "the Negroes, when viewed through their actual characteristics and condition, as through the strong antipathies of the whites, are to say the least, an undesirable population." After advocating colonization of the Negro in Africa as an essential part of the emancipation process, he gives vent to his own preferences in the matter: "if we had the power we would ship them all within the next six months." It is clear then that for Helper abolition of slavery also means the elimination of the Negro and that the second objective vies with the first in importance.[28]

It is even possible to reconcile Helper's assertion in *The Land of Gold* that slavery has a future in tropical America with the antislavery philosophy of *The Impending Crisis.* In attacking the proslavery argument that Negro servitude is necessary in the South because the heat makes it impossible for white men to engage in physical labor, he argues that "instead of its being too hot in the South for white men, it is too cold for negroes, and we long to see the day arrive when the latter shall have entirely receded from their uncongenial homes in America and given full and undivided place to the former." [29] The implication is clear: if the South

[28] Pp. 97, 182.
[29] P. 299.

were indeed too hot for white labor, slavery might be justified. Hence, despite the fact that *The Impending Crisis* recommends African colonization as its plan for Negro removal, the main argument is not incompatible with tropical slavery. It is less an argument against slavery *per se* than an argument against slavery in temperate regions.

In his stress on climatic regions as defining the appropriate habitations for the various races of men, Helper was in accord with the "scientific" racism of the day, as promulgated by Louis Agassiz, Josiah Nott, and others. But there was a substantial debate among racists themselves, as to whether or not the United States was really an appropriate region for Negro labor. Helper and other antislavery or "free soil" racists argued from the theory that all, or most of it, was not; the proslavery racists of course maintained the contrary. The clearest indication of Helper's acceptance of the scientific racism that influenced both sides of the debate on slavery in the 1850's and which would be the basis for his later anti-Negro writings, can be seen in his attack on those who took the doctrine of "the types of mankind" as a justification of slavery. The "American School of Ethnology," headed by scientists like Nott, George

Gliddon, and Samuel G. Morton, had maintained that the Negro race was not descended from Adam and Eve, but had been separately created as a distinct and permanently inferior species.[30] Showing his general agreement with the views of this school, Helper acknowledges that he does "not believe in the unity of the races." He goes on, however, to argue that this is no justification of slavery, because the real issue is slavery as "an impediment to progress." [31] Since he was writing primarily for a Northern antislavery audience, which he was afraid did not fully share his racial beliefs, he did not go all the way and turn the tables on the proslavery racists by maintaining that the Negro, under any system of labor, was an impediment to white progress in temperate regions; but this is clearly what he believed.

This reluctance to spell out his racial beliefs in full would suggest that Helper deliberately kept his anti-Negro sentiments somewhat under wraps in *The Impending Crisis*. They came out sufficiently to show that they still held sway, but he did not

[30] For an excellent study of the racial theories of "the American School of Ethnology," see William Stanton, *The Leopard's Spots: Scientific Attitudes toward Race, 1815–1859* (Chicago, 1960).

[31] *Impending Crisis*, p. 184.

insist upon them. In comparison with *The Land of Gold* and his later anti-Negro books, his strictures on the Negro race seem relatively mild. This would seem to be another case of Helper's principled dishonesty or opportunistic militancy. As his subsequent efforts to promote his book as a Republican campaign document would suggest, Helper the opportunist, the man in search of fame, fortune, and recognition, sought to capitalize on the antislavery sentiment of the North. And like many Southerners, Helper undoubtedly had preconceived notions about Northern racial attitudes that made it seem advisable to tone down his anti-Negro opinions. But the fact that there would be no objection in the North to the racist note that was cautiously but unmistakably sounded indicates that Helper might have underestimated Northern Negrophobia.

Most of *The Impending Crisis* is of course not directly concerned with race at all, but with the incompatibility of slavery and economic progress. But as *The Land of Gold* had clearly revealed, there was a substratum in Helper's thinking which identified racial homogeneity, "democratic" society, and general prosperity. It is only when we realize that race, republicanism, and the gospel of opportunity were indissolubly linked in Helper's

thinking that we can fully understand the intellectual basis of *The Impending Crisis*.

In moving from the muted racism of *The Impending Crisis* to its overt attack on slavery as a
barrier to economic progress, we come to the real
strength of the book—an argument that was exaggerated but essentially valid. Despite all its ex-
cesses of rhetoric and misleading statistics, *The
Impending Crisis* presents a strong economic case
against slavery. It does so, to put the matter simply,
by comparing Southern backwardness and poverty
to Northern prosperity and economic growth and
then attributing the differences to slavery. In making his statistical comparisons, Helper was guilty
of a number of distortions, such as his claim that
the hay crop of the North was of greater value
than the sum total of all the great Southern staples,
and he suppressed economic facts favorable to the
South, such as the importance of the cotton export
trade to the national economy, providing, as it did,
the principal basis of American foreign exchange.
But in arguing that slavery impeded Southern
economic development, he was on firm ground.
Despite more than a century of subsequent argument over the profitability of slavery, there has
been no serious challenge to Helper's theory that
slavery was an important factor in putting a low

ceiling on the prosperity of the mass of the Southern population.[32] Whether or not slavery returned a satisfactory profit to the slaveowner—there has been much contention on this point—it is undeniable that it seriously limited the capital available for the investment in enterprises other than staple agriculture based on slave labor. Whether Southerners invested in slaves and plantations for rational economic reasons or to indulge their taste for an aristocratic way of life, they denied to capitalists, manufacturers, and even those interested in mixed farming based on free labor the resources they needed to give the South a diversified and balanced economy. The result, as Helper pointed out, was economic colonialism to the North, with the South paying a premium for manufactured goods, commercial services, and transportation facilities that they should have provided for themselves. The existence of this colonial relation, which denied the South its fair share of the national wealth, had long been stressed by Southern sectionalists in their efforts to develop a sense of grievance against the North. But in attributing

[32] The most recent study which concerns itself with the economic impact of slavery, Eugene Genovese's, *The Political Economy of Slavery* (New York, 1965), reaches conclusions similar to Helper's.

Southern backwardness solely to Northern economic policies, especially the protective tariff, they were less perceptive than Helper, who maintained that the disparity came from basic differences in economic and social organization, differences rooted in slavery.

It was a short step from this kind of analysis to the argument that the non-slaveholding majority in the South not only lacked an economic stake in the slave system but was actually held back by it. The revolutionary edge of Helper's argument came from its contention that the non-slaveholders could emerge from poverty only through the abolition of slavery. With the overthrow of the slaveholding class, the poor man of the South would have a chance to succeed as a farmer, mechanic, or merchant.

Because he argued along these lines, Helper has been described by historians as a spokesman for the Southern yeomanry. Hugh C. Bailey in his study of Helper describes him as a precursor of later Southern agrarian radicals like Ben Tillman, Cole Blease, and Huey Long. He was, Bailey tells us, a "Southern yeoman," interested in the deliverance of "his people." [33] But this theory is an overly simple one which is subject to important

[33] *Helper*, pp. 29, 81.

modifications. In discussing the capitalist class of the Old South, Eugene Genovese has argued that the genuine class interest of Southern manufacturers and businessmen should have led them to endorse Helper's position. That they did not do so is presented as evidence of the degree to which they were dominated by the planter ethos.[34] Whatever the full merit of such Marxist theorizing about the real but unexpressed interests of classes, it does force reconsideration of Helper's place in the real or potential struggle between groups and classes in the South. As we have seen, Helper had emerged from the class of small farmers, but his first ambition had been to be a merchant and his second had been to "strike it rich quick." These were hardly agrarian aspirations as they are usually understood. In his politics, he identified early in life with the party of commerce and industry. Before becoming a Republican, he indicated in one of his later books, he "was always a Whig of the school of Clay and Webster." [35]

The most strikng evidence that Helper was, to a great extent, an unrecognized and unacknowledged spokesman for an embryonic capitalist class, and consequently outside of the Southern agrarian

[34] *Political Economy*, chap. viii.
[35] *The Negroes in Negroland* (New York, 1868), p. vii.

tradition, comes directly from *The Impending Crisis*. That the book was a capitalist tract was recognized by some observers at the time. The *London Daily News* in its review of the book described it as advocating "a thorough reform in the labor system and *renovation of the fortunes of the capitalists*." [36] That Helper's real social ideal was the successful capitalist, rather than the moderately prosperous independent yeoman, is revealed in his fulsome praise for Abbott Lawrence, the New England cotton manufacturer who at one point allegedly contemplated putting up mills in Virginia. Although Lawrence demonstrated "a shrewdness that will command the admiration of every practical businessman," and an interest in "nothing that did not swell the dimensions of his own purse," he was a "genuine philanthropist" who was "always solicitous to invest his capital in a manner calculated to promote the interest of those around him." Spurned by the slaveholding South, he kept his money in New England "and there employed his capital in building up the cities of Lowell and Lawrence, either of which, in all those elements of material and social prosperity that makes up the greatness of States, is already far in advance of all

[36] Quoted in Gehrke, "Negro Slavery," p. 322. The italics are mine.

the seedy and squalid niggervilles in the Old Dominion." [37]

Elsewhere in *The Impending Crisis*, Helper indicates that his interest in the yeomanry and "poor
whites" is not so much in turning them into prosperous farmers as in making them a source of labor
for future Southern factories. Like Cassius M.
Clay, the Kentucky abolitionist, Helper was more a
spokesman for commerce and industry than for a
healthy agriculture based on small holdings. The
best indication of how far Helper departed from
the yeoman-oriented tradition of Southern agrarian
thought—the "Jeffersonian tradition"—comes in
his hymn of praise to the combination of commerce
and large cities and his assertion that the key to
Southern prosperity lies in urbanization. "In this
age of the world," he writes, "commerce is an indispensable element of national greatness. Without
commerce we can have no great cities, and without
great cities we can have no reliable tenure of distinct nationality. Commerce is the forerunner of
wealth and population . . ." As for the South, its
greatest need, he contends, is "a great Southern
importing, exporting, and manufacturing city." [38]

As the promoter of a capitalist South, therefore,

[37] *Impending Crisis*, pp. 107, 108.
[38] *Ibid.*, pp. 348, 331.

Helper was more the precursor of Henry W. Grady and the postwar advocates, of "a New South," than he was of the Populists and agrarian radicals who opposed them. As a matter of fact, he anticipated the "New South" creed in almost every respect. Grady and his followers were to accept Helper's argument that slavery was economically regressive by arguing that emancipation had been a godsend which had released economic energies heretofore stifled by slavery. Like Helper, they would welcome Northern capital and see employment in manufacturing as the salvation of the poor whites.[39] Helper of course would be a prophet unrecognized in his own land. The New South, because it was forced to pay sentimental homage to the Old South, would be in no position to deify a thoroughgoing enemy of the *ancien regime*.

IV

If Helper's place in Southern intellectual history has been misunderstood, so has his relationship to the general development of American antislavery thought. It has long been recognized that Helper was the heir to a Southern antislavery tradi-

[39] The best treatment of the proponents of "the New South" is in C. Vann Woodward's *Origins of the New South* (Baton Rouge, 1951).

tion. His principal economic arguments and un-
friendly attitude toward the Negro were anticipated
by a number of earlier Southern dissenters. His
fellow North Carolinian, Daniel Goodloe, for example, published a pamphlet in 1846 which advocated emancipation as a cure for the economic
retardation of the South.[40] Lacking the impassioned
rhetoric and revolutionary overtones of *The Impending Crisis,* Goodloe's pamphlet relied heavily
on sectional comparison to make a similar case
against slavery. Other important economic critics
of slavery who anticipated Helper in the South
were Henry Ruffner of Virginia and Cassius M.
Clay of Kentucky.[41] Clay, the most prominent abolitionist who remained in the slave states during the
1840's and '50's, bears a striking resemblance to
Helper in his basic attitudes. More provincial in
his approach than the North Carolinian, Clay centered his attention on the single state of Kentucky
which he dreamed of converting into a great manufacturing region through the gradual abolition of
slavery. Like Helper, he was a Negrophobe with

[40] *Inquiry into the Causes Which Have Retarded the Accumulation of Wealth and Increase of Population in the Southern
States* (Washington, 1846).

[41] See Kenneth Stampp, "The Southern Refutation of the Pro-
slavery Argument," *North Carolina Historical Review,* 21 (January 1944), 35–45.

no interest in the welfare of the slave. His emancipation scheme would have allowed Kentucky slaveholders to increase their liquid capital by selling
their slaves farther South before the completion of
the emancipation process.[42] "I have studied the
Negro character," Clay wrote. "They lack self-
reliance—we can make nothing out of them. God
has made them for the sun and the banana." [43]

In locating Helper within this provincial tradition of Southern self-criticism, Kenneth Stampp
and Clement Eaton have both implied that *The
Impending Crisis* bears only a peripheral relationship to the main current of antislavery thought as
it developed nationally.[44] This conclusion is valid
if attention is limited to the efforts of abolitionists
like William Lloyd Garrison, Wendell Phillips,
Theodore Weld, and James G. Birney. But by the
1850's, opposition to slavery in the North had en-
larged its base and taken on a new character. The
"free soil" movement, although not avowedly abolitionist, was, in the broad sense of the word, antislavery, and Helper's arguments, including his
racism, can be seen as compatible with the free soil

[42] Daniel L. Smiley, *Lion of White Hall: The Life of Cassius M.
Clay* (Madison, 1962), *passim*.
[43] Quoted, *ibid.*, pp. 56–57.
[44] See Stampp, "Southern Refutation," pp. 44–45; and Clement
Eaton, *The Mind of the Old South* (Baton Rouge, 1964), p. 135.

consciousness. It is, in fact, only by recognizing
Helper's centrality in the broadened antislavery
impulse of the 1850's that we can explain both the
general popularity of his book in the North and the
fact that it was endorsed and distributed by prominent Republicans.

Helper of course was concerned with getting rid
of Southern slavery, and the "free soilers," for constitutional and political reasons, limited their immediate objections to the extension of slavery to the
territories. In the preparation of the *Compendium*,
these differences became apparent, and Helper was
prevailed upon to delete a passage explicitly critical
of the free soilers for not going far enough. It is
worthy of note, however, that Helper's plan of
gradual emancipation did not technically violate
the constitutional scruples of the moderate Northern opponents of slavery; for it advocated abolition in the South by individual state action rather
than by some use of federal authority.

The intellectual basis of mainstream Northern
opposition to slavery in the 1850's is badly in need
of extended reevaluation. The belief that the North
was being overwhelmed by humanitarian and egali-
tarian sentiments emanating from the early abolitionists is no longer tenable. When we notice what
was actually being said and advocated by influen-

tial Northern opponents of slavery in the 1850's, we come to realize that Helper's mixture of racism and economic Whiggery was not an unusual form for the antislavery argument to take. Abraham Lincoln's relatively mild racism in a framework of liberal economics is well known. Less recognized is the more blatant vision of a prosperous white America in which the Negro has no place which was promulgated by William H. Seward, the leading figure in the Republican party before the nomination of Lincoln in 1860. In 1858, in attacking the proslavery Lecompton constitution of Kansas, Seward said: "The interest of the white man demands the ultimate emancipation of all men. . . . The white man needs this continent to labor upon." [45] Where this left the Negro was revealed in a Republican campaign speech delivered by Seward in Detroit in September 1860: "The great fact is now fully realized that the African race here is a foreign and feeble element, like the Indians incapable of assimilation . . . and it is a pitiful exotic unnecessarily transplanted into our fields, and which it is unprofitable to cultivate at the cost of the desolation of the native vineyard." [46]

[45] *Cong. Globe*, 35 Cong., 2 Sess., I, 944.
[46] *The Works of William H. Seward*, ed. George E. Baker (Boston, 1884), IV, 317.

The closeness of Helper's racial beliefs to those of influential Northern critics of slavery is further demonstrated by comparing *The Impending Crisis* to George M. Weston's important free soil tract, *The Progress of Slavery in the United States,* which was published in the same year. Weston argued that Northern population was growing rapidly and that "white artisans and farmers" were destined not only to expand into the territories but to carry a civilization based on free labor into the South itself. This expansion of "freedom" would result not only from the economic superiority of free labor—upon which Weston like Helper puts a good deal of emphasis—but was also a natural consequence of the competitive superiority of the white race over the Negro in temperate regions. The future of the Negro in the United States is clear; he "will disappear, perhaps to regions more congenial to him, perhaps to regions where his labors can be made more useful, perhaps by some process of colonization which charity may yet devise; but at all events he will disappear." [47] Such views on the manifest destiny of the white race to become sole occupants of the North American continent were frequently expressed by Northern op-

---

[47] *The Progress of Slavery in the United States* (Washington, D.C., 1857), p. 33.

ponents of slavery. They were endorsed not only
by politicians and publicists, but by clergymen
like Horace Bushnell.[48] Even a humanitarian radical like Theodore Parker was convinced of the
pronounced inferiority of the Negro, and had a
grand vision of a Western hemisphere that was
entirely Anglo-Saxon.[49]

Nor was Helper's advocacy of colonization an
anomaly in the antislavery circles of the 1850's.
Both Henry Ward Beecher, one of the leading antislavery preachers, and his even more famous sister,
Harriet Beecher Stowe, author of *Uncle Tom's
Cabin*, believed in colonization as the ultimate solution of the race problem.[50] In the late 1850's, Frank
P. Blair, Republican politician from Missouri, introduced congressional legislation to subsidize Negro colonization in Central America. Negro inferiority, he argued, did not justify slavery, but was
rather "a conclusive argument against blending the
two races then in the same community, to deteri-
orate the superior by admixture or contact with

[48] See Horace Bushnell, *The Census and Slavery* (Hartford, 1860).
[49] See Theodore Parker, "The Condition of America," Address of
    May 12, 1854, *Collected Works*, ed. Francis Cobbe (London,
    1863), V, 328.
[50] Henry Ward Beecher, "American Slavery," Sermon of May 15,
    1851, in *Patriotic Addresses*, ed. J. R. Howard (New York,
    1888), p. 186; Mrs. Stowe's advocacy of colonization is obvious
    from several passages in *Uncle Tom's Cabin*.

the inferior races. . . ." His solution, he pointed
out, was in accordance with the doctrine that "the
marked distinctions between the races indicate
[an] adaptability to various climates of our earth,
as plainly and conclusively as the vegetable life of
each zone proclaims the climate which produced
it. . . . the races are made for or by the climate
in which they dwell and like the flora and fauna
of a land, will flourish only in a congenial climate." [51] Hence the Negro belonged in the tropics
and not in the United States. Blair's project, and
presumably some of the reasoning behind it, was
endorsed not only by prominent Republicans but
also by such antislavery radicals as Gerrit Smith
and Theodore Parker.[52]

One can only conclude, then, that Helper's opposition to slavery on racist grounds was not anom-
alous or exotic but was fully in tune with much
of the Northern antislavery sentiment of the 1850's.

V

After the furor over *The Impending Crisis* had
died down, Helper embarked on a career as a
fanatical racist and anti-Negro writer. In 1861, he

[51] *The Destiny of the Races of This Continent* (Washington, D.C.,
1859), p. 4.
[52] *Ibid.*, pp. 29–33.

sought a reward for his services to the now triumphant Republican Party by requesting a consular
post, the sort of position which he hoped would
provide an opportunity to write his next major
book—a plea for the expulsion of the Negro from
the United States.[53] In a letter of that year, he
summed up his philosophy: "A trio of unmitigated
and demoralizing nuisances, constituting in the aggregate, a most foul and formidable obstacle to
our high and mighty civilization in America are
Negroes, Slavery, and Slaveholders. . . .

Death to Slavery!
Down with the Slaveholders!
Away with the Negroes!"[54]

Having done justice to the first two imperatives
in *The Impending Crisis,* Helper turned to the
third. But as American Consul in Buenos Aires
during the war years, he apparently found that
the exigencies of wartime diplomacy did not give
him much time to write, and it was not until 1867,
shortly after his return from South America, that
he was able to publish *Nojoque; A Question for a
Continent. Nojoque* may be the most virulent racist
diatribe ever published in the United States. It

[53] Bailey, *Helper,* p. 113.
[54] Letter to "W," June 5, 1861, printed in *Nojoque,* pp. 252–253.

contemplates with relish the impending extermination of not only the Negro but all non-white races. The general flavor of the book is suggested by passages like the following:

> America and all the other continents and islands, for white men! Erebus for the negroes! Limbo for the mulattoes! Hades for the Chinese! and Tophet for all the other swarthy and copper-colored ghouls!
>
> . . . .
>
> at least *one million* of negroes have perished in the South since the dawn of the present decade! Verily, "the lord gave, and the lord hath taken away; blessed be the name of the Lord"—and more especially so in all cases of this kind—for taking away! [55]

Helper's view of the millennium is the time when "the negroes, and all the other swarthy races of mankind" have been "completely fossilized." Then, in a lily-white world, "all will be well; unexampled peace, plenty and prosperity shall every where be the established order of things; and in a single word, the long-talked-of and superlatively good time will come at last." [56]

To speed up the divinely-ordained process of racial extermination, Helper proposed as immediate steps the denial of all rights to Negroes and

[55] *Ibid.*, pp. 207, 236.
[56] *Ibid.*, pp. 298–299.

their complete separation from the whites. Once
they had been removed from the cities and settled
on reservations, plans could be made for their expulsion from the territory of the United States.
Under such a policy, the Negro would go the way
of the Indian, who was widely believed at the time
to be headed for early "fossilization." [57]

All this of course went in the teeth of the emerg-
ing Reconstruction policies of Helper's own party,
and throughout the book he excoriates the "Black
Republicans" for being untrue to their prewar racial attitudes. His heroes are "White Republicans"
like Secretary of State Seward and those Republicans in the House and Senate who had remained
loyal to President Johnson and had joined the
Democrats in efforts to prevent federal action on
behalf of Negro equality.

There is no escaping the sense that *Nojoque* is
the product of an unbalanced mind. Helper's racism was so extreme that it cannot be explained
simply in terms of the conventional anti-Negro sentiment which was widespread during this period.
We know too little about Helper's life to gain
much insight into the most personal roots of his
mania; but there are hints in *Nojoque* and his other
anti-Negro writing which show that his extreme

[57] *Ibid.*, chap. v.

revulsion to Negroes was an exaggerated form of a characteristic reaction of Southern non-slavehold-ing whites—a jealousy of the prerogatives of both the aristocracy and their Negro retainers which expressed itself defensively in a violent disgust at the kind of intimacy that existed between the races on the plantation or in the wealthy urban house-hold. Looked at from this perspective, Helper's combination of extreme racism and opposition to slavery becomes more comprehensible.

There is no doubt that Helper was obsessed with what he regarded as the obscenity of close personal relationships between whites and negroes, even under a system of absolute white dominance. Too prudish to face directly the question of interracial sexual relations, he centered his disgust on the nursing of white infants by Negro slaves or ser-vants. One of the epithets he had directed at the Southern Democrat in *The Impending Crisis* was that he was "a negro-nursed adherent of modern, miscalled democracy." Every Southern "gentle-men" who fought a duel, he continued, was "an abandoned wretch, sucked in the corrupt milk of slavery from the breasts of his father's sable con-cubines." [58] In *Nojoque*, he returns obliquely to the theme of interracial breastfeeding in asking, "Does

[58] P. 169.

there flow, did there ever flow, from the breast of
the negro, even so much as a tea-spoonful of the
Milk of Human Kindness?" And in one of the
oddest passages in the book, he makes it clear that
he himself was not nursed by a Negro. In describing his early life, he recalls that his mother's breast
was "a source of sweet solace and sustenance, which
his elder brothers banteringly allege he did not
desert until he was at least six years of age!" [59]
Yet he also insists on this same page that the family owned four slaves, two of whom were apparently female, a dubious claim for which there
is no other evidence.[60] Why should Helper claim
that the family owned slaves and then emphasize
that he was not, as might normally have been the
case, nursed by one? One suspects a peculiar am-
bivalence here—a suppressed envy of the aristocracy with its prerogative of having close contact
with Negroes, being mastered by an overt revulsion against all intimacy with non-whites.

Elsewhere in *Nojoque,* Helper contends that
Southern slaveholders "ought to have had more
common decency than to wish to be the *centre* (or
anything else) of the exceedingly foul and noxious
surrounding of negroes and negro slavery," and

[59] *Nojoque,* pp. 349, 13.
[60] Lefler, *Hinton Rowan Helper,* p. 31.

congratulates them on "having undergone purification [as a result of emancipation] from their very long and vile association with the negro." [61]

After the publication of *Nojoque,* Helper was attacked by some Radical Republicans for allegedly having changed his mind about the Negro since the publication of *The Impending Crisis.* Helper countered not only by citing the anti-Negro passages from the earlier work but also by presenting testimony from friends and associates to whom he had freely expressed his opinions before the war. A. B. Burdick, the publisher of *The Impending Crisis,* testified that Helper had made it clear to him in 1857 that "one of his greatest objections to slavery" had been "that it kept the two races in juxtaposition," and that Helper, as long as he had known him, had avoided all contacts with Negroes, refusing even to patronize hotels and restaurants which employed Negroes in menial capacities. Another man who knew Helper before the war recalled that "he has always been inflexibly opposed to all the relations and conditions which have kept the two races close together; and this, as I have invariably understood him, was one of the principal grounds of his opposition to slavery." [62]

[61] *Nojoque,* pp. 198, 279.

[62] These letters were printed as appendices to Helper's *Noonday Exigencies in America* (New York, 1871), pp. 204–206.

In a letter to the *National Intelligencer* in 1867, Helper gave his most complete explanation of the relationship between his current Negrophobia and his previous opposition to slavery and suggested the tangle of motives and feelings that lay behind it. He began with a general statement of principle. For the two races to live in "close association . . . together beneath the same roof . . . in juxtaposition within the acknowledged limits of any hamlet, village, town, or city, or even within the boundaries of any farm or plantation, as they did live under the system of slavery, and as they still live under the condition of freedom, is . . . (particularly as it affects the whites), a gross shame, a shocking indecency, and a glaring crime." In the Old South, he noted, " 'having negroes around' was both fashionable and aristocratic," and concluded that Negroes were actually in a favored position in comparison with the poor whites: "The mass of the white population absolutely debarred from the pecuniary profits and other advantages of employment, and forced into the purlieus of poverty and ignorance. The baseborn and incapable blacks, by the force of a vulgar public opinion placed above the meritorious whites." [63] Then, in a remarkable passage, Helper revealed the twisted envy that he

[63] The *National Intelligencer*, November 11, 1867, reprinted as an appendix to *Negroes in Negroland*, pp. 238–240.

must have felt for both the slaveholder and the slave, when, earlier in his life, he had contemplated his chances as a lower-class white in a slaveholding state.

For nearly two hundred and fifty years, the negroes here, as waiters in hotels, and in the families of the most learned and refined, as barbers and body-servants to professional men, pleasure-seekers and others, have had the constant benefit of hearing the intelligent conversation of their masters and mistresses, and also of listening to the interesting and instructive stories in the cities and towns (just where not one of them ought ever to have been, and just where not one of them ought ever to be), they always had free and undisputed admission to the public meetings in the court-houses and in the town halls, and also to the religious meetings held in the churches and elsewhere. As a class, they alone, of all the poor people in the South, had access, at all times, in the families of the rich and refined, to books, magazines, and newspapers. On the other hand, the poor whites, treated as outcasts, merely because they did not own slaves, enjoyed none of the opportunities which were so easily within the reach of the negroes, whether for the enlargement or cultivation of the mind, or for the health and comfort of the body; and what is worse,—ay what, indeed, is very much worse,—the condition of things in this respect is still unchanged.[64]

[64] *Ibid.*, p. 240.

This passage, with its intense note of personal grievance, reveals much about some of the deepest roots of Helper's pathological racism. One can now picture him as a young man with a vision of a bright world to which he was denied access—a world shared by the favored whites and their Negro slaves. As this passage indicates, Helper was profoundly envious of "the refinement," "intelligent conversation," even "the pleasure seeking" of the aristocracy. It was as if the planters and their black retainers, locked in an unholy alliance, were conspiring against him personally to deny him all the advantages of high status. We have no positive evidence that Helper as a boy was ever traumatically affronted by an upper-caste Negro servant, like the young Thomas Sutpen in William Faulkner's historically penetrating novel of the Old South, *Absalom, Absalom;* but he might well have been. It is easy to visualize him as an apprentice shopkeeper dealing with imperious household slaves who were acting for their masters.

If suppressed envy and a sense of personal grievance were really at the core of Helper's racism, one is tempted to jump to the conclusion that he can be taken as a typical representative of the lower class white mentality of the Old South. But only a few men of poor-white origin openly challenged slavery or the dominance of the aristocracy. Most non-slaveholding whites accepted their subservient position in return for personal independence as subsistance farmers and for flattering attention from politicians at election time. What could have made Helper different was his experience as a student at Mocksville Academy, which was patronized largely by children of the planter class. At Mocksville, he would have encountered social snobbery and have glimpsed enough of a tantalizing world he could never enter to have embittered him for life. The subsequent history of extreme Southern racism was to bear out the theory that the most vicious Negro-baiting came not from poor whites, *per se,* but from those of lower class origin who had some access to the higher reaches of society but no firm position there.[65]

Nojoque was followed by two other anti-Negro books, *Negroes in Negroland* (1868) a collection of ethnological materials detrimental to the Negro, and *Noonday Exigencies in America* (1871). In the

[65] Two of the most intensive sociological studies of Southern communities during the segregation era, John Dollard's *Caste and Class in a Southern Town* (New Haven and London, 1937), and Allison Davis, *et al., Deep South* (Chicago, 1941), both conclude that white racial antipathy is strongest not among the lower class but among the insecure middle class of poor white origin, a group which is "straining" for status and respectability.

latter book, Helper revealed that race had become, at least temporarily, his single obsession. He had now abandoned the economic Whiggery of *The Impending Crisis* and was attempting to make a class appeal to the working population on the theory that Radical efforts for Negro equality represented an anti-labor plot by the wealthy capitalists of the North. In a letter of 1869 to the President of the New York Workingmen's Association, which he reprinted as the introduction to the book, he warned of the growing power of wealth and the widening gulf between the rich and the poor, and argued that Radical Reconstruction and Negro equality were denying the untapped wealth of the South to working-class immigrants from the North. In the text of *Noonday Exigencies*, he claimed that Negroes in the North were being given preference for certain kinds of jobs and that it was the poor who were exposed to the danger of racial amalgamation and the daughters of the poor who were assaulted by Negroes and driven into prostitution because of the alleged Negro monopoly on domestic positions. The book amounted to an extended proposal for a new political party based on grievances of class and race—an ominous anticipation of fascism.

During this period Helper was in contact with the leaders of the National Labor Union and actu-

ally exerted some influence on them. The racism
which crept into the Union's policies and pro-
nouncements around 1870 was encouraged and
applauded by Helper, and the Union actually
appointed a committee to examine in full the proposals contained in *Noonday Exigencies*.[66]

In giving his racism a quasi-Populist flavor
Helper anticipated the Southern demagogues of the
early twentieth century who combined the leftover
rhetoric of Populism with virulent race-baiting.
Having been a prophet of the New South in the Old
South, he now foreshadowed the triumph of racism
and legalized segregation at the end of the century.
As far as dominant Southern opinion was concerned, he was always twenty to thirty years ahead
of his time.

Yet his racism of 1870 was, if excessive, not
entirely out of place in the America of that period.
Radical Reconstruction was already being under-
mined, partially at least because of the doubts
of Northerners as to whether the Negro really had
the capacity for self-government. The egalitarians,
if they were genuinely that, had won some battles,
but were losing the war. As time went on, Northerners increasingly took the evidence of corruption
in the Radical governments of the South as indi-

[66] Bailey, *Helper*, p. 152.

cations that the national policy had been mistaken and that the biological inferiority of the Negro rendered him incapable of full citizenship. One of the reasons for the failure of Radical Reconstruction was that a milder version of Helper's racial ideas had wide currency in the North.

VI

The final phase of Helper's career saw him dominated by one last obsession, the promotion of a railroad linking North and South Amerca. This project was cut from the same cloth as his desire for the racial purification of California, his opposition to slavery, and his campaign for Negro expulsion. In a striking way, it summed up his entire career as a publicist and agitator.

His interest in Latin America went back to the period of his consulship in Argentina. As might be expected, Helper had been utterly intolerant of Latin American civilization, objecting in particular to the variety of races and racial mixtures and to the prominence of Catholicism. During the late '70's he came to think increasingly of a Pan American Railroad as an enterprise which would yield a vast profit to the promoters and at the same time be the basis of the economic and cultural salvation of Latin America. The railroad would bring in capital

and immigrants from the United States to develop
the resources of the countries to the South, and, as
a result, white men would "supplant entirely the
cumbersomely and worthlessly base and black and
brown elements [and] the vile-visaged and deleterious forms of human rubbish around them." [67]
Here was the same ambition for simultaneous economic development and racial purification that had
been the basis of his thinking about California and
the Old South. His passion for absolute racial, cultural, and economic homogeneity—for a world in
which Hinton Rowan Helper would feel at home
because everyone looked like him and shared his
views—remained unabated.

One after another, Helper's efforts to interest
business and government in his railroad enterprise
failed, and he spent the last years of his life in
poverty and frustration. On March 8, 1909, he shut
the windows and barricaded the door of his dingy
Washington apartment and turned on the gas. His
death brought a final surge of fame as the press
recalled the historical importance of *The Impending Crisis*.[68]

John Spencer Bassett, the historian, who knew

[67] Bailey, *Helper*, p. 177.
[68] *Ibid.*, pp. 194–195.

Helper in his later years, once discouraged a student from writing a dissertation on him because he regarded Helper as "mentally unbalanced." "He wrote a book which stated a very patent fact in a striking way, but aside from that, he was neither wise nor attractive." [69] One can agree with the essence of Bassett's judgment and yet deny that Helper is unworthy of study. The particular ways in which Helper revealed his lack of wisdom and mental stability cannot be detached from historically important social and intellectual influences which were exerted upon him. His racism and cultural intolerance were extreme manifestations of beliefs which were shared by most Americans of his time. Helper is of interest, therefore, for the same reason that unusually severe and virulent cases of disease are of value in the study of general pathology. By showing the logical extremes of American racism and something of its origin, Helper's career reveals sources of contamination and shows how the disease itself, if not properly treated, can warp the mind of an individual or a society.

[69] Quoted in Eaton, *Mind of the Old South*, p. 130.

A NOTE ON THE TEXT

This John Harvard Library edition of *The Impending Crisis of the South: How to Meet It* has been photographed from the "fourth thousand" of the first edition (1857). Numbers referring to the editor's notes have been inserted.

The editor wishes to thank Miss Judith Ann Dussman for assistance in the research for the notes and Mrs. Danae Cooperman for typing the Introduction and the notes.

THE

IMPENDING CRISIS

OF

THE SOUTH:

HOW TO MEET IT.

BY

HINTON ROWAN HELPER,

OF NORTH CAROLINA.

COUNTRYMEN! I sue for simple justice at your hands,
Naught else I ask, nor less will have;
Act right, therefore, and yield my claim,
Or, by the great God that made all things,
I'll fight, till from my bones my flesh be hack'd!—*Shakspeare.*

The liberal deviseth liberal things,
And by liberal things shall he stand.—*Isaiah.*

FOURTH THOUSAND.

NEW-YORK:
BURDICK BROTHERS, 8 SPRUCE STREET.
1857.

PREFACE.

~~~~~~~~~~~~~~~~

IF my countrymen, particularly my countrymen of the South, still more particularly those of them who are non-slaveholders, shall peruse this work, they will learn that no narrow and partial doctrines of political or social economy, no prejudices of early education have induced me to write it. If, in any part of it, I have actually deflected from the tone of true patriotism and nationality, I am unable to perceive the fault. What I have committed to paper is but a fair reflex of the honest and long-settled convictions of my heart.

In writing this book, it has been no part of my purpose to cast unmerited opprobrium upon slaveholders, or to display any special friendliness or sympathy for the blacks. I have considered my subject more particularly with reference to its economic aspects as regards the whites—not with reference, except in a very slight degree, to its humanitarian or religious aspects. To the latter side of the question, Northern writers have already done full and timely justice. The genius of the North has also most ably and eloquently discussed the subject in the form of novels. Yankee wives have written the most popular anti-slavery literature of the day. Against this I have nothing to say; it is all well enough for women to give the fictions of slavery; men should give the facts.

I trust that my friends and fellow-citizens of the South will read this book—nay, proud as any Southerner though I am, I entreat, I beg of them to do so. And as the work, considered with reference to its author's nativity, is a novelty—the South being my birth-place and my home, and my ancestry having resided there for more than a century—so I indulge the hope that its reception by my fellow-Southrons will also be novel; that is to say, that they will receive it, as it is offered, in a reasonable and friendly spirit, and that they will read it and reflect upon it as an honest and faithful endeavor to treat a subject of enormous import, without rancor or prejudice, by one who naturally comes within the pale of their own sympathies.

An irrepressibly active desire to do something to elevate the South to an honorable and powerful position among the enlightened quarters of the globe, has been the great leading principle that has actuated me in the preparation of the present volume; and so well convinced am I that the plan which I have proposed is the only really practical one for achieving the desired end, that I earnestly hope to see it prosecuted with energy and zeal, until the Flag of Freedom shall wave triumphantly alike over the valleys of Virginia and the mounds of Mississippi.

H. R. H.

June, 1857.

CONTENTS.

~~~~~~~~~

CHAPTER I.

CHAPTER II.

CHAPTER III.

Rights. North Carolina—Mecklenburg Declaration of Independence—Judge Ruffin. South Carolina—Extracts from the Writings of some of her more Sensible Sons. Georgia —Gen. Oglethorpe—Darien Resolutions.

CHAPTER IV.

NORTHERN TESTIMONY............................... 235

Opinions of Franklin—Hamilton—Jay—Adams—Webster —Clinton—Warren—Complimentary Allusions to Garrison, Greeley, Seward, Sumner, and others.

CHAPTER V.

TESTIMONY OF THE NATIONS........................ 245

The Voice of England—Opinions of Mansfield—Locke— Pitt—Fox—Shakspeare—Cowper—Milton—Johnson— Price—Blackstone—Coke—Hampden—Harrington—Fortescue—Brougham—The Voice of Ireland—Opinions of Burke—Curran—Extract from the Dublin University Magazine for December, 1856—The Voice of Scotland—Opinions of Beattie—Miller—Macknight—The Voice of France —Opinions of Lafayette—Montesquieu—Louis X—Buffon —Rousseau—Brissot—The Voice of Germany—Opinions of Grotius—Gœthe—Luther—Extract from the Letter of a living German writer to his Friends in this Country— The Voice of Italy—Opinions of Cicero—Lactantius—Leo X—The Voice of Greece—Opinions of Socrates—Aristotle —Polybius—Plato.

CHAPTER VI.

TESTIMONY OF THE CHURCHES........................ 258

Introductory Remarks—Presbyterian Testimony—Albert Barnes—Thomas Scott—General Assembly in 1818—Synod of Kentucky—Episcopal Testimony—Bishop Horsley —Bishop Butler—Bishop Porteus—John Jay—Antislavery Churchman—Baptist Testimony—Rev. Mr. Brisbane, of South Carolina—Francis Wayland—Abraham Booth—Baptists of Virginia in 1789—Methodist Testimony—John Wesley—Adam Clarke—Extracts from the Discipline for 1784, '85 and '97—Catholic Testimony— Pope Gregory XVI—Pope Leo X—The Abbe Raynal— Henry Kemp.

CONTENTS.

CHAPTER VII.

AGE.

BIBLE TESTIMONY. 275

The Bible an Anti-Slavery Text-book—Selected Precepts and Sayings of the Old Testament—Selected Precepts and Sayings of the New Testament—Irrefragability of the Arguments here and elsewhere introduced against Slavery.

CHAPTER VIII.

FREE FIGURES AND SLAVE. 281

Opening Remarks—General Statistics of the Free and of the Slave States—Tonnage, Exports, and Imports—Products of Manufactures—Miles of Canals and Railroads in Operation—Public Schools—Libraries other than Private —Newspapers and Periodicals—Illiterate White Adults— —National Political Power of the two Sections—Popular Vote for President in 1856—Patents Issued on New Inventions—Value of Church Property—Acts of Benevolence—Contributions for the Bible Cause, Tract Cause, Missionary Cause, and Colonization Cause—Table of deaths in the several States in 1850—Number of Free White Male Persons over fifteen years of age engaged in Agriculture or other out-door Labor in the Slave States— Falsity of the Assertion that White Men cannot cultivate Southern Soil—White Female Agriculturists in North Carolina—Number of Natives of the Slave States in the Free States, and of Natives of the Free States in the Slave States—Value of the Slaves at $400 per head—List of Presidents of the United States—Judges of the Supreme Court—Secretaries of State—Presidents of the Senate— Speakers of the House—Postmasters General—Secretaries of the Interior—Secretaries of the Treasury—Secretaries of War—Secretaries of the Navy—Result of the Presidenial Elections in the United States from 1796 to 1856—Aid or Kansas—Contributions for the Sufferers in Portsnouth, Va., during the Prevalence of the Yellow Fever in he Summer of 1855—Congressional Representation—Custom House Receipts–When the Old States were Settled and he New Admitted into the Union—First European Setlements in America—Freedom and Slavery at the Fair —What Freedom Did—What Slavery Did—Average Value ver Acre of Lands in the States of New York and North Carolina.

CHAPTER IX.

Plea for a great Southern Commercial City—Importance of Cities in General—Letters from the Mayors of sundry American Cities, North and South—Wealth and Population of New-York, Baltimore, Philadelphia, New-Orleans, Boston, St. Louis, Brooklyn, Charleston, Cincinnati, Louisville, Chicago, Richmond, Providence, Norfolk, Buffalo, Savannah, New-Bedford, Wilmington—Wealth Concentrated at Commercial Points—Boston and its Business—Progressive Growth of Cities—A Fleet of Merchantmen—Commerce of Norfolk—Baltimore, Past, Present, and Future—Insignificance of Southern Commerce—Enslavement of Slaveholders to the Products of Northern Industry—Almost Utter Lack of Patrioitsm in Southern Merchants and Slaveholders.

CHAPTER X.

Why this Work was not Published in Baltimore—Legislative Acts Against Slavery—Testimony of a West India Planter to the Advantages of Free over Slave Labor—The True Friends of the South—Slavery Thoughtful—Signs of Contrition—Progress of Freedom in the South—Antislavery Extracts from Southern Journals—A Right Feeling in the Right Quarter—The Illiterate Poor Whites of the South.

CHAPTER XI.

Instances of Protracted Literary Labor—Comparative Insignificance of Periodical and General Literature in the Southern States—The New-York Tribune—Southern System of Publishing—Book-making in America—The Business of the Messrs. Harper—Southern Journals Struggling for Existence—Paucity of Southern Authors—Proportion of White Adults, over Twenty Years of Age, in each State, who cannot Read and Write, to the Whole White Population—Southern Authors Compelled to Seek Northern Publishers—Conclusion.

CHAPTER I.

IT is not our intention in this chapter to enter into an elaborate ethnographical essay, to establish peculiarities of difference, mental, moral, and physical, in the great family of man. Neither is it our design to launch into a philosophical disquisition on the laws and principles of light and darkness, with a view of educing any additional evidence of the fact, that as a general rule, the rays of the sun are more fructifying and congenial than the shades of night. Nor yet is it our purpose, by writing a formal treatise on ethics, to draw a broad line of distinction between right and wrong, to point out the propriety of morality and its advantages over immorality, nor to waste time in pressing a universally admitted truism—that virtue is preferable to vice. Self-evident truths require no argumentative demonstration.

What we mean to do is simply this : to take a survey of the relative position and importance of the several states of this confederacy, from the adoption of the national compact ; and when, of two sections of the country starting under the same auspices, and with equal natural advantages, we find the one rising to a degree of almost unexampled power and eminence, and the other sinking into a state of comparative imbecility and obscurity, it is our determination to trace out the causes which have led to the elevation of the former, and the depression of the latter, and to use our most earnest and honest endeavors to utterly extirpate whatever opposes the progress and prosperity of any portion of the union.

This survey we have already made ; we have also instituted an impartial comparison between the cardinal sections of the country, north, south, east, and west ; and as a true hearted southerner, whose ancestors have resided in North Carolina between one and two hundred years, and as one who would rather have his native clime excel than be excelled, we feel constrained to confess that we are deeply abashed and chagrined at the disclosures of the comparison thus instituted. At the time of the adoption of the Constitution, in 1789, we commenced an even race with the North. All things considered, if either the North or the South had the advantage, it was the latter. In proof of this, let us introduce a few statistics, beginning with the states of

NEW YORK AND VIRGINIA.

In 1790, when the first census was taken, New York contained 340,120 inhabitants ; at the same time the population of Virginia was 748,308, being more than twice the number of New York. Just sixty years afterward, as we learn from the census of 1850, New York had a population of 3,097,394 ; while that of Virginia was only 1,421,661, being less than half the number of New York !

In 1791, the exports of New York amounted to $2,505,-465 ; the exports of Virginia amounted to $3,130,865.   In 1852, the exports of New York amounted to $87,484,456 ; the exports of Virginia, during the same year, amounted to only $2,724,657.   In 1790, the imports of New York and Virginia were about equal ; in 1853, the imports of New York amounted to the enormous sum of $178,270,-999 ; while those of Virginia, for the same period, amount-ed to the pitiful sum of only $399,004.   In 1850, the pro-ducts of manufactures, mining and the mechanic arts in New York amounted to $237,597,249 ; those of Virginia amounted to only $29,705,387.   At the taking of the last census, the value of real and personal property in Vir-ginia, including negroes, was $391,646,438 ; that of New York, exclusive of any monetary valuation of human be-ings, was $1,080,309,216.

In August, 1856, the real and personal estate assessed in the City of New-York amounted in valuation to $511,-740,491, showing that New-York City alone is worth far more than the whole State of Virginia.

What says one of Virginia's own sons ?   He still lives ; hear him speak.   Says Gov. Wise :

"It may be painful, but nevertheless, profitable, to re-cur occasionally to the history of the past ; to listen to the admonitions of experience, and learn lessons of wisdom from the efforts and actions of those who have preceded us in the drama of human life.   The records of former days show that at a period not very remote, Virginia stood pre-eminently the first commercial State in the Union ; when her commerce exceeded in amount that of all the New

England States combined ; when the City of Norfolk owned more than one hundred trading ships, and her direct foreign trade exceeded that of the City of New-York, now the centre of trade and the great emporium of North America. At the period of the war of independence, the commerce of Virginia was four times larger than that of New-York."

The cash value of all the farms, farming implements and machinery in Virginia, in 1850, was $223,423,315 ; the value of the same in New-York, in the same year, was $576,631,568. In about the same ratio does the value of the agricultural products and live stock of New-York exceed the value of the agricultural products and live stock of Virginia. But we will pursue this humiliating comparison no further. With feelings mingled with indignation and disgust, we turn from the picture, and will now pay our respects to

MASSACHUSETTS AND NORTH CAROLINA.

In 1790, Massachusetts contained 378,717 inhabitants ; in the same year North Carolina contained 393,751 ; in 1850, the population of Massachusetts was 994,514, all freemen ; while that of North Carolina was only 869,039, of whom 288,548 were slaves. Massachusetts has an area of only 7,800 square miles ; the area of North Carolina is 50,704 square miles, which, though less than Virginia, is considerably larger than the State of New-York. Massachusetts and North Carolina each have a harbor, Boston and Beaufort, which harbors, with the States that back them, are, by nature, possessed of about equal capacities and advantages for commercial and manufacturing enterprise. Boston has grown to be the second commercial city in the Union ; her ships, freighted with the useful and unique inventions and manufactures of her ingenious artisans and mechanics, and bearing upon their stalwart arms the majestic flag of our country, glide triumphantly through the winds and over the waves of every ocean. She has done, and is now doing, great honor to herself, her State and the nation, and her name and fame are spoken with reverence in the remotest regions of the earth.

How is it with Beaufort, in North Carolina, whose harbor is said to be the safest and most commodious anywhere to be found on the Atlantic coast south of the harbor of New-York, and but little inferior to that? Has anybody ever heard of her? Do the masts of her ships ever cast a shadow on foreign waters? Upon what distant or benighted shore have her merchants and mariners ever hoisted our national ensign, or spread the arts of civilization and peaceful industry? What changes worthy of note have taken place in the physical features of her superficies since "the evening and the morning were the third day?" But we will make no further attempt to draw a comparison between the populous, wealthy, and renowned city of Boston and the obscure, despicable little village of Beaufort, which, notwithstanding "the placid bosom of its deep and well-protected harbor," has no place in the annals or records of the country, and has scarcely ever been heard of fifty miles from home.

In 1853, the exports of Massachusetts amounted to

$16,895,304, and her imports to $41,367,956 ; during the same time, and indeed during all the time, from the period of the formation of the government up to the year 1853, inclusive, the exports and imports of North Carolina were so utterly insignificant that we are ashamed to record them. In 1850, the products of manufactures, mining and the mechanic arts in Massachusetts, amounted to $151,-137,145 ; those of North Carolina, to only $9,111,245. In 1856, the products of these industrial pursuits in Massachusetts had increased to something over $288,000,000, a sum more than twice the value of the entire cotton crop of all the Southern States ! In 1850, the cash value of all the farms, farming implements and machinery in Massachusetts, was $112,285,931 ; the value of the same in North Carolina, in the same year, was only $71,823,298. In 1850, the value of all the real and personal estate in Massachusetts, without recognizing property in man, or setting a monetary price on the head of a single citizen, white or black, amounted to $573,342,286 ; the value of the same in North Carolina, including negroes, amounted to only.$226,800,472. In 1856, the real and personal estate assessed in the City of Boston amounted in valuation to within a fraction of $250,000,000, showing conclusively that so far as dollars and cents are concerned, that single city could buy the whole State of North Carolina, and by right of purchase, if sanctioned by the Constitution of the United States, and by State Constitutions, hold her as a province. In 1850, there were in Massachusetts 1,861 native white and free colored persons over twenty years of age who could not read and write ; in the same year, the same class of persons in North Carolina numbered 80,083 ; while her 288,548 slaves were, by legislative enactments, kept in a state of absolute ignorance and unconditional subordination.

Hoping, however, and believing, that a large majority of the most respectable and patriotic citizens of North Carolina have resolved, or will soon resolve, with unyielding purpose, to cast aside the great obstacle that impedes their progress, and bring into action a new policy which will lead them from poverty and ignorance to wealth and intellectual greatness, and which will shield them not only from the rebukes of their own consciences, but also from the just reproaches of the civilized world, we will, for the present, in deference to their feelings, forbear the further enumeration of these degrading disparities, and turn our attention to

PENNSYLVANIA AND SOUTH CAROLINA.

An old gentleman, now residing in Charleston, told us, but a few months since, that he had a distinct recollection of the time when Charleston imported foreign fabrics for the Philadelphia trade, and when, on a certain occasion, his mother went into a store on Market-street to select a silk dress for herself, the merchant, unable to please her fancy, persuaded her to postpone the selection for a few days, or until the arrival of a new stock of superb styles and fashions which he had recently purchased in the metropolis of South Carolina. This was all very proper Charleston had a spacious harbor, a central position, and a mild climate ; and from priority of settlement and business connections, to say nothing of other advantages, she enjoyed greater facilities for commercial transactions than Philadelphia. She had a right to get custom wherever she could find it, and in securing so valuable a customer as the Quaker City, she exhibited no small degree of laudable enterprise. But why did she not maintain her supremacy? If the answer to this query is not already in the reader's mind, it will suggest itself before he peruses the whole of this work. For the present, suffice it to say, that the cause of her shameful insignificance and decline is essentially the same that has thrown every other Southern city and State in the rear of progress, and rendered them tributary, in a commercial and manufacturing point of view, almost entirely tributary, to the more sagacious and enterprising States and cities of the North.

A most unfortunate day was that for the Palmetto State, and indeed for the whole South, when the course of trade was changed, and she found herself the retailer of foreign and domestic goods, imported and vended by wholesale merchants at the North. Philadelphia ladies no longer look to the South for late fashions, and fine silks and satins ; no Quaker dame now wears drab apparel of Charleston importation. Like all other *niggervilles* in our disreputable part of the confederacy, the commercial emporium of South Carolina is sick and impoverished ; her silver cord has been loosed ; her golden bowl has been broken ; and her unhappy people, without proper or profitable employment, poor in pocket, and few in number, go mourning or loafing about the streets. Her annual importations are actually less now than they were a century ago, when South Carolina was the second commercial province on the continent, Virginia being the first.

In 1760, as we learn from Mr. Benton's "Thirty Years' View," the foreign imports into Charleston were $2,662,-000 ; in 1855, they amounted to only $1,750,0Q0 ! In 1854, the imports into Philadelphia, which, in foreign trade, ranks at present but fourth among the commercial cities of the union, were $21,963,021. In 1850, the products of manufactures, mining, and the mechanic arts, in Pennsylvania, amounted to $155,044,910 ; the products of the same in South Carolina, amounted to only $7,063,513.

As shown by the census report of 1850, which was prepared under the superintendence of a native of South Carolina, who certainly will not be suspected of injustice to his own section of the country, the Southern states, the cash value of all the farms, farming implements, and machinery in Pennsylvania, was $422,598,640 ; the value of the same in South Carolina, in the same year, was only $86,518,038. From a compendium of the same census, we learn that the value of all the real and personal property in Pennsylvania, actual property, no slaves, amounted to $729,144,998 ; the value of the same in South Carolina, including the estimated — we were about to say fictitious — value of 384,925 negroes, amounted to only $288,257,-694. We have not been able to obtain the figures necessary to show the exact value of the real and personal estate in Philadelphia, but the amount is estimated to be not less than $300,000,000 ; and as, in 1850, there were 408,-762 free inhabitants in the single city of Philadelphia, against 283,544 of the same class, in the whole state of South Carolina, it is quite evident that the former is more powerful than the latter, and far ahead of her in all the elements of genuine and permanent superiority. In Pennsylvania, in 1850, the annual income of public schools amounted to $1,348,249 ; the same in South Carolina, in the same year, amounted to only $200,600 ; in the former state there were 393 libraries other than private, in the latter only 26 ; in Pennsylvania 310 newspapers and periodicals were published, circulating 84,898,672 copies annually ; in South Carolina only 46 newspapers and periodicals were published, circulating but 7,145,930 copies per annum.

The incontrovertible facts we have thus far presented are, we think, amply sufficient, both in number and magnitude, to bring conviction to the mind of every candid reader, that there is something wrong, socially, politically and morally wrong, in the policy under which the South has so long loitered and languished. Else, how is it that the North, under the operations of a policy directly the opposite of ours, has surpassed us in almost everything great and good, and left us standing before the world, an object of merited reprehension and derision?

For one, we are heartily ashamed of the inexcusable weakness, inertia and dilapidation everywhere so manifest throughout our native section ; but the blame properly attaches itself to an usurping minority of the people, and we are determined that it shall rest where it belongs. More on this subject, however, after a brief but general survey of the inequalities and disparities that exist between those two grand divisions of the country, which, without reference to the situation that any part of their territory bears to the cardinal points, are every day becoming more familiarly known by the appropriate appellation of

THE FREE AND THE SLAVE STATES.

It is a fact well known to every intelligent Southerner that we are compelled to go to the North for almost every article of utility and adornment, from matches, shoepegs and paintings up to cotton-mills, steamships and statuary; that we have no foreign trade, no princely merchants, nor respectable artists; that, in comparison with the free states, we contribute nothing to the literature, polite arts and inventions of the age; that, for want of profitable employment at home, large numbers of our native population find themselves necessitated to emigrate to the West, whilst the free states retain not only the larger proportion of those born within their own limits, but induce, annually, hundreds of thousands of foreigners to settle and remain amongst them; that almost everything produced at the North meets with ready sale, while, at the same time, there is no demand, even among our own citizens, for the productions of Southern industry; that, owing to the absence of a proper system of business amongst us, the North becomes, in one way or another, the proprietor and dispenser of all our floating wealth, and that we are dependent on Northern capitalists for the means necessary to build our railroads, canals and other public improvements; that if we want to visit a foreign country, even

though it may lie directly South of us, we find no convenient
way of getting there except by taking passage through a
Northern port ; and that nearly all the profits arising from
the exchange of commodities, from insurance and shipping
offices, and from the thousand and one industrial pursuits
of the country, accrue to the North, and are there invested
in the erection of those magnificent cities and stupendous
works of art which dazzle the eyes of the South, and attest
the superiority of free institutions !

The North is the Mecca of our merchants, and to it they
must and do make two pilgrimages per annum—one in the
spring and one in the fall.   All our commercial, mechanical,
manufactural, and literary supplies come from there.   We
want Bibles, brooms, buckets and books, and we go to the
North ; we want pens, ink, paper, wafers and envelopes,
and we go to the North ; we want shoes, hats, handker-
chiefs, umbrellas and pocket knives, and we go to the
North ; we want furniture, crockery, glassware and pianos,
and we go to the North ; we want toys, primers, school
books, fashionable apparel, machinery, medicines, tomb-
stones, and a thousand other things, and we go to the
North for them all.   Instead of keeping our money in circulation at home, by patronizing our own mechanics, manufacturers, and laborers, we send it all away to the North,
and there it remains ; it never falls into our hands again.

In one way or another we are more or less subservient
to the North every day of our lives.   In infancy we are
swaddled in Northern muslin ; in childhood we are hu-
mored with Northern gewgaws ; in youth we are instructed out of Northern books ; at the age of maturity we sow

our " wild oats" on Northern soil ; in middle-life we ex-
haust our wealth, energies and talents in the dishonorable
vocation of entailing our dependence on our children and
on our children's children, and, to the neglect of our own
interests and the interests of those around us, in giving
aid and succor to every department of Northern power ;
in the decline of life we remedy our eye-sight with Nor-
thren spectacles, and support our infirmities with Northern
canes ; in old age we are drugged with Northern physic ;.
and, finally, when we die, our inanimate bodies, shrouded
in Northern cambric, are stretched upon the bier, borne to
the grave in a Northern carriage, entombed with a Northern spade, and memorized with a Northern slab !

But it can hardly be necessary to say more in illustration of this unmanly and unnational dependence, which is
so glaring that it cannot fail to be apparent to even the
most careless and superficial observer. All the world
sees, or ought to see, that in a commercial, mechanical,
manufactural, financial, and literary point of view, we are
as helpless as babes ; that, in comparison with the Free
States, our agricultural resources have been greatly exaggerated, misunderstood and mismanaged ; and that, instead of cultivating among ourselves a wise policy of mutual assistance and co-operation with respect to individuals, and of self-reliance with respect to the South at large,
instead of giving countenance and encouragement to the
industrial enterprises projected in our midst, and instead
of building up, aggrandizing and beautifying our own
States, cities and towns, we have been spending our substance at the North, and are daily augmenting and

strengthening the very power which now has us so completely under its thumb.

It thus appears, in view of the preceding statistical facts and arguments, that the South, at one time the superior of the North in almost all the ennobling pursuits and conditions of life, has fallen far behind her competitor, and now ranks more as the dependency of a mother country than as the equal confederate of free and independent States. Following the order of our task, the next duty that devolves upon us is to trace out the causes which have conspired to bring about this important change, and to place on record the reasons, as we understand them,

WHY THE NORTH HAS SURPASSED THE SOUTH.

And now that we have come to the very heart and soul of our subject, we feel no disposition to mince matters, but mean to speak plainly, and to the point, without any equivocation, mental reservation, or secret evasion whatever. The son of a venerated parent, who, while he lived, was a considerate and merciful slaveholder, a native of the South, born and bred in North Carolina, of a family whose home has been in the valley of the Yadkin for nearly a century and a half, a Southerner by instinct and by all the influences of thought, habits, and kindred, and with the desire and fixed purpose to reside permanently within the limits of the South, and with the expectation of dying there also—we feel that we have the right to express our opinion, however humble or unimportant it may be, on any and every question that affects the public good ; and, so help us God, "sink or swim, live or die, survive or per-ish," we are determined to exercise that right with manly firmness, and without fear, favor or affection.

And now to the point. In our opinion, an opinion which has been formed from data obtained by assiduous re-searches, and comparisons, from laborious investigation, logical reasoning, and earnest reflection, the causes which have impeded the progress and prosperity of the South, which have dwindled our commerce, and other similar pursuits, into the most contemptible insignificance ; sunk a large majority of our people in galling poverty and ig-norance, rendered a small minority conceited and tyran-nical, and driven the rest away from their homes ; entailed upon us a humiliating dependence on the Free States ; dis-graced us in the recesses of our own souls, and brought us under reproach in the eyes of all civilized and enlight-ened nations—may all be traced to one common source, and there find solution in the most hateful and horrible word, that was ever incorporated into the vocabulary of human economy— *Slavery!*

Reared amidst the institution of slavery, believing it to be wrong both in principle and in practice, and having seen and felt its evil influences upon individuals, commu-nities and states, we deem it a duty, no less than a privi-lege, to enter our protest against it, and to use our most strenuous efforts to overturn and abolish it ! Then we are an abolitionist ? Yes ! not merely a freesoiler, but an abolitionist, in the fullest sense of the term. We are not only in favor of keeping slavery out of the territories, but, carrying our opposition to the institution a step further,

2

we here unhesitatingly declare ourself in favor of its im·
mediate and unconditional abolition, in every state in this
confederacy, where it now exists ! Patriotism makes us
a freesoiler ; state pride makes us an emancipationist ; a
profound sense of duty to the South makes us an abolition
ist ; a reasonable degree of fellow feeling for the negro,
makes us a colonizationist. With the free state men in
Kanzas and Nebraska, we sympathize with all our heart
We love the whole country, the great family of states and
territories, one and inseparable, and would have the word
Liberty engraved as an appropriate and truthful motto, on
the escutcheon of every member of the confederacy. We
love freedom, we hate slavery, and rather than give up
the one or submit to the other, we will forfeit the pound
of flesh nearest our heart. Is this sufficiently explicit and
categorical ? If not, we hold ourself in readiness at all
times, to return a prompt reply to any proper question
that may be propounded.[1]

Our repugnance to the institution of slavery, springs
from no one-sided idea, or sickly sentimentality. We have
not been hasty in making up our mind on the subject ; we
have jumped at no conclusions ; we have acted with perfect calmness and deliberation ; we have carefully considered, and examined the reasons for and against the institution, and have also taken into account the propable consequences of our decision. The more we investigate the
matter, the deeper becomes the conviction that we are right;
and with this to impel and sustain us, we pursue our labor
with love, with hope, and with constantly renewing vigor.

That we shall encounter opposition w ᵼ consider as certain ; perhaps we may even be subjected to insult and violence. From the conceited and cruel oligarchy of the South, we could look for nothing less. But we shall shrink from no responsibility, and do nothing unbecoming a man ; we know how to repel indignity, and if assaulted, shall not fail to make the blow recoil upon the aggressor's head. The road we have to travel may be a rough one, but no impediment shall cause us to falter in our course. The line of our duty is clearly defined, and it is our intention to follow it faithfully, or die in the attempt.

But, thanks to heaven, we have no ominous forebodings of the result of the contest now pending between Liberty and Slavery in this confederacy. Though neither a prophet nor the son of a prophet, our vision is sufficiently penetrative to divine the future so far as to be able to see that the " peculiar institution" has but a short, and, as heretofore, inglorious existence before it. Time, the righter of every wrong, is ripening events for the desired consummation of our labors and the fulfillment of our cherished hopes. Each revolving year brings nearer the inevitable crisis. The sooner it comes the better ; may heaven, through our humble efforts, hasten its advent.

The first and most sacred duty of every Southerner, who has the honor and the interest of his country at heart, is to declare himself an unqualified and uncompromising abolitionist. No conditional or half-way declaration will avail ; no mere threatening demonstration will succeed. With those who desire to be instrumental in bringing about the triumph of liberty over slavery, there should be neither evasion, vacillation, nor equivocation. We should

listen to no modifying terms or compromises that may be
proposed by the proprietors of the unprofitable and ungod-
ly institution.   Nothing short of the complete abolition of
slavery can save the South from falling into the vortex of
utter ruin.   Too long have we yielded a submissive obedience to the tyrannical domination of an inflated oligarchy ; too long have we tolerated their arrogance and self-
conceit ; too long have we submitted to their unjust and
savage exactions.   Let us now wrest from them the sceptre of power, establish liberty and equal rights throughout the land, and henceforth and forever guard our legislative halls from the pollutions and usurpations of pro-
slavery demagogues.

   We have stated, in a cursory manner, the reasons, as
we understand them, why the North has surpassed the
South, and have endeavored to show, we think successfully, that the political salvation of the South depends upon the speedy and unconditional abolition of slavery.   We
will not, however, rest the case exclusively on our own
arguments, but will again appeal to incontrovertible facts
and statistics to sustain us in our conclusions.   But before we do so, we desire to fortify ourself against a charge
that is too frequently made by careless and superficial
readers.   We allude to the objections so often urged
against the use of tabular statements and statistical facts.
It is worthy of note, however, that those objections never
come from thorough scholars or profound thinkers.   Among
the majority of mankind, the science of statistics is only
beginning to be appreciated ; when well understood, it
will be recognized as one of the most important branches

of knowledge, and, as a matter of course, be introduced and taught as an indispensable element of practical education in all our principal institutions of learning. One of the most vigorous and popular transatlantic writers of the day, Wm. C. Taylor, LL.D., of Dublin,[2] says :

"The cultivation of statistics must be the source of all future improvement in the science of political economy, because it is to the table of the statistician that the economist must look for his facts ; and all speculations not founded upon facts, though they may be admired and applauded when first propounded, will, in the end, assuredly be forgotten. Statistical science may almost be regarded as the creation of this age. The word statistics was invented in the middle of the last century by a German professor,* to express a summary view of the physical, moral, and social conditions of States ; he justly remarked, that a numerical statement of the extent, density of population, imports, exports, revenues, etc., of a country, more perfectly explained its social condition than general statements, however graphic or however accurate. When such statements began to be collected, and exhibited in a popular form, it was soon discovered that the political and economical sciences were likely to gain the position of physical sciences ; that is to say, they were about to obtain records of observation, which would test the accuracy of recognized principles, and lead to the discovery of new modes of action. But the great object of this new science is to lead to the knowledge of human nature ; that

---

* Achenwall, a native of Elbing, Prussia. Born 1719, died 1792.

is, to ascertain the general course of operation of man's mental and moral faculties, and to furnish us with a correct standard of judgment, by enabling us to determine the average amount of the past as a guide to the average probabilities of the future. This science is yet in its infancy, but has already produced the most beneficial effects. The accuracy of the tables of life have rendered the calculations of rates of insurance a matter of much greater certainty than they were heretofore ; the system of keeping the public accounts has been simplified and improved; and finally, the experimental sciences of medicine and political economy, have been fixed on a firmer foundation than could be anticipated in the last century. Even in private life this science is likely to prove of immense advantage, by directing attention to the collection and registration of facts, and thus preventing the formation of hasty judgments and erroneous conclusions."

The compiler, or rather the superintendent of the seventh United States census, Prof. De Bow,[3] a gentleman of more than ordinary industry and practical learning, who, in his excellent Review, has, from time to time, displayed much commendable zeal in his efforts to develop the industrial resources of the Southern and South-western states, and who is, perhaps, the greatest statistician in the country, says :—

" Statistics are far from being the barren array of figures ingeniously and laboriously combined into columns and tables, which many persons are apt to suppose them. They constitute rather the ledger of a nation, in which, like the merchant in his books, the citizen can read, at one view, all of the results of a year or of a period of years, as compared with other periods, and deduce the profit or the loss which has been made, in morals, education, wealth or power."

Impressed with a sense of the propriety of introducing, in this as well as in the succeeding chapters of our work, a number of tabular statements exhibiting the comparative growth and prosperity of the free and slave states, we have deemed it eminently proper to adduce the testimony of these distinguished authors in support of the claims which official facts and accurate statistics lay to our consideration. And here we may remark that the statistics which we propose to offer, like those already given, have been obtained from official sources, and may, therefore, be relied on as correct. The object we have in view in making a free use of facts and figures, if not already apparent, will soon be understood. It is not so much in its moral and religious aspects that we propose to discuss the question of slavery, as in its social and political character and influences. To say nothing of the sin and the shame of slavery, we believe it is a most expensive and unprofitable institution ; and if our brethren of the South will but throw aside their unfounded prejudices and preconceived opinions, and give us a fair and patient hearing, we feel confident that we can bring them to the same conclusion. Indeed, we believe we shall be enabled—not alone by our own contributions, but with the aid of incontestable facts and arguments which we shall introduce from other sources —to convince all true-hearted, candid and intelligent Southerners, who may chance to read our book, (and we hope their name may be legion) that slavery, and nothing but slavery, has retarded the progress and prosperity of our portion of the Union ; depopulated and impoverished our cities by forcing the more industrious and enterprising natives of the soil to emigrate to the free states ; brought our domain under a sparse and inert population by preventing foreign immigration ; made us tributary to the North, and reduced us to the humiliating condition of mere provincial subjects in fact, though not in name. We believe, moreover, that every patriotic Southerner thus convinced will feel it a duty he owes to himself, to his country, and to his God, to become a thorough, inflexible, practical abolitionist. So mote it be !

Now to our figures. Few persons have an adequate idea of the important part the cardinal numbers are now playing in the cause of Liberty. They are working wonders in the South. Intelligent, business men, from the Chesapeake to the Rio Grande, are beginning to see that slavery, even in a mercenary point of view, is impolitic, because it is unprofitable. Those unique, mysterious little Arabic sentinels on the watch-towers of political economy, 1, 2, 3, 4, 5, 6, 7, 8, 9, 0, have joined forces, allied themselves to the powers of freedom, and are hemming in and combatting the institution with the most signal success. If let alone, we have no doubt the digits themselves would soon terminate the existence of slavery ; but we do not mean to let them alone ; they must not have all the honor of annihilating the monstrous iniquity. We want to become an auxiliary in the good work, and facilitate it. The liberation of five millions of " poor white trash" from the second degree of slavery, and of three millions of miserable kidnapped negroes from the first degree, cannot be accomplished too soon. That it was not accomplished many years ago is our misfortune. It now behooves us to take a bold and determined stand in defence of the inalienable rights of ourselves and of our fellow men, and to avenge the multiplicity of wrongs, social and political, which we have suffered at the hands of a villainous oligarchy. It is madness to delay. We cannot be too hasty in carrying out our designs. Precipitance in this matter is an utter impossibility. If to-day we could emancipate all the slaves in the Union, we would do it, and the country and everybody in it would be vastly better off to-morrow. Now is the time for action ; let us work.

By taking a sort of inventory of the agricultural products of the free and slave States in 1850, we now propose to correct a most extraordinary and mischievous error into which the people of the South have unconsciously fallen. Agriculture, it is well known, is the sole boast of the South ; and, strange to say, many pro-slavery Southerners, who, in our latitude, pass for intelligent men, are so puffed up with the idea of our importance in this respect, that they speak of the North as a sterile region, unfit for cultivation, and quite dependent on the South for the necessaries of life ! Such rampant ignorance ought to be knocked in the head ! We can prove that the North produces greater quantities of bread-stuffs than the South ! Figures shall show the facts. Properly, the South has nothing left to boast of ; the North has surpassed her in everything, and is going farther and farther ahead of her every day.

2*

We ask the reader's careful attention to the following tables, which we have prepared at no little cost of time and trouble, and which, when duly considered in connection with the foregoing and subsequent portions of our work, will, we believe, carry conviction to the mind that the downward tendency of the South can be arrested only by the abolition of slavery.

TABLE NO. I.

AGRICULTURAL PRODUCTS OF THE FREE STATES—1850.

States.	Wheat, bushels.	Oats, bushels.	Indian Corn, bushels.
California	17,228		12,236
Connecticut.....	41,762	1,258,738	1,935,043
Illinois...	9,414,575	10,087,241	57,646,984
Indiana...	6,214,458	5,655,014	52,964,363
Iowa.....	1,530,581	1,524,345	8,656,799
Maine.....	296,259	2,181,037	1,750,056
Massachusetts....	31,211	1,165,146	2,345,490
Michigan...............	4,925,889	2,866,056	5,641,420
New Hampshire..	185,658	973,381	1,573,670
New Jersey.............	1,601,190	3,378,063	8,759,704
New York.................	13,121,498	26,552,814	17,858,400
Ohio....	14,487,351	13,472,742	59,078,695
Pennsylvania..	15,367,691	21,538,156	19,835,214
Rhode Island....	49	215,232	539,201
Vermont.....	535,955	2,307,784	2,032,396
Wisconsin...	4,286,131	3,414,672	1,988,979
	72,157,486	96,590,371	242,618,650

TABLE NO. II.

AGRICULTURAL PRODUCTS OF THE SLAVE STATES—1850.

States.	Wheat, bushels.	Oats, bushels.	Indian Corn, bushels.
Alabama....	294,044	2,965,696	28,754,048
Arkansas.... ...... , ...	199,639	656,183	8,893,939
Delaware....	482,511	604,518	3,145,542
Florida.....	1,027	66,586	1,996,809
Georgia...	1,088,534	3,820,044	30,080,099
Kentucky...	2,142,822	8,201,311	58,672,591
Louisiana	417	89,637	10,266,373
Maryland....	4,494,680	2,242,151	10,749,858
Mississippi..	137,990	1,503,288	22,446,552
Missouri...	2,981,652	5,278,079	36,214,537
North Carolina...	2,130,102	4,052,078	27;941,051
South Carolina...	1,066,277	2,322,155	16,271,454
Tennessee ,.....	1,619,386	7,703,086	52,276,223
Texas. ...,.	41,729	199,017	6,028,876
Virginia.	11,212,616	10,179,144	35,254,319
	27,904,476	49,882,979	348,992,282

TABLE NO. III.

AGRICULTURAL PRODUCTS OF THE FREE STATES—1850.

States.	Potatoes, (I. & S.) bush.	Rye, bushels.	Barley, bushels.
California	10,292		9,712
Connecticut	2,689,805	600,893	19,099
Illinois	2,672,294	83,364	110,795
Indiana	2,285,048	78,792	45,483
Iowa	282,363	19,916	25,093
Maine	3,436,040	102,916	151,731
Massachusetts	3,585,384	481,021	112,385
Michigan	2,361,074	105,871	75,249
New Hampshire	4,307,919	183,117	70,256
New Jersey	3,715,251	1,255,578	6,492
New York	15,403,997	4,148,182	3,585,059
Ohio	5,245,760	425,918	354,358
Pennsylvania	6,032,904	4,805,160	165,584
Rhode Island	651,029	26,409	18,875
Vermont	4,951,014	176,233	42,150
Wisconsin	1,402,956	81,253	209,692
	59,033,170	12,574,623	5,002,013

TABLE NO. IV.

AGRICULTURAL PRODUCTS OF THE SLAVE STATES—1850.

States.	Potatoes, (I. & S.) bush.	Rye, bushels.	Barley, bushels.
Alabama	5,721,205	17,261	3,958
Arkansas	981,981	8,047	177
Delaware	305,985	8,066	56
Florida	765,054	1,152	
Georgia	7,213,807	53,750	11,501
Kentucky	2,490,666	415,073	95,343
Louisiana	1,524,085	475	
Maryland	973,932	226,014	745
Mississippi	5,003,277	9,606	228
Missouri	1,274,511	44,268	9,631
North Carolina	5,716,027	229,563	2,735
South Carolina	4,473,960	43,790	4,583
Tennessee	3,845,560	89,137	2,737
Texas	1,426,803	3,108	4,776
Virginia	3,130,567	458,930	25,437
	44,847,420	1,608,240	161,907

TABLE NO. V.

AGRICULTURAL PRODUCTS OF THE FREE STATES—1850.

States.	Buckwheat, bushels.	Beans & Peas, bushels.	Clov. & Grass seeds, bush.
California		2,292	
Connecticut...............	229,297	19,090	30,469
Illinois..........	184,509	82,814	17,807
Indiana.	149,740	35,773	30,271
Iowa......	52,516	4,475	2,438
Maine...	104,523	205,541	18,311
Massachusetts.	105,895	43,709	6,087
Michigan......	472,917	74,254	26,274
New Hampshire..	65,265	70,856	8,900
New Jersey..	878,934	14,174	91,331
New York...	3,183,955	741,546	184,715
Ohio....	638,060	60,168	140,501
Pennsylvania....	2,193,692	55,231	178,943
Rhode Island....	1,245	6,846	5,036
Vermont.....	209,819	104,649	15,696
Wisconsin.	79,878	20,657	5,486
	8,550,245	1,542,295	762,265

TABLE NO. VI.

AGRICULTURAL PRODUCTS OF THE SLAVE STATES—1850.

States.	Buckwheat, bushels.	Beans & Peas, bushels.	Clov. & Grass seeds, bush.
Alabama....	348	892,701	685
Arkansas..	175	285,738	526
Delaware.......	8,615	4,120	3,928
Florida.....	55	135,359	2
Georgia	250	1,142,011	560
Kentucky	16,097	202,574	24,711
Louisiana...	3	161,732	99
Maryland.....	103,671	12,816	17,778
Mississippi	1,121	1,072,757	617
Missouri	23,641	46,017	4,965
North Carolina....	16,704	1,584,252	1,851
South Carolina..	283	1,026,900	406
Tennessee.	19,427	369,321	14,214
Texas.....	59	179,351	10
Virginia....	214,898	521,579	53,155
	405,357	7,637,227	123,517

TABLE NO. VII.

AGRICULTURAL PRODUCTS OF THE FREE STATES—1850.

States.	Flaxseed, bushels.	Val. of Garden products.	Val. of Orchard prod'ts.
California		$75,275	$17,700
Connecticut....	703	196,874	175,118
Illinois...	10,787	127,494	446,049
Indiana...	36,888	72,864	324,940
Iowa....	1,959	8,848	8,434
Maine....	580	122,387	342,865
Massachusetts....	72	600,020	463,995
Michigan....	519	14,738	132,650
New Hampshire..	189	56,810	248,560
New Jersey....	16,525	475,242	607,268
New York....	57,963	912,047	1,761,950
Ohio...	188,880	214,004	695,921
Pennsylvania..	41,728	688,714	723,389
Rhode Island...		98,298	63,994
Vermont....	939	18,853	315,255
Wisconsin...	1,191	32,142	4,823
	358,923	$3,714,605	$6,332,914

TABLE NO. VIII.

AGRICULTURAL PRODUCTS OF THE SLAVE STATES—1850.

States.	Flaxseed, bushels.	Val. of Garden products.	Val. of Orchard prod'ts.
Alabama....	69	$84,821	$15,408
Arkansas....	321	17,150	40,141
Delaware..	904	12,714	46,574
Florida....		8,721	1,280
Georgia..	622	76,500	92,776
Kentucky....	75,801	303,120	106,230
Louisiana		148,329	22,259
Maryland....	2,446	200,869	164,051
Mississippi....	26	46,250	50,405
Missouri...	13,696	99,454	514,711
North Carolina..	38,196	39,462	34,348
South Carolina..	55	47,286	35,108
Tennessee....	18,904	97,183	52,894
Texas.	26	12,354	12,505
Virginia....	52,318	183,047	177,137
	203,484	$1,377,260	$1,355,827

RECAPITULATION—FREE STATES.

Wheat	72,157,486	bush.	@	1.50	$108,236,229
Oats	96,590,371	"	"	40	38,636,148
Indian Corn	242,618,650	"	"	60	145,571,190
Potatoes (I. & S.)	59,033,170	"	"	38	22,432,604
Rye	12,574,623	"	"	1.00	12,574,623
Barley	5,002,013	"	"	90	4,501,811
Buckwheat	8,550,245	"	"	50	4,275,122
Beans & Peas	1,542,295	"	"	1.75	2,699,015
Clov. & Grass seeds	762,265	"	"	3.00	2,286,795
Flax Seeds	358,923	"	"	1.25	448,647
Garden Products					3,714,605
Orchard Products					6,332,914

Total,......499,190,041 bushels, valued as above, at $351,709,703

RECAPITULATION—SLAVE STATES.

Wheat	27,904,476	bush.	@	1.50	$ 41,856,714
Oats	49,882,799	"	"	40	19,953,191
Indian Corn	348,992,282	"	"	60	209,395,369
Potatoes (I. & S.)	44,847,420	"	"	38	17,042,019
Rye	1,608,240	"	"	1.00	1,608,240
Barley	161,907	"	"	90	145,716
Buckwheat	405,357	"	"	50	202,678
Beans & Peas	7,637,227	"	"	1.75	13,365,147
Clov. & Grass seeds	123,517	"	"	3.00	370,551
Flax Seeds	203,484	"	"	1.25	254,355
Garden Products					1,377,260
Orchard Products					1,355,827

Total......481,766,889 bushels, valued as above, at $306,927,067

TOTAL DIFFERENCE—BUSHEL-MEASURE PRODUCTS.

	Bushels.	Value.
Free States	499,190,041	$351,709,703
Slave States	481,766,889	306,927,067

Balance in bushels 17,423,152 Difference in value...$44,782,636

So much for the boasted agricultural superiority of the South! Mark well the balance in bushels, and the difference in value! Is either in favor of the South? No! Are both in favor of the North? Yes! Here we have unquestionable proof that of all the bushel-measure products of the nation, the free states produce far more than one-half; and it is worthy of particular mention, that *the excess of Northern products is of the most valuable kind.* The account shows a balance against the South, in favor of the North, of *seventeen million four hundred and twenty-three thousand one hundred and fifty-two bushels,* and a difference in value of *forty-four million seven hundred and eighty-two thousand six hundred and thirty-six dollars.* Please bear these facts in mind, for, in order to show positively how the free and slave States do stand upon the great and important subject of rural economy, we intend to take an account of all the other products of the soil, of the live-stock upon farms, of the animals slaughtered, and, in fact, of every item of husbandry of the two sections; and if, in bringing our tabular exercises to a close, we find slavery gaining upon freedom — a thing it has never yet been known to do — we shall, as a matter of course, see that the above amount is transferred to the credit of the side to which it of right belongs.

In making up these tables we have two objects in view; the first is to open the eyes of the non-slaveholders of the South, to the system of deception, that has so long been practiced upon them, and the second is to show slaveholders themselves — we have reference only to those who are not too perverse, or ignorant, to perceive naked truths

—that free labor is far more respectable, profitable, and productive, than slave labor. In the South, unfortunately, no kind of labor is either free or respectable. Every white man who is under the necessity of earning his bread, by the sweat of his brow, or by manual labor, in any capacity, no matter how unassuming in deportment, or exemplary in morals, is treated as if he was a loathsome beast, and shunned with the utmost disdain. His soul may be the very seat of honor and integrity, yet without slaves — himself a slave — he is accounted as nobody, and would be deemed intolerably presumptuous, if he dared to open his mouth, even so wide as to give faint utterance to a three-lettered monosyllable, like yea or nay, in the presence of an august knight of the whip and the lash.

There are few Southerners who will not be astonished at the disclosures of these statistical comparisons, between the free and the slave States. That the astonishment of the more intelligent and patriotic non-slaveholders will be mingled with indignation, is no more than we anticipate. We confess our own surprise, and deep chagrin, at the result of our investigations. Until we examined into the matter, we thought and hoped the South was really ahead of the North in *one* particular, that of agriculture ; but our thoughts have been changed, and our hopes frustrated, for instead of finding ourselves the possessors of a single advantage, we behold our dear native South stripped of every laurel, and sinking deeper and deeper in the depths of poverty and shame ; while, at the same time, we see the North, our successful rival, extracting and absorbing the few elements of wealth yet remaining amongst us, and rising higher and higher in the scale of fame, fortune, and invulnerable power. Thus our disappointment gives way to a feeling of intense mortification, and our soul involuntarily, but justly, we believe, cries out for retribution against the treacherous, slave-driving legislators, who have so basely and unpatriotically neglected the interests of their poor white constituents and bargained away the rights of posterity. Notwithstanding the fact that the white non-slaveholders of the South, are in the majority, as five to one, they have never yet had any part or lot in framing the laws under which they live. There is no legislation except for the benefit of slavery, and slaveholders. As a general rule, poor white persons are regarded with less esteem and attention than negroes, and though the condition of the latter is wretched beyond description, vast numbers of the former are infinitely worse off. A cunningly devised mockery of freedom is guarantied to them, and that is all. To all intents and purposes they are disfranchised, and outlawed, and the only privilege extended to them, is a shallow and circumscribed participation in the political movements that usher slaveholders into office.

We have not breathed away seven and twenty years in the South, without becoming acquainted with the demagogical manœuverings of the oligarchy. Their intrigues and tricks of legerdemain are as familiar to us as household words ; in vain might the world be ransacked for a more precious junto of flatterers and cajolers. It is amusing to ignorance, amazing to credulity, and insulting to intelligence, to hear them in their blattering efforts to mystify and pervert the sacred principles of liberty, and turn the curse of slavery into a blessing. To the illiterate poor whites — made poor and ignorant by the system of slavery — they hold out the idea that slavery is the very bulwark of our liberties, and the foundation of American independence ! For hours at a time, day after day, will they expatiate upon the inexpressible beauties and excellencies of this great, *free* and *independent* nation ; and finally, with the most extravagant gesticulations and rhetorical flourishes, conclude their nonsensical ravings, by attributing all the glory and prosperity of the country, from Maine to Texas, and from Georgia to California, to the " invaluable institutions of the South !" With what patience we could command, we have frequently listened to the incoherent and truth-murdering declamations of these champions of slavery, and, in the absence of a more politic method of giving vent to our disgust and indignation, have involuntarily bit our lips into blisters.

The lords of the lash are not only absolute masters of the blacks, who are bought and sold, and driven about like so many cattle, but they are also the oracles and arbiters of all non-slaveholding whites, whose freedom is merely nominal, and whose unparalleled illiteracy and degradation is purposely and fiendishly perpetuated. How little the " poor white trash," the great majority of the Southern people, know of the real condition of the country is, indeed, sadly astonishing. The truth is, they know nothing of public measures, and little of private affairs, except what their imperious masters, the slave-drivers, condescend to tell, and that is but precious little, and even that little, always garbled and one-sided, is never told except in public harangues ; for the haughty cavaliers of shackles and handcuffs will not degrade themselves by holding private converse with those who have neither dimes nor hereditary rights in human flesh.

Whenever it pleases, and to the extent it pleases, a slaveholder to become communicative, poor whites may hear with fear and trembling, but not speak. They must be as mum as dumb brutes, and stand in awe of their august superiors, or be crushed with stern rebukes, cruel oppressions, or downright violence. If they dare to think for themselves, their thoughts must be forever concealed. The expression of any sentiment at all conflicting with the gospel of slavery, dooms them at once in the community in which they live, and then, whether willing or unwilling, they are obliged to become heroes, martyrs, or exiles. They may thirst for knowledge, but there is no Moses among them to smite it out of the rocks of Horeb. The black veil, through whose almost impenetrable meshes light seldom gleams, has long been pendent over their eyes, and there, with fiendish jealousy, the slave-driving ruffians sedulously guard it. Non-slaveholders are not only kept in ignorance of what is transpiring at the North, but they are continually misinformed of what is going on even in the South. Never were the poorer classes of a people, and those classes so largely in the majority, and all inhabiting the same country, so basely duped, so adroitly swindled, or so damnably outraged.

It is expected that the stupid and sequacious masses, the white victims of slavery, will believe, and, as a general thing, they do believe, whatever the slaveholders tell them ; and thus it is that they are cajoled into the notion that they are the freest, happiest and most intelligent people in the world, and are taught to look with prejudice and disapprobation upon every new principle or progressive movement. Thus it is that the South, woefully inert and inventionless, has lagged behind the North, and is now weltering in the cesspool of ignorance and degradation.

We have already intimated that the opinion is prevalent throughout the South that the free States are quite sterile and unproductive, and that they are mainly dependent on us for breadstuffs and other provisions. So far as the cereals, fruits, garden vegetables and esculent roots are concerned, we have, in the preceding tables, shown the utter falsity of this opinion ; and we now propose to show that it is equally erroneous in other particulars, and very far from the truth in the general reckoning. We can prove, and we intend to prove, from facts in our possession, that the hay crop of the free States is worth considerably more in dollars and cents than all the cotton, tobacco, rice, hay and hemp produced in the fifteen slave States. This statement may strike some of our readers with amazement, and others may, for the moment, regard it as quite incredible ; but it is true, nevertheless, and we shall soon proceed to confirm it. The single free State of New-York produces more than *three times* the quantity of hay that is produced in all the slave States. Ohio produces a larger number of tons than all the Southern and Southwestern States, and so does Pennsylvania. Vermont, little and unpretending as she is, does the same thing, with the exception of Virginia. Look at the facts as presented in the tables, and let your own eyes, physical and intellectual, confirm you in the truth.

And yet, forsooth, the slave-driving oligarchy would whip us into the belief that agriculture is not one of the leading and lucrative pursuits of the free States, that the soil there is an uninterrupted barren waste, and that our Northern brethren, having the advantage in nothing except wealth, population, inland and foreign commerce, manufactures, mechanism, inventions, literature, the arts and sciences, and their concomitant branches of profitable industry,—miserable objects of charity—are dependent on us for the necessaries of life.

Next to Virginia, Maryland is the greatest Southern hay-producing State ; and yet, it is the opinion of several of the most extensive hay and grain dealers in Baltimore, with whom we have conversed on the subject, that the domestic crop is scarcely equal to one-third the demand, and that the balance required for home consumption, about two-thirds, is chiefly brought from New-York, Pennsylvania and Massachusetts. At this rate, Maryland receives and consumes not less than three hundred and fifteen thousand tons of Northern hay every year ; and this, as we are informed by the dealers above-mentioned, at an average cost to the last purchaser, by the time it is stowed in the mow, of at least twenty-five dollars per ton ; it would thus appear that this most popular and valuable provender, one of the staple commodities of the North, commands a market in a single slave State, to the amount of seven million eight hundred and seventy-five thousand dollars per annum.

In this same State of Maryland, less than one million of dollar's worth of cotton finds a market, the whole number of bales sold here in 1850 amounting to only twenty-three thousand three hundred and twenty-five, valued at seven hundred and forty-six thousand four hundred dollars. Briefly, then, and in round numbers, we may state the case thus : Maryland buys annually seven millions of dollars worth of hay from the North, and one million of dollars worth of cotton from the South. Let slaveholders and their fawning defenders read, ponder and compare.

The exact quantities of Northern hay, rye, and buck-wheat flour, Irish potatoes, fruits, clover and grass seeds, and other products of the soil, received and consumed in all the slaveholding States, we have no means of ascertaining; but for all practical purposes, we can arrive sufficiently near to the amount by inference from the above data, and from what we see with our eyes and hear with our ears wherever we go. Food from the North for man or for beast, or for both, is for sale in every market in the South. Even in the most insignificant little villages in the interior of the slave States, where books, newspapers and other mediums of intelligence are unknown, where the poor whites and the negroes are alike bowed down in heathenish ignorance and barbarism, and where the news is received but once a week, and then only in a Northern-built stage-coach, drawn by horses in Northern harness, in charge of a driver dressed *cap-a-pie* in Northern habili-ments, and with a Northern whip in his hand,—the agricultural products of the North, either crude, prepared, pickled or preserved, are ever to be found.

Mortifying as the acknowledgment of the fact is to us, it is our unbiased opinion—an opinion which will, we believe, be endorsed by every intelligent person who goes into a careful examination and comparison of all the facts in the case—that the profits arising to the North from the sale of provender and provisions to the South, are far greater than those arising to the South from the sale of cotton, tobacco and breadstuffs to the North. It follows, then, that the agricultural interests of the North being not only equal but actually superior to those of the South, the hundreds of millions of dollars which the commerce and manufactures of the former annually yield, is just so much clear and independent gain over the latter. It follows, also, from a corresponding train or system of deduction, and with all the foregoing facts in view, that the difference between freedom and slavery is simply the difference between sense and nonsense, wisdom and folly, good and evil, right and wrong.

Any observant American, from whatever point of the compass he may hail, who will take the trouble to pass through the Southern markets, both great and small, as we have done, and inquire where this article, that and the other came from, will be utterly astonished at the variety and quantity of Northern agricultural productions kept for sale. And this state of things is growing worse and worse every year. Exclusively agricultural as the South is in her industrial pursuits, she is barely able to support her sparse and degenerate population. Her men and her domestic animals, both dwarfed into shabby objects of commiseration under the blighting effects of slavery, are constantly feeding on the multifarious products of Northern soil.   And if the whole truth must be told, we may here add, that these products, like all other articles of merchandize purchased at the North, are generally bought on a credit, and, in a great number of instances, by far too many, never paid for—not, as a general rule, because the purchasers are dishonest or unwilling to pay, but because they are impoverished and depressed by the retrogressive and deadening operations of slavery, that most unprofitable and pernicious institution under which they live.

To show how well we are sustained in our remarks upon hay and other special products of the soil, as well as to give circulation to other facts of equal significance, we quote a single passage from an address by Paul C. Cameron, before the Agricultural Society of Orange County, North Carolina.   This production is, in the main, so powerfully conceived, so correct and plausible in its statements and conclusions, and so well calculated, though, perhaps, not intended, to arouse the old North State to a sense of her natural greatness and acquired shame, that we could wish to see it published in pamphlet form, and circulated throughout the length and breadth of that unfortunate and degraded heritage of slavery.   Mr. Cameron says :

"I know not when I have been more humiliated, as a North Carolina farmer, than when, a few weeks ago, at a railroad depot at the very doors of our State capital, I saw

3

wagons drawn by Kentucky mules, loading with Northern hay, for the supply not only of the town, but to be taken to the country. Such a sight at the capital of a State whose population is almost exclusively devoted to agriculture, is a most humiliating exhibition. Let us cease to use every thing, as far as it is practicable, that is not the product of our own soil and workshops—not an axe, or a broom, or bucket, from Connecticut. By every consideration of self-preservation, we are called to make better efforts to expel the Northern grocer from the State with his butter, and the Ohio and Kentucky horse, mule and hog driver, from our county at least. It is a reproach on us as farmers, and no little deduction from our wealth, that we suffer the population of our towns and villages to supply themselves with butter from another Orange County in New-York."

We have promised to prove that the hay crop of the free states is worth considerably more than all the cotton, tobacco, rice, hay and hemp produced in the fifteen slave States. The compilers of the last census, as we learn from Prof. De Bow, the able and courteous superintendent, in making up the hay-tables, allowed two thousand two hundred and forty pounds to the ton. The price per ton at which we should estimate its value has puzzled us to some extent. Dealers in the article in Baltimore think it will average twenty-five dollars, in their market. Four or five months ago they sold it at thirty dollars per ton. At the very time we write, though there is less activity in the article than usual, we learn, from an examination of sundry prices-current and commercial journals, that hay is selling in Savannah at $33 per ton ; in Mobile and New Orleans at $26 ; in Charleston at $25 ; in Louisville at $24 ; and in Cincinnati at $23. The average of these prices is *twenty-six dollars sixteen and two-third cents;* and we suppose it would be fair to employ the figures which would indicate this amount, the net value of a single ton, in calculating the total market value of the entire crop. Were we to do this—and, with the foregoing facts in view, we submit to intelligent men whether we would not be justifiable in doing it,—the hay crop of the free states, 12,690,982 tons, in 1850, would amount in valuation to the enormous sum of $331,081,695—more than four times the value of all the cotton produced in the United States during the same period !

But we shall not make the calculation at what we have found to be the average value per ton throughout the country. What rate, then, shall be agreed upon as a basis of comparison between the value of the hay crop of the North and that of the South, and as a means of testing the truth of our declaration—that the former exceeds the aggregate value of all the cotton, tobacco, rice, hay and hemp produced in the fifteen slave States ? Suppose we take $13,08⅓—just half the average value—as the multiplier in this arithmetical exercise. This we can well afford to do ; indeed, we might reduce the amount per ton to much less than half the average value, and still have a large margin left for triumphant demonstration. It is not our purpose, however, to make an overwhelming display of the incomparable greatness of the free States.

In estimating the value of the various agricultural pro-

ducts of the two great sections of the country, we have
been guided by prices emanating from the Bureau of Agriculture in Washington ; and in a catalogue of those prices
now before us, we perceive that the average value of hay
throughout the nation is supposed to be not more than
half a cent per pound—$11.20 per ton—which, as we have
seen above, is considerably less than half the present
market value ;—and this, too, in the face of the fact that
prices generally rule higher than they do just now. It
will be admitted on all sides, however, that the prices fixed
upon by the Bureau of Agriculture, taken as a whole, are
as fair for one section of the country as for the other, and
that we cannot blamelessly deviate from them in one particular without deviating from them in another.   Eleven
dollars and twenty cents ($11.20) per ton shall therefore
be the price ; and, notwithstanding these greatly reduced
figures, we now renew, with an addendum, our declaration
and promise, that—*We can prove, and we shall now proceed to
prove, that the annual hay crop of the free States is worth considerably more in dollars and cents than all the cotton, tobacco, rice,
hay, hemp and cane sugar annually produced in the fifteen slave
States.*

HAY CROP OF THE FREE STATES — 1850.

12,690,982 tons *a* 11,20 .... $142,138,998

SUNDRY PRODUCTS OF THE SLAVE STATES — 1850.

Cotton	2,445,779 bales	*a* 32,00	$78,264,928
Tobacco	185,023,906 lbs.	" 10	18,502,390
Rice (rough)	215,313,497 lbs.	" 4	8,612,539
Hay	1,137,784 tons	" 11,20	12,743,180
Hemp	34,673 tons	" 112,00	3,883,376
Cane Sugar	237,133,000 lbs.	" 7	16,599,310

$138,605,723

RECAPITULATION.

Hay crop of the free States $142,138,998
Sundry products of the slave States 138,605,723

Balance in favor of the free States $3,533,275

There is the account ; look at it, and let it stand in attestation of the exalted virtues and surpassing powers of freedom. Scan it well, Messieurs lords of the lash, and learn from it new lessons of the utter inefficiency, and despicable imbecility of slavery. Examine it minutely, liberty-loving patriots of the North, and behold in it additional evidences of the beauty, grandeur, and super-excellence of free institutions. Treasure it up in your minds, outraged friends and non-slaveholders of the South, and let the recollection of it arouse you to an inflexible determination to extirpate the monstrous enemy that stalks abroad in your land, and to recover the inalienable rights and liberties, which have been filched from you by an unprincipled oligarchy.

In deference to truth, decency and good sense, it is to

be hoped that negro-driving politicians will never more have the effrontery to open their mouths in extolling the agricultural achievements of slave labor. Especially is it desirable, that, as a simple act of justice to a basely deceived populace, they may cease their stale and senseless harangues on the importance of cotton. The value of cotton to the South, to the North, to the nation, and to the world, has been so grossly exaggerated, and so extensive have been the evils which have resulted in consequence of the extraordinary misrepresentations concerning it, that we should feel constrained to reproach ourself for remissness of duty, if we failed to make an attempt to explode the popular error. The figures above show what it is, and what it is not. Recur to them, and learn the facts.

So hyperbolically has the importance of cotton been magnified by certain pro-slavery politicians of the South, that the person who would give credence to all their fustian and bombast, would be under the necessity of believing that the very existence of almost everything, in the heaven above, in the earth beneath, and in the water under the earth, depended on it. The truth is, however, that the cotton crop is of but little value to the South. New England and Old England, by their superior enterprise and sagacity, turn it chiefly to their own advantage. It is carried in their ships, spun in their factories, woven in their looms, insured in their offices, returned again in their own vessels, and, with double freight and cost of manufacturing added, purchased by the South at a high premium. Of all the parties engaged or interested in its transportation and manufacture, the South is the only one that

does not make a profit. Nor does she, as a general thing,
make a profit by producing it.

We are credibly informed that many of the farmers in
the immediate vicinity of Baltimore, where we now write,
have turned their attention exclusively to hay, and that
from one acre they frequently gather two tons, for which
they receive fifty dollars. Let us now inquire how many
dollars may be expected from an acre planted in cotton.
Mr. Cameron, from whose able address before the Agricultural Society of Orange County, North Carolina, we have
already gleaned some interesting particulars, informs us,
that the cotton planters in his part of the country, "have
contented themselves with a crop yielding only *ten or
twelve dollars per acre*," and that "the summing up of a large
surface gives but a living result." An intelligent resident
of the Palmetto State, writing in De Bow's Review,
not long since, advances the opinion that the cotton
planters of South Carolina are not realizing more than one
per cent. on the amount of capital they have invested.
While in Virginia, very recently, an elderly slaveholder,
whose religious walk and conversation had recommended
and promoted him to an eldership in the Presbyterian
church, and who supports himself and family by raising
niggers and tobacco, told us that, for the last eight or ten
years, aside from the increase of his human chattels, he
felt quite confident he had not cleared as much even as
one per cent. per annum on the amount of his investment.
The real and personal property of this aged *Christian* consists chiefly in a large tract of land and about thirty negroes, most of whom, according to his own confession, are

more expensive than profitable. The proceeds arising from the sale of the tobacco they produce, are all absorbed in the purchase of meat and bread for home consumption, and when the crop is stunted by drought, frost, or otherwise cut short, one of the negroes must be sold to raise funds for the support of the others. Such are the agricultural achievements of slave labor ; such are the results of " the sum of all villainies." The diabolical institution subsists on its own flesh. At one time children are sold to procure food for the parents, at another, parents are sold to procure food for the children. Within its pestilential atmosphere, nothing succeeds ; progress and prosperity are unknown ; inanition and slothfulness ensue ; everything becomes dull, dismal and unprofitable ; wretchedness and desolation run riot throughout the land; an aspect of most melancholy inactivity and dilapidation broods over every city and town ; ignorance and prejudice sit enthroned over the minds of the people ; usurping despots wield the sceptre of power ; everywhere, and in everything, between Delaware Bay and the Gulf of Mexico, are the multitudinous evils of slavery apparent.

The soil itself soon sickens and dies beneath the unnatural tread of the slave. Hear what the Hon. C. C. Clay, of Alabama, has to say upon the subject. His testimony is eminently suggestive, well-timed, and truthful ; and we heartily commend it to the careful consideration of every spirited Southron who loves his country, and desires to see it rescued from the fatal grasp of " the mother of harlots :" Says he :

"I can show you, with sorrow, in the older portions of

Alabama, and in my native county of Madison, the sad memorials of the artless and exhausting culture of cotton. Our small planters, after taking the cream off their lands, unable to restore them by rest, manures, or otherwise, are going further West and South, in search of other virgin lands, which they may and will despoil and impoverish in like manner.   Our wealthier planters, with greater means and no more skill, are buying out their poorer neighbors, extending their plantations, and adding to their slave force.   The wealthy few, who are able to live on smaller profits, and to give their blasted fields some rest, are thus pushing off the many who are merely independent.   Of the $20,000,000 annually realized from the sales of the cotton crop of Alabama, nearly all not expended in supporting the producers, is re-invested in land and negroes.   Thus the white population has decreased and the slave increased almost *pari passu* in several counties of our State.   In 1825, Madison county cast about 3,000 votes ; now, she cannot cast exceeding 2,300.   In traversing that county, one will discover numerous farm-houses, once the abode of industrious and intelligent freemen, now occupied by slaves, or tenantless, deserted and dilapidated ; he will observe fields, once fertile, now unfenced, abandoned, and covered with those evil harbingers, fox-tail and broom-sedge ; he will see the moss growing on the mouldering walls of once thrifty villages, and will find ' one only master grasps the whole domain,' that once furnished happy homes for a dozen white families.   Indeed, a country in its infancy, where fifty years ago scarce a forest tree had been felled by the axe of the pioneer, is already exhibiting the painful signs of senility and decay, apparent in Virginia and the Carolinas."

Some one has said that " an honest confession is good for the soul," and if the adage be true, as we have no doubt it is, we think Mr. C. C. Clay is entitled to a quiet conscience on one score at least. In the extract quoted above, he gives us a graphic description of the ruinous operations and influences of slavery in the Southwest ; and we, as a native of Carolina, and a traveler through Virginia, are ready to bear testimony to the fitness of his remarks when he referred to those States as examples of senility and decay. With equal propriety, however, he might have stopped nearer home for a subject of comparison. Either of the States bordering upon Alabama, or, indeed, any other slave States, would have answered his purpose quite as well as Virginia and the Carolinas. Wherever slavery exists there he may find parallels to the destruction that is sweeping with such deadly influence over his own unfortunate State.

As for examples of vigorous, industrious and thrifty communities, they can be found anywhere beyond the Upas-shadow of slavery—nowhere else. New-York and Massachusetts, which, by nature, are confessedly far inferior to Virginia and the Carolinas, have, by the more liberal and equitable policy which they have pursued, in substituting liberty for slavery, attained a degree of eminence and prosperity altogether unknown in the slave States.

Amidst all the hyperbole and cajolery of slave-driving politicians who, as we have already seen, are ' the books, the arts, the academies, that show, contain, and govern all the South,' we are rejoiced to see that Mr. Clay, Mr. Cameron, and a few others, have had the boldness and honesty to step forward and proclaim the truth. All such frank admissions are to be hailed as good omens for the South. Nothing good can come from any attempt to conceal the unconcealable evidences of poverty and desolation everywhere trailing in the wake of slavery. Let the truth be told on all occasions, of the North as well as of the South, and the people will soon begin to discover the egregiousness of their errors, to draw just comparisons, to inquire into cause and effect, and to adopt the more utile measures, manners and customs of their wiser cotemporaries.

In wilfully traducing and decrying everything North of Mason and Dixon's line, and in excessively magnifying the importance of everything South of it, the oligarchy have, in the eyes of all liberal and intelligent men, only made an exhibition of their uncommon folly and dishonesty. For a long time, it is true, they have succeeded in deceiving the people, in keeping them humbled in the murky sloughs of poverty and ignorance, and in instilling into their untutored minds passions and prejudices expressly calculated to strengthen and protect the accursed institution of slavery ; but, thanks to heaven, their inglorious reign is fast drawing to a close ; with irresistible brilliancy, and in spite of the interdict of tyrants, light from the pure fountain of knowledge is now streaming over the dark places of our land, and, ere long—mark our words—there will ascend from Delaware, and from Texas, and from all the intermediate States, a huzza for Freedom and for Equal Rights, that will utterly confound the friends of despotism, set at defiance the authority of usurpers, and carry consternation to the heart of every slavery-propagandist.

To undeceive the people of the South, to bring them to a knowledge of the inferior and disreputable position which they occupy as a component part of the Union, and to give prominence and popularity to those plans which, if adopted, will elevate us to an equality, socially, morally, intellectually, industrially, politically, and financially, with the most flourishing and refined nation in the world, and, if possible, to place us in the van of even that, is the object of this work.   Slaveholders, either from ignorance or from a wilful disposition to propagate error, contend that the South has nothing to be ashamed of, that slavery has proved a blessing to her, and that her superiority over the North in an agricultural point of view makes amends for all her shortcomings in other respects.   On the other hand, we contend that many years of continual blushing and severe penance would not suffice to cancel or annul the shame and disgrace that justly attaches to the South in consequence of slavery —the direst evil that e'er befell the land—that the South bears nothing like even a respectable approximation to the North in navigation, commerce, or manufactures, and that, contrary to the opinion entertained by ninety-nine hundredths of her people, she is far behind the free States in the only thing of which she has ever dared to boast—agriculture.   We submit the question to the arbitration of figures, which, it is said, do not lie.   With regard to the bushel-measure products of the soil, of which we have already taken an inventory, we have seen that there is a balance against the South in favor of the North of *seventeen million four hundred and twenty-three thousand one hundred and fifty-two bushels*, and a difference in the value of the same, also in favor of the North, of *forty-four million seven hundred and eighty-two thousand six hundred and thirty-six dollars.* It is certainly a most novel kind of agricultural superiority that the South claims on that score !

Our attention shall now be directed to the twelve principal pound-measure products of the free and of the slave States—hay, cotton, butter and cheese, tobacco, cane, sugar, wool, rice, hemp, maple sugar, beeswax and honey, flax, and hops—and in taking an account of them, we shall, in order to show the exact quantity produced in each State, and for the convenience of future reference, pursue the same plan as that adopted in the preceding tables. Whether slavery will appear to better advantage on the scales than it did in the half-bushel, remains to be seen. It is possible that the rickety monster may make a better show on a new track ; if it makes a more ridiculous display, we shall not be surprised. A careful examination of its precedents, has taught us the folly of expecting anything good to issue from it in any manner whatever. It has no disposition to emulate the magnanimity of its betters, and as for a laudable ambition to excel, that is a characteristic altogether foreign to its nature. Languor and inertia are the insalutary viands upon which it delights to satiate its morbid appetite ; and "from bad to worse" is the ill-omened motto under which, in all its feeble efforts and achievements, it ekes out a most miserable and deleterious existence.

TABLE NO. IX.

AGRICULTURAL PRODUCTS OF THE FREE STATES—1850.

States.	Hay, tons.	Hemp, tons.	Hops, lbs.
California	2,038		
Connecticut..............	516,131		554
Illinois..................	601,952		3,551
Indiana.	403,230		92,796
Iowa.....................	89,055		8,242
Maine...	755,889		40,120
Massachusetts.	651,807		121,595
Michigan.....	404,934		10,663
New Hampshire..	598,854		257,174
New Jersey..	435,950		2,133
New York..............	3,728,797	4	2,536,299
Ohio....	1,443,142	150	63,731
Pennsylvania............	1,842,970	44	22,088
Rhode Island..	74,418		277
Vermont.....	866,153		288,023
Wisconsin.	275,662		15,930
	12,690,982	198	3,463,176

TABLE NO. X.

AGRICULTURAL PRODUCTS OF THE SLAVE STATES—1850.

States.	Hay, tons.	Hemp, tons.	Hops, lbs.
Alabama....	32,685		276
Arkansas..	3,976	15	157
Delaware......	30,159		348
Florida.....	2,510		14
Georgia.....	23,449		261
Kentucky	113,747	17,787	4,309
Louisiana.....	25,752		125
Maryland............. ..	157,956	63	1,870
Mississippi...	12,504	7	473
Missouri....	116,925	16,028	4,130
North Carolina....	145,653	39	9,246
South Carolina...........	20,925		26
Tennessee.	74,091	595	1,032
Texas.....	8,354		7
Virginia..	369,098	139	11,506
	1,137,784	34,673	33,780

TABLE NO. XI.

AGRICULTURAL PRODUCTS OF THE FREE STATES—1850.

States.	Flax, lbs.	Maple Sugar, lbs.	Tobacco, lbs.
California			1,000
Connecticut	17,928	50,796	1,267,624
Illinois	160,063	248,904	841,394
Indiana	584,469	2,921,192	1,044,620
Iowa	62,660	78,407	6,041
Maine	17,081	93,542	
Massachusetts	1,162	795,525	138,246
Michigan	7,152	2,439,794	1,245
New Hampshire	7,652	1,298,863	50
New Jersey	182,965	2,197	310
New York	940,577	10,357,484	83,189
Ohio	446,932	4,588,209	10,454,449
Pennsylvania	530,307	2,326,525	912,651
Rhode Island	85	28	
Vermont	20,852	6,349,357	
Wisconsin	68,393	610,976	1,268
	3,048,278	32,161,799	14,752,087

TABLE NO. XII.

AGRICULTURAL PRODUCTS OF THE SLAVE STATES—1850.

States.	Flax, lbs.	Maple Sugar, lbs.	Tobacco, lbs.
Alabama	3,921	643	164,990
Arkansas	12,291	9,330	218,936
Delaware	17,174		
Florida	50		998,614
Georgia	5,387	50	423,924
Kentucky	2,100,116	437,405	55,501,196
Louisiana		255	26,878
Maryland	35,686	47,740	21,407,497
Mississippi	665		49,960
Missouri	627,160	178,910	17,113,784
North Carolina	593,796	27,932	11,984,786
South Carolina	333	200	74,285
Tennessee	368,131	158,557	20,148,932
Texas	1,048		66,897
Virginia	1,000,450	1,227,665	56,803,227
	4,765,198	2,088,687	185,023,906

TABLE NO. XIII.

ANIMAL PRODUCTS OF THE FREE STATES—1850.

States.	Wool, lbs.	Butter and Cheese, lbs.	Beeswax and Honey, lbs.
California	5,520	855	
Connecticut..............	497,454	11,861,396	93,304
Illinois.............	2,150,113	13,804,768	869,444
Indiana.	2,610,287	13,506,099	935,329
Iowa.......	373,898	2,381,028	321,711
Maine...	1,364,034	11,678,265	189,618
Massachusetts.	585,136	15,159,512	59,508
Michigan......	2,043,283	8,077,390	359,232
New Hampshire..	1,108,476	10,173,619	117,140
New Jersey..	375,396	9,852,966	156,694
New York..	10,071,801	129,507,507	1,755,830
Ohio.... ....:	10,196,371	55,268,921	804,275
Pennsylvania....	4,481,570	42,383,452	839,509
Rhode Island....	129,692	1,312,178	6,347
Vermont.....	3,400,717	20,858,814	249,422
Wisconsin.	253,963	4,034,033	131,005
	39,647,211	349,860,783	6,888,368

TABLE NO. XVI.

ANIMAL PRODUCTS OF THE SLAVE STATES—1850.

States.	Wool, lbs.	Butter and Cheese, lbs.	Beeswax and Honey, lbs.
Alabama....	657,118	4,040,223	897,021
Arkansas.... ....₀	182,595	1,884,327	192,338
Delaware..	57,768	1,058,495	41,248
Florida....	23,247	389,513	18,971
Georgia.	990,019	4,687,535	732,514
Kentucky...	2,297,433	10,161,477	1,158,019
Louisiana	109,897	685,026	96,701
Maryland..	477,438	3,810,135	74,802
Mississippi....	559,619	4,367,425	397,460
Missouri....	1,627,164	8,037,931	1,328,972
North Carolina... ..-	970,738	4,242,211	512,289
South Carolina...	487,233	2,986,820	216,281
Tennessee....	1,364,378	8,317,266	1,036,572
Texas....	131,917	2,440,199	380,825
Virginia	2,860,765	11,525,651	880,767
	12,797,329	68,634,224	7,964,760

TABLE NO. XV.

AGRICULTURAL PRODUCTS OF THE SLAVE STATES—1850.

States.	Cotton, bales of 400 lbs.	Cane Sugar, hhds. 1000 lbs.	Rough Rice, lbs.
Alabama............	564,429	87	2,312,252
Arkansas..	65,344		63,179
Delaware.......			
Florida.....	45,131	2,750	1,075,090
Georgia....	499,091	846	38,950,691
Kentucky	758	10	5,688
Louisiana....	178,737	226,001	4,425,349
Maryland....			
Mississippi	484,292	8	2,719,856
Missouri....			700
North Carolina....	50,545		5,465,868
South Carolina..........	300,901	77	159,930,613
Tennessee.	194,532	3	258,854
Texas.....	58,072	7,351	88,203
Virginia....	3,947		17,154
	2,445,779	237,133	215,313,497

RECAPITULATION—FREE STATES.

Hay...............	28,427,799,680 lbs.	@	1-2 c.	$142,138,998
Hemp....	443,520	"	"	5 "	22,176
Hops.....	3,463,176	"	"	15 "	519,476
Flax.	3,048,278	"	"	10 "	304,827
Maple Sugar.........	32,161,799	"	"	8 "	2,572,943
Tobacco............	14,752,087	"	"	10 "	1,475,208
Wool...............	39,647,211	"	"	35 "	13,876,523
Butter and Cheese...	349,860,783	"	"	15 "	52,479,117
Beeswax and Honey..	6,888,368	"	"	15 "	1,033,255

Total,..... ..28,878,064,902 lbs., valued as above, $214,422,523

RECAPITULATION — SLAVE STATES.

Hay	2,548,636,160	lbs. @	1-2	c.	...$12,743,180
Hemp	77,667,520	" "	5	"	3,883,376
Hops	33,780	" "	15	"	5,067
Flax	4,766,198	" "	10	"	476,619
Maple Sugar	2,088,687	" "	8	"	167,094
Tobacco	185,023,906	" "	10	"	.:....18,502,390
Wool	12,797,329	" "	35	"	4,479,065
Butter and Cheese	68,634,224	" "	15	"	10,295,133
Beeswax and Honey	7,964,760	" "	15	"	1,194,714
Cotton	978,311,600	" "	8	"	78,264,928
Cane Sugar	237,133,000	" "	7	"	16,599,310
Rice (rough)	215,313,497	" "	4	"	8,612,539

Total.......4,338,370,661 lbs. valued as above, at $155,223,415

TOTAL DIFFERENCE — POUND-MEASURE PRODUCTS.

	Pounds.	*Value.*
Free States	28,878,064,902	$214,422,523
Slave States	4,338,370,661	155,223,415

Balance in pounds, 24,539,694,241 Difference in value, $59,199,108

Both quantity and value again in favor of the North !
Behold also the enormousness of the difference ! In this
comparison with the South, neither hundreds, thousands,
nor millions, according to the regular method of computation, are sufficient to exhibit the excess of the pound-
measure products of the North. Recourse must be had to
an almost inconceivable number ; billions must be called
into play ; and there are the figures telling us, with unmistakable emphasis and distinctness, that, in this department of agriculture, as in every other, the North is vastly
the superior of the South—the figures showing a total
balance in favor of the former of *twenty-four billion five hun-*

dred and thirty-nine million six hundred and ninety-four thousand two hundred and forty-one pounds, valued · at *fifty-nine million one hundred and ninety-nine thousand one hundred and eight dollars.* And yet, the North is a poor, God-forsaken country, bleak, inhospitable, and unproductive!

What next? Is it necessary to adduce other facts in order to prove that the rural wealth of the free States is far greater than that of the slave States? Shall we make a further demonstration of the fertility of northern soil, or bring forward new evidences of the inefficient and desolating system of terra-culture in the South? Will nothing less than "confirmations strong as proofs of holy writ," suffice to convince the South that she is standing in her own light, and ruining both body and soul by the retention of slavery? Whatever duty and expedience require to be done, we are willing to do. Additional proofs are at hand. Slaveholders and slave-breeders shall be convinced, confuted, convicted, and converted. They shall, in their hearts and consciences, if not with their tongues and pens, bear testimony to the triumphant achievements of free labor. In the two tables which immediately follow these remarks, they shall see how much more vigorous and fruitful the soil is when under the prudent management of free white husbandmen, than it is when under the rude and nature-murdering tillage of enslaved negroes; and in two subsequent tables they shall find that the live stock, slaughtered animals, farms, and farming implements and machinery, in the free States, are worth at least *one thousand million of dollars* more than the market value of the same in the slave States! In the face, however, of all these most significant and incontrovertible facts, the oligarchy have the unparalleled audacity to tell us that the South is the greatest agricultural country in the world, and that the North is a dreary waste, unfit for cultivation, and quite dependent on us for the necessaries of life. How preposterously false all such babble is, the following tables will show :—

TABLE NO. XVI.

ACTUAL CROPS PER ACRE ON THE AVERAGE IN THE FREE STATES—1850.

States.	Wheat, bushels.	Oats, bushels.	Rye. bushels.	Ind. Corn, bushels.	Irish Potatoes, bush.
Connecticut..		21		40	85
Illinois..	11	29	14	33	115
Indiana.	12	20	18	33	100
Iowa...	14	36		32	100
Maine...	10			27	120
Massachusetts....	16	26	13	31	170
Michigan..	10	26		32	140
New Hampshire...	11	30		30	220
New Jersey..	11	26		33	
New York...	12	25	17	27	100
Ohio....	12	21	25	36	
Pennsylvania.....	15			20	75
Rhode Island.....		30			100
Vermont.	13		20	32	178
Wisconsin........	14	35		30	
	161	325	107	436	1,503

TABLE NO. XVII.

ACTUAL CROPS PER ACRE ON THE AVERAGE IN THE SLAVE STATES—1850.

States.	Wheat, bushels.	Oats, bushels.	Rye, bushels.	Ind. Corn, bushels.	Irish Potatoes, bush.
Alabama.........	5	12		15	60
Arkansas........		18		22	
Delaware.........	11	20		20	
Florida	15				175
Georgia..........	5	18	7	16	125
Kentucky........	8	18	11	24	130
Louisiana.				16	
Maryland.........	13	21	18	23	75
Mississippi.......	9	12		18	105
Missouri.........	11	26		34	110
North Carolina....	7	10	15	17	65
South Carolina...:	8	12		11	70
Tennessee........	7	19	7	21	120
Texas......	15			20	250
Virginia...	7	13	5	18	75
	121	199	63	275	1,360

RECAPITULATION OF ACTUAL CROPS PER ACRE ON THE
AVERAGE — 1850.

FREE STATES.	SLAVE STATES.
Wheat ...... 12 bushels per acre.	Wheat ...... 9 bushels per acre.
Oats........27 " "	Oats........17 " "
Rye ....18 " "	Rye ....11 " "
Indian Corn 31 " "	Indian Corn .20 " "
Irish Potatoes 125 " "	Irish Potatoes 113 " "

What an obvious contrast between the vigor of Liberty
and the impotence of Slavery! What an unanswerable
argument in favor of free labor! Add up the two columns
of figures above, and what is the result? Two hundred
and thirteen bushels as the products of five acres in the
North, and only one hundred and seventy bushels as the
products of five acres in the South. Look at each item
separately, and you will find that the average crop per
acre of every article enumerated is greater in the free
States than it is in the slave States. Examine the table
at large, and you will perceive that while Massachusetts
produces sixteen bushels of wheat to the acre, Virginia
produces only seven; that Pennsylvania produces fifteen
and Georgia only five: that while Iowa produces thirty-
six bushels of oats to the acre, Mississippi produces only
twelve; that Rhode Island produces thirty, and North Carolina only ten: that while Ohio produces twenty-five
bushels of rye to the acre, Kentucky produces only eleven;
that Vermont produces twenty, and Tennessee only seven:
that while Connecticut produces forty bushels of Indian
corn to the acre, Texas produces only twenty; that New
Jersey produces thirty-three, and South Carolina only
eleven: that while New Hampshire produces two hundred
and twenty bushels of Irish potatoes to the acre, Maryland
produces only seventy-five; that Michigan produces one
hundred and forty, and Alabama only sixty. Now for
other beauties of slavery in another table.

TABLE NO. XVIII.

VALUE OF FARMS AND DOMESTIC ANIMALS IN THE FREE STATES
—1850.

States.	Value of Live Stock.	Val. of Animals Slaughtered.	Cash Val. of Farms, Farm. Imp. & Mac.
California	$3,351,058	$107,173	$3,977,524
Connecticut	7,467,490	2,202,266	74,618,963
Illinois..........	24,209,258	4,972,286	102,538,851
Indiana.	22,478,555	6,567,935	143,089,617
Iowa............	3,689,275	821,164	17,830,436
Maine...	9,705,726	1,646,778	57,146,305
Massachusetts...	9,647,710	2,500,924	112,285,931
Michigan........	8,008,734	1,328,327	54,763,817
New Hampshire..	8,871,901	1,522,873	57,560,122
New Jersey......	10,679,291	2,638,552	124,663,014
New York.......	73,570,499	13,573,883	576,631,568
Ohio.....	44,121,741	7,439,243	371,509,188
Pennsylvania....	41,500,053	8,219,848	422,598,640
Rhode Island....	1,532,637	667,486	17,568,003
Vermont.........	12,643,228	1,861,336	66,106,509
Wisconsin.	4,897,385	920,178	30,170,131
	$286,376,541	$56,990,237	$2,233,058,619

TABLE NO. XIX.

VALUE OF FARMS AND DOMESTIC ANIMALS IN THE SLAVE STATES
—1850.

States.	Value of Live Stock.	Val. of Animals Slaughtered.	Cash Val. of Farms, Farm. Imp. & Mac.
Alabama........	$21,690,112	$4,823,485	$69,448,887
Arkansas........	6,647,969	1,163,313	16,866,541
Delaware........	1,849,281	373,665	19,390,310
Florida	2,880,058	514,685	6,981,904
Georgia.........	25,728,416	6,339,762	101,647,595
Kentucky.......	29,661,436	6,462,598	160,190,299
Louisiana.	11,152,275	1,458,990	87,391,336
Maryland........	7,997,634	1,954,800	89,641,988
Mississippi......	19,403,662	3,636,582	60,501,561
Missouri........	19,887,580	3,367,106	67,207,068
North Carolina...	17,717,647	5,767,866	71,823,298
South Carolina...	15,060,015	3,502,637	86,568,038
Tennessee.......	29,978,016	6,401,765	103,211,422
Texas.......	10,412,927	1,116,137	18,701,712
Virginia..	33,656,659	7,502,986	223,423,315
	$253,723,687	$54,388,377	$1,183,995,274

RECAPITULATION—FREE STATES.

Value of live Stock $286,376,541
Value of Animals slaughtered,.................... 56,990,237
Value of Farms, Farming-Implements and Machinery, 2,233,058,619
—————
$2,576,425,397

RECAPITULATION—SLAVE STATES.

Value of Live Stock........................... $253,723,687
Value of Animals slaughtered 54,388,377
Value of Farms, Farming Implements and Machinery, 1,183,995,274
—————
$1,492,107,338

DIFFERENCE IN VALUE—FARMS AND DOMESTIC ANIMALS.

Free States, ... $2,576,425,397
Slave States 1,492,107,338

Balance in favor of the Free States............. $1,084,318,059

By adding to this last balance in favor of the free States the differences in value which we found in their favor in our account of the bushel-and-pound-measure products, we shall have a very correct idea of the extent to which the undivided agricultural interests of the free States preponderate over those of the slave States. Let us add the differences together, and see what will be the result.

BALANCES—ALL IN FAVOR OF THE NORTH.

Difference in the value of bushel-measure products.. $44,782,636
Difference in the value of pound-measure products.. 59,199,108
Difference in the value of farms and domestic animals 1,084,318,059

Total...................$1,188,299,803

No figures of rhetoric can add emphasis or significance to these figures of arithmetic. They demonstrate conclusively the great moral triumph of Liberty over Slavery. They show unequivocally, in spite of all the blarney and boasting of slave-driving politicians, that the entire value of all the agricultural interests of the free States is very nearly twice as great as the entire value of all the agricultural interests of the slave States—the value of those interests in the former being twenty-five hundred million of dollars, that of those in the latter only fourteen hundred million, leaving a balance in favor of the free States of *one billion one hundred and eighty-eight million two hundred and ninety-nine thousand eight hundred and three dollars !* That is what we call a full, fair and complete vindication of Free Labor. Would we not be correct in calling it a total eclipse of the Black Orb? Can it be possible that the slavocracy will ever have the hardihood to open their mouths again on the subject of terra-culture in the South? Dare they ever think of cotton again? Ought they not, as a befitting confession of their crimes and misdemeanors, and as a reasonable expiation for the countless evils which they have inflicted on society, to clothe themselves in sackcloth, and, after a suitable season of contrition and severe penance, follow the example of one Judas Iscariot, and go and hang themselves?

It will be observed that we have omitted the Territories and the District of Columbia in all the preceding tables. We did this purposely. Our object was to draw an equitable comparison between the value of free and slave labor in the thirty-one sovereign States, where the two systems, comparatively unaffected by the wrangling of politicians, and, as a matter of course, free from the interference of

4

the general government, have had the fullest opportunities to exert their influence, to exhibit their virtues, and to commend themselves to the sober judgments of enlightened and discriminating minds. Had we counted the Territories on the side of the North, and the District of Columbia on the side of the South, the result would have been still greater in behalf of free labor. Though "the sum of all villanies" has but a mere nominal existence in Delaware and Maryland, we have invariably counted those States on the side of the South ; and the consequence is, that, in many particulars, the hopeless fortunes of slavery have been propped up and sustained by an imposing array of figures which of right ought to be regarded as the property of freedom. But we like to be generous to an unfortunate foe, and would utterly disdain the use of any unfair means of attack or defence.

We shall take no undue advantage of slavery. It shall have a fair trial, and be judged according to its deserts. Already has it been weighed in the balance, and found wanting ; it has been measured in the half-bushel, and found wanting ; it has been apprized in the field, and found wanting. Whatever redeeming traits or qualities it may possess, if any, shall be brought to light by subjecting it to other tests.

It was our desire and intention to furnish a correct table of the gallon-measure products of the several States of the Union ; but we have not been successful in our attempt to procure the necessary statistics. Enough is known, however, to satisfy us that the value of the milk, wine, ardent spirits, malt liquors, fluids, oils, and molasses, annually

produced and sold in the free States, is at east fifty millions of dollars greater than the value of the same articles
annually produced and sold in the slave States. Of sweet
milk alone, it is estimated that the monthly sales in three
Northern cities, New York, Philadelphia and Boston,
amount to a larger sum than the marketable value of all
the rosin, tar, pitch, and turpentine, annually produced in
the Southern States.

Our efforts to obtain reliable information respecting
another very important branch of profitable industry, the
lumber business, have also proved unavailing ; and we are
left to conjecture as to the amount of revenue annually
derived from it in the two grand divisions of our country.
The person whose curiosity prompts him to take an
account of the immense piles of Northern lumber now lying
on the wharves and houseless lots in Baltimore, Richmond,
and other slaveholding cities, will not, we imagine, form
a very flattering opinion of the products of Southern forests. Let it be remembered that nearly all the clippers,
steamers, and small craft, are built at the North ; that
large cargoes of Eastern lumber are exported to foreign
countries ; that nine-tenths of the wooden-ware used in the
Southern States is manufactured in New England ; that,
in outrageous disregard of the natural rights and claims
of Southern mechanics, the markets of the South are forever filled with Northern furniture, vehicles, ax helves,
walking canes, yard-sticks, clothes-pins and pen-holders ;
that the extraordinary number of factories, steam-engines,
forges and machine-shops in the free States, require an
extraordinary quantity of cord-wood ; that a large majority

of the magnificent edifices and other structures, both private and public, in which timber, in its various forms, is extensively used, are to be found in the free States— we say, let all these things be remembered, and the truth will at once flash across the mind that the forests of the North are a source of far greater income than those of the South. The difference is simply this : At the North everything is turned to advantage. When a tree is cut down, the main body is sold or used for lumber, railing or paling, the stump for matches and shoepegs, the knees for shipbuilding, and the branches for fuel. At the South everything is either neglected or mismanaged. Whole forests are felled by the ruthless hand of slavery, the trees are cut into logs, rolled into heaps, covered with the limbs and brush, and then burned on the identical soil that gave them birth. The land itself next falls a prey to the fell destroyer, and that which was once a beautiful, fertile and luxuriant woodland, is soon despoiled of all its treasures, and converted into an eye-offending desert.

Were we to go beneath the soil and collect all the mineral and lapidarious wealth of the free States, we should find it so much greater than the corresponding wealth of the slave States, that no ordinary combination of figures would suffice to express the difference. To say nothing of the gold and quicksilver of California, the iro.. and coal of Pennsylvania, the copper of Michigan, the lead of Illinois, or the salt of New-York, *the marble and free-stone quarries of New England are, incredible as it may seem to those unacquainted with the facts, far more important sources of revenue than all the subterranean deposits in the slave States.* From the most reliable statictics within our reach, we are led to the inference that the total value of all the precious metals, rocks, minerals, and medicinal waters, annually extracted from the bowels of the free States, is not less than eighty-five million of dollars ; the whole value of the same sub-stances annually brought up from beneath the surface of the slave States does not exceed twelve millions. In this respect to what is our poverty ascribable? To the same cause that has impoverished and dishonored us in all other respects—the thriftless and degrading institution of slavery.

Nature has been kind to us in all things. The strata and substrata of the South are profusely enriched with gold and silver, and precious stones, and from the natural orifices and aqueducts in Virgina and North Carolina, flow the purest healing waters in the world. But of what avail is all this latent wealth? Of what avail will it ever be, so long as slavery is permitted to play the dog in the manger? To these queries there can be but one reply. Slavery must be suppressed ; the South, so great and so glorious by nature, must be reclaimed from her infamy and degradation ; our cities, fields and forests, must be kept intact from the unsparing monster ; the various and ample resources of our vast domain, subterraneous as well as superficial, must be developed, and made to con-tribute to our pleasures and to the necessities of the world.

A very significant chapter, and one particularly perti-nent to many of the preceding pages, might be written on the Decline of Agriculture in the Slave States ; but as the press of other subjects admonishes us to be concise upon this point, we shall present only a few of the more striking instances. In the first place, let us compare the crops of wheat and rye in Kentucky, in 1850, with the corresponding crops in the same State in 1840 — after which, we will apply a similar rule of comparison to two or three other slaveholding states.

KENTUCKY.

	Wheat, bus.	Rye, bus.
Crop of 1840	4,803,152	1,321,373
" " 1850	2,142,822	415,073

Decrease 2,660,330 bus.   Decrease 906,300 bus.

TENNESSEE.

	Wheat, bus.	Tobacco, lbs.
Crop of 1840	4,569,692	29,550,432
" " 1850	1,619,386	20,148,932

Decrease 2,950,306 bus. Decrease 9,401,500 lbs.

VIRGINIA.

	Rye, bus.	Tobacco, lbs.
Crop of 1840	1,482,799	75,347,106
" " 1850	458,930	56,803,227

Decrease 1,023,869 bus. Decrease 18,543,879 lbs.

ALABAMA.

	Wheat, bus.	Rye, bus.
Crop of 1840	838,052	51,000
" " 1850	294,044	17,261

Decrease 544,008 bus.   Decrease 33,739 bus.

The story of these figures is too intelligible to require words of explanation ; we shall, therefore, drop this part of our subject, and proceed to compile a couple of tables that will exhibit on a single page the wealth, revenue and expenditure, of the several states of the confederacy. Let it be distinctly understood, however, that, in the compilation of these tables, three million two hundred and four thousand three hundred and thirteen negroes are valued as personal property, and credited to the Southern States as if they were so many horses and asses, or bridles and blankets — and that no monetary valuation whatever is placed on any creature, of any age, color, sex or condition, that bears the upright form of man in the free States.

TABLE NO. XX.

WEALTH, REVENUE AND EXPENDITURE OF THE FREE STATES—
1850.

States.	Real and Personal property.	Revenue.	Expenditure.
California	$22,161,872	$366,825	$925,625
Connecticut......	155,707,980	150,189	137,326
Illinois...	156,265,006	736,030	192,940
Indiana..........	202,650,264	1,283,064	1,061,605
Iowa......... ..	23,714,638	139,681	131,631
Maine...........	122,777,571	744,879	624,101
Massachusetts....	573,342,286	598,170	674,622
Michigan........	59,787,255	548,326	431,918
New Hampshire..	103,652,835	141,686	149,890
New Jersey......	153,151,619	139,166	180,614
New York........	1,080,309,216	2,698,310	2,520,932
Ohio............	504,726,120	3,016,403	2,736,060
Pennsylvania.....	729,144,998	7,716,552	6,876,480
Rhode Island.....	80,508,794	124,944	115,835
Vermont...... ...	92,205,049	185,830	183,058
Wisconsin...	42,056,595	135,155	136,096
	$4,102,172,108	$18,725,211	$17,076,733

TABLE NO. XXI.

WEALTH, REVENUE AND EXPENDITURE OF THE SLAVE STATES—
1850.

States.	Real and Personal property.	Revenue.	Expenditure.
Alabama...	$228,204,332	$658,976	$513,559
Arkansas..	39,841,025	68,412	74,076
Delaware.........	18,855,863		
Florida..........	23,198,734	60,619	55,234
Georgia.........	335,425,714	1,142,405	597,882
Kentucky.......	301,628,456	779,293	674,697
Louisiana....... .	233,998,764	1,146,568	1,098,911
Maryland........	219,217,364	1,279,953	1,360,458
Mississippi.....	228,951,130	221,200	223,637
Missouri...	137,247,707	326,579	207,656
North Carolina...	226,800,472	219,000	228,173
South Carolina...	288,257,694	532,152	463,021
Tennessee.	207,454,704	502,126	623,625
Texas....	55,362,340	140,688	156,622
Virginia....	391,646,438	1,265,744	1,272,382
	$2,936,090,737	$8,343,715	$7,549,933

Entire Wealth of the Free States,................ $4,02,172,108
Entire Wealth of the Slave States, including Slaves, 2,836,090,737

Balance in favor of the Free States,.......... $1,166,081,371

What a towering monument to the beauty and glory of
Free Labor ! What irrefragable evidence of the unequaled
efficacy and grandeur of free institutions ! These figures
are, indeed, too full of meaning to be passed by without
comment. The two tables from which they are borrowed
are at least a volume within themselves ; and, after all the
pains we have taken to compile them, we shall, perhaps,
feel somewhat disappointed if the reader fails to avail himself of the important information they impart.

Human life, in all ages, has been made up of a series of
adventures and experiments, and even at this stage of the
world's existence, we are almost as destitute of a perfect
rule of action, secular or religious, as were the erratic cotemporaries of Noah. It is true, however, that we have
made some progress in the right direction ; and as it seems
to be the tendency of the world to correct itself, we may
suppose that future generations will be enabled, by intui-
tion, to discriminate between the true and the false, the
good and the bad, and that with the development of this fac-
ulty of the mind, error and discord will begin to wane, and
finally cease to exist. Of all the experiments that have
been tried by the people in America, slavery has proved
the most fatal ; and the sooner it is abolished the better it
will be for us, for posterity, and for the world. One of
the evils resulting from it, and that not the least, is apparent in the figures above. Indeed, the *unprofitableness* of

slavery is a monstrous evil, when considered in all its bearings ; it makes us poor ; poverty makes us ignorant ; ignorance makes us wretched ; wretchedness makes us wicked, and wickedness leads to the devil !

> "Ignorance is the curse of God,
> Knowledge the wing wherewith we fly to heaven."

Facts truly astounding are disclosed in the two last tables, and we could heartily wish that every intelligent American would commit them to memory. The total value of all the real and personal property of the free States, with an area of only 612,597 square miles, is one billion one hundred and sixty-six million eighty-one thousand three hundred and seventy-one dollars greater than the total value of all the real and personal property, including the price of 3,204,313 negroes, of the slave States, which have an area of 851,508 square miles ! But extraordinary as this difference is in favor of the North, it is much less than the true amount. *On the authority of Southrons themselves, it is demonstrable beyond the possibility of refutation that the intrinsic value of all the property in the free States is more than three times greater than the intrinsic value of all the property in the slave States.*

James Madison, a Southern man, fourth President of the United States, a most correct thinker, and one of the greatest statesmen the country has produced, " thought it wrong to admit the idea that there could be property in man," and we indorse, to the fullest extent, this opinion of the profound editor of the *Federalist*. We shall not recognize property in man : the slaves of the South are not worth a groat in any civilized community ; no man of genuine decency and refinement would hold them as property on any terms ; in the eyes of all enlightened nations and individuals, they are men, not merchandize. Southern pro-slavery politicians, some of whom have not hesitated to buy and sell their own sons and daughters, boast that the slaves of the South are worth sixteen hundred million of dollars, and we have seen the amount estimated as high as two thousand million. Mr. De Bow, the Southern superintendent of the seventh census, informs us that the value of all the property in the slave States, real and personal, including slaves, was, in 1850, only $2,936,090,737; while, according to the same authority, the value of all the real and personal property in the free States, genuine property, property that is everywhere recognized as property, was, at the same time, $4,102,172,108. Now all we have to do in order to ascertain the real value of all the property of the South, independent of negroes, whose value, if valuable at all, is of a local and precarious character, is to subtract from the sum total of Mr. De Bow's return of the entire wealth of the slave States the estimated value of the slaves themselves ; and then, by deducting the difference from the intrinsic value of all the property in the free States, we shall have the exact amount of the overplus of wealth in the glorious land of free soil, free labor, free speech, free presses, and free schools. And now to the task.

Entire Wealth of the Slave States, including Slaves, $2,936,090,737
Estimated Value of the Slaves,.................. 1,600,000,000

True Wealth of the Slave States,............ $1,336,090,737

True Wealth of the Free States,................... $4,102,172,108
True Wealth of the Slave States,................ 1,336,090,737

    Balance in favor of the Free States,........ .. $2,766,081,371

There, friends of the South and of the North, you have
the conclusion of the whole matter. Liberty and slavery
are before you ; choose which you will have ; as for us, in
the memorable language of the immortal Henry, we say,
" give us liberty, or give us death !" In the great struggle
for wealth that has been going on between the two rival
systems of free and slave labor, the balance above exhibits
the net profits of the former. The struggle on the one side
has been calm, laudable, and eminently successful ; on the
other, it has been attended by tumult, unutterable cruelties
and disgraceful failure. We have given the slave drivers
every conceivable opportunity to vindicate their domestic
policy, but for them to do it is a moral impossibility.

    Less than three-quarters of a century ago—say in 1789,
for that was about the average time of the abolition of
slavery in the Northern States—the South, with advantages in soil, climate, rivers, harbors, minerals, forests,
and, indeed, almost every other natural resource, began an
even race with the North in all the important pursuits of
life ; and now, in the brief space of scarce three score
years and ten, we find her completely distanced, enervated,
dejected and dishonored. Slave-drivers are the sole authors
of her disgrace ; as they have sown so let them reap.

    As we have seen above, a careful and correct inventory
of all the real and personal *property* in the two grand divisions of the country, discloses the astounding fact that, in
1850, the free States were worth precisely *two thousand*

seven hundred and sixty-six million eighty-one thousand three hundred and seventy-one dollars more than the slave States! Twenty-seven hundred and sixty-six million of dollars!— Think of it! What a vast and desirable sum, and how much better off the South would be with it than without it! Such is the enormous amount out of which slavery has defrauded us during the space of sixty-one years— from 1789 to 1850—being an average of about forty-five million three hundred and fifty thousand dollars per annum. During the last twenty-five or thirty years, however, our annual losses have been far greater than they were formerly. There has been a gradual increase every year, and now the ratio of increase is almost incredible. No patriotic Southerner can become conversant with the facts without experiencing a feeling of alarm and indignation. Until the North abolished slavery, she had no advantage of us whatever; the South was more than her equal in every respect. But no sooner had she got rid of that hampering and pernicious institution than she began to absorb our wealth, and now it is confidently believed that the merchants and negro-driving pleasure-seekers of the South annually pour one hundred and twenty million of dollars into her coffers! Taking into account, then, the probable amount of money that has been drawn from the South and invested in the North within the last six years, and adding it to the grand balance above—the net profits of the North up to 1850—it may be safely assumed that, in the present year of grace, 1857, *the free States are worth at least thirty-four hundred million of dollars more than the slave States!* Let him who dares, gainsay these remarks and calculations ; no truthful tongue will deny them ; no honorable pen can controvert them.

One more word now as to the valuation of negroes. Were our nature so degraded, or our conscience so elastic as to permit us to set a price upon men, as we would set a price upon cattle and corn, we should be content to abide by the appraisement of the slaves of the South, and would then enter into a calculation to ascertain the value of foreigners to the North. Not long since, it was declared in the South that "one free laborer is equal to five slaves," and as there are two million five hundred thousand Europeans in the free States, all of whom are free laborers, we might bring Southern authority to back us in estimating their value at *sixty-two hundred million of dollars* — a handsome sum wherewithal to offset the account of *sixteen hundred million of dollars*, brought forward as the value of Southern slaves! It is obvious, therefore, that if we were disposed to follow the barbarian example of the traffickers in human flesh, we could prove the North vastly richer than the South in bone and sinew — to say nothing of mind and morals, which shall receive our attention hereafter. The North has just as good a right to appraise the Irish immigrant, as the South has to set a price on the African slave. But as it would be wrong to do either, we shall do neither. It is not our business to think of man as a merchantable commodity ; and we will not, even by implication, admit "the wild and guilty fantasy," that the condition of chattelhood may rightfully attach to sentient and immortal beings.

In this connection, we would direct the special attention of the reader to the following eloquent passage, exhibiting the philosophy of free and slave labor, from the facile pen of the editor of the *North American and United States Gazette* :

" In the very nature of things, the freeman must produce more than the slave. There is no conclusion of science more certain. Under a system which gives to a laboring man the fruit of his toil, there is every motive to render him diligent and assiduous. If he relies on being employed by others, his wages rise with his reputation for industry, skill, and faithfulness. And as owner of the soil, there is every assurance that he will do what he can to cultivate it to the best advantage, and develope its latent wealth. Self-interest will call forth what powers of intellect and of invention he has to aid him in his work, and employ his physical strength to the greatest possible advantage. Free labor receives an immediate reward, which cheers and invigorates it ; and above all, it has that chief spring of exertion, hope, whose bow always spans the heaven before it. It has an inviolate hearth ; it has a home. But it looks forward to a still better condition, to brighter prospects in the future, to which its efforts all contribute. The children in such a household are chief inducements to nerve the arm of labor, that they may be properly cared for, fed, clothed, educated, accomplished, instructed in some useful and honorable calling, and provided for when they shall go out upon the world. All its sentiments, religious and otherwise, all its affections for parents and kindred, all its tastes are so many impelling and stimulating forces. It is disposed to read.

to ornament its home, to travel, to enjoy social intercourse, and to attain these ends, it rises to higher exertions and a stricter economy of time ; it explores every path of employment, and is, therefore, in the highest degree productive.

"How different is it with slave labor ! The slave toils for another, and not for himself. Whether he does little or much, whether his work is well or ill performed, he has a subsistence, nothing less, nothing more ; and why should he toil beyond necessity ? He cannot accumulate any property for the decline of his years, or to leave to his children when he is departed. Nay, he cannot toil to better the present condition of his children. They belong to another, and not to him. He cannot supply his hut with comforts, or embellish it with the adornments of taste. He does not read. He does not journey for pleasure. Inducements to exertion, he has none. That he may adapt himself to his condition, and enjoy the present hour, he deadens those aspirations that must always be baffled in his case, and sinks down into ease and sensuality. His mind is unlighted and untutored ; dark with ignorance. Among those who value him most, he is proverbially indolent, thievish, and neglectful of his master's interests. It is common for even the advocates of slavery to declare that one freeman is worth half a dozen slaves. With every cord to exertion thus sundered, the mind benighted, the man nearly lost in the animal, it requires no deep philosophy to see why labor cannot be near as productive as it would be were these conditions all reversed. Though ever so well directed by the superior skill, and urged forward by the strong arm of the master, slave labor is necessarily a blight to the soil—sterility follows in its steps, and not afar off.

"What a difference, plain and heaven-wide, between the outward and interior life of a slave and of a free community, resulting directly and palpably from this difference in its labor. The cottage-home, amid trees and shrubbery, its apartments well adorned and furnished, books on its shelves, and the passing literature of the day scattered around ; the few, perhaps, but well-tilled acres, belonging to the man who tills them ; the happy children with sunny prospects ; the frequent school ; the church arrayed with beauty ; the thriving, handsome village ; the flourishing cities and prosperous marts of trade ; the busy factories ; railroads, traffic, travel—where free labor tills the ground, how beautiful it all is in contrast to the forlorn and dreary aspect of a country tilled by slaves. The villages of such a country are mainly groups of miserable huts. Its comparatively few churches are too often dilapidated and unsightly. The common school-house, the poor man's college, is hardly known, showing how little interest is felt in the chief treasures of the State, the immortal minds of the multitude who are not born to wealth. The signs of premature old age are visibly impressed upon everything that meets the eye. The fields present a dread monotony. Everywhere you see lands that are worn out, barren and deserted, in consequence of slave tillage, left for more fertile lands in newer regions, which are also, in their turn, to be smitten with sterility and forsaken. The free community may increase its population almost without limit.

The capacity of slave countries to sustain a population is soon at an end, and then it diminishes. In all the elements of essential prosperity, in all that elevates man, how striking the contrast between the region that is tilled by slave, and the region that is tilled by free labor."

For the purpose of showing what Virginia, once the richest, most populous, and most powerful of the States, has become under the blight of slavery, we shall now introduce an extract from one of the speeches delivered by Henry A. Wise, during the last gubernatorial campaign in that degraded commonwealth. Addressing a Virginia audience, in language as graphic as it is truthful, he says :—

" Commerce has long ago spread her sails, and sailed away from you. You have not, as yet, dug more than coal enough to warm yourselves at your own hearths; you have set no tilt-hammer of Vulcan to strike blows worthy of gods in your own iron-foundries ; you have not yet spun more than coarse cotton enough, in the way of manufacture, to clothe your own slaves. You have no commerce, no mining, no manufactures. You have relied alone on the single power of agriculture, and *such agriculture !* Your sedge-patches outshine the sun. Your inattention to your only source of wealth, has seared the very bosom of mother earth. Instead of having to feed cattle on a thousand hills, you have had to chase the stump-tailed steer through the sedge-patches to procure a tough beef-steak. The present condition of things has existed too long in Virginia. The landlord has skinned the tenant, and the tenant has skinned the land, until all have grown poor together."

With tears in its eyes, and truth on its lips, for the first time after an interval of twenty years, the *Richmond Enquirer* helps to paint the melancholy picture. In 1852, that journal thus bewailed the condition of Virginia :—

"We have cause to feel deeply for our situation. Philadelphia herself contains a population far greater than the whole free population of Eastern Virginia. The little State of Massachusetts has an aggregate wealth exceeding that of Virginia by more than $126,000,000."

Just a score of years before these words were penned, the same paper, then edited by the elder Ritchie[4] made a most earnest appeal to the intelligence and patriotism of Virginia, to adopt an effectual measure for the speedy over-throw of the damnable institution of human bondage Here is an extract from an article which appeared in its editorial column under date of January 7th, 1832 :

"Something must be done, and it is the part of no honest man to deny it—of no free press to affect to conceal it. When this dark population is growing upon us ; when every new census is but gathering its appalling numbers upon us ; when, within a period equal to that in which this Federal Constitution has been in existence, these numbers will increase to more than two millions within Virginia ; when our sister States are closing their doors upon our blacks for sale, and when our whites are moving westwardly in greater numbers than we like to hear of ; when this, the fairest land on all this continent, for soil, and climate, and situation, combined, might be-

come a sort of garden spot, if it were worked by the hands
of white men alone, can we, ought we, to sit quietly down,
fold our arms, and say to each other, ' Well, well ; this
thing will not come to the worst in our days ; we will
leave it to our children, and our grandchildren, and great-
grandchildren, to take care of themselves, and to brave
the storm !' Is this to act like wise men ? Means, sure
but gradual, systematic but discreet, ought to be adopted,
for reducing the mass of evil which is pressing upon the
South, and will still more press upon her, the longer it is
put off. We say now, in the utmost sincerity of our hearts,
that our wisest men cannot give too much of their attention to this subject, nor can they give it too soon."

Better abolition doctrine than this is seldom heard.
Why did not the *Enqurier* continue to preach it ? What
potent influence hushed its clarion voice, just as it began
to be lifted in behalf of a liberal policy and an enlightened
humanity ? Had Mr. Ritchie continued to press the truth
home to the hearts of the people, as he should have done,
Virginia, instead of being worth only $392,000,000 in 1850
—negroes and all—would have been worth at least $800,-
000,000 in genuine property ; and if the State had emancipated her slaves at the time of the adoption of the Constitution, the last census would no doubt have reported her
wealth, and correctly, at a sum exceeding a thousand
millions of dollars.

Listen now to the statement of a momentous fact. The
value of all the property, real and personal, including
slaves, in seven slave States, Virginia, North Carolina,
Tennessee, Missouri, Arkansas, Florida and Texas, is less

than the real and personal estate, which is unquestionable property, in the single State of New-York   Nay, worse; if eight entire slave States, Arkansas, Delaware, Florida, Maryland, Missouri, Mississippi, Tennessee and Texas, and the District of Columbia—with all their hordes of human merchandize—were put up at auction, New-York could buy them all, and then have one hundred and thirty-three millions of dollars left in her pocket ! Such is the amazing contrast between freedom and slavery, even in a pecuniary point of view.   When we come to compare the North with the South in regard to literature, general intelligence, inventive genius, moral and religious enterprises, the discoveries in medicine, and the progress in the arts and sciences, we shall, in every instance, find the contrast equally great on the side of Liberty.

It gives us no pleasure to say hard things of the Old Dominion, the mother of Washington, Jefferson, Henry, and other illustrious patriots, who, as we shall prove hereafter, were genuine abolitionists ; but the policy which she has pursued has been so utterly inexcusable, so unjust to the non-slaveholding whites, so cruel to the negroes, and so disregardful of the rights of humanity at large, that it becomes the duty of every one who makes allusion to her history, to expose her follies, her crimes, and her poverty, and to publish every fact, of whatever nature, that would be instrumental in determining others to eschew her bad example.   She has wilfully departed from the faith of the founders of this Republic.   She has not only turned a deaf ear to the counsel of wise men from other States in the Union, but she has, in like manner, ignored the teachings of the great warriors and statesmen who have sprur from her own soil.　In a subsequent chapter, we expect to show that all, or nearly all, the distinguished Virginians, whose bodies have been consigned to the grave, but whose names have been given to history, and whose memoirs have a place in the hearts of their countrymen, were the friends and advocates of universal freedom—that they were inflexibly opposed to the extension of slavery into the Territories, devised measures for its restriction, and, with hopeful anxiety, looked forward to the time when it should be eradicated from the States themselves.　With them, the rescue of our country from British domination, and the establishment of the General Government upon a firm basis, were considerations of paramount importance ; they supposed, and no doubt earnestly desired, that the States, in their sovereign capacities, would soon abolish an institution which was so palpably in conflict with the principles enunciated in the Declaration of Independence.　Indeed, it would seem that, among the framers of that immortal instrument and its equally immortal sequel, the Constitution of the United States, there was a tacit understanding to this effect ; and the Northern States, true to their implied faith, abolished it within a short period after our national independence had been secured.　Not so with the South.　She has pertinaciously refused to perform her duty. She has apostatized from the faith of her greatest men, and even at this very moment repudiates the sacred principle that " all men are endowed by their Creator with certain unalienable rights," among which " are life, liberty, and the pursuit of happiness "　It is evident, therefore, that the free States are the only members of this confederacy that have established republican forms of government based upon the theories of Washington, Jefferson, Madison, Henry, and other eminent statesmen of Virginia.

The great revolutionary movement which was set on foot in Charlotte, Mecklenburg county, North Carolina, on the 20th day of May, 1775, has not yet been terminated, nor will it be, until every slave in the United States is freed from the tyranny of his master.[5] Every victim of the vile institution, whether white or black, must be reinvested with the sacred rights and privileges of which he has been deprived by an inhuman oligarchy. What our noble sires of the revolution left unfinished it is our duty to complete. They did all that true valor and patriotism could accomplish. Not one iota did they swerve from their plighted faith; the self-sacrificing spirit which they evinced will command the applause of every succeeding age. Not in vindication of their own personal rights merely, but of the rights of humanity; not for their own generation and age simply, but for all ages to the end of time, they gave their toil, their treasure and their blood, nor deemed them all too great a price to pay for the establishment of so comprehensive and beneficent a principle. Let their posterity emulate their courage, their disinterestedness, and their zeal, and especially remember that it is the duty of every existing generation so to provide for its individual interests, as to confer superior advantages on that which is to follow. To this principle the North has adhered with the strictest fidelity. How has it been with the South? Has she imitated the praiseworthy example of our illustrious ancestors? No! She has treated it with the utmost contempt; she has been extremely selfish—so selfish, indeed, that she has robbed posterity of its natural rights. From the period of the formation of the government down to the present moment, her policy has been downright suicidal, and, as a matter of course, wholly indefensible. She has hugged a viper to her breast; her whole system has been paralyzed, her conscience is seared, and she is becoming callous to every principle of justice and magnanimity. Except among the non-slaveholders, who, besides oeing kept in the grossest ignorance, are under the restraint of all manner of iniquitous laws, patriotism has ceased to exist within her borders. And here we desire to be distinctly understood, for we shall have occasion to refer to this matter again. We repeat, therefore, the substance of our averment, that, at this day, there is not a grain of patriotism in the South, except among the non-slaveholders. Subsequent pages shall testify to the truth of this assertion. Here and there, it is true, a slaveholder, disgusted with the institution, becomes ashamed of himself, emancipates his negroes, and enters upon the walks of honorable life; but these cases are exceedingly rare, and do not, in any manner, disprove the general correctness of our remark. All persons who do voluntarily manumit their slaves, as mentioned above, are undeniably actuated by principles of pure patriotism, justice and humanity; and so believing, we delight to do them honor.

Once more to the Old Dominion. At her door we lay the bulk of the evils of slavery. The first African sold in America was sold on James River, in that State, on the

20th of A 1gust, 1620[6]; and although the institution was fastened upon her and the other colonies by the mother country, she was the first to perceive its blighting and degrading influences, her wise men were the first to denounce it, and, after the British power was overthrown at York Town, she should have been the first to abolish it. Fifty-seven years ago she was the Empire State ; now, with half a dozen other slaveholding states thrown into the scale with her, she is far inferior to New-York, which, at the time Cornwallis surrendered his sword to Washington, was less than half her equal. Had she obeyed the counsels of the good, the great and the wise men of our nation—especially of her own incomparable sons, the extendible element of slavery would have been promptly arrested, and the virgin soil of nine Southern States, Kentucky, Tennessee, Louisiana, Mississippi, Alabama, Missouri, Arkansas, Florida, and Texas, would have been saved from its horrid pollutions. Confined to the original states in which it existed, the institution would soon have been disposed of by legislative enactments, and long before the present day, by a gradual process that could have shocked no interest and alarmed no prejudice, we should have rid ourselves not only of African slavery, which is an abomination and a curse, but also of the negroes themselves, who, in our judgment, whether viewed in relation to their actual characteristics and condition, or through the strong antipathies of the whites, are, to say the least, an undesirable population.

This, then, is the ground of our expostulation with Virginia : that, in stubborn disregard of the advice and

5

friendly warnings of Washington, Jefferson, Madison, Henry, and a host of other distinguished patriots who sprang from her soil—patriots whose voices shall be heard before we finish our task—and in utter violation of every principle of justice and humanity, *she still persists* in fostering an institution which is so manifestly detrimental to her vital interests. Every Virginian, whether living or dead, whose name is an honor to his country, has placed on record his abhorrence of slavery, and in doing so, has borne testimony to the blight and degradation that everywhere follow in its course.' One of the best abolition speeches we have ever read was delivered in the Virginia House of Delegates, January 20th, 1832, by Charles James Faulkner, who still lives, and who has, we understand, generously emancipated several of his slaves, and sent them to Liberia. Here follows an extract from his speech ; let Southern politicians read it attentively, and imbibe a moiety of the spirit of patriotism which it breathes :—

" Sir, I am gratified to perceive that no gentleman has yet risen in this Hall, the avowed advocate of slavery. *The day has gone by when such a voice could be listened to with patience, or even with forbearance.* I even regret, Sir, that we should find those amongst us who enter the lists of discussion as its *apologists*, except alone upon the ground of uncontrollable necessity. And yet, who could have listened to the very eloquent remarks of the gentleman from Brunswick, without being forced to conclude that he at least considered slavery, however *not to be defended upon principle*, yet as being divested of much of its enormity, as you approach it in practice.

" Sir, if there be one who concurs with that gentleman in the harmless character of this institution, let me request him to compare the condition of the slaveholding portion of this commonwealth—*barren, desolate, and seared as it were by the avenging hand of Heaven*—with the descriptions which we have of this country from those who first broke its virgin soil. To what is this change ascribable? *Alone to the withering and blasting effects of slavery.* If this does not satisfy him, let me request him to extend his travels to the *Northern States of this Union,* and beg him to contrast the happiness and contentment which prevail throughout that country, the busy and cheerful sound of industry, the rapid and swelling growth of their population, their means and institutions of education, their skill and proficiency in the useful arts, their enterprise and public spirit, the monuments of their commercial and manufacturing industry ; and, above all, their devoted attachment to the government from which they derive their protection, *with the derision, discontent, indolence, and poverty of the Southern country.* To what, Sir, is all this ascribable? *To that vice in the organization of society, by which one-half of its inhabitants are arrayed in interest and feeling against the other half*—to that unfortunate state of society in which freemen regard labor as disgraceful, and slaves shrink from it as a burden tyrannically imposed upon them—to that condition of things in which half a million of your population can feel no sympathy with the society in the prosperity of which they are forbidden to participate, and no attachment to a government at whose hands they receive nothing but injustice.

" If this should not be sufficient, and the curious and incredulous inquirer should suggest that the contrast which has been adverted to, and which is so manifest, might be traced to a difference of climate, or other causes distinct from slavery itself, permit me to refer him to the two States of Kentucky and Ohio. No difference of soil, no diversity of climate, no diversity in the original settlement of those two States, can account for the remarkable disproportion in their natural advancement. Separated by a river alone, *they seem to have been purposely and providentially designed to exhibit in their future histories the difference which necessarily results from a country free from, and a country afflicted with, the curse of slavery.*

" Vain and idle is every effort to strangle this inquiry. As well might you attempt to chain the ocean, or stay the avenging thunderbolts of Heaven, as to drive the people from any inquiry which may result in their better condition. This is too deep, too engrossing a subject of consideration. It addresses itself too strongly to our interests, to our passions, and to our feelings. I shall advocate no scheme that does not respect the right of property, *so far as it is entitled to be respected,* with a just regard to the safety and resources of the State. I would approach the subject as one of great magnitude and delicacy, as one whose varied and momentous consequences demand the calmest and most deliberate investigation. But still, Sir, I would approach it—aye, delicate as it may be, encompassed as it may be with difficulties and hazards, I would still approach it. The people demand it. Their security requires it. In the language of the wise and prophetic Jefferson, ' You must approach it—you must bear it—you must adopt some plan of emancipation, or worse will follow.'"

Mr. Curtis, in a speech in the Virginia Legislature in 1832, said:

"There is a malaria in the atmosphere of these regions, which the new comer shuns, as being deleterious to his views and habits. See the wide-spreading ruin which the avarice of our ancestral government has produced in the South, as witnessed in a sparse population of freemen, deserted habitations, and fields without culture ! Strange to tell, even the wolf, driven back long since by the approach of man, now returns, after the lapse of a hundred years, to howl over the desolations of slavery."

Mr. Moore, also a member of the Legislature of Virginia, in speaking of the evils of slavery, said :

"The first I shall mention is the irresistible tendency which it has to undermine and destroy everything like virtue and morality in the community. If we look back through the long course of time which has elapsed since the creation to the present moment, we shall scarcely be able to point out a people whose situation was not, in many respects, preferable to our own, and that of the other States, in which negro slavery exists.

"In that part of the State below tide-water, the whole face of the country wears an appearance of almost utter desolation, distressing to the beholder. The very spot on which our ancestors landed, a little more than two hundred years ago, appears to be on the eve of again becoming the haunt of wild beasts."

Mr. Rives, of Campbell county, said :

" On the multiplied and desolating evils of slavery, he was not disposed to say much. The curse and deteriorating consequence were within the observation and experience of the members of the House and the people of Virginia, and it did not seem to him that there could be two opinions about it."

Mr. Powell said :

" I can scarcely persuade myself that there is a solitary gentleman in this House who will not readily admit that slavery is an evil, and that its removal, if practicable, is a consummation most devoutly to be wished. I have not heard, nor do I expect to hear, a voice raised in this Hall to the contrary."

In the language of another, " we might multiply extracts almost indefinitely from Virginia authorities — testifying to the blight and degradation that have overtaken the Old Dominion, in every department of her affairs. Her commerce gone, her agriculture decaying, her land falling in value, her mining and manufactures nothing, her schools dying out,—she presents, according to the testimony of her own sons, the saddest of all pictures — that of a sinking and dying State." Every year leaves her in a worse condition than it found her ; and as it is with Virginia, so it is with the entire South. In the terse language of Governor Wise, " all have grown poor together." The black god of slavery, which the South has worshipped for two hundred and thirty-seven years, is but a devil in disguise ; and if we would save ourselves from being engulphed in utter ruin we must repudiate this foul god, for a purer deity, and abandon his altars for a holier shrine. No time is to be lost ; his fanatical adorers, the despotic adversaries of human liberty, are concocting schemes for the enslavement of all the laboring classes' irrespective of race or color. The issue is before us ; we cannot evade it ; we must meet it with firmness, and with unflinching valor.

What it was that paralyzed the tongues of all those members of the Virgina Legislature, who, at the session of 1831–'32, distinguished themselves by advocating a system of emancipation, is a mystery that has never yet been solved. Whether any oɪ all of them shared a division of spoils with a certain newspaper editor, we have no means of knowing ; but if all accounts be true, there was consummated in Richmond, in the latter part of the year 1832, one of the blackest schemes of bribery and corruption that was ever perpetrated in this or any other country. We are assured, however, that one thing is certain, and it is this : that the negro population of Virginia was very considerably and suddenly decreased by forcible emigration—that a large gang was driven further South, sold, and the proceeds divided among certain renegades and traitors, who, Judas-like, had agreed to serve the devil for a price.[8]

We would fain avoid all personalities and uncomplimentary allusions to the dead, but when men, from love of lucre, from mere selfish motives, or from sheer turpitude of heart, inflict great injuries and outrages on the public, their villainy ought to be exposed, so that others may be deterred from following in their footsteps. As a general rule, man's moral nature is, we believe, so strong

that it invariably prompts him to eschew vice and practice virtue—in other words, to do right ; but this rule,
like all others, has its exceptions, as might be most strik·
ingly illustrated in the character of ———— ————, and
some half-dozen or more of his pro-slavery coadjutors.
From whose hands did this man receive fifty thousand
dollars—improperly, if not illegally, taken from the
public funds in Washington ?   When did he receive it ?—
and for what purpose ?—and who was the arch-dema-
gogue through whose agency the transfer was made ?
He was an oligarchical member of the Cabinet under Mr.
Polk's administration in 1845,—and the money was
used,—and who can doubt *intended* ?—for the express
purpose of establishing another negro-driving journal to
support the tottering fortunes of slavery. From the
second volume of a valuable political work, "by a Senator of thirty years," we make the following pertinent
extract :—

" The *Globe* was sold, and was paid for, and how ? becomes a question of public concern to answer ; for it was
paid for out of public money—those same $50,000 which
were removed to the village bank in the interior of Pennsylvania by a Treasury order on the fourth of November,
1844.   Three annual installments made the payment, and
the Treasury did not reclaim the money for these three
years ; and, though traveling through tortuous channels,
the sharpsighted Mr. Rives traced the money back to its
starting point from that deposit.   Besides, Mr. Cameron,
who had control of the village bank, admitted before a
committee of Congress, that he had furnished money for

the payments--an admission which the obliging Committee, on request, left out of their report. Mr. Robert J. Walker was Secretary of the Treasury during these three years, and the conviction was absolute, among the close observers of the course of things, that he was the prime contriver and zealous manager of the arrangements which displaced Mr. Blair and installed Mr. Ritchie."

Thus, if we are to believe Mr. Benton, in his "Thirty Year's View," and we are disposed to regard him as good authority, the Washington *Union* was brought into existence under the peculiar auspices of the ostensible editor of the Richmond *Enquirer ;* and the two papers, fathered by the same individual, have gone hand in hand for the last dozen or thirteen years, the shameless advocates and defenders of human bondage. To suppose that either has been sustained by fairer means than it was commenced with, would be wasting imagination on a great improbability. Both have uniformly and pertinaciously opposed every laudable enterprise that the white non-slaveholder has projected ; indeed, so unmitigated has been their hostility to all manual pursuits in which their stupid and vulgar slaves can not be employed to advantage—and if there is any occupation under the sun in which they can be employed to good advantage, we known not what it is— that it is an extremely difficult matter to find a respectable merchant, mechanic, manufacturer, or business man of any calling whatever, within the bounds of their circulation.[9]

We have been credibly informed by a gentleman from Powhattan county, in Virginia, that in the year 1836 or

5*

'37, or about that time, the Hon. Abbott Lawrence, of Boston, backed by his brother Amos and other millionaires of New England, went down to Richmond with the sole view of reconnoitering the manufacturing facilities of that place —fully determined, if pleased with the water-power, to erect a large number of cotton-mills and machine-shops. He had been in the capital of Virginia only a day or two before he discovered, much to his gratification, that nature had shaped everything to his liking ; and as he was a business man who transacted business in a business-like manner, he lost no time in making preliminary arrangements for the consummation of his noble purpose. His mission was one of peace and promise ; others were to share the benefits of his laudable and concerted scheme ; thousands of poor boys and girls in Virginia, instead of growing up in extreme poverty and ignorance, or of having to emigrate to the free States of the West, were to have avenues of profitable employment opened to them at home ; thus they would be enabled to earn an honest and reputable living, to establish and sustain free schools, free libraries, free lectures, and free presses, to become useful and exemplary members of society, and to die fit candidates for heaven. The magnanimous New Englander was in ecstasies with the prospect that opened before him. Individually, so far as mere money was concerned, he was perfectly independent ; his industry and economy in early life had secured to him the ownership and control of an ample fortune. With the aid of eleven other men, each equal to himself, he could have bought the whole city of Richmon 1—negroes and all—though it is not to be presumed that he would have disgraced his name by becoming a trader in human flesh. But he was not selfish ; unlike the arrogant and illiberal slaveholder, he did not regard himself as the centre around whom everybody else should revolve. On the contrary, he was a genuine philanthropist. While, with a shrewdness that will command the admiration of every practical business man, he engaged in nothing that did not swell the dimensions of his own purse, he was yet always solicitous to invest his capital in a manner calculated to promote the interest of those around him. Nor was he satisfied with simply furnishing the means whereby his less fortunate neighbors were to become prosperous, intelligent and contented. With his generous heart and sagacious mind, he delighted to aid them in making a judicious application of his wealth to their own use. Moreover, as a member of society, he felt that the community had some reasonable claims upon him, and he made it obligatory on himself constantly to devise plans and exert his personal efforts for the public good. Such was the character of the distinguished manufacturer who honored Richmond with his presence nineteen or twenty years ago ; such was the character of the men whom he represented, and such were the grand designs which they sought to accomplish.

To the enterprising and moneyed descendant of the Pilgrim Fathers it was a matter of no little astonishment, that the immense water-power of Richmond had been so long neglecte l. He expressed his surprise to a number of Virginians, and was at a loss to know why they had not, long prior to the period of his visit amongst them,

availed themselves of the powerful element that is eter·
nally gushing and foaming over the falls of James River.
Innocent man ! He was utterly unconscious of the fact
that he was " interfering with the beloved institutions of
the South," and little was he prepared to withstand the
terrible denunciations that were immediately showered on
his head through the columns of the Richmond *Enquirer*.
Few words will suffice to tell the sequel. That negro-
worshipping sheet, whose hireling policy, for the last four
and twenty years, has been to support the worthless black
slave and his tyrannical master at the expense of the free
white laborer, wrote down the enterprise ! and the noble
son of New England, abused, insulted and disgusted,
quietly returned to Massachusetts, and there employed
his capital in building up the cities of Lowell and Lawrence, either of which, in all those elements of material
and social prosperity that make up the greatness of States,
is already far in advance of the most important of all the
seedy and squalid niggervilles in the Old Dominion. Such
is an inkling of the infamous means that have been resort-
ed to, from time to time, for the purpose of upholding and
perpetuating in America the accursed institution of
slavery.[10]

Having in view all the foregoing facts, we were not in
the least surprised when, while walking through Hollywood Cemetery, in the western suburbs of Richmond, not
long since, our companion, a Virginian of the true school,
directed our attention to a monument of some pretentions,
and exclaimed, " There lie the remains of a man upon
whose monument should be inscribed in everlasting prom-

inence the finger of scorn pointing downward." The reader
scarcely needs to be told that we were standing at the
tomb of ———— ————, who in the opinion of our friend,
had, by concentrating within himself the views and purposes of all the evil spirits in Virginia, greatly retarded
the abolition of slavery; so greatly, indeed, as, thereby,
to throw the State at least fifty years behind her free
competitors of the North, of the East, and of the West.
It is to be hoped that Virginia may never give birth to
another man whose evil influence will so justly entitle him
to the reprobation of posterity.[11]

How any rational man in this or any other country,
with the astounding contrasts between Freedom and Slavery ever looming in his view, can offer an apology for
the existing statism of the South, is to us a most inexplicable mystery. Indeed, we cannot conceive it possible
that the conscience of any man, who is really sane, would
permit him to become the victim of such an egregious
and diabolical absurdity. Therefore, at this period of our
history, with the light of the past, the reality of the present, and the prospect of the future, all so prominent
and so palpable, we infer that every person who sets up
an unequivocal defence of the institution of slavery, must,
of necessity, be either a fool, a knave, or a madman.

It is much to be regretted that the slavocrats look at
but one side of the question. Of all the fanatics in the
country, they have, of late, become the most unreasonable
and ridiculous. Let them deliberately view the subject
of slavery in all its aspects and bearings, and if they are
possessed of honest hearts and convincible minds, they

will readily perceive the grossness of their past errors, renounce their allegiance to a cause so unjust and disgraceful, and at once enroll themselves among the hosts of Freedom and the friends of universal Liberty. There are thirty-one States in the Union ; let them drop California, or any other new free State, and then institute fifteen comparisons, first comparing New-York with Virginia, Pennsylvania with Carolina, Massachusetts with Georgia, and so on, until they have exhausted the catalogue. Then, for once, let them be bold enough to listen to the admonitions of their own souls, and if they do not soon start to their feet *demanding* the abolition of slavery, it will only be because they have reasons for suppressing their inmost sentiments. Whether we compare the old free States with the old slave States, or the new free States with the new slave States, the difference, unmistakable and astounding, is substantially the same. All the free States are alike, and all the slave States are alike. In the former, wealth, intelligence, power, progress, and prosperity, are the prominent characteristics ; in the latter, poverty, ignorance, embecility, inertia, and extravagance, are the distinguishing features. To be convinced, it is only necessary for us to open our eyes and look at facts —to examine the *statistics* of the country, to free ourselves from obstinacy and prejudice, and to unbar our minds to convictions of truth. Let figures be the umpire. Close attention to the preceding and subsequent tables is all we ask ; so soon as they shall be duly considered and understood, the primary object of this work will have been accomplished.

Not content with eating out the vitals of the South, slavery, true to the character which it has acquired for insatiety and rapine, is beginning to make rapid encroachments on new territory ; and as a basis for a few remarks on the blasting influence which it is shedding over the broad and fertile domains of the West, which in accordance with the views and resolutions offered by the immortal Jefferson, should have been irrevocably dedicated to freedom, we beg leave to call the attention of the reader to another presentation of the philosophy of free and slave labor.   Says the *North American and United States Gazette* :

"We have but to compare the States, possessing equal natural advantages, in which the two kinds of labor are employed, in order to decide with entire confidence as to which kind is the more profitable.   At the origin of the government, Virginia, with a much larger extent of territory than New-York, contained a population of seven hundred and fifty thousand, and sent ten representatives to Congress ; while New-York contained a population of three hundred and forty thousand, and sent six representatives to Congress.   Behold how the figures are reversed.   The population of New-York is three and a half millions, represented by thirty-three members in Congress ; while the population of Virginia is but little more than one and a half millions, represented by thirteen members in Congress.   It is the vital sap of free labor that makes the one tree so thrifty and vigorous, so capable of bearing with all ease the fruit of such a population.   And it is slave labor which strikes a decadence through the other, drying up many of its branches with a fearful sterility, and rendering the

rest but scantily fruitful ; really incapable of sustaining
more. Look at Ohio, teeming with inhabitants, its soil
loaded with every kind of agricultural wealth, its people
engaged in every kind of freedom's diversified employments, abounding with numberless happy homes, and with
all the trophies of civilization, and it exhibits the magic
effect of free labor, waking a wilderness into life and
beauty ; while Kentucky, with equal or superior natural
advantages, nature's very garden in this Western world,
which commenced its career at a much earlier date, and
was in a measure populous when Ohio was but a slumber-
ing forest, but which in all the elements of progress, is
now left far, very far, behind its young rival, shows how
slave labor hinders the development of wealth among a
people, and brings a blight on their prosperity. The one
is a grand and beautiful poem in honor of free labor. The
other is an humble confession to the world of the inferiority
of slave labor."

Equally significant is the testimony of Daniel R. Goodloe,
of North Carolina,[12] who says :—

" The history of the United States shows, that while the
slave States increase in population less rapidly than the
free, there is a tendency in slave society to diffusion,
greater than is exhibited by free society. In fact, diffusion,
or extension of area, is one of the necessities of slavery ;
the prevention of which is regarded as directly and immediately menacing to the existence of the institutior. This
arises from the almost exclusive application of slave labor
to the one occupation of agriculture, and the difficulty, if
not impossibility, of diversifying employments. Free soci-

ety, on the contrary, has indefinite resources of development within a restricted area. It will far excel slave
society in the cultivation of the ground—first, on account
of the superior intelligence of the laborers ; and secondly,
in consequence of the greater and more various demands
upon the earth's products, where commerce, manufactures,
and the arts, abound. Then, these arts of life, by bringing
men together in cities and towns, and employing them in
the manufacture or transportation of the raw materials of
the farmer, give rise to an indefinite increase of wealth
and population. The confinement of a free people within
narrow limits seems only to develop new resources of
wealth, comfort and happiness ; while slave society, pent
up, withers and dies. It must continually be fed by new
fields and forests, to be wasted and wilted under the poisonous tread of the slave."

Were we simply a freesoiler, or anything else less than
a thorough and uncompromising abolitionist, we should
certainly tax our ability to the utmost to get up a cogent
argument against the extension of slavery over any part
of our domain where it does not now exist ; but as our
principles are hostile to the institution even where it does
exist, and, therefore, by implication and in fact, more hostile still to its introduction into new territory, we forbear
the preparation of any special remarks on this particular
subject.

With regard to the unnational and demoralizing institution of slavery, we believe the majority of Northern people
are too scrupulous. They seem to think that it is enough
for them to be mere freesoilers, to keep in check the diffu-

sive element of slavery, and to prevent it from crossing over the bounds within which it is now regulated by municipal law. Remiss in their *national* duties, as we contend, they make no positive attack upon the institution in the Southern States. Only a short while since, one of their ablest journals—the *North American and United States Gazette*, published in Philadelphia—made use of the following language :—

" With slavery in the States, we make no pretence of having anything politically to do. For better or for worse, the system belongs solely to the people of those States ; and is separated by an impassable gulf of State sovereignty from any legal intervention of ours. We cannot vote it down any more than we can vote down the institution of caste in Hindostan, or abolish polygamy in the Sultan's dominions. Thus, precluded from all political action in reference to it, prevented from touching one stone of the edifice, not the slightest responsibility attaches to us as citizens for its continued existence. But on the question of extending slavery over the free Territories of the United States, it is our right, it is our imperative duty to think, to feel, to speak and to vote. We cannot interfere to cover the shadows of slavery with the sunshine of freedom, but we can interfere to prevent the sunshine of freedom from being eclipsed by the shadows of slavery. We can interpose to stay the progress of that institution, which aims to drive free labor from its own heritage. Kansas should be divided up into countless homes for the ownership of men who have a right to the fruit of their own labors. Free labor would make it bud and blossom like the rose ;

would cover it with beauty, and draw from it boundless wealth ; would throng it with population ; would make States, nations, empires out of it, prosperous, powerful, intelligent and free, illustrating on a wide theatre the beneficent ends of Providence in the formation of our government, to advance and elevate the millions of our race, and, like the heart in the body, from its central position, sending out on every side, far and near, the vital influences of freedom and civilization. May that region, therefore, be secured to free labor."

Now we fully and heartily indorse every line of the latter part of this extract ; but, with all due deference to our sage cotemporary, we do most emphatically dissent from the sentiments embodied in the first part. Pray, permit us to ask—have the people of the North no interest in the United States as a *nation*, and do they not see that slavery is a great injury and disgrace to the *whole country* ? Did they not, in " the days that tried men's souls," strike as hard blows to secure the independence of Georgia as they did in defending the liberties of Massachusetts, and is it not notoriously true that the Toryism of South Carolina prolonged the war two years at least ? Is it not, moreover, equally true that the oligarchs of South Carolina have been unmitigated pests and bores to the General Government ever since it was organized, and that the free and conscientious people of the North are virtually excluded from her soil, in consequence of slavery ? It is a well-known and incontestible fact, that the Northern States furnished about two-thirds of all the American troops engaged in the Revolutionary War ; and, though they were neither more nor less brave or patriotic than their fellow-soldiers of the South, yet, inasmuch as the independence of our country was mainly secured by virtue of their numerical strength, we think they ought to consider it not only their right but their *duty* to make a firm and decisive effort to save the States which they fought to free, from falling under the yoke of a worse tyranny than that which overshadowed them under the reign of King George the Third. Freemen of the North! we earnestly entreat you to think of these things. Hitherto, as mere freesoilers, you have approached but half-way to the line of your duty ; now, for your own sakes and for ours, and for the purpose of perpetuating this glorious Republic, which your fathers and our fathers founded in septennial streams of blood, we ask you, in all seriousness, to organize yourselves as *one man* under the banners of Liberty, and to aid us in *exterminating* slavery, which is the only thing that militates against our complete aggrandizement as a nation.

In this extraordinary crisis of affairs, no man can be a true patriot without first becoming an abolitionist. (A freesoiler is only a tadpole in an advanced state of transformation ; an abolitionist is the full and perfectly developed frog.) And here, perhaps, we may be pardoned for the digression necessary to show the exact definition of the terms *abolish*, *abolition* and *abolitionist*. We have looked in vain for an explanation of the signification of these words in any Southern publication ; for no dictionary has ever yet been published in the South, nor is there the least probability that one ever will be published within her borders, until slavery is *abolished;* but, thanks to Heaven, a portion of this continent is what our Revolutionary Fathers and the Fathers of the Constitution fought and labored and prayed to make it—a land of freedom, of power, of progress, of prosperity, of intelligence, of religion, of literature, of commerce, of science, of arts, of agriculture, of manufactures, of ingenuity, of enterprise, of wealth, of renown, of goodness, and of grandeur. From that glorious part of our confederacy—from the North, whence, on account of slavery in the South, we are under the humiliating necessity of procuring almost everything that is useful or ornamental, from primers to Bibles, from wafers to printing-presses, from ladles to locomotives, and from portfolios to portraits and pianos—comes to us a huge volume bearing the honored name of Webster—Noah Webster, who, after thirty-five years of unremitting toil, completed a work which is, we believe, throughout Great Britain and the United States, justly regarded as the standard vocabulary of the English language—and in it the terms *abolish, abolition,* and *abolitionist,* are defined as follows :—

"Abolish, *v. t.* To make void; to annul; to abrogate; applied chiefly and appropriately to establish laws, contracts, rites, customs and institutions; as to *abolish* laws by a repeal, actual or virtual. To destroy or put an end to; as to *abolish* idols."

"Abolition, *n.* The act of abolishing; or the state of being abolished; an annulling; abrogation; utter destruction; as the *abolition* of laws, decrees, or ordinances, rites, customs, &c. The putting an end to slavery; emancipation."

"Abolitionist, *n.* A person who favors abolition, or the immediate emancipation of slaves."

There, gentlemen of the South, you have the definitions of the transitive verb *abolish* and its two derivative nouns, *abolition* and *abolitionist;* can you, with the keenest possible penetration of vision, detect in either of these words even a tittle of the opprobrium which the oligarchs, in their wily and inhuman efforts to enslave all working classes irrespective of race or color, have endeavored to attach to them? We know you cannot; abolition is but another name for patriotism, and its other special synonyms are generosity, magnanimity, reason, prudence, wisdom, religion, progress, justice, and humanity.

And here, by the way, we may as well explain whom we refer to when we speak of gentlemen of the South. We say, therefore, that, deeply impressed with the conviction that slavery is a great social and political evil, a *sin and a crime,* in the fullest sense, whenever we speak of gentlemen of the South, or of gentlemen anywhere, or at whatever time, or in whatever connection we may speak of gentlemen, we seldom allude to slaveholders, for the simple reason that, with few exceptions, we cannot conscientiously recognize *them* as gentlemen. It is only in those rare instances where the crime is mitigated by circumstances over which the slaveholder has had no control, or where he himself, convinced of the impropriety, the folly and the wickedness of the institution, is anxious to abolish it, that we can sincerely apply to him the sacred appellation in question—an appellation which we would no sooner think of applying to a *pro-slavery* slaveholder, or any other pro-slavery man, than we would think of applying it to a border-ruffian, a thief or a murderer. Let it be understood, however, that the rare instances of which we speak are less rare than many persons may suppose. We are personally acquainted with several slaveholders in North Carolina, South Carolina, Maryland and Virginia, who have unreservedly assured us that they were disgusted with the institution, and some of them went so far as to say they would be glad to acquiesce in the provision of a statute which would make it obligatory on them all to manumit their slaves, without the smallest shadow or substance of compensation. These, we believe, are the sentiments of all the respectable and patriotic slaveholders, who have eyes to see, and see—ears to hear, and hear ; who, perceiving the impoverishing and degrading effects of slavery, are unwilling to entail it on their children, and who, on account of their undeviating adherence to truth and justice, are, like the more intelligent non-slaveholders, worthy of being regarded as gentlemen in every sense of the term. Such slaveholders were Washington, Jefferson, Madison, and other illustrious Virginians, who, in the language of the great chief himself, declared it among their "*first wishes* to see some plan adopted by which slavery, in this country, may be abolished by law." The words embraced within this quotation were used by Washington, in a letter to John F. Mercer, dated September 9th, 1786—a letter from which we shall quote more freely hereafter ; and we think his emphatic use of the participle *abolished*, at that early day, is proof positive that the glorious " Father of his Country" is entitled to the first place in the calendar of primitive American abolitionists.

It is against slavery on the whole, and against slave-holders as a body, that we wage an exterminating war. Those persons who, under the infamous slave-laws of the South—laws which have been correctly spoken of as a "disgrace to civilization," and which must be annulled simultaneously with the abolition of slavery—have had the vile institution entailed on them contrary to their wills, are virtually on our side ; we may, therefore, very properly strike them off from the black list of three hundred and forty-seven thousand slaveholders, who, as a body, have shocked the civilized world with their barbarous conduct, and from whose conceited and presumptuous ranks are selected the officers who do all the legislation, town, county, state and national, for (against) five millions of poor outraged whites, and three millions of enslaved negroes.

Non-slaveholders of the South ! farmers, mechanics and workingmen, we take this occasion to assure you that the slaveholders, the arrogant demagogues whom you have elected to offices of honor and profit, have hoodwinked you, trifled with you, and used you as mere tools for the consummation of their wicked designs. They have purposely kept you in ignorance, and have, by moulding your passions and prejudices to suit themselves, induced you to act in direct opposition to your dearest rights and interests. By a system of the grossest subterfuge and misrepresentation, and in order to avert, for a season, the vengeance that will most assuredly overtake them ere long, they have taught you to hate the abolitionists, who are your best and only true friends. Now, as one of your own number, we appeal to you to join us in our patriotic endeavors to rescue the generous soil of the South from the usurped and desolating control of these political vampires. Once and forever, at least so far as this country is concerned, the infernal question of slavery must be disposed of ; a speedy and perfect abolishment of the whole institution is the true policy of the South—and this is the policy which we propose to pursue. Will you aid us, will you assist us, will you be freemen, or will you be slaves ? These are questions of vital importance ; weigh them well in your minds ; come to a prudent and firm decision, and hold yourselves in readiness to act in accordance therewith. You must either be for us or against us—antislavery or pro-slavery ; it is impossible for you to occupy a neutral ground ; it is as certain as fate itself, that if you do not voluntarily oppose the usurpations and outrages of the slavocrats, they will force you into involuntary compliance with their infamous measures. Consider well the aggressive, fraudulent and despotic power which they have exercised in the affairs of Kanzas ; and remember that, if, by adhering to erroneous principles of neutrality or non-resistance, you allow them to force the curse of slavery on that vast and fertile field, the broad area of all the surrounding States and Territories—the whole nation, in fact—will soon fall a prey to their diabolical intrigues and machinations. Thus, if you are not vigilant, will they take advantage of your neutrality, and make you and others the victims of their inhuman despotism. Do not reserve the strength of your arms until you shall have been rendered powerless to strike ; the present is the

6

proper time for action ; under all the circumstances, apathy or indifference is a crime. First ascertain, as nearly as you can, the precise nature and extent of your duty, and then, without a moment's delay, perform it in good faith. To facilitate you in determining what considerations of right, justice and humanity require at your hands, is one of the primary objects of this work ; and we shall certainly fail in our desire if we do not accomplish our task in a manner acceptable to God and advantageous to man.

But we are carrying this chapter beyond all ordinary bounds ; and yet, there are many important particulars in which we have drawn no comparison between the free and the slave States. The more weighty remarks which we intended to offer in relation to the new States of the West and Southwest, free and slave, shall appear in the succeeding chapter. With regard to agriculture, and all the multifarious interests of husbandry, we deem it quite unnecessary to say more. Cotton has been shorn of its magic power, and is no longer King ; *dried grass*, commonly called hay, is, it seems, the rightful heir to the throne. Commerce, Manufactures, Literature, and other important subjects, shall be considered as we progress.

CHAPTER II.

HOW SLAVERY CAN BE ABOLISHED.

PRELIMINARY to our elucidation of what we conceive to be the most discreet, fair and feasible plan for the abolition of slavery, we propose to offer a few additional reasons why it should be abolished.   Among the thousand and one arguments that present themselves in support of our position — which, before we part with the reader, we shall endeavor to define so clearly, that it shall be regarded as ultra only by those who imperfectly understand it — is the influence which slavery invariably exercises in depressing the value of real estate ; and as this is a matter in which the non-slaveholders of the South, of the West, and of the Southwest, are most deeply interested, we shall discuss it in a sort of preamble of some length.

The oligarchs say we cannot abolish slavery without infringing on the right of property.   Again we tell them we do not recognize property in man ; but even if we did, and if we were to inventory the negroes at quadruple, the value of their last assessment, still, impelled by a sense of duty to others, and as a matter of simple justice to ourselves, we, the non-slaveholders of the South, would be fully warranted in emancipating all the slaves at once, and that, too, without any compensation whatever to

those who claim to be their absolute masters and owners
We will explain. In 1850, the average value per acre, of
land in the Northern States was $28,07 ; in the North-
western $11,39 ; in the Southern $5,34 ; and in the Southwestern $6,26. Now, in consequence of numerous natural
advantages, among which may be enumerated the greater
mildness of climate, richness of soil, deposits of precious
metals, abundance and spaciousness of harbors, and super-
excellence of water-power, we contend that, had it not
been for slavery, the average value of land in all the
Southern and Southwestern States, would have been *at
least* equal to the average value of the same in the Northern States. We conclude, therefore, and we think the
conclusion is founded on principles of equity, that you,
the slaveholders, are indebted to us, the non-slaveholders,
in the sum of $22,73, which is the difference between
$28,07 and $5,34, on every acre of Southern soil in our
possession. This claim we bring against you, because
slavery, which has inured exclusively to your own benefit,
if, indeed, it has been beneficial at all, has shed a blighting influence over our lands, thereby keeping them out of
market, and damaging every acre to the amount specified.
Sirs ! are you ready to settle the account ? Let us see
how much it is. There are in the fifteen slave States,
346,048 slaveholders, and 544,926,720 acres of land. Now
the object is to ascertain how many acres are owned by
slaveholders, and now many by non-slaveholders. Suppose we estimate five hundred acres as the average landed
property of each slaveholder ; will that be fair ? We
think it will, taking into consideration the fact that 174,503

of the whole number of slaveholders hold less than five slaves each—68,820 holding only one each. According to this hypothesis, the slaveholders own 173,024,000 acres, and the non-slaveholders the balance, with the exception of about 40,000,000 of acres, which belong to the General Government. The case may be stated thus :

Area of the Slave States 544,926,720 acres.

Estimates
{
Acres owned by slaveholders.. 173,024,000
Acres owned by the government 40,000,000—213,024,000
Acres owned by non-slaveholders.... 331,902,720

Now, chevaliers of the lash, and worshippers of slavery, the total value of three hundred and thirty-one million nine hundred and two thousand seven hundred and twenty acres, at twenty-two dollars and seventy-three cents per acre, is *seven billion five hundred and forty-four million one hundred and forty-eight thousand eight hundred and twenty-five dollars;* and this is our account against you on a single score. Considering how your villainous institution has retarded the development of our commercial and manufacturing interests, how it has stifled the aspirations of inventive genius ; and, above all, how it has barred from us the heaven-born sweets of literature and religion—concernments too sacred to be estimated in a pecuniary point of view—might we not, with perfect justice and propriety, duplicate the amount, and still be accounted modest in our demands ? Fully advised, however, of your indi-gent circumstances, we feel it would be utterly useless to call on you for the whole amount that is due us ; we shall, therefore, in your behalf, make another draft on the fund of non-slaveholding generosity, and let the account, meagre as it is, stand as above. Though we have given you all the offices, and you have given us none of the benefits of legislation ; though we have fought the battles of the South, while you were either lolling in your piazzas, or playing the tory, and endeavoring to filch from us our birthright of freedom ; though you have absorbed the wealth of our communities in sending your own children to Northern seminaries and colleges, or in employing Yankee teachers to officiate exclusively in your own families, and have refused to us the limited privilege of common schools ; though you have scorned to patronize our mechanics and industrial enterprises, and have passed to the North for every article of apparel, utility, and adornment ; and though you have maltreated, outraged and defrauded us in every relation of life, civil, social, and political, yet we are willing to forgive and *forget* you, if you will but do us justice on a single count. Of you, the introducers, aiders and abettors of slavery, we demand indemnification for the damage our lands have sustained on account thereof ; the amount of that damage is $7,544,148,825 ; and now, Sirs, we are ready to receive the money, and if it is perfectly convenient to you, we would be glad to have you pay it in specie ! It will not avail you, Sirs, to parley or prevaricate. We must have a settlement. Our claim is just and overdue. We have already indulged you too long. Your criminal extravagance has almost ruined us. We are determined that you shall no longer play the profligate, and fair sumptuously every day at our expense. How do you propose to settle ? Do you offer us your negroes in part payment ? We do not want your negroes. We would not have all of them, nor any number of them, even as a gift. We hold ourselves above the disreputable and iniquitous practices of buying, selling, and owning slaves. What we demand is damages in money, or other absolute property, as an equivalent for the pecuniary losses we have suffered at your hands. You value your negroes at sixteen hundred millions of dollars, and propose to sell them to us for that sum ; we should consider ourselves badly cheated, and disgraced for all time, here and hereafter, if we were to take them off your hands at sixteen farthings ! We tell you emphatically, we are firmly resolved never to degrade ourselves by becoming the mercenary purchasers or proprietors of human beings. Except for the purpose of liberating them, we would not give a handkerchief or a tooth-pick for all the slaves in the world. But, in order to show how brazenly absurd are the howls and groans which you invariably set up for compensation, whenever we speak of the abolition of slavery, we will suppose your negroes are worth all you ask for them, and that we are bound to secure to you every cent of the sum before they can become free—in which case, our accounts would stand thus :

Non-slaveholder's account against Slaveholders......$7,544,148,825
Slaveholder's account against Non-slaveholders.......1,600,000,000

Balance due Non-slaveholders.............$5,944,148,825

Now, Sirs, we ask you in all seriousness, Is it not true that you have filched from us nearly five times the amount of the assessed value of your slaves ? Why, then, do you still clamor for more ? Is it your purpose to make the game perpetual ? Think you that we will ever continue to b w at the wave of your wand, that we will bring

humanity into everlasting disgrace by licking the hand
that smites us, and that with us there is no point beyond
which forbearance ceases to be a virtue ?   Sirs, if these be
your thoughts, you are laboring under a most fatal delusion.   You can goad us no further ; you shall oppress us
no longer ; heretofore, earnestly but submissively, we
have asked you to redress the more atrocious outrages
which you have perpetrated against us ; but what has
been the invariable fate of our petitions ?   With scarcely
a perusal, with a degree of contempt that added insult to
injury, you have laid them on the table, and from thence
they have been swept into the furnance of oblivion.   Henceforth, Sirs, we are demandants, not suppliants.   We demand our rights, nothing more, nothing less.   It is for you
to decide whether we are to have justice peaceably or by
violence, for whatever consequences may follow, we are
determined to have it one way or the other.   Do you aspire to become the victims of white non-slaveholding vengeance by day, and of barbarous massacre by the negroes
at night ?   Would you be instrumental in bringing upon
yourselves, your wives, and your children, a fate too horrible to contemplate ? shall history cease to cite, as an
instance of unexampled cruelty, the Massacre of St. Bar-
tholomew, because the world—the South—shall have furnished a more direful scene of atrocity and carnage ?   Sirs,
we would not wantonly pluck a single hair from your
heads ; but we have endured long, we have endured
much ; slaves only of the most despicable class would
endure more.   An enumeration or classification of all the
abuses, insults, wrongs, injuries, usurpations, and oppres-

sions, to which you have subjected us, would fill a larger
volume than this ; it is our purpose, therefore, to speak
only of those that affect us most deeply.   Out of our effects
your have long since overpaid yourselves for your negroes ;
and now, Sirs, you *must* emancipate them—speedily emancipate them, or we will emancipate them for you !   Every
non-slaveholder in the South is, or ought to be, and will
be, against you.   You yourselves ought to join us at once
in our laudable crusade against " the mother of harlots."[13]
Slavery has polluted and impoverished your lands ; freedom will restore them to their virgin purity, and add from
twenty to thirty dollars to the value of every acre.   Correctly speaking, emancipation will cost you nothing ; the
moment you abolish slavery, that very moment will the
putative value of the slave become actual value in the
soil.   Though there are ten millions of people in the South,
and though you, the slaveholders, are only three hundred
and forty-seven thousand in number, you have within a
fraction of one-third of all the territory belonging to the
fifteen slave States.   You have a landed estate of 173,-
024,000 acres, the present average market value of which
is only $5,34 per acre ; emancipate your slaves on Wednes-
day morning, and on the Thursday following the value of
your lands, and ours too, will have increased to an average of at least $28,07 per acre.   Let us see, therefore,
even in this one particular, whether the abolition of
slavery will not be a real pecuniary advantage to you.
The present total market value of all your landed property,
at $5,34 per acre, is only $923,248,160 !   With the beauty
and sunlight of freedom beaming on the same estate, it

would be worth, at $28,07 per acre, $4,856,873,680 ! The
former sum, deducted from the latter, leaves a balance of
$3,933,535,520, and to the full extent of this amount will
your lands be increased in value whenever you abolish
slavery ; that is, provided you abolish it before it completely "dries up all the organs of increase." Here is a
more manifest and distinct statement of the case :—

Estimated value of slaveholders' lands after slavery } $4,856,783,680
    shall have been abolished.................... }

Present value of slaveholders' lands.............   923,248,160

Probable aggregate enhancement of value........ $3,933,535,520

Now, Sirs, this last sum is considerably more than twice
as great as the estimated value of your negroes ; and those
of you, if any there be, who are yet heirs to sane minds
and honest hearts, must, it seems to us, admit that the
bright prospect which freedom presents for a wonderful
increase in the value of real estate, ours as well as yours,
to say nothing of the thousand other kindred considerations,
ought to be quite sufficient to induce all the Southern
States, in their sovereign capacities, to abolish slavery at
the earliest practical period. You yourselves, instead of
losing anything by the emancipation of your negroes—
even though we suppose them to be worth every dime of
$1,600,000,000—would, in this one particular, the increased
value of land, realize a *net profit* of over *twenty three hundred
millions of dollars !* Here are the exact figures :—

Net increment of value which it is estimated will
    accrue to slaveholders' lands in consequence { $3,933,535,520
    of the abolition of slavery..............

Putative value of the slaves..................   1,600,000,000

Slaveholders' estimated net landed profits of eman. $2,333,535,520

What is the import of these figures ? They are full of meaning. They proclaim themselves the financial intercessors for freedom, and, with that open-hearted liberality which is so characteristic of the sacred cause in whose behalf they plead, they propose to pay you upward of three thousand nine hundred millions of dollars for the very "property" which you, in all the reckless extravagance of your inhuman avarice, could not find a heart to price at more than one thousand six hundred millions. In other words, your own lands, groaning and languishing under the monstrous burden of slavery, announce their willingness to pay you all you ask for the negroes, and offer you, besides, a bonus of more than twenty-three hundred millions of dollars, if you will but convert those lands into free soil ! *Our* lands, also, cry aloud to be spared from the further pollutions and desolations of slavery ; and now, Sirs, we want to know explicitly whether, or not, it is your intention to heed these lamentations of the ground ? We want to know whether you are men or devils—whether you are entirely selfish and cruelly dishonest, or whether you have any respect for the rights of others. We, the non-slaveholders of the South, have many very important interests at stake—interests which, heretofore, you have steadily despised and trampled under foot, but which, henceforth, we shall foster and defend in utter defiance of all the unhallowed influences which it is possible for you, or any other class of slaveholders or slavebreeders to bring against us. Not the least among these interests is our landed property, which, to command a decent price, only needs to be disencumbered of slavery.

In his present condition, we believe man exercises one of the noblest virtues with which heaven has endowed him, when, without taking any undue advantage of his fellow-men, and with a firm, unwavering purpose to confine his expenditures to the legitimate pursuits and pleasures of life, he covets money and strives to accumulate it. Entertaining this view, and having no disposition to make an improper use of money, we are free to confess that we have a greater penchant for twenty-eight dollars than for five; for ninety than for fifteen; for a thousand than for one hundred. South of Mason and Dixon's line we, the non-slaveholders, have 331,902,720 acres of land, the present average market value of which, as previously stated, is only $5,34 per acre; by abolishing slavery we expect to enhance the value to an average of at least $28,07 per acre, and thus realize an average net increase of wealth of more than *seventy-five hundred millions of dollars*. The hope of realizing smaller sums has frequently induced men to perpetrate acts of injustice; we can see no reason why the certainty of becoming immensely rich in real estate, or other property, should make us falter in the performance of a *sacred duty*.

As illustrative of our theme, a bit of personal history may not be out of place in this connection. Only a few months have elapsed since we sold to an elder brother an interest we held in an old homestead which was willed to us many years ago by our dear departed father. The tract of land, containing two hundred acres, or thereabouts, is situated two and a half miles west of Mocksville, the capital of Davie county, North Carolina, and is very nearly equally divided by Bear Creek, a small tributary of the South Yadkin. More than one-third of this tract—on which we have plowed, and hoed, and harrowed, many a long summer without ever suffering from the effects of *coup de soleil*—is under cultivation ; the remaining portion is a well-timbered forest, in which, without being very particular, we counted, while hunting through it not long since, sixty-three different kinds of indigenous trees—to say nothing of either coppice, shrubs or plants—among which the hickory, oak, ash, beech, birch, and black walnut, were most abundant. No turpentine or rosin is produced in our part of the State ; but there are, on the place of which we speak, several species of the genus Pinus, by the light of whose flammable knots, as radiated on the contents of some half-dozen old books, which, by hook or by crook, had found their way into the neighborhood, we have been ena-bled to turn the long winter evenings to our advantage, and have thus *partially* escaped from the prison-grounds of those loathsome dungeons of illiteracy in which it has been the constant policy of the oligarchy to keep the masses, the non-slaveholding whites and the negroes, forever con-fined. The fertility of the soil may be inferred from the quality and variety of its natural productions ; the meadow and the bottom, comprising, perhaps, an area of forty acres, are hardly surpassed by the best lands in the valley of the Yadkin. A thorough examination of the orchard will disclose the fact that considerable attention has been paid to the selection of fruits ; the buildings are tolerable ; the water is good. Altogether, to be frank, and nothing more, it is, for its size, one of the most desirable farms in the county, and will, at any time, command the maximum price of land in Western Carolina. Our brother, anxious to become the sole proprietor, readily agreed to give us the highest market price, which we shall publish by-and-bye. While reading the Baltimore *Sun*, the morning after we had made the sale, our attention was allured to a paragraph headed "Sales of Real Estate," from which, among other significant items, we learned that a tract of land containing exactly two hundred acres, and occupying a portion of one of the rural districts in the southeastern part of Pennsylvania, near the Maryland line, had been sold the week before, at *one hundred and five dollars and fifty cents* per acre. Judging from the succinct account given in the *Sun*, we are of the opinion that, with regard to fertility of soil, the Pennsylvania tract always has been, is now, and perhaps always will be, rather inferior to the one under special consideration. One is of the same size as the other ; both are used for agricultural purposes ; in all probability the only *essential* difference between them is this : one is blessed with the pure air of freedom, the other is cursed with the malaria of slavery. For our interest in the old homestead we received a nominal sum, amounting to an average of precisely *five dollars and sixty cents* per acre. No one but our brother, who was keen for the purchase, would have given us quite so much.

And, now, pray let us ask, what does this narrative teach ? We shall use few words in explanation : there is an extensive void, but it can be better filled with reflection. The aggregate value of the one tract is $21,100 ; that of the other is only $1,120 ; the difference is $19,980. We

contend, therefore, in view of all the circumstances detailed, that the advocates and retainers of slavery, have,
to all intents and purposes, defrauded our family out of
this last-mentioned sum.   In like manner, and on the same
basis of deduction, we contend that almost every non-
slaveholder, who either is or has been the owner of real
estate in the South, would, in a court of strict justice, be
entitled to damages — the amount in all cases to be determined with reference to the quality of the land in question.   We say this because, in violation of every principle
of expediency, justice, and humanity, and in direct opposition to our solemn protests, slavery was foisted upon us,
and has been thus far perpetuated, by and through the
diabolical intrigues of the oligarchs, and by them alone ;
and furthermore, because the very best agricultural lands
in the Northern States being worth from one hundred to
one hundred and seventy-five dollars per acre, there is no
possible reason, except slavery, why the more fertile and
congenial soil of the South should not be worth at least
as much.   If, on this principle, we could ascertain, in the
matter of real estate, the total indebtedness of the slaveholders to the non-slaveholders, we should doubtless find
the sum quite equivalent to the amount estimated on a
preceding page — $7,544,148,825.

We have recently conversed with two gentlemen who,
to save themselves from the poverty and disgrace of
slavery, left North Carolina six or seven years ago, and
who are now residing in the territory of Minnesota, where
they have accumulated handsome fortunes.   One of them
had traveled extensively in Kentucky, Missouri, Ohio,

Indiana, and other adjoining States ; and, according to his account, and we know him to be a man of veracity, it is almost impossible for persons at a distance, to form a proper conception of the magnitude of the difference between the current value of lands in the Free and the Slave States of the West. On one occasion, embarking at Wheeling, he sailed down the Ohio ; Virgina and Kentucky on the one side, Ohio and Indiana on the other. He stopped at several places along the river, first on the right bank, then on the left, and so on, until he arrived at Evansville ; continuing his trip, he sailed down to Cairo, thence up the Mississippi to the mouth of the Des Moines ; having tarried at different points along the route, sometimes in Missouri, sometimes in Illinois. Wherever he landed on free soil, he found it from one to two hundred per cent. more valuable than the slave soil on the opposite bank. If, for instance, the maximum price of land was eight dollars in Kentucky, the minimum price was sixteen in Ohio ; if it was seven dollars in Missouri, it was fourteen in Illinois. Furthermore, he assured us, that, so far as he could learn, two years ago, when he traveled through the States of which we speak, the range of prices of agricultural lands, in Kentucky, was from three to eight dollars per acre ; in Ohio, from sixteen to forty ; in Missouri, from two to seven ; in Illinois, from fourteen to thirty ; in Arkansas, from one to four ; in Iowa, from six to fifteen.

In all the old slave States, as is well known, there are vast bodies of land that can be bought for the merest trifle. We know an enterprising capitalist in Philadelphia, who owns in his individual name, in the State of

Virginia, *one hundred and thirty thousand acres*, for which he paid only *thirty-seven and a half cents* per acre ! Some years ago, in certain parts of North Carolina, several large tracts were purchased at the rate of *twenty-five cents* per acre !

Hiram Berdan, the distinguished inventor, who has frequently seen freedom and slavery side by side, and who is, therefore, well qualified to form an opinion of their relative influence upon society, says :

"Many comparisons might be drawn between the free and the slave States, either of which should be sufficient to satisfy any man that slavery is not only ruinous to free labor and enterprise, but injurious to morals, and blighting to the soil where it exists. The comparison between the States of Michigan and Arkansas, which were admitted into the Union at the same time, will fairly illustrate the difference and value of free and slave labor, as well as the difference of moral and intellectual progress in a free and in a slave State.

In 1836 these young Stars were admitted into the constellation of the Union. Michigan, with one-half the extent of territory of Arkansas, challenged her sister State for a twenty years' race, and named as her rider, 'Neither slavery, nor involuntary servitude, unless for the punishment of crime, shall ever be tolerated in this State.' Arkansas accepted the challenge, and named as her rider, 'The General Assembly shall have no power to pass laws for the emancipation of slaves without the consent of the owners.' Thus mounted, these two States, the one free and the other slave, started together twenty years ago, and now, having arrived at the end of the proposed race, let us review and mark the progress of each. Michigan comes out in 1856 with three times the population of slave Arkansas, with five times the assessed value of farms, farming implements and machinery, and with eight times the number of public schools."

In the foregoing part of our work, we have drawn comparisons between the old free States and the old slave States, and between the new free States and the new slave States ; had we sufficient time and space, we might with the most significant results, change this method of comparison, by contrasting the new free States with the old slave States. Can the slavocrats compare Ohio with Virginia, Illinois with Georgia, or Indiana with South Carolina, without experiencing the agony of inexpressible shame ? If they can, then indeed has slavery debased them to a lower deep than we care to contemplate. Herewith we present a brief contrast, as drawn by a Maryland abolitionist, between the most important old slave State and the most important new free State :

" Virginia was a State, wealthy and prosperous, when Ohio was a wilderness belonging to her. She gave that territory away, and what is the result ? Ohio supports a population of two million souls, and the mother contains but one and a half millions ; yet Virginia is one-third larger than the Buckeye State. Virginia contains 61,000 square miles, Ohio but 40,000. The latter sustains 50 persons to the square mile, while Virginia gives employment to but 25 to the square mile. Notwithstanding Virginia's superiority in years and in soil—for she grows tobacco, as well as corn and wheat—notwithstanding her immense coal-fields, and her splendid Atlantic ports, Ohio, the infant State, had 21 representatives in Congress in 1850, while Virginia had but 13—the latter having *commenced* in the Union with 10 Congressmen. Compare the progress of these States, and then say, what is it but Free Labor that has advanced Ohio ? and to what, except slavery, can we attribute the non-progression of the Old Dominion ?"

As a striking illustration of the selfish and debasing influences which slavery exercises over the hearts and minds of slaveholders themselves, we will here state the fact that, when we, the non-slaveholders, remonstrate against the continuance of such a manifest wrong and inhumanity—a system of usurpation and outrage so obviously detrimental to *our* interests—they fly into a terrible passion, exclaiming, among all sorts of horrible threats, which are not unfrequently executed, "It's none of your business !"—meaning to say thereby that their slaves do not annoy us, that slavery affects no one except the masters and their chattels personal, and that *we* should give ourselves no concern about it, whatever ! To every man of common sense and honesty of purpose the preposterousness of this assumption is so evident, that any studied attempt to refute it would be a positive insult. Would it be none of our business, if they were to bring the small-pox into the neighborhood, and, with premeditated design, let "foul contagion spread ?" Or, if they were to throw a pound of strychnine into a public spring, would that be none of our business ? Were they to turn a pack of mad dogs loose on the community, would we be performing the part of good citizens by closing ourselves within doors for the space of nine days, saying nothing to anybody ? Small-pox is a nuisance ; strychnine is a nuisance ; mad dogs are a nuisance ; slavery is a nuisance ; slaveholders are a nuisance, and so are slave-breeders ; it is our business, nay, it is our imperative duty, to abate nuisances ; we propose, therefore, with the exception of strychnine, which is the least of all these nuisances, to exterminate this catalogue from beginning to end.

We mean precisely what our words express, when we say we believe thieves are, as a general rule, less amenable to the moral law than slaveholders ; and here is the basis of our opinion :   Ordinarily, thieves wait until we acquire a considerable amount of property, and then they steal a dispensable part of it ; but they deprive no one of physical liberty, nor do they fetter the mind ; slaveholders, on the contrary, by clinging to the most barbarous relic of the most barbarous age, bring disgrace on themselves, their neighbors, and their country, depreciate the value of their own and others' lands, degrade labor, discourage energy and progress, prevent non-slaveholders from accumulating wealth, curtail their natural rights and privileges, doom their children to ignorance, and all its attendant evils, rob the negroes of their freedom, throw a damper on every species of manual and intellectual enterprise, that is not projected under their own roofs and for their own advantage, and, by other means equally at variance with the principles of justice, though but an insignificant fractional part of the population, they constitute themselves the sole arbiters and legislators for the entire South.   Not merely so ; the thief rarely steals from more than one man out of an hundred ; the slaveholder defrauds ninety and nine, and the hundredth does not escape him.   Again, thieves steal trifles from rich men ; slaveholders oppress poor men, and enact laws for the perpetuation of their poverty. Thieves practice deceit on the wise ; slaveholders take advantage of the ignorant.

We contend, moreover, that slaveholders are more criminal than common murderers. We know all slaveholders would not wilfully imbue their hands in the blood of their fellow-men ; but it is a fact, nevertheless, that all slaveholders are under the shield of a perpetual license to murder. This license they have issued to themselves. According to their own infamous statutes, if the slave raises his hand to ward off an unmerited blow, they are permitted to take his life with impunity. We are personally acquainted with three ruffians who have become actual murderers under circumstances of this nature. One of them killed two negroes on one occasion ; the other two have murdered but one each. Neither of them has ever been subjected to even the preliminaries of a trial ; not one of them has ever been arrested ; their own private explanations of the homicides exculpated them from all manner of blame in the premises. They had done nothing wrong in the eyes of the community. The negroes made an effort to shield themselves from the tortures of a merciless flagellation, and were shot dead on the spot Their murderers still live, and are treated as honorable members of society ! No matter how many slaves or free negroes may witness the perpetration of these atrocious homicides, not one of them is ever allowed to lift up his voice in behalf of his murdered brother. In the South, negroes, whether bond or free, are never, under any circumstances, permitted to utter a syllable under oath, except for or against persons of their own color ; their testimony against white persons is of no more consequence than the idle zephyr of the summer.[14]

We shall now introduce four tables of valuable and interesting statistics, to which philosophic and discriminating readers will doubtless have frequent occasions to refer. Tables 22 and 23 will show the area of the several

States, in square miles and in acres, and the number of
inhabitants to the square mile in each State ; also the
grand total, or the average, of every statistical column ;
tables 24 and 25 will exhibit the total number of inhabitants residing in each State, according to the census of
1850, the number of whites, the number of free colored,
and the number of slaves. The recapitulations of these
tables will be followed by a complete list of the number
of slaveholders in the United States, showing the exact
number in each Southern State, and in the District of
Columbia. Most warmly do we commend all these statis
tics to the *studious* attention of the reader. Their lan·
guage is more eloquent than any possible combination of
Roman vowels and consonants. We have spared no pains
in arranging them so as to express at a single glance the
great truths of which they are composed ; and we doubt
not that the plan we have adopted will meet with general
approbation. Numerically considered, it will be perceived
that the slaveholders are, in reality, a very insignificant
class. Of them, however, we shall have more to say hereafter.

TABLE NO. XXII.

AREA OF THE FREE STATES.

States.	Square Miles.	Acres.	Inhabit'nts to square mile.
California	155,980	99,827,200	.59
Connecticut..	4,674	2,991,360	79.83
Illinois.. ....,..	55,405	35,359,200	15.37
Indiana.	33,809	21,637,760	29.24
Iowa....	50,914	32,584,960	3.78
Maine.................	31,766	20,330,240	18.36
Massachusetts..........	7,800	4,992,000	127.50
Michigan..............	56,243	35,995,520	7.07
New Hampshire..	9,280	5,939,200	34.26
New Jersey..	8,320	5,324,800	58.84
New York............	47,000	30,080,000	65.90
Ohio....	39,964	26,576,960	49.55
Pennsylvania....	46,000	29,440,000	50.26
Rhode Island....	1,306	835,840	112.97
Vermont.............	10,212	6,535,680	30.76
Wisconsin.......	53,924	34,511,360	5.66
	612,597	392,062,082	21,91

TABLE NO. XXIII.

AREA OF THE SLAVE STATES.

States.	Square Miles.	Acres.	Inhabit'nts to square mile.
Alabama....	50,722	32,027,490	15.21
Arkansas.... ....,.	52,198	33,406,720	4.02
Delaware..	2,120	1,356,800	43.18
Florida......	59,268	37,931,520	1.48
Georgia..	58,000	37,120,000	15.62
Kentucky....	37,680	24,115,200	26.07
Louisiana	41,255	26,403,200	12.55
Maryland.............	11,124	7,119,360	52.41
Mississippi..	47,156	30,179,840	12.86
Missouri...	67,380	43,123,200	10.12
North Carolina...	50,704	32,450,560	17.14
South Carolina...	29,385	18,805,400	22.75
Tennessee........	45,600	29,184,000	21.99
Texas.	237,504	152,002,560	.89
Virginia...	61,352	39,165,280	23.17
	851,448	544,926,720	11.29

TABLE NO. XXIV.

POPULATION OF THE FREE STATES—1850.

States.	Whites.	Free Colored.	Total.
California	91,635	962	92,597
Connecticut	363,099	7,693	370,792
Illinois	846,034	5,436	851,470
Indiana	977,154	11,262	988,416
Iowa	191,881	333	192,214
Maine	581,813	1,356	583,169
Massachusetts	985,450	9,064	994,514
Michigan	395,071	2,583	397,654
New Hampshire	317,456	520	317,976
New Jersey	465,509	23,810	489,555
New York	3,048,325	49,069	3,097,394
Ohio	1,955,050	25,279	1,980,329
Pennsylvania	2,258,160	53,626	2,311,786
Rhode Island	143,875	3,670	147,545
Vermont	313,402	718	314,120
Wisconsin	304,756	635	305,391
	13,233,670	196,116	13,434,922

TABLE NO. XXV.

POPULATION OF THE SLAVE STATES—1850.

States.	Whites.	Free Colored.	Slaves.	Total.
Alabama	426,514	2,265	342,844	771,623
Arkansas	162,189	608	47,100	209,897
Delaware	71,169	18,073	2,290	91,532
Florida	47,203	932	39,310	87,445
Georgia	521,572	2,931	381,622	906,185
Kentucky	761,413	10,011	210,981	982,405
Louisiana	255,491	17,462	244,809	517,762
Maryland	417,943	74,723	90,368	583,034
Mississippi	295,718	930	309,878	606,326
Missouri	592,004	2,618	87,422	682,044
North Carolina	553,028	27,463	288,548	869,039
South Carolina	274,563	8,960	384,984	668,507
Tennessee	756,836	6,422	239,459	1,002,717
Texas	154,034	397	58,161	212,592
Virginia	894,800	54,333	472,528	1,421,661
	6,184,477	228,138	3,200,364	9,612,979

RECAPITULATION——AREA.

	Square Miles.	Acres.
Area of the Slave States............851,448		544,926,720
Area of the Free States............612,597		392,062,082
Balances in favor of Slave States...238,851		152,864,638

RECAPITULATION——POPULATION——1850.

	Whites.	Total.
Population of the Free States.....13,233,670		13,434,922
Population of the Slave States ... 6,184,477		9,612,976
Balances in favor of the Free States 7,049,193		3,821,946

FREE COLORED AND SLAVE——1850.

Free Negroes in the Slave States........................228,138
Free Negroes in the Free States........................196,116

Excess of Free Negroes in the Slave States............... 32,022

Slaves in the Slave States..............................3,200,364
Free Negroes in the Slave States.......................228,138

Aggregate Negro Population of the Slave States in 1850...3,428,502

THE TERRITORIES AND THE DISTRICT OF COLUMBIA.

	Area in Square Miles.	Population.
Indian Territory....................71,127		
Kansas " 114,798		
Minnesota " 166,025		6,077
Nebraska " 335,882		
N. Mexico " 207,007		61,547
Oregon " 185,030		13,294
Utah " 269,170		11,380
Washington " 123,022		
Columbia, Dist. of.............. 60		*51,687
Aggregate of Area and Population, 1,472,121		143,985

*Of the 51,687 inhabitants in the District of Columbia, in 1850, 10,057 were Free Colored, and 3,687 were slaves.

7

NUMBER OF SLAVEHOLDERS IN THE UNITED STATES—1850.

Alabama...29,295
Arkansas... 5,999
Columbia, District of,................................ 1,477
Delaware... 809
Florida... 3,520
Georgia...38,456
Kentucky..38,385
Louisiana...20,670
Maryland..16,040
Mississippi...23,116
Missouri..19,185
North Carolina......................................28,303
South Carolina......................................25,596
Tennessee...33,864
Texas... 7,747
Virginia..55,063

Total Number of Slaveholders in the United States.........347,525

CLASSIFICATION OF THE SLAVEHOLDERS—1850.

Holders of   1 slave............................... 68,820
Holders of   1 and under   5....................105,683
Holders of   5 and under   10.................... 80,765
Holders of   10 and under   20.................... 54,595
Holders of   20 and under   50.................... 29,733
Holders of   50 and under   100.................... 6,196
Holders of   100 and under   200.................... 1,479
Holders of   200 and under   300.................... 187
Holders of   300 and under   500.................... 56
Holders of   500 and under 1,000.................... 9
Holders of 1,000 and over   2

Aggregate Number of Slaveholders in the United States....347,525

It thus appears that there are in the United States, three hundred and forty-seven thousand five hundred and twenty-five slaveholders. But this appearance is deceptive. The actual number is certainly less than two hundred thousand. Professor De Bow, the Superintendent of the Census, informs us that "the number includes slave-hirers," and furthermore, that "where the party owns slaves in different counties, or in different States, he will be entered more than once." Now every Southerner, who has any practical knowledge of affairs, must know, and does know, that every New Year's day, like almost every other day, is desecrated in the South, by publicly hiring out slaves to large numbers of non-slaveholders. The slave-owners, who are the exclusive manufacturers of public sentiment, have popularized the dictum that white servants, decency, virtue, and justice, are unfashionable ; and there are, we are sorry to say, nearly one hundred and sixty thousand non-slaveholding sycophants, who have subscribed to this false philosophy, and who are giving constant encouragement to the infamous practices of slaveholding and slave-breeding, by hiring at least one slave every year.

In the Southern States, as in all other slave countries, there are three odious classes of mankind ; the slaves themselves, who are cowards ; the slaveholders, who are tyrants ; and the non-slaveholding slave-hirers, who are lickspittles. Whether either class is really entitled to the regards of a gentleman is a matter of grave doubt. The slaves are pitiable ; the slaveholders are detestable ; the slave-hirers are contemptible.[15]

With the statistics at our command, it is impossible for us to ascertain the exact numbers of slaveholders and non-slaveholding slave-hirers in the slave States; but we have data which will enable us to approach very near to the facts. The town from which we hail, Salisbury, the capital of Rowan county, North Carolina, contains about twenty-three hundred inhabitants, including three hundred and seventy-two slaves, fifty-one slaveholders, and forty-three non-slaveholding slave-hirers. Taking it for granted that this town furnishes a fair relative proportion of all the slaveholders, and non-slaveholding slave-hirers in the slave States, the whole number of the former, including those who have been " entered more than once," is one hundred and eighty-eight thousand five hundred and fifty-one; of the latter, one hundred and fifty-eight thousand nine hundred and seventy-four; and, now, estimating that there are in Maryland, Virginia, and other grain-growing States, an aggregate of two thousand slave-owners, who have cotton plantations *stocked* with negroes in the far South, and who have been " entered more than once," we find, as the result of our calculations, that the total number of actual slaveholders in the Union, is precisely one hundred and eighty-six thousand five hundred and fifty-one—as follows :

Number of actual slaveholders in the United States..   186,551
Number " entered more than once"......   2,000
Number of non-slaveholding slave-hirers...........   158,974

Aggregate number, according to De Bow........ ...   347,525

The greater number of non-slaveholding slave-hirers, are

a kind of third-rate aristocrats—persons who formerly owned slaves, but whom slavery, as is its custom, has dragged down to poverty, leaving them, in their false and shiftless pride, to eke out a miserable existence over the hapless chattels personal of other men.

So it seems that the total number of actual slave-owners, including their entire crew of cringing lickspittles, against whom we have to contend, is but three hundred and forty-seven thousand five hundred and twenty-five. Against this army for the defense and propagation of slavery, we think it will be an easy matter—independent of the negroes, who, in nine cases out of ten, would be delighted with an opportunity to cut their masters' throats, and without accepting of a single recruit from either of the free States, England, France or Germany—to muster one at least three times as large, and far more respectable for its utter extinction. We hope, however, and believe, that the matter in dispute may be adjusted without arraying these armies against each other in hostile attitude. We desire peace, not war—justice, not blood. Give us fair-play, secure to us the right of discussion, the freedom of speech, and we will settle the difficulty at the ballot-box, not on the battle-ground—by force of reason, not by force of arms. But we are wedded to one purpose from which no earthly power can ever divorce us. We are determined to abolish slavery at all hazards—in defiance of all the opposition, of whatever nature, which it is possible for the slavocrats to bring against us. Of this they may take due notice, and govern themselves accordingly.[16]

Before we proceed further, it may be necessary to call

attention to the fact that, though the ostensible proprietorship of the slaves is vested in fewer individuals than we have usually counted in our calculations concerning them, the force and drift of our statistics remain unimpaired. In the main, all our figures are correct. The tables which we have prepared, especially, and the recapitulations of those tables, may be relied on with all the confidence that is due to American official integrity; for, as we have substantially remarked on a previous occasion, the particulars of which they are composed have been obtained from the returns of competent census agents, who, with Prof. De Bow as principal, were expressly employed to collect them. As for our minor labors in the science of numbers, we cheerfully submit them to the candid scrutiny of the impartial critic.

A majority of the slaveholders with whom we are acquainted—and we happen to know a few dozen more than we care to know—own, or pretend to own, at least fifteen negroes each; some of them are the masters of more than fifty each; and we have had the *honor (!)* of an introduction to one man who is represented as the owner of sixteen hundred! It is said that if all the lands of this latter worthy were in one tract, they might be formed into two counties of more than ordinary size; he owns plantations and woodlands in three cotton-growing States.

The quantity of land owned by the slaveholder is generally in proportion to the number of negroes at his " quarter ;" the master of only one or two slaves, if engaged in agriculture, seldom owns less than three hundred acres; the holder of eight or ten slaves usually owns from a thousand to fifteen hundred acres ; five thousand acres are not unfrequently found in the possession of the master of fifty slaves ; while in Columbia, South Carolina, about twelve months ago, a certain noted slaveholder was pointed out to us, and reported as the owner of nearly two hundred thousand acres in the State of Mississippi.   How the great mass of illiterate poor whites, a majority of whom are the indescribably wretched tenants of these slavocratic land-sharks, are specially imposed upon and socially outlawed, we shall, if we have time and space, take occasion to explain in a subsequent chapter.

Thus far, in giving expression to our sincere and settled opinions, we have endeavored to show, in the first place, that slavery is a great moral, social, civil, and political evil—a dire enemy to true wealth and national greatness, and an atrocious crime against both God and man ; and, in the second place, that it is a paramount duty which we owe to heaven, to the earth, to America, to humanity, to our posterity, to our consciences, and to our pockets, to adopt effectual and judicious measures for its immediate abolition.   The questions now arise, How can the evil be averted ?   What are the most prudent and practical means that can be devised for the abolition of slavery ?   In the solution of these problems it becomes necessary to deal with a multiplicity of stubborn realities.   And yet, we can see no reason why North Carolina, in her sovereign capacity, may not, with equal ease and success, do what forty-five other States of the world have done within the last forty-five years.   Nor do we believe any good reason exists why Virginia should not perform as great a deed in 1859 as did New-York in 1799.   Massachusetts abolished slavery in 1780 ; would it not be a masterly stroke of policy in Tennessee, and every other slave State, to abolish it in or before 1860 ?[17]

Not long since, a slavocrat, writing on this subject, said, apologetically, " we frankly admit that slavery is a monstrous evil ; but what are we to do with an institution which has baffled the wisdom of our greatest statesmen ?" Unfortunately for the South, since the days of Washington, Jefferson, Madison, and their illustrious compatriots, she has never had more than half a dozen statesmen, all told ; of mere politicians, wire-pullers, and slave-driving demagogues, she has had enough, and to spare ; but of statesmen, in the true sense of the term, she has had, and now has, but precious few—fewer just at this time, perhaps, than ever before.   It is far from a matter of surprise to us that slavery has, for such a long period, baffled the " wisdom" of the oligarchy ; but our surprise is destined to culminate in amazement, if the wisdom of the non-slaveholders does not soon baffle slavery.

From the eleventh year previous to the close of the eighteenth century down to the present moment, slaveholders and slave-breeders, who, to speak naked truth, are, as a general thing, unfit to occupy any honorable station in life, have, by chicanery and usurpation, wielded all the official power of the South ; and, excepting the patriotic services of the noble abolitionists above-mentioned, the sole aim and drift of their legislation has been to aggrandize themselves, to strengthen slavery, and to keep the poor whites, the constitutional majority, bowed down in the deepest depths of degradation. We propose to subvert this entire system of oligarchal despotism. We think there should be *some* legislation for decent white men, not alone for negroes and slaveholders. Slavery lies at the root of all the shame, poverty, ignorance, tyranny and imbecility of the South ; slavery must be thoroughly eradicated ; let this be done, and a glorious future will await us.

The statesmen who are to abolish slavery in Kentucky, must be mainly and independently constituted by the non-slaveholders of Kentucky ; so in every other slave State. Past experience has taught us the sheer folly of ever expecting voluntary justice from the slaveholders. Their illicit intercourse with "the mother of harlots" has been kept up so long, and their whole natures have, in consequence, become so depraved, that there is scarcely a spark of honor or magnanimity to be found amongst them. As well might one expect to hear highwaymen clamoring for a universal interdict against traveling, as to expect slaveholders to pass laws for the abolition of slavery Under all the circumstances, it is the duty of the non-slaveholders to mark out an independent course for themselves, to steer entirely clear of the oligarchy, and to utterly contemn and ignore the many vile imstruments of power, animate and inanimate, which have been so freely and so effectually used for their enslavement. Now is the time for them to assert their rights and liberties ; never before was there such an appropriate period to strike for Freedom in the South.[18]

Had it not been for the better sense, the purer patriotism, and the more practical justice of the non-slaveholders,

7*

the Middle States and New England would still be groaning and groveling under the ponderous burden of slavery ;
New-York would never have risen above the dishonorable
level of Virginia ; Pennsylvania, trampled beneath the
iron-heel of the black code, would have remained the un-
progressive parallel of Georgia ; Massachusetts would
have continued till the present time, and Heaven only
knows how much longer, the contemptible coequal of
South Carolina.

Succeeded by the happiest moral effects and the grandest physical results, we have seen slavery crushed beneath the wisdon of the non-slaveholding statesmen of
the North ; followed by corresponding influences and
achievements, many of us who have not yet passed the
meridian of life, are destined to see it equally crushed
beneath the wisdom of the non-slaveholding Statesmen of
the South. With righteous indignation, we enter our disclaimer against the base yet baseless admission that
Louisiana and Texas are incapable of producing as great
statesmen as Rhode Island and Connecticut. What has
been done for New Jersey by the statesmen of New Jersey, can be done for North Carolina by the statesmen of
North Carolina ; the wisdom of the former State has abolished slavery ; as sure as the earth revolves on its axis,
the wisdom of the latter will not do less.

That our plan for the abolition of slavery, is the best
that can be devised, we have not the vanity to contend ;
but that it is a good one, and will do to act upon until a
better shall have been suggested, we do firmly and conscientiously believe. Though but little skilled in the deli-

cate art of surgery, we have pretty thoroughly probed slavery, the frightful tumor on the body politic, and have, we think, ascertained the precise remedies requisite for a speedy and perfect cure. Possibly the less ardent friends of freedom may object to our prescription, on the ground that some of its ingredients are too griping, and that it will cost the patient a deal of most excruciating pain. But let them remember that the patient is exceedingly refractory, that the case is a desperate one, and that drastic remedies are indispensably necessary. When they shall have invented milder yet equally efficacious ones, it will be time enough to discontinue the use of ours — then no one will be readier than we to discard the infallible strong recipe for the infallible mild. Not at the persecution of a few thousand slaveholders, but at the restitution of natural rights and prerogatives to several millions of non-slaveholders, do we aim.

Inscribed on the banner, which we herewith unfurl to the world, with the full and fixed determination to stand by it or die by it, unless one of more virtuous efficacy shall be presented, are the mottoes which, in substance, embody the principles, as we conceive, that should govern us in our patriotic warfare against the most subtle and insidious foe that ever menaced the inalienable rights and liberties and dearest interests of America :

1st. Thorough Organization and Independent Political Action on the part of the Non-Slaveholding whites of the South.

2nd. Ineligibility of Slaveholders — Never another vote to the Trafficker in Human Flesh.

3rd. No Co-operation with Slaveholders in Politics—No
Fellowship with them in Religion—No Affiliation with
them in Society.

4th. No Patronage to Slaveholding Merchants—No Guest-
ship in Slave-waiting Hotels—No Fees to Slaveholding
Lawyers—No Employment of Slaveholding Physicians
—No Audience to Slaveholding Parsons.

5th. No Recognition of Pro-slavery Men, except as Ruffians, Outlaws, and Criminals.

6th. Abrupt Discontinuance of Subscription to Pro-slavery
Newspapers.

7th. The Greatest Possible Encouragement to Free White
Labor.

8. No more Hiring of Slaves by Non-slaveholders.

9th. Immediate Death to Slavery, or if not immediate,
unqualified Proscription of its Advocates during the Period of its Existence.

10th. A Tax of Sixty Dollars on every Slaveholder for each
and every Negro in his Possession at the present time,
or at any intermediate time between now and the 4th
of July, 1863—said Money to be Applied to the transportation of the Blacks to Liberia, to their Colonization
in Central or South America, or to their Comfortable
Settlement within the Boundaries of the United States.

11th. An additional Tax of Forty Dollars per annum to be
levied annually, on every Slaveholder for each and every
Negro found in his possession after the 4th of July,
1863—said Money to be paid into the hands of the Negroes so held in Slavery, or, in cases of death, to their
next of kin, and to be used by them at their own option[19]

This, then, is the outline of our scheme for the abolition
of slavery in the Southern States. Let it be acted upon
with due promptitude, and, as certain as truth is mightier
than error, fifteen years will not elapse before every foot
of territory, from the mouth of the Delaware to the embog-
uing of the Rio Grande, will glitter with the jewels of
freedom. Some time during this year, next, or the year
following, let there be a general convention of non-slaveholders from every slave State in the Union, to deliberate
on the momentous issues now pending. First, let them
adopt measures for holding in restraint the diabolical ex-
cesses of the oligarchy ; secondly, in order to cast off the
thraldom which the infamous slave-power has fastened
upon them, and, as the first step necessary to be taken to
regain the inalienable rights and liberties with which they
were invested by Nature, but of which they have been
divested by the accursed dealers in human flesh, let them
devise ways and means for the complete annihilation of
slavery ; thirdly, let them put forth an equitable and comprehensive platform, fully defining their position, and in-
viting the active sympathy and co-operation of the millions of down-trodden non-slaveholders throughout the
Southern and Southwestern States. Let all these things
be done, not too hastily, but with calmness, deliberation,
prudence, and circumspection ; if need be, let the delegates to the convention continue in session one or two
weeks ; only let their labors be wisely and thoroughly performed ; let them, on Wednesday morning, present to the
poor whites of the South, a well-digested scheme for the
reclamation of their ancient rights and prerogatives, and,

on the Thursday following, slavery in the United States will be worth absolutely less than nothing ; for then, besides being so vile and precarious that nobody will want it, it will be a lasting reproach to those in whose hands it is lodged.

Were it not that other phases of the subject admonish us to be economical of space, we could suggest more than a dozen different plans, either of which, if scrupulously carried out, would lead to a wholesome, speedy, and perfect termination of slavery. Under all the circumstances, however, it might be difficult for us—perhaps it would not be the easiest thing in the world for any body else— to suggest a better plan than the one above. Let it, or one embodying its principal features, be adopted forthwith, and the last wail of slavery will soon be heard, growing fainter and fainter, till it dies utterly away, to be succeeded by the jubilant shouts of emancipated millions.

Henceforth, let it be distinctly understood that ownership in slaves constitutes ineligibility—that it is a crime, as we verily believe it is, to vote for a slavocrat for any office whatever. Indeed, it is our honest conviction that all the pro-slavery slaveholders, who are alone responsible for the continuance of the baneful institution among us, deserve to be at once reduced to a parallel with the basest criminals that lie fettered within the cells of our public prisons. Beyond the power of computation is the extent of the moral, social, civil, and political evils which they have brought, and are still bringing, on the country. Were it possible that the whole number could be gathered together and transformed into four equal gangs of licensed robbers, ruffians, thieves, and murderers, society, we feel assured,

would suffer less from their atrocities then than it does
now. Let the wholesome public sentiment of the non-
slaveholders be vigilant and persevering in bringing them
down to their proper level. Long since, and in the most
unjust and cruel manner, have they socially outlawed the
non-slaveholders ; now security against further oppression,
and indemnity for past grievances, make it incumbent on
the non-slaveholders to cast them into the identical pit
that they dug for their betters—thus teaching them how to
catch a Tartar !

At the very moment we write, as has been the case ever
since the United States have had a distinct national existence, and as will always continue to be the case, unless
right triumphs over wrong, all the civil, political, and other
offices, within the gift of the South, are filled with negro-
nursed incumbents from the ranks of that execrable band
of misanthropes—three hundred and forty-seven thousand
in number—who, for the most part, obtain their living by
breeding, buying and selling slaves. The magistrates in
the villages, the constables in the districts, the commis-
sioners of the towns, the mayors of the cities, the sheriffs
of the counties, the judges of the various courts, the members of the legislatures, the governors of the States, the
representatives and senators in Congress—are all slaveholders. Nor does the catalogue of their usurpations end
here. Through the most heart-sickening arrogance and
bribery, they have obtained control of the General Government, and all the consuls, ambassadors, envoys extraordinary and ministers plenipotentiary, who are chosen from
the South, and commissioned to foreign countries, are

selected with special reference to the purity of their pro-
slavery antecedents.   If credentials have ever been issued
to a single non-slaveholder of the South, we are ignorant
of both the fact and the hearsay ; indeed, it would be very
strange if this much abused class of persons were permitted to hold important offices abroad, when they are not
allowed to hold unimportant ones at home.

And, then, there is the Presidency of the United States,
which office has been held *forty-eight* years by slaveholders
from the South, and only *twenty* years by non-slaveholders
from the North.   Nor is this the full record of oligarchal
obtrusion.   On an average, the offices of Secretary of
State, Secretary of the Treasury, Secretary of the Interior,
Secretary of the Navy, Secretary of War, Postmaster-Gen-
eral and Attorney-General, have been under the control of
slave-drivers nearly two-thirds of the time.   The Chief Justices and the Associate Justices of the Supreme Court of
the United States, the Presidents pro tem. of the Senate,
and the Speakers of the House of Representatives, have,
in a large majority of instances, been slave-breeders from
the Southern side of the Potomac.   Five slaveholding Presidents have been reëlected to the chief magistracy of the
Republic, while no non-slaveholder has ever held the office
more than a single term.   Thus we see plainly that even
the non-slaveholders of the North, to whose freedom, energy, enterprise, intelligence, wealth, population, power,
progress, and prosperity, our country is almost exclusively
indebted for its high position among the nations of the
earth, have been arrogantly denied a due participation in
the honors of federa ɔffice.   When " the sum of all villain-

ies" shall have ceased to exist, then the rights of the non-slaveholders of the North, of the South, of the East, and of the West, will be duly recognized and respected; not before.

With all our heart, we hope and believe it is the full and fixed determination of a majority of the more intelligent and patriotic citizens of this Republic, that the Presidential chair shall never again be filled by a slavocrat. Safely may we conclude that the doom of the oligarchy is already sealed with respect to that important and dignified station; it now behooves us to resolve, with equal firmness and effect, that, after a certain period during the next decade of years, no slaveholder shall occupy any position in the Cabinet, that no slave-breeder shall be sent as a diplomatist to any foreign country, that no slave-driver shall be permitted to bring further disgrace on either the Senate or the House of Representatives, that the chief justices, associate justices, and judges of the several courts, the governors of the States, the members of the legislatures, and all the minor functionaries of the land, shall be free from the heinous crime of ownership in man.

For the last sixty-eight years, slaveholders have been the sole and constant representatives of the South, and what have they accomplished? It requires but little time and few words, to tell the story of their indiscreet and unhallowed performances. In fact, with what we have already said, gestures alone would suffice to answer the inquiry. We can make neither a more truthful nor emphatic reply than to point to our thinly inhabited States, to our fields despoiled of their virgin soil, to the despicable price of lands to our unvisited cities and towns, to our

vacant harbors and idle water-power, to the dreary absence of shipping and manufactories, to our unpensioned
soldiers of the revolution, to the millions of living monuments of ignorance, to the poverty of the whites, and to
the wretchedness of the blacks.

Either directly or indirectly, are slave-driving demagogues, who have ostentatiously set up pretensions to
statesmanship, responsible for every dishonorable weakness and inequality that exists between the North and the
South. Let them shirk the responsibility if they can ; but
it is morally impossible for them to do so. We know
how ready they have always been to cite the numerical
strength of the North, as a valid excuse for their inability
to procure appropriations from the General Government,
for purposes of internal improvement, for the establishment of lines of ocean steamers to South American and
European ports, and for the accomplishment of othe: objects. Before that apology ever escapes from their lips
again, let them remember that the numerical weakness of
the South is wholly attributable to their own villainous
statism. Had the Southern States, in accordance with
the principles enunciated in the Declaration of Independence, abolished slavery at the same time the Northern
States abolished it, there would have been, long since,
and most assuredly at this moment, a larger, wealthier,
wiser, and more powerful population, south of Mason and
Dixon's line, than there now is north of it. This fact being so well established that no reasonable man denies it,
it is evident that the oligarchy will have to devise another subterfuge for even temporary relief.

Until slavery and slaveholders cease to be the only favored objects of legislation in the South, the North will continue to maintain the ascendency in every important particular. With those loathsome objects out of the way, it would not take the non-slaveholders of the South more than a quarter of a century to bring her up, in all respects, to a glorious equality with the North ; nor would it take them much longer to surpass the latter, which is the most vigorous and honorable rival that they have in the world. Three quarters of a century hence, if slavery is abolished within the next ten years, as it ought to be, the South will, we believe, be as much greater than the North, as the North is now greater than the South. Three quarters of a century hence, if the South retains slavery, which God forbid ! she will be to the North much the same that Poland is to Russia, that Cuba is to Spain, or that Ireland is to England.

What we want and must have, as the only sure means of attaining to a position worthy of Sovereign States in this eminently progressive and utilitarian age, is an energetic, intelligent, enterprising, virtuous, and unshackled population ; an untrammeled press, and the Freedom of Speech. For ourselves, as white people, and for the negroes and other persons of whatever color or condition, we demand all the rights, interests and prerogatives, that are guarantied to corresponding classes of mankind in the North, in England, in France, in Germany, or in any other civilized and enlightened country. Any proposition that may be offered conceding less than this demand, will be promptly and disdainfully rejected.

Speaking of the non-slaveholders of the South, George M. Weston, a zealous co-laborer in the cause of Freedom, says :—

"The non-slaveholding whites of the South, being not less than seven-tenths of the whole number of whites, would seem to be entitled to some enquiry into their actual condition; and especially, as they have no real political weight or consideration in the country, and little opportunity to speak for themselves. I have been for twenty years a reader of Southern newspapers, and a reader and hearer of Congressional debates ; but, in all that time, I do not recollect ever to have seen or heard these non-slaveholding whites referred to by Southern 'gentlemen,' as constituting any part of what they call 'the South.' When the rights of the South, or its wrongs, or its policy, or its interests, or its institutions, are spoken of, reference is always intended to the rights, wrongs, policy, interests, and institutions of the three hundred and forty-seven thousand slaveholders. Nobody gets into Congress from the South but by their direction ; nobody speaks at Washington for any Southern interest except theirs. Yet there is, at the South, quite another interest than theirs ; embracing from two to three times as many white people ; and, as we shall presently see, entitled to the deepest sympathy and commiseration, in view of the material, intellectual, and moral privations to which it has been subjected, the degradation to which it has already been reduced, and the still more fearful degradation with which it is threatened by the inevitable operation of existing causes and influences."

The following extract, from a paper on "Domestic Manufactures in the South and West," published by M. Tarver, of Missouri, may be appropriately introduced in this connection :—

"The non-slaveholders possess, generally, but very small means, and the land which they possess is almost universally poor, and so sterile that a scanty subsistence is all that can be derived from its cultivation ; and the more fertile soil, being in the possession of the slaveholders, must ever remain out of the power of those who have none. This state of things is a great drawback, and bears heavily upon and depresses the moral energies of the poorer classes. The acquisition of a respectable position in the scale of wealth appears so difficult, that they decline the hopeless pursuit, and many of them settle down into habits of idleness, and become the almost passive subjects of all its consequences. And I lament to say that I have observed of late years, that an evident deterioration is taking place in this part of the population, the younger portion of it being less educated, less industrious, and in every point of view less respectable than their ancestors.'

Equally worthy of attention is the testimony of Gov. Hammond, of South Carolina, who says :—

" According to the best calculation, which, in the absence of statistic facts, can be made, it is believed, that of the three hundred thousand white inhabitants of South Carolina, there are not less than fifty thousand whose industry, such as it is, and compensated as it is, is not, in the present condition of things, and does not promise to be hereafter, adequate to procure them, honestly, such a support as every white person is, and feels himself entitled to. And this, next to emigration, is, perhaps, the heaviest of the weights that press upon the springs of our prosperity. Most of these now follow agricultural pursuits, in feeble, yet injurious competition with slave labor. Some, perhaps, not more from inclination, than from the want of due encouragement, can scarcely be said to work at all. They obtain a precarious subsistence, by occasional jobs, by hunting, by fishing, sometimes by plundering fields or folds, and too often by what is, in its effects, far worse—trading with slaves, and seducing them to plunder for their benefit."

Conjoined with the sundry plain straightforward facts which have issued from our own pen, these extracts show con 'usively that immediate and independent political action on the part of the non-slaveholding whites of the South, is, with them, a matter, not only of positive duty, but also of the utmost importance. As yet, it is in their power to rescue the South from the gulf of shame and guilt, into which slavery has plunged her ; but if they do not soon arouse themselves from their apathy, this power will be wrenched from them, and then, unable to resist the strong arm of the oppressor, they will be completely degraded to a social and political level with the negroes, whose condition of servitude will, in the meantime, become far more abject and forlorn than it is now.

In addition to the reasons which we have already assigned why no slavocrat should, in the future, be elected to any office whatever, there are others that deserve to be carefully considered. Among these may be mentioned the illbreeding and the ruffianism of slaveholding officials. Tedious indeed would be the task to enumerate all the homicides, duels, assaults and batteries, and other crimes, of which they are the authors in the course of a single year. To the general reader their career at the seat of government is well known ; there, on frequent occasions, choking with rage at seeing their wretched sophistries scattered to the winds by the sound, logical reasoning of the champions of Freedom, they have overstepped the bounds of common decency, vacated the chair of honorable controversy, and, in the most brutal and cowardly manner, assailed their unarmed opponents with bludgeons, bowie knives and pistols. Compared with some of their barbarisms at home, however, their frenzied onslaughts at the national Capital have been but the simplest breaches

of civil deportment; and it is only for the purpose of
avoiding personalities that we now refrain from divulging
a few instances of the unparalleled atrocities which they
have perpetrated in legislative halls South of the Potomac.   Nor is it alone in the national and State legislatures that they substitute brute force for genteel behavior
and acuteness of intellect.   Neither court-houses nor public streets, hotels nor private dwellings, rum-holes nor
law-offices, are held sacred from their murderous conflicts.
About certain silly abstractions that no practical business
man ever allows to occupy his time or attention, they are
eternally wrangling ; and thus it is that rencounters,
duels, homicides, and other demonstrations of personal
violence, have become so popular in all slaveholding communities.   A few years of entire freedom from the cares
and perplexities of public life, would, we have no doubt,
greatly improve both their manners and their morals ; and
we suggest that it is a Christian duty, which devolves on
the non-slaveholders of the South, to disrobe them of the
mantle of office, which they have so long worn with disgrace to themselves, injustice to their constituents, and
ruin to their country.

But what shall we say of such men as Botts, Stuart, and
Macfarland of Virginia ; of Raynor, Morehead, Miller,
Stanly, Graves, and Graham of North Carolina ; of Davis
and Hoffman of Maryland ; of Blair and Benton of Missouri ; of the Marshalls of Kentucky ; and of Etheridge of
Tennessee ?[20] All these gentlemen, and many others of the
same school, entertain, we believe, sentiments similar to
those that were entertained by the immortal Fathers of the

Republic—that slavery is a great moral, social, civil, and political evil, to be got rid of at the earliest practical period—and if they do, in order to secure our votes, it is only necessary for them to " have the courage of their opinions," to renounce slavery, and to come out frankly, fairly and squarely, in favor of freedom.   To neither of these patriotic sons of the South, nor to any one of the class to which they belong, would we give any offence whatever.   In our strictures on the criminality of pro-slavery demagogues we have had heretofore, and shall have hereafter, no sort of reference to any respectable slaveholder—by which we mean, any slaveholder who admits the injustice and inhumanity of slavery, and who is not averse to the discussion of measures for its speedy and total. extinction.   Such slaveholders are virtually on our side, that is, on the side of the non-slaveholding whites, with whom they may very properly be classified.   On this point, once for all, we desire to be distinctly understood ; for it would be manifestly unjust not to discriminate between the anti-slavery proprietor who owns slaves by the law of entailment, and the pro-slavery proprietor who engages in the traffic and becomes an aider and abettor of the institution from sheer turpitude of heart ; hence the propriety of this special disclaimer.

If we have a correct understanding of the positions which they assumed, some of the gentlemen whose names are written above, gave, during the last presidential campaign, ample evidence of their unswerving devotion to the interests of the great majority of the people, the non-slaveholding whites ; and it is our unbiassed opinion that a more positive truth is no where recorded in Holy Writ, than Kenneth Raynor uttered, when he said, in substance, that the greatest good that could happen to this country would be the complete overthrow of slave-driving democracy, *alias* the nigger party, which has for its head and front the Ritchies and Wises of Virginia, and for its caudal termination the Butlers and Quatlebums of South Carolina.

And this, by the way, is a fit occasion to call attention to the fact, that slave-driving Democrats have been the perpetrators of almost every brutal outrage that ever disgraced our halls of legislation. Of countless instances of assault and battery, affrays, and fatal rencounters, that have occurred in the court-houses, capitols, and other public buildings in the Southern States, we feel safe in saying that the aggressor, in at least nine cases out of ten, has been a negro-nursed adherent of modern, miscalled democracy. So, too, the challenger to almost every duel has been an abandoned wretch, who, on many occasions during infancy, sucked in the corrupt milk of slavery from the breasts of his father's sable concubines, and who has never been known to become weary of boasting of a fact that invariably impressed itself on the minds of his auditors or observers, the very first moment they laid their eyes upon him, namely, that *he* was a member of the Democratic party. Brute violence, however, can hardly be said to be the worst characteristic of the slave-driving Democrat; his ignorance and squalidity are proverbial; his senseless enthusiasm is disgusting.[21]

Peculiarly illustrative of the material of which sham democracy is composed was the vote polled at the Five Points precinct, in the city of New-York, on the 4th of November,

8

1856, when James Buchanan was chosen President by a *minority* of the people.   We will produce the figures :

Five Points Precinct, New-York City, 1856.

Votes cast for James Buchanan			574
" " " John C. Fremont			16
" " " Millard Fillmore			9

It will be recollected that Col. Fremont's majority over Buchanan, in the State of New-York, was between seventy-eight and seventy-nine thousand, and that he ran ahead of the Fillmore ticket to the number of nearly one hundred and fifty-one thousand.   We have not the shadow of a doubt that he is perfectly satisfied with Mr. Buchanan's triumph at the Five Points, which, with the exception of the slave-pens in Southern cities, is, perhaps, the most vile and heart-sickening locality in the United States.

One of the most noticeable and commendable features of the last general election is this : almost every State, whose inhabitants have enjoyed the advantages of free soil, free labor, free speech, free presses, and free schools, and who have, in consequence, become great in numbers, in virtue, in wealth, and in wisdom, voted for Fremont, the Republican candidate, who was pledged to use his influence for the extension of like advantages to other parts of the country.   On the other hand, with a single honorable exception, all the States which "have got to hating everything with the prefix Free, from free negroes down and up through the whole catalogue—free farms, free labor, free society, free will, free thinking, free children, and free schools," and which have exposed their citizens to all the perils of numerical weakness, absolute ignorance, and hopeless poverty, voted for Buchanan, the Democratic candidate, who, in reply to the overtures of his slave-driving partisans, had signified his willingness to pursue a policy that would perpetuate and disseminate, without limit, the multitudinous evils of human bondage.

Led on by a huckstering politician, whose chief vocation, at all times, is the rallying of ragamuffins, shoulder-strikers, and liquor-house vagabonds, into the ranks of his party, and who, it is well known, receives from the agents of the slave power, regular installments of money for this infamous purpose, a Democratic procession, exceedingly motley and unrefined, marched through the streets of one of the great cities of the North, little less than a fortnight previous to the election of Mr. Buchanan to the Presidency ; and the occasion gave rise, on the following day, to a communication in one of the morning papers, from which we make the following pertinent extract :

" While the Democratic procession was passing through the streets of this city, a few days since, I could not but think how significant the exultation of that ignorant multitude was of the ferocious triumphs which would be displayed if ever false Democracy should succeed in throwing the whole power of the country into the hands of the Slave Oligarchy. It is melancholy to think that every individual in that multitude, ignorant and depraved though he may be, foreign perhaps in his birth, and utterly unacquainted with the principles upon which the welfare of the country depends, and hostile it may be to those principles, if he does understand them, is equal in the power which he may exercise by his vote to the most intelligent and upright man in the community.

" Of this, indeed, it is useless to complain. We enjoy our freedom with the contingency of its loss by the acts of a numerical majority. It behooves all men, therefore, who have a regard to the common good, to look carefully at the influences which may pervert the popular mind; and this, I think, can only be done by guarding against the corruption of individual character. A man who has nothing but political business to attend to—I mean the management of elections—ought to be shunned by all honest men. If it were possible, he should have the mark of Cain put upon him, that he might be known as a plotter against the welfare of his country."

That less than *three* per cent. of those who voted for Col. Fremont, that only about *five* per cent. of those who gave their suffrages to Mr. Fillmore, and that more than *eighteen* per cent. of those who supported Mr. Buchanan, were persons over one and twenty years of age who could not read and write, are estimates which we have no doubt are not far from the truth, and which, in the absence of reliable statistics, we venture to give, hoping, by their publicity, to draw closer attention to the fact, that the illiterate foreigners of the North, and the unlettered natives of the South, were cordially united in their suicidal adherence to the Nigger party. With few exceptions, all the intelligent non-slaveholders of the South, in concert with the more respectable slaveholders, voted for Mr. Fillmore ; certain rigidly patriotic persons of the former class, whose hearts were so entirely with the gallant Fremont that they refused to vote at all—simply because they did not dare to express their preference for him—form the exceptions to which we allude.

Though the Whig, Democratie, and Know-Nothing newspapers, in all the States, free and slave, denounced Col. Fremont as an intolerant Catholic, it is now generally conceded that he was nowhere supported by the peculiar friends of Pope Pius IX. The votes polled at t.he Five Points precinct, which is almost exclusively inhabited by low Irish Catholics, show how powerfully the Jesuitical influence was brought to bear against him. At that delectable local'ty, as we have already shown, the timid Sage of Wheatland received five hundred and seventy-four votes ; whereas the dauntless Finder of Empire received only sixteen.

True to their instincts for Freedom, the Germans, generally, voted the right ticket, and they will do it again, and continue to do it. With the intelligent Protestant element of the Fatherland on our side, we can well afford to dispense with the ignorant Catholic element of the Emerald Isle. In the influences which they exert on society, there is so little difference between Slavery, Popery, and Negro-driving Democracy, that we are not at all surprised to see them going hand in hand in their diabolical works of inhumanity and desolation.

There is, indeed, no lack of evidence to show that the Democratic party of to-day is simply and unreservedly a sectional Nigger party. On the 15th of December, 1856, but a few weeks subsequent to the appearance of a scandalous message from an infamous governor of South Carolina, recommending the reöpening of the African slave trade, Emerson Etheridge of Tennessee—honor to his name !—submitted, in the House of Representatives, the following timely resolution :—

"Resolved, That this House regard all suggestions or propositions of every kind, by whomsoever made, for a revival of the slave trade, as shocking to the moral sentiments of the enlightened portion of mankind, and that any act on the part of Congress, legislating for, conniving at, or legalizing that horrid and inhuman traffic, would justly subject the United States to the reproach and execration of all civilized and Christian people throughout the world."

Who voted *for* this resolution? and who voted *against* it? Let the yeas and nays answer; they are on record, and he who takes the trouble to examine them will find that the resolution encountered no opposition worth mentioning, except from members of the Democratic party. Scrutinize the yeas and nays on any other motion or resolution affecting the question of slavery, and the fact that a majority of the members of this party have uniformly voted for the retention and extension of the "sum of all villanies," will at once be apparent.

For many years the slave-driving Democrats of the South have labored most strenuously, both by day and by night —we regret to say how unsuccessfully—to point out abolition proclivities in the Whig and Know-Nothing parties, the latter of which is now buried, and deservedly, so deep in the depths of the dead, that it is quite preposterous to suppose it will ever see the light of resurrection.

For its truckling concessions to the slave power, the Whig party merited defeat, and defeated it was, and that, too, in the most decisive and overwhelming manner. But there is yet in this party much vitality, and if its friends will reorganize, detach themselves from the burden of slavery, espouse the cause of the white man, and hoist the fair flag of freedom, the time may come, at a day by no means remote, when their hearts will exult in triumph over the ruins of miscalled Democracy.

It is not too late, however, for the Democratic party to secure to itself a pure renown and an almost certain perpetuation of its power. Let it at once discard the worship of slavery, and do earnest battle for the principles of freedom, and it will live victoriously to a period far in the future. On the other hand, if it does not soon repudiate the fatal heresies which it has incorporated into its creed, its doom will be inevitable. Until the black flag entirely disappears from its array, we warn the non-slaveholders of the South to repulse and keep it at a distance, as they would the emblazoned skull and cross-bones that flout them from the flag of the pirate.

With regard to the sophistical reasoning which teaches that abolitionists, before abolishing slavery, should compensate the slaveholders for all or any number of the negroes in their possession, we have, perhaps, said quite enough ; but wishing to brace our arguments, in every important particular, with unequivocal testimony from men whom we are accustomed to regard as models of political sagacity and integrity—from Southern men as far as possible—we herewith present an extract from a speech delivered in the Virginia House of Delegates, January 20, 1832, by Charles James Faulkner, whose sentiments, as then and there expressed, can hardly fail to find a response in the heart of every intelligent, upright man :—

" But, Sir, it is said that society having conferred this property on the slaveholder, it cannot *now* take it from him without an adequate compensation, by which is meant full value. I may be singular in the opinion, but I defy the legal research of the House to point me to a principle recognized by the law, even in the ordinary course of its adjudications, where the community pays for property which is removed or destroyed because t is a nuisance, and found injurious to that society. There is, I humbly apprehend, no such principle. There is no obligation upon society to continue your right one moment after it becomes injurious to the best interests of society; nor to compensate you for the loss of that, the deprivation of which is demanded by the safety of the State, and in which general benefit you participate as members of the community. Sir, there is to my mind a manifest distinction between condemning private property to be applied to some beneficial public purpose, and condemning or removing private property which is ascertained to be a positive wrong to society. It is a distinction which pervades the whole genius of the law; and is founded upon the idea, that any man who holds property injurious to the peace of that society of which he is a member, thereby violates the condition upon the observance of which his right to the property is alone guarantied. For property of the first class condemned, there ought to be compensation; but for property of the latter class, none can be demanded upon principle, none accorded as matter of right.

"It is conceded that, at this precise moment of our legislation, slaves are injurious to the interests and threaten the subversion and ruin of this Commonwealth. Their present number, their increasing number, all admonish us of this. In different terms, and in more measured language, the same fact has been conceded by all who have yet addressed this House. '*Something must be done*,' emphatically exclaimed the gentleman from Dinwiddie; and I thought I could perceive a response to that declaration, in the countenance of a large majority of this body. And why must something be done? Because if not, says the gentleman from Campbell, the throats of all the *white* people of Virginia will be cut. No, says the gentleman from Dinwiddie—'The whites cannot be conquered—the throats of the *blacks* will be cut.' It is a trifling difference, to be sure, Sir, and matters not to the argument. For the fact is conceded, that one race or the other must be exterminated.

"Sir, such being the actual condition of this Commonwealth, I ask if we would not be justified *now*, supposing all considerations of po icy and humanity concurred, without even a moment's delay, in staving off this appalling and overwhelming calamity? Sir, if this immense negro population were now in arms, gathering into black and formidable masses of attack, would that man be listened to, who spoke about property, who prayed you not to direct your artillery to such or such a point, for you would destroy some of *his* property? Sir, to the eye of the Statesman, as to the eye of Omniscience, dangers pressing, and dangers that must *necessarily* press, are alike present. With a single glance he embraces Virginia now, with the elements of destruction reposing quietly upon her bosom, and Virginia is lighted from one extremity to the other with the torch of servile insurrection and massacre. It is not sufficient for him that the match is not yet applied. It is enough that the magazine is open, and the match will shortly be applied.

"Sir, it is true in national as it is in private contracts, that loss and injury to one party may constitute as fair a consideration as gain to the other. Does the slaveholder, while he is enjoying his slaves, reflect upon the deep injury and incalculable loss which the possession of that property inflicts upon the true interests of the country? Slavery, it is admitted, is an evil—it is an institution which presses heavily against the best interests of the State. It banishes free white labor, it exterminates the mechanic, the artisan, the manufacturer. It deprives them of occupation. It deprives them of bread. It converts the energy of a community into indolence, its power into imbecility, its efficiency into weakness. Sir, being thus injurious, have we not a right to demand its extermination? shall society suffer, that the slaveholder may continue to gather his *crop* of human flesh? What is his mere pecuniary claim, compared with the great interests of the common weal? Must the country languish, droop, die, that the slaveholder may flourish? Shall all interests be subservient to one—all rights subordinate to those of the slaveholder? Has not the mechanic, have not the middle classes their rights—rights incompatible with the existence of slavery?

"Sir, so great and overshadowing are the evils of slavery—so sensibly are they felt by those who have traced the causes of our national decline—so perceptible is the poisonous operation of its principles in the va ed and diversified interests of this Common-

8*

wealth, that all, whose minds are not warped by prejudice or interest, must admit that the disease has now assumed that mortal tendency, as to justify the application of any remedy which, under the great law of State necessity, we might consider advisable."

From the abstract of our plan for the abolition of slavery, it will be perceived that, so far from allowing slaveholders any compensation for their slaves, we are, and we think justly, in favor of imposing on them a tax of sixty dollars for each and every negro now in their possession, as also for each and every one that shall be born to them between now and the 4th of July, 1863; after which time, we propose that they shall be taxed forty dollars per annum, annually, for every person by them held in slavery, without regard to age, sex, color, or condition —the money, in both instances, to be used for the sole advantage of the slaves. As an addendum to this proposition, we would say that, in our opinion, if slavery is not totally abolished by the year 1869, the annual tax ought to be increased from forty to one hundred dollars; and furthermore, that if the institution does not then almost immediately disappear under the onus of this increased taxation, the tax ought in the course of one or two years thereafter, to be augmented to such a degree as will, in harmony with other measures, prove an infallible death-blow to slavery on or before the 4th of July, 1876.[22]

At once let the good and true men of this country, the patriot sons of the patriot fathers, determine that the sun which rises to celebrate the centennial anniversary of our national independence, shall not set on the head of any slav within the limits of our Republic. Will not the non-slaveholders of the North, of the South, of the East, and of the West, heartily, unanimously sanction this proposition ? Will it not be cheerfully indorsed by many of the slaveholders themselves ? Will any *respectable* man enter a protest against it ? On the 4th of July, 1876— sooner, if we can—let us make good, at least so far as we are concerned, the Declaration of Independence, which was proclaimed in Philadelphia on the 4th of July, 1776 —that " all men are endowed by their Creator with certain inalienable rights ; that among these, are life, liberty, and the pursuit of happiness ; that to secure these rights, governments are instituted among men, deriving their just powers from the consent of the governed ; that whenever any form of government becomes destructive of these ends, it is the right of the people to alter or to abolish it, and to institute a new government, laying its foundation on such principles, and organizing its powers in such form, as to them shall seem most likely to effect their safety and happiness." In purging our land of the iniquity of negro slavery, we will only be carrying on the great work that was so successfully commenced by our noble sires of the Revolution ; some future generation may possibly complete the work by annulling the last and least form of oppression.

To turn the slaves away from their present homes— away from all the property and means of support which their labor has mainly produced, would be unpardonably cruel—exceedingly unjust. Still more cruel and unjust would it be, however, to the non-slaveholding whites no less than to the negroes, to grant further toleration to the existence of slavery. In any event, come what will, transpire what may, the institution must be abolished. The evils, if any, which are to result from its abolition, cannot, by any manner of means, be half as great as the evils which are certain to overtake us in case of its continuance. The perpetuation of slavery is the climax of iniquity.

Two hundred and thirty-seven years have the negroes in America been held in inhuman bondage. During the whole of this long period they have toiled unceasingly from the gray of dawn till the dusk of eve, for their cruel task-masters, who have rewarded them with scanty allowances of the most inferior qualities of victuals and clothes, with heartless separations of the tenderest ties of kindred, with epithets, with scoldings, with execrations, and with the lash—and, not unfrequently, with the fatal bludgeon or the more deadly weapon. From the labor of their hands, and from the fruit of their loins, the human-mongers of the South have become wealthy, insolent, corrupt, and tyrannical. In reason and in conscience the slaves might claim from their masters a much larger sum than we have proposed to allow them. If they were to demand an equal share of all the property, real and personal, which has been accumulated or produced through their efforts, Heaven, we believe, would recognize them as honest claimants.

Elsewhere we have shown, by just and liberal estimates, that, on the single score of damages to lands, the slave-holders are, at this moment, indebted to the non-slaveholding whites in the extraordinary sum of $7,544,148,825.

Considered in connection with the righteous claim of wages for services which the negroes might bring against their masters, these figures are the heralds of the significant fact that, if strict justice could be meted out to all parties in the South, the slaveholders would not only be stripped of every dollar, but they would become in law as they are in reality, the hopeless debtors of the myriads of unfortunate slaves, white and black, who are now cringing, and fawning, and festering around them.   In this matter, however, so far has wrong triumphed over right, that the slaveholders—a mere handful of tyrants, whose manual exercises are wholly comprised in the use they make of instruments of torture, such as whips, clubs, bowie-knives and pistols —have, as the result of a series of acts of their own villainous legislation, become the sole and niggardly proprietors of almost every important item of Southern wealth ; not only do they own all the slaves—none of whom any really respectable person cares to own—but they are also in possession of the more valuable tracts of land and the appurtenances thereto belonging ; while the non-slaveholding whites and the negroes, who compose at least ninetenths of the entire population, and who are the actual producers of every article of merchandize, animal, vegetable, and mineral, that is sold from the South, are most wickedly despoiled of the fruits of their labors, and cast into the dismal abodes of extreme ignorance, destitution and misery.

For the services of the blacks from the 20th of August, 1620, up to the 4th of July, 1863—an interval of precisely two hundred and forty-two years ten months and fourteen days—their masters, if unwilling, ought, in our judgment, to be compelled to grant them their freedom, and to pay each and every one of them at least sixty dollars cash in hand. The aggregate sum thus raised would amount to about two hundred and forty-five millions of dollars, which is less than the total market value of two entire crops of cotton—one-half of which sum would be amply sufficient to land every negro in this country on the coast of Liberia, whither, if we had the power, we would ship them all within the next six months. As a means of protection against the exigencies which might arise from a sudden transition from their present homes in America to their future homes in Africa, and for the purpose of enabling them there to take the initiatory step in the walks of civilized life, the remainder of the sum—say about one hundred and twenty-two millions of dollars—might, very properly, be equally distributed amongst them after their arrival in the land of their fathers.

Dr. James Hall, the Secretary of the Maryland Colonization Society, informs us that the average cost of sending negroes to Liberia does not exceed thirty dollars each ; and it is his opinion that arrangements might be made on an extensive plan for conveying them thither at an average expense of not more than twenty-five dollars each.

The American colonization movement, as now systematized and conducted, is simply an American humane farce. At present the slaves are increasing in this country at the rate of nearly one hundred thousand per annum ; within the last ten years, as will appear below, the American Colonization Society has sent to Liberia less than five thousand negroes.

Emigrants sent to Liberia by the American Colonization Society, during the ten years ending January 1st, 1857.

```
        In 1847..... .... .... ......    39 ⎫
        In 1848.... .... .... .... .....213  ⎪
        In 1849.... .... .... .... .....474  ⎪
        In 1850.... .... .... .... .....590  ⎪
        In 1851.... .... .... .... .....279  ⎪
        In 1852.... .... .... .... .....568  ⎬ Emigrants.
        In 1853.... .... .... .... .....583  ⎪
        In 1854.... .... .... .... .....783  ⎪
        In 1855.... .... .... .... .....207  ⎪
        In 1856.... .... .... .... .....544  ⎪
                                       ----  ⎪
           Total.... .... .... .....4280    ⎭
```

The average of this total is precisely four hundred and twenty-eight, which may be said to be the number of negroes annually colonized by the society ; while the yearly increase of slaves, as previously stated, is little less than one hundred thousand ! Fiddlesticks for such colonization ! Once for all, within a reasonably short period, let us make the slaveholders do something like justice to their negroes by giving each and every one of them his freedom, and sixty dollars in current money ; then let us charter all the ocean steamers, packets and clipper ships that can be had on liberal terms, and keep them constantly plying between the ports of America and Africa, until all slaves shall enjoy freedom in the land of their fathers. Under a well-devised and properly conducted system of operations, but a few years would be required to redeem the United States from the monstrous curse of negro slavery.

Some few years ago, when certain ethnographical oligarchs proved to their own satisfaction that the negro was an inferior "type of mankind," they chuckled wonderfully, and avowed, in substance, that it was right for the stronger race to kidnap and enslave the weaker—that because Nature had been pleased to do a trifle more for the Caucasian race than for the African, the former, by virtue of its superiority, was perfectly justifiable in holding the latter in absolute and perpetual bondage ! No system of logic could be more antagonistic to the spirit of true democracy. It is probable that the world does not contain two persons who are exactly alike in all respects ; yet "*all* men are endowed by their Creator with certain *inalienable* rights, among which are life, *liberty*, and the pursuit of happiness." All mankind may or may not be the descendants of Adam and Eve. In our own humble way of thinking, we are frank to confess, we do not believe in the unity of the races. This is a matter, however, which has little or nothing to do with the great question at issue. Aside from any theory concerning the original parentage of the different races of men, facts, material and immaterial, palpable and impalpable—facts of the eyes and facts of the conscience—crowd around us on every hand, heaping proof upon proof, that slavery is a shame, a crime, and a curse—a great moral, social, civil, and political evil—an oppressive burden to the blacks, and an incalculable injury to the whites—a stumbling-block to the nation, an impediment to progress, a damper on all the nobler instincts, principles, aspirations and enterprises of man, and à dire enemy to every true interest.

Waiving all other counts, we have, we think, shown to the satisfaction of every impartial reader, that, as elsewhere stated, on the single score of damages to lands, the slaveholders are, at this moment, indebted to us, the non-slaveholding whites, in the enormous sum of nearly seventy-six hundred millions of dollars. What shall be done with this amount? It is just; shall payment be demanded? No; all the slaveholders in the country could not pay it; nor shall we ever ask them for even a moiety of the amount—no, not even for a dime, nor yet for a cent; we are willing to forfeit every farthing for the sake of freedom; for ourselves we ask no indemnification for the past : we only demand justice for the future.

But, Sirs, knights of bludgeons, chevaliers of bowie-knives and pistols, and lords of the lash, we are unwilling to allow you to swindle the slaves out of all the rights and claims to which, as human beings, they are most sacredly entitled. Not alone for ourself as an individual, but for others also—particularly for five or six millions of Southern non-slaveholding whites, whom your iniquitous statism has debarred from almost all the mental and material comforts of life—do we speak, when we say, you *must* emancipate your slaves, and pay each and every one of them at least sixty dollars cash in hand. By doing this, you will be restoring to them their natural rights, and remunerating them at the rate of less than twenty-six cents per annum for the long and cheerless period of their servitude, from the 20th of August, 1620, when, on James River, in Virginia, they became the unhappy slaves of heartless masters. Moreover, by doing this you will be performing but a simple act of justice to the non-slave holding whites, upon whom the institution of slavery has weighed scarcely less heavily than upon the negroes themselves. You will also be applying a saving balm to your own outraged hearts and consciences, and your children—yourselves in fact—freed from the accursed stain of slavery, will become respectable, useful, and honorable members of society.

And now, Sirs, we have thus laid down our ultimatum. What are you going to do about it? Something dreadful, as a matter of course! Perhaps you will dissolve the Union *again*. Do it, if you dare ! Our motto, and we would have you to understand it, is *the abolition of slavery, and the perpetuation of the American Union.* If, by any means, you do succeed in your treasonable attempts to take the South out of the Union to-day, we will bring her back to-morrow—if she goes away with you, she will return without you.

Do not mistake the meaning of the last clause of the last sentence ; we could elucidate it so thoroughly that no intelligent person could fail to comprehend it ; but, for reasons which may hereafter appear, we forego the task.

Henceforth there are other interests to be consulted in the South, aside from the interests of negroes and slaveholders. A profound sense of duty incites us to make the greatest possible efforts for the abolition of slavery ; an equally profound sense of duty calls for a continuation of those efforts until the very last foe to freedom shall have been utterly vanquished. To the summons of the righteous monitor within, we shall endeavor to prove faithful ;

no opportunity for inflicting a mortal wound in the side of slavery shall be permitted to pass us unimproved. Thus, terror-engenderers of the South, have we fully and frankly defined our position; we have no modifications to propose, no compromises to offer, nothing to retract. Frown, Sirs, fret, foam, prepare your weapons, threat, strike, shoot, stab, bring on civil war, dissolve the Union, nay, annihilate the solar system if you will—do all this, more, less, better, worse, anything—do what you will, Sirs, you can neither foil nor intimidate us; our purpose is as firmly fixed as the eternal pillars of Heaven; we have determined to abolish slavery, and, so help us God, abolish it we will ! Take this to bed with you to-night, Sirs, and think about it, dream over it, and let us know how you feel to-morrow morning.

CHAPTER III.

SOUTHERN TESTIMONY AGAINST SLAVERY.

IF it please the reader, let him forget all that we have written on the subject of slavery; if it accord with his inclination, let him ignore all that we may write hereafter. We seek not to give currency to our peculiar opinions ; our greatest ambition, in these pages, is to popularize the sayings and admonitions of wiser and better men. Miracles, we believe, are no longer wrought in this bedeviled world ; but if, by any conceivable or possible supernatural event, the great Founders of the Republic, Washington, Jefferson, Henry, and others, could be reinvested with corporeal life, and returned to the South, there is scarcely a slaveholder between the Potomac and the mouth of the Mississippi, that would not burn to pounce upon them with bludgeons, bowie-knives and pistols ! Yes, without adding another word, Washington would be *mobbed* for what he has already said. Were Jefferson now employed as a professor in a Southern college, he would be dismissed and driven from the State, perhaps murdered before he reached the border. If Patrick Henry were a bookseller in Alabama, though it might be demonstrated beyond the shadow of a doubt that he had never bought,

sold, received, or presented, any kind of literature except
Bibles and Testaments, he would first be subjected to the
ignominy of a coat of tar and feathers, and then limited
to the option of unceremonious expatriation or death.
How seemingly impossible are these statements, and yet
how true ! Where do we stand ? What is our faith ?
Are we a flock without a shepherd ? a people, without a
prophet ? a nation without a government?

Has the past, with all its glittering monuments of
genius and patriotism, furnished no beacon by which we
may direct our footsteps in the future ? If we but prove
true to ourselves, and worthy of our ancestry, we have
nothing to fear ; our Revolutionary sires have devised and
bequeathed to us an almost perfect national policy. Let
us cherish, and defend, and build upon, the fundamental
principles of that polity, and we shall most assuredly
reap the golden fruits of unparalleled power, virtue and
prosperity. Heaven forbid that a desperate faction of
slaveholding criminals should succeed in their infamous
endeavors to quench the spirit of liberty, which our forefathers infused into those two sacred charts of our political faith, the Declaration of Independence, and the Constitution of the United States. Oligarchal politicians are
alone responsible for the continuance of African slavery in
the South. For purposes of self-aggrandizement, they
have kept learning and civilization from the people ; they
have wilfully misinterpreted the national compacts, and
have outraged their own consciences by declaring to their
illiterate constituents, that the Founders of the Republic
were not abolitionists. When the dark clouds of slavery,

error and ignorance shall have passed away,—and we believe the time is near at hand when they are to be dissi-
pated,—the freemen of the South, like those of other sections, will learn the glorious truth, that inflexible opposition to Human Bondage has formed one of the distinguishing characteristics of every really good or great
man that our country has produced.

The principles, aims and objects that actuated the
framers of the Constitution, are most graphicallly and
eloquently set forth, in the following extract from a
speech recently delivered by the Hon. A. H. Cragin, of
New Hampshire, in the House of Representatives :

" When our forefathers reared the magnificent structure of a
free Republic in this Western land, they laid its foundations
broad and deep in the eternal principles of right. Its materials
were all quarried from the mountain of truth ; and, as it rose
majestically before an astonished world, it rejoiced the hearts and
hopes of mankind. Tyrants only cursed the workmen and their
workmanship. Its architecture was new. It had no model in
Grecian or Roman history. It seemed a paragon, let down from
Heaven to inspire the hopes of men, and to demonstrate the favor
of God to the people of a new world. The builders recognized
the rights of human nature as universal. Liberty, the great first
right of man, they claimed for ' all men,' and claimed it from
' God himself.' Upon this foundation they erected the temple,
and dedicated it to Liberty, Humanity, Justice, and Equality.
Washington was crowned its patron saint."

" The work completed was the noblest effort of human wisdom.
But it was not perfect. It had one blemish—a little spot—the
black stain of slavery. The workmen—the friends of freedom
everywhere—deplored this. They labored long and prayerfully
to remove this deformity. They applied all the skill of their
art ; but they labored in vain. Self-interest was too strong for
patriotism and love of liberty. The work stood still, and for a

time it was doubtful whether the experiment would succeed. The blot must remain, or the whole must fail. The workmen revarnished their work, to conceal and cover up the stain. Slavery was recognized, but not sanctioned. The word slave or slavery must not mar the Constitution. So great an inconsistency must not be proclaimed to the world."

"All agreed, at that time, that the anomaly should not increase, and all concurred in the hope and belief that the blemish would gradually disappear. Those noble men looked forward to the time when slavery would be abolished in this land of ours. They believed that the principles of liberty were so dear to the people, that they would not long deny to others what they claimed for themselves. They never dreamed that slavery would be extended, but firmly believed it would be wholly blotted out. *I challenge any man to show me a single patriot of the Revolution who was in favor of slavery, or who advocated its extension.* So universal was the sentiment of liberty then, that no man, North or South, could be found to justify it. Some palliated the evil, and desired that it might be gradually extinguished; but none contemplated it as a permanent institution."

"Liberty was then the national goddess, worshiped by all the people. They sang of liberty, they harangued for liberty, they prayed for liberty, and they sacrificed for liberty. Slavery was then hateful. It was denounced by all. The British king was condemned for foisting it upon the Colonies. Southern men were foremost in entering their protest against it. It was then everywhere regarded as an evil, and a crime against humanity."

The fact is too palpable to be disguised, that slavery and slaveholders have always been a clog and a dead-weight upon the government—a disgrace and a curse to humanity. The slaveholding Tories of the South, particularly of South Carolina, in their atrocious hostility to freedom, prolonged the arduous war of the Revolution from two to three years; and since the termination of that momentous struggle, in which, thank Heaven, they were most signally defeated, it has been their constant aim and effort to subvert the dear-bought liberties which were achieved by the non-slaveholding patriots.

Non-slaveholders of the South ! up to the present period, neither as a body, nor as individuals, have you ever had an independent existence ; but, if true to yourselves and to the memory of your fathers, you, in equal copartnership with the non-slaveholders of the North, will soon become the honored rulers and proprietors of the most powerful, prosperous, virtuous, free, and peaceful nation, on which the sun has ever shone.   Already has the time arrived for you to decide upon what basis you will erect your political superstructure.   Upon whom will you depend for an equitable and judicious form of constitutional government ? Whom will you designate as models for your future statesmen ?   Your choice lies between the dead and the living— between the Washingtons, the Jeffersons and the Madisons of the past, and the Quattlebums, the Quitmans and the Butlers of the present.   We have chosen ; choose ye, remembering that freedom or slavery is to be the issue of your option.

As the result of much reading and research, and at the expenditure of no inconsiderable amount of time, labor and money, we now proceed to make known the anti-slavery sentiments of those noble abolitionists, the Fathers of the Republic, whose liberal measures of public policy have been so criminally perverted by the treacherous advocates of slavery.

Let us listen, in the first place, to the voice of him who

was "first in war, first in peace, and first in the hearts of his countrymen," to

THE VOICE OF WASHINGTON.

In a letter to John F. Mercer, dated September 9th, 1786, General Washington says :—

"I never mean, unless some particular circumstances should compel me to it, to possess another slave by purchase, it being among my *first wishes* to see some plan adopted by which slavery, in this country, may be abolished by law."

In a letter to Robert Morris, dated Mount Vernon, April 12, 1786, he says :—

"I can only say that there is not a man living who wishes more sincerely than I do to see a plan adopted for the abolition of it. But there is only one proper and effectual mode by which it can be accomplished, and that is by legislative authority ; and this, as far as my suffrage will go, shall never be wanting."

He says, in a letter

"To the MARQUIS DE LAFAYETTE—April 5th, 1783:—
The scheme, my dear Marquis, which you propose as a precedent, to encourage the emancipation of the black people in this country from the state of bondage in which they are held, is a striking evidence of the benevolence of your heart. I shall be happy to join you in so laudable a work ; but will defer going into a detail of the business till I have the pleasure of seeing you."

In another letter to Lafayette, he says :—

"The benevolence of your heart, my dear Marquis, is so conspicuous on all occasions, that I never wonder at any fresh proofs of it ; but your late purchase of an estate in the Colony of Cayenne, with the view of emancipating the slaves on it, is a generous
9

and noble proof of your humanity. Would to God a like spirit might diffuse itself generally into the minds of the people of this country."

In a letter to Sir John Sinclair, he further said :—

" There are in Pennsylvania laws for the gradual abolition of slavery, which neither Virginia nor Maryland have at present, but which nothing is more certain than they must have, and at a period *not remote.*"

From his last will and testament we make the following extract :

"Upon the decease of my wife, it is my will and desire that all the slaves which I hold in my own right shall receive their freedom. To emancipate them during her life would, though earnestly wished by me, be attended with such insuperable difficulties, on account of their intermixture by marriage with the dower negroes, as to excite the most painful sensation, if not disagreeable consequences, from the latter, while both descriptions are in the occupancy of the same proprietor, it not being in my power, under the tenure by which the dower negroes are held, to manumit them."

It is said that, "when Mrs. Washington learned, from the will of her deceased husband, that the only obstacle to the immediate perfection of this provision was her right of dower, she at once gave it up, and the slaves were made free." A man might possibly concentrate within himself more real virtue and influence than ever Washington possessed, and yet he would not be too good for such a wife.

From the Father of his Country, we now turn to the author of the Declaration of Independence. We will listen to

THE VOICE OF JEFFERSON.

On the 39th and 40th pages of his Notes on Virginia, Jefferson says :—

"There must doubtless be an unhappy influence on the manners of our people, produced by the existence of slavery among us. The whole commerce between master and slave is a perpetual exercise of the most boisterous passions—the most unremitting despotism on the one part, and degrading submissions on the other. Our children see this, and learn to imitate it; for man is an imitative animal. This quality is the germ of all education in him. From his cradle to his grave, he is learning to do what he sees' others do. If a parent could find no motive, either in his philanthropy or his self-love, for restraining the intemperance of passion towards his slave, it should always be a sufficient one that his child is present. But generally it is not sufficient. The parent storms, the child looks on, catches the lineaments of wrath, puts on the same airs in the circle of smaller slaves, gives a loose rein to the worst of passions ; and, thus nursed, educated, and daily exercised in tyranny, cannot but be stamped by it with odious peculiarities. The man must be a prodigy who can retain his manners and morals undepraved by such circumstances. And with what execration should the Statesman be loaded, who, permitting one half the citizens thus to trample on the rights of the other, transforms those into despots and these into enemies, destroys the morals of the one part, and the *amor patriae* of the other ; for if a slave can have a country in this world, it must be any other in preference to that in which he is born to live and labor for another ; in which he must look up the faculties of his nature, contribute, as far as depends on his individual endeavors, to the evanishment of the human race, or entail his own miserable condition on the endless generations proceeding from him. With the morals of the people, their industry also is destroyed ; for, in a warm climate, no man will labor for himself who can make another labor for him. This is so true, that of the proprietors of slaves a very small proportion, indeed, are ever seen to labor. And can the liberties of a nation be thought secure, when we have remov d their only firm basis—a conviction in the minds of the people that these liberties are of the gift of God ? that they are not to be violated but with his wrath ? Indeed, I tremble for my country when I reflect that God is just; that his justice cannot sleep forever ; that considering numbers, nature, and natural means only, a revolution of the wheel of fortune, an exchange of situation is among possible events ; that it may become probable by supernatural interference ! The Almighty has no attribute which can take side with us in such a contest."

While Virginia was yet a Colony, in 1774, she held a Convention to appoint delegates to attend the first general Congress, which was to assemble, and did assemble, in Philadelphia, in September of the same year. Before that Convention, Mr. Jefferson made an exposition of the rights of British America, in which he said :—

"The abolition of domestic slavery is the greatest object of desire in these Colonies, where it was unhappily introduced in their infant State. But previous to the enfranchisement of the slaves, it is necessary to exclude further importations from Africa. Yet our repeated attempts to effect this by prohibitions, and by imposing duties which might amount to prohibition, have been hitherto defeated by his Majesty's negative ; thus preferring the immediate advantage of a few African corsairs to the lasting interests of the American States, and the rights of human nature, deeply wounded by this infamous practice."

In the original draft of the Declaration of Independence, of which it is well known he was the author, we find this charge against the King of Great Britain :—

"He has waged cruel war against human nature itself, violating its most sacred rights of life and liberty, in the persons of a distant people who never offended him, captivating and carrying them into slavery in another hemisphere, or to incur miserable death in their transportation thither.   This piratical waifare, the opprobrium of infidel powers, is the warfare of the Christian King of Great Britain.   Determined to keep a market where men should be bought and sold, he has at length prostituted his negative for suppressing any legislative attempt to prohibit and restrain this execrable commerce."

Hear him further ; he says :—

" We hold these truths to be self-evident, that all men are created equal ; that they are endowed by their Creator with certain unalienable rights ; that among these are life, liberty, and the pursuit of happiness ; that to secure these rights, governments are instituted among men, deriving their just powers from the consent of the governed."

Under date of August 7th, 1785, in a letter to Dr. Price of London, he says :—

" Northward of the Chesapeake you may find, here and there, an opponent of your doctrine, as you may find, here and there, a robber and murderer ; but in no great number.   Emancipation is put into such a train, that in a few years there will be no slaves northward of Maryland.   In Maryland I do not find such a disposition to begin the redress of this enormity, as in Virginia. This is the next State to which we may turn our eyes for the interesting spectacle of justice in conflict with avarice and oppression ; a conflict wherein the sacred side is gaining daily recruits from the influx into office of young men grown up, and growing up.   These have sucked in the principles of liberty, as it were, with their mother's milk ; and it is to them I look with anxiety to turn the fate of the question."

In another letter, written to a friend in 1814, he made use of the following emphatic language :—

" Your favor of July 31st was duly received, and read with peculiar pleasure.   The sentiments do honor to the head and heart of the writer. Mine on the subject of the slavery of negroes have long since been in the possession of the public, and time has only served to give them stronger root. The love of justice and the love of country plead equally the cause of these people, and it is a reproach to us that they should have pleaded it so long in vain."

Again, he says :—·

" What an incomprehensible machine is man ! who can endure toil, famine, stripes, imprisonment, and death itself, in vindication of his own liberty ; and the next moment be deaf to all those motives whose power supported him through his trial, and inflict on his fellow man a bondage, one hour of which is fraught with more misery than ages of that which he rose in rebellion to oppose."

Throughout the South, at the present day, especially among slaveholders, negroes are almost invariably spoken of as " goods and chattels," " property," " human cattle." In our first quotation from Jefferson's works, we have seen that he spoke of the blacks as *citizens*. We shall now hear him speak of them as *brethren*. He says :—

" We must wait with patience the workings of an overruling Providence, and hope that that is preparing the deliverance of these our brethren. When the measure of their tears shall be full, when their groans shall have involved Heaven itself in darkness, doubtless a God of justice will awaken to their distress. Nothing is more certainly written in the Book of Fate, than that this people shall be free."

In a letter to James Heaton, on this same subject, dated May 20, 1826, only six weeks before his death, he says :—

" My sentiments have been forty years before the public. Had

I repeated them forty times, they would have only become the more stale and threadbare. Although I shall not live to see them consummated, they will not die with me."

From the Father of the Declaration of Independence, we now turn to the Father of the Constitution. We will listen to

THE VOICE OF MADISON.

Advocating the abolition of the slave-trade, Mr. Madison said :—

"The dictates of humanity, the principles of the people, the national safety and happiness, and prudent policy, require it of us. It is to be hoped, that by expressing a national disapprobation of the trade, we may *destroy* it, and save our country from reproaches, and our posterity from the imbecility ever attendant on a country filled with slaves."

Again, he says :—

"It is wrong to admit into the Constitution the idea that there can be property in man."

In the 39th No. of " The Federalist," he says :—

"The first question that offers itself is, whether the general form and aspect of the government be strictly Republican. It is evident that no other form would be reconcilable with the genius of the people of America, and with the fundamental principles of the Revolution, or with that honorable determination which animates every votary of freedom, to rest all our political experiments on the capacity of mankind for self-government."

In the Federal Convention, he said —

"And in the third place, where slavery exists, the Republican theory becomes still more fallacious."

On another occasion, he says :—

"We have seen the mere distinction of color made, in the most enlightened period of time, a ground of the most oppressive dominion ever exercised by man over man."

THE VOICE OF MONROE.

In a speech in the Virginia Convention, Mr. Monroe said :—

"We have found that this evil has preyed upon the very vitals of the Union, and has been prejudicial to all the States, in which it has existed."

THE VOICE OF HENRY.

The eloquent Patrick Henry says, in a letter dated January 18, 1773 :—

"Is it not a little surprising that the professors of Christianity, whose chief excellence consists in softening the human heart, in cherishing and improving its finer feelings, should encourage a practice so totally repugnant to the first impressions of right and wrong? What adds to the wonder is, that this abominable practice has been introduced in the most enlightened ages. Times that seem to have pretensions to boast of high improvements in the arts and sciences, and refined morality, have brought into general use, and guarded by many laws, a species of violence and tyranny which our more rude and barbarous, but more honest ancestors detested. Is it not amazing that at a time when the rights of humanity are defined and understood with precision, in a country above all others fond of liberty—that in such an age and in such a country, we find men professing a religion the most mild, humane, gentle, and generous, adopting such a principle, as repugnant to humanity as it is inconsistent with the Bible, and destructive to liberty? Every thinking, honest man rejects it in speculation. How free in practice from conscientious motives! Would any one believe that I am master of slaves of my own purchase? I am drawn along by the general inconvenience of living here without them. I will not, I cannot justify it. However culpable my conduct, I will so far pay my devoir to virtue as to own the excellence and rectitude of her precepts, and lament my want of conformity to them. I believe a time will come when an opportunity will be offered to abolish this lamentable evil. Everything we can do is to improve it, if it happens in our day; if not, let us transmit to our descendants, together with our slaves, a pity for their unhappy lot, and an abhorrence for slavery. If we cannot reduce this wished-for reformation to practice, let us treat the unhappy victims with lenity. It is the furthest advance we can make towards justice. It is a debt we owe to the purity of our religion, to show that it is at variance with that law which warrants slavery."

Again, this great orator says:—

"It would rejoice my very soul, that every one of my fellow-beings was emancipated. We ought to lament and deplore the necessity of holding our fellow-men in bondage. Believe me; I shall honor the Quakers for their noble efforts to abolish slavery."

THE VOICE OF RANDOLPH.

That excentric genius, John Randolph, of Roanoke, in a letter to William Gibbons, in 1820, says:—

"With unfeigned respect and regard, and as sincere a deprecation on the extension of slavery and its horrors, as any other man, be him whom he may, I am your friend, in the literal sense of that much abused word. I say much abused, because it is applied to the leagues of vice and avarice and ambition, instead of good will toward man from love of him who is the Prince of Peace."

While in Congress, he said:

"Sir, I envy neither the heart nor the head of that man from the North who rises here to defend slavery on principle."

It is well known that he emancipated all his negroes. The following lines from his will are well worth perusing and preserving :—

"I give to my slaves their freedom, to which my conscience tells me they are justly entitled. It has a long time been a matter of the deepest regret to me that the circumstances under which I inherited them, and the obstacles thrown in the way by the laws of the land, have prevented my emancipating them in my life-time, which it is my full intention to do in case I can accomplish it."

THOMAS M. RANDOLPH.

In an address to the Virginia Legislature, in 1820, Gov. Randolph said :—

"We have been far outstripped by States to whom nature has been far less bountiful. It is painful to consider what might have been, under other circumstances, the amount of general wealth in Virginia."

THOMAS JEFFERSON RANDOLPH.

In 1832, Mr. Randolph, of Albemarle, in the Legislature of Virginia, used the following most graphic and emphatic language :—

"I agree with gentlemen in the necessity of arming the State for internal defence. I will unite with them in any effort to restore confidence to the public mind, and to conduce to the sense of the safety of our wives and our children. Yet, Sir, I must ask upon whom is to fall the burden of this defence ? Not upon the lordly masters of their hundred slaves, who will never turn out except to retire with their families when danger threatens. No, Sir ; it is to fall upon the less wealthy class of our citizens.

chiefly upon the non-slaveholder. I have known patrols turned out when there was not a slaveholder among them ; and this is the practice of the country. I have slept in times of alarm quiet in bed, without having a thought of care, while these individuals, owning none of this property themselves, were patrolling under a compulsory process, for a pittance of seventy-five cents per twelve hours, the very curtilage of my house, and guarding that property which was alike dangerous to them and myself. After all, this is but an expedient. As this population becomes more numerous, it becomes less productive. Your guard must be increased, until finally its profits will not pay for the expense of its subjection. Slavery has the effect of lessening the free population of a country.

" The gentleman has spoken of the increase of the female slaves being a part of the profit. It is admitted ; but no great evil can be averted, no good attained, without some inconvenience. It may be questioned how far it is desirable to foster and encourage this branch of profit. It is a practice, and an increasing practice, in parts of Virginia, to rear slaves for market. How can an honorable mind, a patriot, and a lover of his country, bear to see this Ancient Dominion, rendered illustrious by the noble devotion and patriotism of her sons in the cause of liberty, converted into one grand menagerie, where men are to be reared for the market, like oxen for the shambles ? Is it better, is it not worse, than the slave trade—that trade which enlisted the labor of the good and wise of every creed, and every clime, to abolish it ? The trader receives the slave, a stranger in language, aspect, and manners, from the merchant who has brought him from the interior. The ties of father, mother, husband, and child, have all been rent in twain ; before he receives him, his soul has become callous. But here, Sir, individuals whom the master has known from infancy, whom he has seen sporting in the innocent gambols of childhood, who have been accustomed to look to him for protection, he tears from the mother's arms and sells into a strange country among strange people, subject to cruel taskmasters.

" He has attempted to justify slavery here, because it exists in Africa, and has stated that it exists all over the world. Upon the same principle, he could justify Mahometanism, with its plurality of wives, petty wars for plunder, robbery, and murder, or any other of the abominations and enormities of savage tribes. Does slavery exist in any part of civilized Europe ? No, Sir, in no part of it."

PEYTON RANDOLPH.

On the 20th of October, 1774, while Congress was in session in Philadelphia, Peyton Randolph, President, the following resolution, among others, was unanimously adopted :—

"That we will neither import nor purchase any slave imported after the first day of December next; after which time we will wholly discontinue the slave-trade, and will neither be concerned in it ourselves, nor will we hire our vessels, nor sell our commodities or manufactures, to those who are concerned in it."

EDMUND RANDOLPH.

The Constitution of the United States contains the following provision :—

"No person held to service or labor in another State, under the laws thereof, escaping to another, shall, in consequence of any law or regulation therein, be discharged from such service or labor, but shall be delivered up on claim of the party to whom such service or labor may be due."

To the studious attention of those vandals who contend that the above provision requires the rendition of fugitive *slaves*, we respectfully commend the following resolution, which, it will be observed, was *unanimously* adopted :—

"On motion of Mr. Randolph, the word '*servitude*' was struck out, and '*service*' unanimously inserted — the former being thought to express the condition of *slaves*, and the latter the obligation of *free* persons."—*Madison Papers, vol.* III., *p.* 1569.

Well done for the Randolphs !

THE VOICE OF CLAY.

Henry Clay, whom everybody loved, and at the mention of whose name the American heart always throbs with emotions of grateful remembrance, said, in an address before the Kentucky Colonization Society, in 1829 :—

"It is believed that nowhere in the *farming* portion of the United States would slave-labor be generally employed, if the proprietor were not tempted to raise slaves by the high price of the Southern market, which keeps it up in his own."

In the United States Senate, in 1850, he used the following memorable words :—

"I am extremely sorry to hear the Senator from Mississippi say that he requires, first the extension of the Missouri Compromise line to the Pacific, and also that he is not satisfied with that, but requires, if I understand him correctly, a positive provision for the admission of slavery South of that line. And now, Sir, coming from a slave State, as I do, I owe it to myself, I owe it to truth, I owe it to the subject to say that no earthly power could induce me to vote for a specific measure for the introduction of slavery where it had not before existed, either South or North of that line. Coming as I do from a slave State, it is my solemn, deliberate and well-matured determination that no power, no earthly power, shall compel me to vote for the positive introduction of slavery either South or North of that line. Sir, while you reproach, and justly too, our British ancestors for the introduction of this institution upon the continent of America, I am, for one, unwilling that the posterity of the present inhabitants of California and of New Mexico, shall reproach us for doing just what we reproach Great Britain for doing to us. If the citizens of those territories choose to establish slavery, and if they come here with Constitutions establishing slavery, I am for admitting them with such provisions in their Constitutions; but then it will be their own work, and not ours, and their posterity will have to reproach them, and not us, for forming Constitutions allowing the institution of slavery to exist among them. These are my views, Sir, and I choose to express them; and I care not how extensively or universally they are known."

Hear him further ; he says :—

"So long as God allows the vital current to flow through my veins, I will never, never, never, by word, or thought, by mind or will, aid in admitting one rood of free territory to the everlasting curse of human bondage."

A bumper to the memory of noble Harry of the West !

CASSIUS M. CLAY.

Of the great number of good speeches made by members of the Republican party during the late Presidential campaign, it is, we believe, pretty generally admitted that the best one was made by Cassius M. Clay, of Kentucky,[23] at the Tabernacle, in New-York City, on the 24th of October, 1856. From the speech of that noble champion of freedom, then and there delivered, we make the following graphic extract :—

"If there are no manufactures, there is no commerce. In vain do the slaveholders go to Knoxville, to Nashville, to Memphis and to Charleston, and resolve that they will have nothing to do with these abolition eighteen millions of Northern people; that they will build their own vessels, manufacture their own goods, ship their own products to foreign countries, and break down

New-York, Philadelphia and Boston! Again they resolve and reresolve, and yet there is not a single ton more shipped and not a single article added to the wealth of the South. But, gentlemen, they never invite such men as I am to attend their Conventions. They know that I would tell them that slavery is the cause of their poverty, and that I will tell them that what they are aiming at is the dissolution of the Union—that they may be prepared to strike for that whenever the nation rises. They well know that by slave labor the very propositions which they make can never be realized; yet when we show these things, they cry out, 'Oh, Cotton is King!' But when we look at the statistics, we find that so far from Cotton being King, Grass is King. There are nine articles of staple productions which are larger than that of cotton in this country."

"I suppose it does not follow because slavery is endeavoring to modify the great dicta of our fathers, that cotton and free labor are incompatible. In the extreme South, at New Orleans, the laboring men—the stevedores and hackmen on the levee, where the heat is intensified by the proximity of the red brick buildings, are all white men, and they are in the full enjoyment of health. But how about cotton? I am informed by a friend of mine—himself a slaveholder, and therefore good authority—that in Northwestern Texas, among the German settlements, who, true to their national instincts, will not employ the labor of a slave—they produce more cotton to the acre, and of a better quality, and selling at prices from a cent to a cent and a half a pound higher than that produced by slave labor. This is an experiment that illustrates what I have always held, that whatever is right is expedient."

THE VOICE OF BENTON.

In his "Thirty Years' View," Thomas H. Benton says:—

"My opposition to the extension of slavery dates further back than 1844—forty years further back; and as this is a suitable time for a general declaration, and a sort of general conscience delivery, I will say that my opposition to it dates from 1804, when

I was a student at law in the State of Tennessee, and studied the subject of African slavery in an American book—a Virginia book —Tucker's edition of Blackstone's Commentaries."

Again, in a speech delivered in St. Louis, on the 3rd of November, 1856, he says :—

"I look at white people, and not at black ones; I look to the peace and reputation of the race to which I belong. I look to the peace of this land—the world's last hope for a free government on the earth. One of the occasions on which I saw Henry Clay rise higher than I thought I ever saw him before, was when in the debate on the admission of California, a dissolution was apprehended if slavery was not carried into this Territory, where it never was. Then Mr. Clay, rising, loomed colossally in the Senate of the United States, as he rose declaring that for no earthly purpose, no earthly object, could he carry slavery into places where it did not exist before. It was a great and proud day for Mr. Clay, towards the latter days of his life, and if an artist could have been there to catch his expression as he uttered that sentiment, with its reflex on his face, and his countenance beaming with firmness of purpose, it would have been a glorious moment in which to transmit him to posterity—his countenance all alive and luminous with the ideas that beat in his bosom. That was a proud day. I could have wished that I had spoken the same words. I speak them now, telling you they were his, and adopting them as my own."

THE VOICE OF MASON.

Colonel Mason, a leading and distinguished member of the Convention that formed the Constitution, from Virginia, when the provision for prohibiting the importation of slaves was under consideration, said :—

" The present question concerns not the importing States alone,

but the whole Union. Slavery discourages arts and manufactures.
The poor despise labor when performed by slaves. They prevent
the emigration of whites who really enrich and strengthen a
country. They produce the most pernicious effect on manners.
Every master of slaves is born a petty tyrant. They bring the
judgment of Heaven on a country. As nations cannot be rewarded or punished in the next world, they must be in this. By
an inevitable chain of causes and effects, Providence punishes national sins by national calamities. He lamented that some of our
Eastern brethren had, from a lust of gain, embarked in this nefa-
rious traffic. As to the States being in possession of the right
to import, this was the case with many other rights, now to be
properly given up. He held it essential, in every point of view,
that the General Government should have power to prevent the
increase of slavery."

THE VOICE OF MCDOWELL.

In 1832, Gov. McDowell used this language in the Virginia Legislature :—

" Who that looks to this unhappy bondage of an unhappy people, in the midst of our society, and thinks of its incidents or issues, but weeps over it as a curse as great upon him who inflicts
as upon him who suffers it ? Sir, you may place the slave where
you please—you may dry up, to your uttermost, the fountains of
his feelings, the springs of his thought—you may close upon his
mind every avenue of knowledge, and cloud it over with artificial
night—you may yoke him to your labors, as the ox, which liveth
only to work and worketh only to live—you may put him under
any process which, without destroying his value as a slave, will
debase and crush him as a rational being—you may do this, and
the idea that he was born to be free will survive it all. It is
allied to his hope of immortality—it is the etherial part of his
nature which oppression cannot rend. It is a torch lit up in his
soul by the hand of Deity, and never meant to be extinguished
by the hand of man."

THE VOICE OF IREDELL.

In the debates of the North Carolina Convention, Mr. Iredell, afterwards a Judge of the United States Supreme Court, said :—

"When the entire abolition of slavery takes place, it will be an event which must be pleasing to every generous mind, and every friend of human nature."

THE VOICE OF PINKNEY.

William Pinkney, of Maryland, in the House of Delegates in that State, in 1789, made several powerful arguments in favor of the abolition of slavery. Here follows a brief extract from one of his speeches :—

"Iniquitous and most dishonorable to Maryland, is that dreary system of partial bondage which her laws have hitherto supported with a solicitude worthy of a better object, and her citizens by their practice, countenanced. Founded in a disgraceful traffic, to which the parent country lent its fostering aid, from motives of interest, but which even she would have disdained to encourage, had England been the destined mart of such inhuman merchandize, its continuance is as shameful as its origin.

I have no hope that the stream of general liberty will forever flow unpolluted through the mire of partial bondage, or that they who have been habituated to lord it over others, will not, in time, become base enough to let others lord it over them. If they resist, it will be the struggle of pride and selfishness, not of principle."

THE VOICE OF LEIGH.

In the Legislature of Virginia, in 1832, Mr. Leigh said :—

I thought, till very lately that it was known to every body

that, during the Revolution, and for many years after, the abolition of slavery was a favorite topic with many of our ablest
Statesmen, who entertained with respect all the schemes which
wisdom or ingenuity could suggest for its accomplishment."

THE VOICE OF MARSHALL.

Thomas Marshall, of Fauquier, said, in the Virginia
Legislature, in 1832 :—

"Wherefore, then, object to slavery ?   Because it is ruinous to
the whites—retards improvements, roots out an industrious population, banishes the yeomanry of the country—deprives the spin-
ner, the weaver, the smith, the shoemaker, the carpenter, of employment and support."

THE VOICE OF BOLLING.

Philip A. Bolling, of Buckingham, a member of the Legislature of Virginia in 1832, said :—

"The time will come—and it may be sooner than many are
willing to believe—when this oppressed and degraded race cannot be held as they now are—when a change will be effected,
abhorrent, Mr. Speaker, to you, and to the feelings of every good
man.
The wounded adder will recoil, and sting the foot that tram-
ples upon it.   The day is fast approaching, when those who oppose all action upon this subject, and, instead of aiding in devis-
ing some feasible plan for freeing their country from an acknowledged curse, cry '*impossible,*' to every plan suggested, will curse
their perverseness, and lament their folly."

THE VOICE OF CHANDLER.

Mr. Chandler, of Norfolk, member of the Virginia Legislature, in 1832, took occasion to say :—

"It is admitted, by all who have addressed this House, that

slavery is a curse, and an increasing one. That it has been destructive to the lives of our citizens, history, with unerring truth, will record. That its future increase will create commotion, cannot be doubted."

THE VOICE OF SUMMERS.

Mr. Summers, of Kanawha, member of the Legislature of Virginia, in 1832, said :—

" The evils of this system cannot be enumerated. It were unnecessary to attempt it. They glare upon us at every step. When the owner looks to his wasted estate, he knows and feels them."

THE VOICE OF PRESTON.

In the Legislature of Virginia, in 1832, Mr. Preston said :—

" Sir, Mr. Jefferson, whose hand drew the preamble to the Bill of Rights, has eloquently remarked that we had invoked for ourselves the benefit of a principle which we had denied to others. He saw and felt that slaves, as men, were embraced within this principle."

THE VOICE OF FREMONT.

John Charles Fremont, one of the noblest sons of the South, says :—

" I heartily concur in all movements which have for their object to repair the mischiefs arising from the violation of good faith in the repeal of the Missouri Compromise. I am opposed to slavery in the abstract, and upon principles sustained and made habitual by long settled convictions. I am inflexibly opposed to its extension on this continent beyond its present limits."

" The great body of non-slaveholding Freemen, including those of the South, upon whose welfare slavery is an oppression, will discover that the power of the General Government over the Public Lands may be beneficially exerted to advance their interests, and secure their independence; knowing this, their suffrages will not be wanting to maintain that authority in the Union, which is absolutely essential to the maintenance of their own liberties, and which has more than once indicated the purpose of disposing of the Public Lands in such a way as would make every settler upon them a freeholder."

THE VOICE OF BLAIR.

In an Address to the Republicans of Maryland, in 1856, Francis P. Blair says :—

" In every aspect in which slavery among us can be considered, it is pregnant with difficulty. Its continuance in the States in which it has taken root has resulted in the monopoly of the soil, to a great extent, in the hands of the slaveholders, and the entire control of all departments of the State Government; and yet a majority of people in the slave States are not slave-owners. This produces an anomaly in the principle of our free institutions, which threatens in time to bring into subjugation to slave-owners the great body of the free white population."

THE VOICE OF MAURY.

Lieut. Maury, to whom has been awarded so much well-merited praise in the world of science, says :—

" The fact must be obvious to the far-reaching minds of our Statesmen, that unless some means of relief be devised, some channel afforded, by which the South can, when the time comes, get rid of the excess of her slave population, she will be ultimately found with regard to this institution, in the predicament of the man with the wolf by the ears; too dangerous to hold on any longer, and equally dangerous to let go. To our mind, the event is as certain to happen as any event which depends on the contingencies of the future, viz.: that unless means be devised for gradually relieving the slave States from the undue pressure ⸳ ᐧ this class upon them—unless some way be opened by which they may be rid of their surplus black population—the time will come—it may not be in the next nor in the succeeding generation—but, sooner or later, come it will, and come it must—when the two races will join in the death struggle for the mastery."

THE VOICE OF BIRNEY.

James G. Birney, of Kentucky, under whom the Abolitionists first became a National Party, and for whom they voted for President in 1844, giving him 66,304 votes, says :

" We have so long practiced injustice, adding to it hypocrisy, in the treatment of the colored race, both negroes and Indians, that we begin to regard injustice as an element—a chief element —the chief element of our government. But no government which admits injustice as an element can be a harmonious one or a permanent one. Harmony is the antagonist of injustice, ever has been, and ever will be ; that is, so long as injustice lasts, which cannot always be, for it is a lie, a semblance, therefore, perishable. True, from the imperfection of man, his ambition and selfishness, injustice often finds its way incidentally into the administration of public affairs, and maintains its footing a long time before it is cast out by the legitimate elements of government."

" Our slave States, especially the more southern of them, in which the number of slaves is greater, and in which, of course the sentiment of injustice is stronger than in the more northern ones, are to be placed on the list of decaying communities. To a philosophic observer, they seem to be falling back on the scale of civilization. Even at the present point of retrogression, the cause of civilization and human improvement would lose nothing by their annihilation."

THE VOICE OF DELAWARE.

Strong anti-slavery sentiment had become popular in

Delaware as early as 1785. With Maryland and Missouri, it may now be ranked as a semi-slave State. Mr. McLane, a member of Congress from this State in 1825, said :—

"I shall not imitate the example of other gentlemen by making professions of my love of liberty and abhorrence of slavery, not, however, because I do not entertain them. I am an enemy to slavery."

THE VOICE OF MARYLAND.

Slavery has little vitality in Maryland. Baltimore, the greatest city of the South—greatest because freest—has a population of more than two hundred thousand souls, and yet less than three thousand of these are slaves. In spite of all the unjust and oppressive statutes enacted by the oligarchy, the non-slaveholders, who with the exception of a small number of slaveholding emancipationists, may in truth be said to be the only class of respectable and patriotic citizens in the South, have wisely determined that their noble State shall be freed from the sin and the shame, the crime and the curse of slavery ; and in accordance with this determination, long since formed, they are giving every possible encouragement to free white labor, thereby, very properly, rendering the labor of slaves both unprofitable and disgraceful. The formation of an Abolition Society in this State, in 1789, was the result of the influence of the masterly speeches delivered in the House of Delegates, by the Hon. William Pinkney, whose undying testimony we have already placed on record. Nearly seventy years ago, this eminent lawyer and Statesman declared to the people of America, that if they did not

mark out the bounds of slavery, and adopt measures for
its total extinction, it would finally "work a decay of the
spirit of liberty in the free States." Further, he said that,
"by the eternal principles of natural justice, no master in
the State has a right to hold his slave in bondage a single
hour." In 1787, Luther Martin, of this State, said :—

"Slavery is inconsistent with the genius of republicanism, and
has a tendency to destroy those principles on which it is supported, as it lessens the sense of the equal rights of mankind,
and habituates us to tyranny and oppression."

THE VOICE OF VIRGINIA.

After introducing the unreserved and immortal testimony of Washington, Jefferson, Madison, Henry, and the
other great men of the Old Dominion, against the institution of slavery, it may to some, seem quite superfluous to
back the cause of Freedom by arguments from other Virginia abolitionists ; but this State, notwithstanding all
her more modern manners and inhumanity, has been so
prolific of just views and noble sentiments, that we deem
it eminently fit and proper to blazon many of them to the
world as the redeeming features of her history. An Abolition Society was formed in this State in 1791. In a memorial which the members of this Society presented to
Congress, they pronounced slavery "not only an odious
degradation, but an outrageous violation of one of the most
essential rights of human nature, and utterly repugnant
to the precepts of the Gospel." A Bill of Rights, unanimously agreed upon by the Virginia Convention of June
12, 1776, holds—

" That all men are, by nature, equally free and independent;

That Government is, or ought to be, instituted for the common benefit, protection, and security, of the People, Nation, or Community ;

That elections of members to serve as representatives of the people in assembly ought to be free ;

That all men having sufficient evidence of permanent common interest with, and attachment to, the community, have the right of suffrage, and cannot be taxed or deprived of their property, for public uses, without their own consent or that of their representatives so elected, nor bound by any law to which they have not in like manner assented, for the public good ;

That the freedom of the Press is one of the greatest bulwarks of Liberty, and can never be restrained but by despotic Governments ;

That no free Government or the blessing of Liberty can be preserved to any people, but by a firm adherence to justice, moderation, temperance, frugality, and virtue, and by a frequent recurrence to fundamental principles."

The " Virginia Society for the Abolition of Slavery," organized in 1791, addressed Congress in these words :—

" Your memorialists, fully aware that righteousness exalteth a nation, and that slavery is not only an odious degradation, but an outrageous violation of one of the most essential rights of human nature, and utterly repugnant to the precepts of the gospel, which breathes ' peace on earth and good will to men,' lament that a practice so inconsistent with true policy and the inalienable rights of men, should subsist in so enlightened an age, and among a people professing that all mankind are, by nature, equally entitled to freedom."

THE VOICE OF NORTH CAROLINA.

If the question, *slavery* or *no slavery*, could be fairly presented for the decision of the legal voters of North Carolina at the next popular election, we believe at least two-

10

thirds of them would deposite the *no slavery* ticket. Perhaps one-fourth of the slaveholders themselves would vote it, for the slaveholders in this State are more moderate, decent, sensible, and honorable, than the slaveholders in either of the adjoining States, or the States further South ; and we know that many of them are heartily ashamed of the vile occupations of slaveholding and slave-breeding in which they are engaged, for we have the assurance from their own lips. As a matter of course, all the non-slaveholders, who are so greatly in the majority, would vote to suppress the degrading institution which has kept them so long in poverty and ignorance, with the exception of those who are complete automatons to the beck and call of their imperious lords and masters, the major-generals of the oligarchy.

How long shall it be before the citizens of North Carolina shall have the privilege of expressing, at the ballot-box, their true sentiments with regard to this vexed question ? Why not decide it at the next general election ? Sooner or later, it must and will be decided—decided correctly, too—and the sooner the better. The first Southern State that abolishes slavery will do herself an immortal honor. God grant that North Carolina may be that State, and soon ! There is at least one plausible reason why this good old State should be the first to move in this important matter, and we will state it. On the 20th of May, 1775, just one year one month and fourteen days prior to the adoption of the Jeffersonian Declaration of Independence, by the Continental Congress in Philadelphia, July 4, 1776, 'he Mecklenburg Declaration of Independence, the authorship of which is generally attributed to Ephraim Brevard, was proclaimed in Charlotte, Mecklenburg county, North Carolina, and fully ratified in a second Convention of the people of said county, held on the 31st of the same month. And here, by the way, we may remark, that it is supposed Mr. Jefferson made use of this last-mentioned document as the basis of his draft of the indestructible title-deed of our liberties. There is certainly an identical-ness of language between the two papers that is well cal-culated to strengthen this hypothesis. This, however, is a controversy about which we are but little concerned. For present purposes, it is, perhaps, enough for us to know, that on the 20th of May, 1775, when transatlantic tyranny and oppression could no longer be endured, North Carolina set her sister colonies a most valorous and praise-worthy example, and that they followed it. To her infa-mous slaveholding sisters of the South, it is now meet that she should set another noble example of decency, virtue, and independence. Let her at once inaugurate a policy of common justice and humanity—enact a system of equitable laws, having due regard to the rights and inter-ests of all classes of persons, poor whites, negroes, and nabobs, and the surrounding States will ere long applaud her measures, and adopt similar ones for the governance of themselves.

Another reason, and a cogent one, why North Carolina should aspire to become the first free State of the South is this : The first slave State that makes herself respectable by casting out " the mother of harlots," and by rendering enterprise and industry honorable, will immediately receive a large accession of most worthy citizens from other States in the Union, and thus lay a broad foundation of permanent political power and prosperity. Intelligent white farmers from the Middle and New England States will flock to our more congenial clime, eager to give thirty dollars per acre for the same lands that are now a drug in the market because nobody wants them at the rate of five dollars per acre ; an immediate and powerful impetus will be given to commerce, manufactures, and all the industrial arts ; science and literature will be revived, and every part of the State will reverberate with the triumphs of manual and intellectual labor.

At this present time, we of North Carolina are worth less than either of the four adjoining States ; let us abolish slavery at the beginning of the next regular decade of years, and if our example is not speedily followed, we shall, on or before the first day of January, 1870, be enabled to purchase the whole of Virginia and South Carolina, including, perhaps, the greater part of Georgia. An exclusive lease of liberty for ten years would unquestionably make us the Empire State of the South. But we have no disposition to debar others from the enjoyment of liberty or any other inalienable right ; we ask no special favors ; what we demand for ourselves we are willing to concede to our neighbors. Hereby we make application for a lease of freedom for ten years ; shall we have it ? May God enable us to secure it, as we believe He will. We give fair notice, however, that if we get it for ten years, we shall, with the approbation of Heaven, keep it twenty—forty— a thousand—forever !

We transcribe the Mecklenburg Resolutions, which, it will be observed, acknowledge the " inherent and inalienable rights of man," and " declare ourselves a free and independent people, are, and of right ought to be, a sovereign and self-governing association, under the control of no power other than that of our God, and the general government of the Congress."

MECKLENBURG DECLARATION OF INDEPENDENCE,

As proclaimed in the town of Charlotte, North Carolina, May 20th, 1775, and ratified by the County of Mecklenburg, in Convention, May 31st, 1775.

" I. *Resolved*—That whosoever, directly or indirectly, abetted, or in any way, form or manner, countenanced the unchartered and dangerous invasion of our rights as claimed by Great Britain, is an enemy to this country, to America. and to the inherent and inalienable rights of man.

" II. *Resolved*—That we the citizens of Mecklenburg County, do hereby dissolve the political bands which have connected us to the mother country, and hereby absolve ourselves from all allegiance to the British Crown, and abjure all political connection, contract or association with that nation, who have wantonly trampled on our rights and liberties, and inhumanly shed the blood of American patriots at Lexington.

" III. *Resolved*—That we do hereby declare ourselves a free and independent people, are, and of right ought to be, a sovereign and self-governing association, under the control of no power other than that of our God, and the general government of the Congress ; to the maintenance of which independence, we solemnly pledge to each other our mutual co-operation, our lives, our fortunes, and our most sacred honor.

" IV. *Resolved*—That as we now acknowledge the existence and control of no law or legal officer, civil or military, within this county, we do hereby ordain and adopt, as a rule of life, all, each, and every of our former laws—wherein, nevertheless, the crown of Great Britain never can be considered as holding rights, privileges, immunities or authority therein."

Had it not been for slavery, which, with all its other blighting and degrading influences, stifles and subdues every noble impulse of the heart, this consecrated spot would long since have been marked by an enduring monument, whose grand proportions should bear witness that the virtues of a noble ancestry are gratefully remembered by an emulous and appreciative posterity. Yet, even as things are, we are not without genuine consolation. The star of hope and promise is beginning to beam brightly over the long-obscured horizon of the South ; and we are firm in the belief, that freedom, wealth, and magnanimity, will soon do justice to the memory of those fearless patriots, whose fair fame has been suffered to moulder amidst the multifarious abominations of slavery, poverty, ignorance and grovelling selfishness.

Judge Iredell's testimony, which will be found on a preceding page, and to which we request the reader to recur, might have been appropriately introduced under our present heading.

In the Provincial Convention held in North Carolina, in August, 1774, in which there were sixty-nine delegates, representing nearly every county in the province, it was—

"*Resolved*—That we will not import any slave or slaves, or purchase any slave or slaves imported or brought into the Province by others, from any part of the world, after the first day of November next."

In Iredell's Statutes, revised by Martin, it is stated that,

SOUTHERN TESTIMONY AGAINST SLAVERY.223

'In North Carolina, no general law at all was passed, prior to the revolution, declaring who might be slaves."

That there is no *legal* slavery in the Southern States, and that slavery no where can be legalized, any more than theft, arson or murder can be legalized, has been virtually admitted by some of the most profound Southern jurists themselves ; and we will here digress so far as to furnish the testimony of one or two eminent lawyers, not of North Carolina, upon this point.

In the debate in the United States Senate, in 1850, on the Fugitive Slave Bill, Mr. Mason, of Virginia, objected to Mr. Dayton's amendment, providing for a trial by jury, because, said he :—

" A trial by jury necessarily carries with it a trial of the whole right, and a trial of the right to service will be gone into, according to all the forms of the Court, in determining upon any other fact. Then, again, it is proposed, as a part of the proof to be adduced at the hearing, after the fugitive has been re-captured, that evidence shall be brought by the claimant to show that slavery is established in the State from which the fugitive has absconded. Now this very thing, in a recent case in the city of New-York, was required by one of the judges of that State, which case attracted the attention of the authorities of Maryland, and against which they protested. In that case the State judge went so far as to say that the only mode of proving it was by reference to the Statute book. Such proof is required in the Senator's amendment ; and if he means by this that proof shall be brought that slavery is established by existing laws, it is impossible to comply with the requisition, for no such law can be produced, I apprehend, in any of the slave States. I am not aware that there is a single State in which the institution is established by positive law."

Judge Clarke, of Mississippi, says :—

" In this State the legislature have considered slaves as reasonable and accountable beings ; and it would be a stigma upon the
character of the State, and a reproach to the administration of
justice, if the life of a slave could be taken with impunity, or if
he could be murdered in cold blood, without subjecting the offen-
der to the highest penalty known to the criminal jurisprudence
of the country. Has the slave no rights, because he is deprived
of his freedom ? He is still a human being, and possesses all
those rights of which he is not deprived by the positive provisions of the law. The right of the master exists not by force of
the law of nature or nations, but by virtue only of the positive
law of the State."

The Hon. Judge Ruffin, of North Carolina, says :—

" Arguments drawn from the well-established principles, which
confer and restrain the authority of the parent over the child,
the tutor over the pupil, the master over the apprentice, have
been pressed on us. The Court does not recognize their application ; there is no likeness between the cases ; they are in opposition to each other, and there is an impassable gulf between them.
The difference is that which exists between freedom and slavery,
and a greater cannot be imagined. In the one, the end in view
is the happiness of the youth, born to equal rights with that governor on whom the duty devolves of training the young to use-
fulness, in a station which he is afterwards to assume among freemen. To such an end, and with such a subject, moral and intellectual instruction seem the natural means, and, for the most
part, they are found to suffice. Moderate force is superadded
only to make the others effectual. If that fail, it is better to
leave the party to his own headstrong passions, and the ultimate
correction of the law, than to allow it to be immoderately inflicted by a private person. With slavery it is far otherwise.
The end is the profit of the master, his security, and the public
safety ; the subject, one doomed, in his own person and his pos
terity, to live without knowledge, and without the capacity to
make anything his own, and to toil that another may reap the
fruits. What moral considerations shall be addressed to such a

being to convince him, what it is impossible but that the most stupid must feel and know can never be true, that he is thus to labor upon a principle of natural duty, or for the sake of his own personal happiness ? Such services can only be expected from one who has no will of his own ; who surrenders his will in implicit obedience to that of another. Such obedience is the consequence only of uncontrolled authority over the body. There is nothing else which can operate to produce the effect. The power of the master must be absolute to render the submission of the slave perfect. I most freely confess my sense of the harshness of this proposition. I feel it as deeply as any man can ; and as a principle of moral right, every person in his retirement must repudiate it."

An esteemed friend, a physician, who was born and bred in Rowan county, North Carolina, and who now resides there, informs us that Judge Gaston, who was one of the half dozen Statesmen whom the South has produced since the days of the venerable fathers of the Republic, was an avowed abolitionist, and that he published an address to the people of North Carolina, delineating, in a masterly manner, the material, moral, and social disadvantages of slavery. Where is that address? Has it been suppressed by the oligarchy? The fact that slaveholders have, from time to time, made strenuous efforts to expunge the sentiments of freedom which now adorn the works of nobler men than the noble Gaston, may, perhaps, fully account for the oblivious state into which his patriotic address seems to have fallen.[24]

THE VOICE OF SOUTH CAROLINA.

Poor South Carolina ! Folly is her nightcap ; fanaticism is her day-dream ; fire-eating is her pastime. She has

lost her better judgment ; the dictates of reason and phi
losophy have no influence upon her actions. Like the wife
who is pitiably infatuated with a drunken, worthless husband, she still clings, with unabated love, to the cause of
her shame, her misery, and her degradation.

A Kentuckian has recently expressed his opinion of this
State in the following language :—

" South Carolina is bringing herself irrecoverably in the public
contempt. It is impossible for any impartial lover of his country, for any just thinking man, to witness her senseless and
quenchless malignancy against the Union without the most im-
measurable disgust and scorn. She is one vast hot-bed of disunion. Her people think and talk of nothing else. She is a festering mass of treason."

In 1854, there were assessed for taxation in

SOUTH CAROLINA,

Acres of Land..17,289,359
Valued at..$22,836,374
Average value per acre....................................$1,32

At the same time there were in

NEW JERSEY,

Acres of Land...5,324,800
Valued at..$153,161,619
Average value per acre....................................$28,76

We hope the Slavocrats will look, first on that picture,
and then on this ; from one or the other, or both, they may
glean a ray or two of wisdom, which, if duly applied, will
be of incalculable advantage to them and their posterity
We trust, also, that the non-slaveholding whites will view,

with discriminating minds, the different lights and shades of these two pictures ; they are the parties most deeply interested ; and it is to them we look for the glorious revolution that is to substitute Freedom for Slavery. They have the power to retrieve the fallen fortunes of South Carolina, to raise her up from the loathsome sink of iniquity into which slavery has plunged her, and to make her one of the most brilliant stars in the great constellation of States. While their minds are occupied with other considerations, let them not forget the difference between *twenty-eight dollars and seventy-six cents*, the value of land per acre in New Jersey, which is a second-rate free State, and *one dollar and thirty-two cents*, the value of land per acre in South Carolina, which is, *par excellence*, the model slave State. The difference between the two sums is twenty-seven dollars and forty-four cents, which would amount to precisely two thousand seven hundred and forty-four dollars on every hundred acres. To present the subject in another form, the South Carolina tract of land, containing two hundred acres, is worth now only two hundred and sixty-four dollars, and is depreciating every day. Let slavery be abolished, and in the course of a few years, the same tract will be worth five thousand seven hundred and fifty-two dollars, with an upward tendency. At this rate, the increment of value on the total area of the State will amount to more than three times as much as the present estimated value of the slaves !

South Carolina has not always been, nor will she always continue to be, on the wrong side. From Ramsay's History of the State, we learn that, in 1774, she—

" *Resolved*—That His Majesty's subjects in North America (without respect to color or other accidents) are entitled to all the inherent rights and liberties of his natural born subjects within the Kingdom of Great Britain ; that it is their fundamental right, that no man should suffer in his person or property without a fair trial, and judgment given by his peers, or by the law of the land."

One of her early writers, under the *non de plume* of Philodemus, in a political pamphlet published in Charleston in 1784, declares that—

" Such is the fatal influence of slavery on the human mind, that it almost wholly effaces from it even the boasted characteristic of rationality."

This same writer, speaking of the particular interests of South Carolina, says :—

" It has been too common with us to search the records of other nations, to find precedents that may give sanction to our own errors, and lead us unwarily into confusion and ruin. It is our business to consult their histories, not with a view to tread right or wrong in their steps, but in order to investigate the real sources of the mischiefs that have befallen them, and to endeavor to escape the rocks which they have all unfortunately split upon. It is paying ourselves but a poor compliment, to say that we are incapable of profiting by others, and that, with all the information which is to be derived from their fatal experience, it is in vain for us to attempt to excel them. If, with all the peculiar advantages of our present situation, we are incapable of surpassing our predecessors, we must be a degenerate race indeed, and quite unworthy of those singular bounties of Heaven, which we are so unskilled or undesirous to turn to our benefit."

A recent number of Frazer's Magazine contains a well-timed and well-written article from the pen of Wm. Henry

Hurlbut,[25] of this State ; and from it we make the following extract :—

" As all sagacious observers of the operation of the system of slavery have demonstrated, the profitable employment of slave-labor is inconsistent with the development of agricultural science, and demands a continual supply of new and unexhausted soil. The slaveholder, investing his capital in the purchase of the laborers themselves, and not merely in soil and machines, paying his free laborers out of the profit, must depend for his continued and progressive prosperity upon the cheapness and facility with which he can transfer his slaves to fresh and fertile lands. An enormous additional item, namely, the price of slaves, being added to the cost of production, all other elements of that cost require to be proportionably smaller, or profits fail."

In an address delivered before the South Carolina Institute, in Charleston, Nov. 20th, 1856, Mr. B. F. Perry,[26] of Greenville, truthfully says :—

"It has been South Carolina's misfortune, in this utilitarian age, to have her greatest talents and most powerful energies directed to pursuits, which avail her nothing, in the way of wealth and prosperity. In the first settlement of a new country, agricultural industry necessarily absorbs all the time and occupation of its inhabitants. They must clear the forests and cultivate the earth, in order to make their bread. This is their first consideration. Then the mechanical arts, and manufactures, and commerce, must follow in the footsteps of agriculture, to insure either individual or national prosperity. No people can be highly prosperous without them. No people ever have been. Agriculture, alone, will not make or sustain a great people. The true policy of every people is to cultivate the earth, manufacture its products, and send them abroad, in exchange for those comforts and luxuries, and necessaries, which their own country and their own industry cannot give or make. The dependence of South Carolina on Europe and the Northern States for all the necessaries, comforts and luxuries, which the mechanic arts afford, has, in fact, drained her of her wealth, and made her positively poor, when compared with her sister States of the Confederacy. It is at once mortifying and alarming, to see and reflect on our own dependence in the mechanic arts and manufactures, on strangers and foreigners. In the Northern States their highest talents and energy have been diversified, and more profitably employed in developing the resources of the country, in making new inventions in the mechanic arts, and enriching the community with science and literature, commerce and manufactures."

THE VOICE OF GEORGIA.

Of the States strictly Southern, Georgia is, perhaps, the most thrifty. This prosperous condition of the State is mainly ascribable to her hundred thousand free white laborers—more than eighty-three thousand of whom are engaged in agricultural pursuits. In few other slave States are the non-slaveholders so little under the domination of the oligarchy. At best, however, even in the most liberal slave States, the social position of the non-slaveholding whites is but one short step in advance of that of the negroes ; and as there is, on the part of the oligarchy, a constantly increasing desire and effort to usurp greater power, the more we investigate the subject the more fully are we convinced that nothing but the speedy and utter annihilation of slavery from the entire nation, can save the masses of white people in the Southern States from ultimately falling to a political level with the blacks —both occupying the most abject and galling condition of servitude of which it is possible for the human mind to conceive.

Gen. Oglethorpe, under whose management the Colony

of Georgia was settled, in 1733, was bitterly opposed to the institution of slavery. In a letter to Granville Sharp, dated Oct. 13th, 1776, he says :—

"My friends and I settled the Colony of Georgia, and by charter were established trustees, to make laws, &c. We determined not to suffer slavery there. But the slave merchants and their adherents occasioned us not only much trouble, but at last got the then government to favor them. We would not suffer slavery, (which is against the Gospel, as well as the fundamental law of England,) to be authorized under our authority ; we refused, as trustees, to make a law permitting such a horrid crime. The government, finding the trustees resolved firmly not to concur with what they believed unjust, took away the charter by which no law could be passed without our consent."

On the 12th of January, 1775, in indorsing the proceedings of the first American Congress, among other resolutions, "the Representatives of the extensive District of Darien, in the Colony of Georgia" adopted the following :—

"5. To show the world that we are not influenced by any contracted or interested motives, but a general philanthropy for all mankind, of whatever climate, language, or complexion, we hereby declare our disapprobation and abhorrence of the unnatural practice of slavery in America, (however the uncultivated state of our country or other specious arguments may plead for it,) a practice founded in injustice and cruelty, and highly dangerous to our liberties, (as well as lives,) debasing part of our fellow creatures below men, and corrupting the virtue and morals of the rest; and is laying the basis of that liberty we contend for, (and which we pray the Almighty to continue to the latest posterity,) upon a very wrong foundation. We therefore resolve, at all times, to use our utmost endeavors for the manumission of our slaves in this Colony, upon the most safe and equitable footing for the masters and themselves

The Hon. Mr. Reid, of this State, in a speech delivered in Congress, Feb. 1, 1820, says :—

"I am not the panegyrist of slavery. It is an unnatural state, a dark cloud, which obscures half the lustre of our free institutions. For my own part, though surrounded by slavery from my cradle to the present moment, yet—

> 'I hate the touch of servile hands,
> I loathe the slaves who cringe around.' "

As an accompaniment to those lines, he might have uttered these :—

> "I would not have a slave to till my ground ;
> To carry me, to fan me while I sleep
> And tremble when I wake, for all the wealth
> That sinews bought and sold have ever earned."

Thus have we presented a comprehensive summary of the most unequivocal and irrefragable testimony of the South against the iniquitous institution of human slavery. What more can we say ? What more can we do ? We might fill a folio volume with similar extracts ; but we must forego the task ; the remainder of our space must be occupied with other arguments. In the foregoing excerpts is revealed to us, in language too plain to be misunderstood, the important fact that every truly great and good man the South has ever produced, has, with hopeful confidence, looked forward to the time when this entire continent shall be redeemed from the crime and the curse of slavery. Our noble self-sacrificing forefathers have performed their part, and performed it well. They have laid us a foundation as enduring as the earth itself ; in their dying moments they admonished us to carry out their designs in the upbuilding and completion of the superstructure. Let us obey their patriotic injunctions.

From each of the six original Southern States we have introduced the most ardent aspirations for liberty—the most positive condemnations of slavery. From each of the nine slave States which have been admitted into the Union since the organization of the General Government, we could introduce, from several of their wisest and best citizens, anti-slavery sentiments equally as strong and convincing as those that emanated from the great founders of our movement—Washington, Jefferson, Madison, Patrick Henry and the Randolphs. As we have already remarked, however, the limits of this chapter will not admit of the introduction of additional testimony from either of the old or of the new slave States.

The reader will not fail to observe that, in presenting these solid abolition doctrines of the South, we have been careful to make such quotations as triumphantly refute, in every particular, the more specious sophistries of the oligarchy.

The mention of the illustrious names above, reminds us of the fact, that the party newspapers, whose venal columns are eternally teeming with vituperation and slander, have long assured us that the Whig ship was to be steered by the Washington rudder, that the Democratic barque was to sail with the Jefferson compass, and that the Know-Nothing brig was to carry the Madison chart. Imposed upon by these monstrous falsehoods, we have, from time to time, been induced to engage passage on each of these corrupt and rickety old hulks ; but, in every instance, we have been basely swamped in the sea of slavery, and are alone indebted for our lives to the kindness of Heaven and the art of swimming. Washington the founder of the Whig party ! Jefferson the founder of the Democratic party ! Voltaire the founder of Christianity ! God forbid that man's heart should always continue to be the citadel of deception—that he should ever be to others the antipode of what he is to himself.

There is now in this country but one party that promises, in good faith, to put in practice the principles of Washington, Jefferson, Madison, and the other venerable Fathers of the Republic—the Republican party. To this party we pledge unswerving allegiance, so long as it shall continue to pursue the statism advocated by the great political prototypes above-mentioned, but no longer. We believe it is, as it ought to be, the desire, the determination, and the destiny of this party, to give the death-blow to slavery ; should future developments prove the party at variance with this belief—a belief, by the bye, which it has recently inspired in the breasts of little less than one and a half millions of the most intelligent and patriotic voters in America—we shall shake off the dust of our feet against it, and join one that will, in a summary manner, extirpate the intolerable grievance.

CHAPTER IV.

NORTHERN TESTIMONY.

THE best evidence that can be given of the enlightened patriotism and love of liberty in the Free States, is the fact that, at the Presidential election in 1856, they polled thirteen hundred thousand votes for the Republican candidate, JOHN C. FREMONT. This fact of itself seems to preclude the necessity of strengthening our cause with the individual testimony of even their greatest men. Having, however, adduced the most cogent and conclusive anti-slavery arguments from the Washingtons, the Jeffersons, the Madisons, the Randolphs, and the Clays of the South, we shall now proceed to enrich our pages with gems of Liberty from the Franklins, the Hamiltons, the Jays, the Adamses, and the Websters of the North. Too close attention cannot be paid to the words of wisdom which we have extracted from the works of these truly eminent and philosophic Statesmen. We will first listen to

THE VOICE OF FRANKLIN.

Dr. Franklin was the first president of "The Pennsylvania Society for promoting the Abolition of Slavery ;"

and it is now generally conceded that this was the first
regularly organized American abolition Society—it having
been formed as early as 1774, while we were yet subjects
of the British government. In 1790, in the name and on
behalf of this Society, Dr. Franklin, who was then within
a few months of the close of his life, drafted a memorial
"to the Senate and House of Representatives of the
United States," in which he said :—

"Your memorialists, particularly engaged in attending to the
distresses arising from slavery, believe it to be their indispensable duty to present this subject to your notice. They have observed, with real satisfaction, that many important and salutary
powers are vested in you, for 'promoting the welfare and securing the blessings of liberty to the people of the United States;
and as they conceive that these blessings ought rightfully to be
administered, without distinction of color, to all descriptions of
people, so they indulge themselves in the pleasing expectation
that nothing which can be done for the relief of the unhappy objects of their care, will be either omitted or delayed.

From a persuasion that equal liberty was originally the portion, and is still the birthright of all men, and influenced by the
strong ties of humanity and the principles of their institution,
your memorialists conceive themselves bound to use all justifiable endeavors to loosen the bonds of slavery, and promote a general enjoyment of the blessings of freedom. Under these impressions, they earnestly entreat your attention to the subject
of slavery ; that you will be pleased to countenance the restora-
tion to liberty of those unhappy men, who, alone, in this land of
freedom, are degraded into perpetual bondage, and who, amid the
general joy of surrounding freemen, are groaning in servile subjection ; that you will devise means for removing this inconsistency of character from the American people ; that you will promote mercy and justice towards this distressed race ; and that
you will step to the very verge of the power vested in you for

discouraging every species of traffic in the persons of our fellow-men."

On another occasion, he says:—"Slavery is an atrocious debasement of human nature."

THE VOICE OF HAMILTON.

Alexander Hamilton, the brilliant Statesman and financier, tells us that—

"The sacred rights of mankind are not to be rummaged for among old parchments or musty records. They are written as with a sunbeam, in the whole volume of human nature, by the hand of the Divinity itself, and can never be erased or obscured by mortal power."

Again, in 1774, addressing himself to an American Tory, he says :—

"The fundamental source of all your errors, sophisms, and false reasonings, is a total ignorance of the natural rights of mankind. Were you once to become acquainted with these, you could never entertain a thought, that all men are not, by nature, entitled to equal privileges. You would be convinced that natural liberty is the gift of the beneficent Creator to the whole human race ; and that civil liberty is founded on that."

THE VOICE OF JAY.

John Jay, first Chief Justice of the United States under the Constitution of 1789, in a letter to the Hon. Elias Boudinot, dated Nov. 17, 1819, says :—

"Little can be added to what has been said and written on the subject of slavery. I concur in the opinion that it ought not to be introduced nor permitted in any of the new States. and that it ought to be gradually diminished and finally abolished in all of them.

" To me, the constitutional authority of the Congress to prohi bit the migration and importation of slaves into any of the States, does not appear questionable.

" The first article of the Constitution specifies the legislative powers committed to the Congress. The 9th section of that article has these words : ' The *migration* or *importation* of such persons as any of the *now-existing* States shall think proper to admit, shall not be prohibited by the Congress prior to the year 1808, but a tax or duty may be imposed on such importation, not exceeding ten dollars for each person.'

" I understand the sense and meaning of this clause to be, that the power of the congress, although competent to prohibit such migration and importation, was to be exercised with respect to the *then* existing States, and them only, until the year 1808, but the Congress were at liberty to make such prohibitions as to any *new* State, which might in the *mean* time be established. And further, that from and after *that* period, they were authorized to make such prohibitions as to *all* the States, whether *new* or *old*.

" It will, I presume, be admitted, that slaves were the persons intended. The word slaves was avoided, probably on account of the existing toleration of slavery, and its discordancy with the principles of the Revolution, and from a consciousness of its being repugnant to the following positions in the Declaration of Independence : ' We hold these truths to be self-evident : that all men are created equal ; that they are endowed by their Creator with certain inalienable rights ; that among these are life, liberty, and the pursuit of happiness.' "

In a previous letter, written from Spain, whither he had been appointed as minister plenipotentiary, he says, speaking of the abolition of slavery :—

" Till America comes into this measure, her prayers to Heaven will be impious. This is a strong expression, but it is just. I believe that God governs the world, and I believe it to be a maxim in His, as in our Courts, tha those who ask for equity ought to do it."

WILLIAM JAY.

The Hon. Wm. Jay, a noble son of Chief Justice John Jay, says :—

" A crisis has arrived in which we must maintain our rights, or surrender them for ever. I speak not to abolitionists alone, but to all who value the liberty our fathers achieved. Do you ask what we have to do with slavery ? Let our muzzled presses answer—let the mobs excited against us by the merchants and politicians answer—let the gag laws threatened by our governors and legislatures answer, let the conduct of the National Government answer."

THE VOICE OF ADAMS.

From the Diary of John Quincy Adams, " the old man eloquent," we make the following extract :—

" It is among the evils of slavery, that it taints the very sources of moral principle. It establishes false estimates of virtue and vice ; for what can be more false and more heartless than this doctrine, which makes the first and holiest rights of humanity to depend upon the color of the skin ? It perverts human reason, and induces men endowed with logical powers to maintain that slavery is sanctioned by the Christian religion ; that slaves are happy and contented in their condition ; that between master and slave there are ties of mutual attachment and affection ; that the virtues of the master are refined and exalted by the degradation of the slave, while at the same time they vent execrations upon the slave-trade, curse Britain for having given them slaves, burn at the stake negroes convicted of crimes, for the terror of the example, and writhe in agonies of fear at the very mention of human rights as applicable to men of color."

THE VOICE OF WEBSTER.

In a speech wh'ch he delivered at Niblo's Garden, in

the city of New-York, on the 15th of March, 1847. Daniel
Webster, the great Expounder of the Constitution, said :—

"On the general question of slavery, a great part of the community is already strongly excited. The subject has not only
attracted attention as a question of politics, but it has struck a
far deeper one ahead. It has arrested the religious feeling of
the country, it has taken strong hold on the consciences of men.
He is a rash man, indeed, and little conversant with human nature, and especially has he an erroneous estimate of the character of the people of this country, who supposes that a feeling of
this kind is to be trifled with or despised. It will assuredly
cause itself to be respected. But to endeavor to coin it into silver, or retain its free expression, to seek to compress and confine it, warm as it is, and more heated as such endeavors would
inevitably render it—should this be attempted, I know nothing,
even in the Constitution or Union itself, which might not be en-
dangered by the explosion which might follow."

When discussing the Oregon Bill in 1848, he said :—

"I have made up my mind, for one, that under no circumstances will I consent to the further extension of the area of slavery
in the United States, or to the further increase of slave representation in the House of Representatives."

Under date of February 15th, 1850, in a letter to the
Rev. Mr. Furness, he says :—

"From my earliest youth I have regarded slavery as a great
moral and political evil. I think it unjust, repugnant to the natural equality of mankind, founded only in superior power ; a
standing and permanent conquest by the stronger over the
weaker. All pretense of defending it on the ground of different
races, I have ever condemned. I have even said that if the black
race is weaker, that is a reason against, not for, its subjection
and oppression. In a religious point of view I have ever regarded it, and even spoken of it, not as subject to any express denun-

ciation, either in the Old Testament or the New, but as opposed to the whole spirit of the Gospel and to the teachings of Jesus Christ. The religion of Jesus Christ is a religion of kindness, justice, and brotherly love. But slavery is not kindly affectionate; it does not seek anothers, and not its own; it does not let the oppressed go free. It is, as I have said, but a continual act of oppression. But then, such is the influence of a habit of thinking among men, and such is the influence of what has been long established, that even minds, religious and tenderly conscientious, such as would be shocked by any single act of oppression, in any single exercise of violence and unjust power, are not always moved by the reflection that slavery is a continual and permanent violation of human rights."

While delivering a speech at Buffalo, in the State of New York, in the summer of 1851, only about twelve months prior to his decease, he made use of the following emphatic words :—

"I never would consent, and never have consented, that there should be one foot of slave territory beyond what the old thirteen States had at the formation of the Union. Never, never ."

NOAH WEBSTER.

Noah Webster, the great American vocabulist, says :—

"That freedom is the sacred right of every man, whatever be his color, who has not forfeited it by some violation of municipal law, is a truth established by God himself, in the very creation of human beings. No time, no circumstance, no human power or policy can change the nature of this truth, nor repeal the fundamental laws of society, by which every man's right to liberty is guarantied. The act of enslaving men is always a violation of those great primary laws of society, by which alone, the master himself holds every particle of his own freedom."

11

THE VOICE OF CLINTON.

DeWitt Clinton, the father of the great system of internal improvements in the State of New York, speaking of despotism in Europe, and of slavery in America, asks :—

"Have not prescription and precedent—patriarchal dominion —divine right of kings and masters, been alternately called in to sanction the slavery of nations ? And would not all the despotisms of the ancient and modern world have vanished into air, if the natural equality of mankind had been properly understood and practiced ? * * * This declares that the same measure of justice ought to be measured out to all men, without regard to adventitious inequalities, and the intellectual and physical disparities which proceed from inexplicable causes."

THE VOICE OF WARREN.

Major General Joseph Warren, one of the truest patriots of the Revolution, and the first American officer of rank that fell in our contest with Great Britain, says :—

" That personal freedom is the natural right of every man, and that property, or an exclusive right to dispose of what he has honestly acquired by his own labor, necessarily arises therefrom, are truths that common sense has placed beyond the reach of contradiction. And no man, or body of men, can, without being guilty of flagrant injustice, claim a right to dispose of the persons or acquisitions of any other man or body of men, unless it can be proved that such a right has arisen from some compact between the parties, in which it has been explicitly and freely granted."

Otis, Hancock, Ames, and others, should be heard, but for the want of space. Volumes upon volumes might be filled with extracts similar to the above, from the works of the deceased Statesmen and sages of the North, who,

while living, proved themselves equal to the task of exterminating from their own States the matchless curse of
human slavery.   Such are the men who, though no longer
with us in the flesh, " still live."   A living principle—an
immortal interest—have they, invested in every great and
good work that distinguishes the free States.   The railroads, the canals, the telegraphs, the factories, the fleets
of merchant vessels, the magnificent cities, the scientific
modes of agriculture, the unrivaled institutions of learning,
and other striking evidences of progress and improvement
at the North, are, either directly or indirectly, the offspring of their gigantic intellects.   When, if ever, commerce, and manufactures, and agriculture, and great enterprises, and truth, and liberty, and justice, and magnanimity, shall have become obsolete terms, then their names
may possibly be forgotten, but not tell then.

An army of brave and worthy successors—champions
of Freedom now living, have the illustrious forefathers of
the North, in the persons of Garrison, Greeley, Giddings,
Goodell, Grow, and Gerrit Smith ; in Seward, Sumner,
Stowe, Raymond, Parker, and Phillips ; in Beecher, Banks,
Burlingame, Bryant, Hale, and Hildreth ; in Emerson,
Dayton, Thompson, Tappan, King and Cheever ; in Whittier, Wilson, Wade, Wayland, Weed, and Burleigh.   These
are the men whom, in connection with their learned and
eloquent compatriots, the Everetts, the Bancrofts, the
Prescotts, the Chapins, the Longfellows, and the Danas,
future historians, if faithful to their calling, will place on
record as America's true statesmen, literati, preachers,
philosophers, and philanthropists, of the present age.

In this connection, however, it may not be amiss to re-mark that the Homers, the Platos, the Bacons, the New-tons, the Shakspeares, the Miltons, the Blackstones, the Cuviers, the Humboldts, and the Macaulays of Amercia, have not yet been produced ; nor, in our humble judgment, will they be, until slavery shall have been overthrown and freedom established in the States of Virginia, Kentucky, and Tennessee. Upon the soil of those States, when free, or on other free soil crossed by about the same degrees of latitude, and not distant from the Appalachian chain of mountains, will, we believe, be nurtured into manhood, in the course of one or two centuries, perhaps, as great men as those mentioned above—greater, possibly, than any that have ever yet lived. Whence their ancestors may come, whether from Europe, from Asia, from Africa, from Oceanica, from North or South America, or from the islands of the sea, or whatever honorable vocation they may now be engaged in, matters nothing at all. For ought we know, their great-grandfathers are now humble artisans in Maine, or moneyed merchants in Massachu setts ; illiterate poor whites in Mississippi, or slave-driv-ing lordlings in South Carolina ; frugal farmers in Michi-gan, or millionaires in Illinois ; daring hunters in the Rocky Mountains, or metal-diggers in California ; peasants in France, or princes in Germany—no matter where, or what, the scope of country above-mentioned is, in our opinion, destined to be the birth-place of their illustrious offspring—the great savans of the New World, concern-ing whom we should console ourselves with the hope that they are not buried deeply in the matrix of the future.

CHAPTER V.

TESTIMONY OF THE NATIONS.

T. the true friends of freedom throughout the world, it is a pleasing thought, and one which, by being communicated to others, is well calculated to universalize the principles of liberty, that the great heroes, statesmen, and sages, of all ages and nations, ancient and modern, who have ever had occasion to speak of the institution of human slavery, have entered their most unequivocal and positive protests against it. To say that they disapproved of the system would not be sufficiently expressive of the utter detestation with which they uniformly regarded it. That they abhorred it as the vilest invention that the Evil-One has ever assisted bad men to concoct, is quite evident from the very tone and construction of their language.

Having, with much pleasure and profit, heard the testimony of America, through her representative men, we will now hear that of other nations, through their representative men—doubting not that we shall be more than remunerated for our time and trouble. We will first listen to

THE VOICE OF ENGLAND.

In the case of James Somerset, a negro who had been kidnapped in Africa, transported to Virginia, there sold into slavery, thence carried to England, as a waiting-boy, and there induced to institute proceedings against his master for the recovery of his freedom,

MANSFIELD says :—

"The state of slavery is of such a nature that it is incapable of being introduced on any reasons, moral or political, but only by positive law, which preserves its force long after the reasons, occasion, and time itself whence it was created, is erased from the memory. It is so odious that nothing can be sufficient to support it but positive law. Whatever inconveniences, therefore, may follow from the decision, I cannot say this case is allowed or approved by the law of England, and therefore the black must be discharged."

LOCKE says :—

"Slavery is so vile, so miserable a state of man, and so directly opposite to the generous temper and courage of our nation, that it is hard to be convinced that an Englishman, much less a gentleman, should plead for it."

Again, he says :—

"Though the earth, and all inferior creatures be common to all men, yet every man has a property in his own person ; this nobody has any right to but himself."

PITT says :—

"It is injustice to permit slavery to remain for a single hour."

FOX says :—

"With regard to a regulation of slavery, my detestation of its existence induces me to know no such thing as a regulation of robbery, and a restriction of murder. Personal freedom is a right of which he who deprives a fellow-creature is criminal in so depriving him, and he who withholds is no less criminal in withholding."

SHAKSPEARE says :—

" A man is master of his liberty."

Again, he says :—

"It is the curse of Kings, to be attended
By slaves, that take their humors for a warrant
To break within the bloody house of life,
And, on the winking of authority,
To understand a law; to know the meaning
Of dangerous majesty, when, perchance, it frowns
More upon humor than advised respect."

Again :—

" Heaven will one day free us from this slavery."

Again :—

"Liberty! Freedom! Tyranny is dead!—
Run hence, proclaim, cry it about the streets;
Some to the common pulpits, and cry out,
Liberty, freedom, and enfranchisement"

COWPER says :—

" Slaves cannot breathe in England; if their lungs
Receive our air, that moment they are free.
They touch our country and their shackles fall.
That's noble, and bespeaks a nation proud
And jealous of the blessing. Spread it then,
And let it circulate through every vein
Of all your Empire, that where Britain's power
Is felt, mankind may feel her mercy too!"

MILTON asks :—

" Where is the beauty to see,
    Like the sun-brilliant brow of a nation when free ?"

Again, he says :—

" If our fathers promised for themselves, to make themselves
slaves, they could make no such promise for us."

Again :—

" Since, therefore, the law is chiefly right reason, if we are
bound to obey a magistrate as a minister of God, by the very same
reason and the very same law, we ought to resist a tyrant, and
minister of the devil."

DR. JOHNSON says :—

" No man is by nature the property of another.   The rights of
nature must be some way forfeited before they can justly be taken
away."

DR. PRICE says :—

" If you have a right to make another man a slave, he has a
right to make you a slave."

BLACKSTONE says :—

" If neither captivity nor contract can, by the plain law of nature and reason, reduce the parent to a state of slavery, much
less can they reduce the offspring."

Again, he says :—

" The primary aim of society is to protect individuals in the
enjoyment of those absolute rights which were vested in them by
the immutable laws of nature.   Hence it follows that the first
and primary end of human laws is to maintain those absolute
rights of individuals."

Again :—

" If any human law shall allow or require us to commit crime, we are bound to transgress that human law, or else we must offend both the natural and divine."

COKE says :—

" What the Parliament doth, shall be holden for naught, whenever it shall enact that which is contrary to the rights of nature."

HAMPDEN says :—

" The essence of all law is justice. What is not justice is not law ; and what is not law, ought not to be obeyed."

HARRINGTON says :—

" All men naturally, are equal ; for though nature with a noble variety has made different features and lineaments of men, yet as to freedom, she has made every one alike, and given them the same desires."

FORTESCUE says :—

" Those rights which God and nature have established, and which are therefore called natural rights, such as life and liberty, need not the aid of human laws to be more effectually invested in every man than they are ; neither do they receive any additional strength when declared by the municipal laws to be inviolable. On the contrary, no human power has any authority to abridge or destroy them, unless the owner himself shall commit some act that amounts to a forfeiture."

Again, he says :—

" The law, therefore, which supports slavery and opposes liberty, must necessarily be condemned as cruel, for every feeling of human nature advocates liberty. Slavery is introduced by human wickedness, but God advocates liberty, by the nature which he has given to man '

11*

BROUGHAM says :—

" Tell me not of rights—talk not of the property of the planter in his slaves. I deny the right ; I acknowledge not the property. In vain you tell me of laws that sanction such a claim. There is a law above all the enactments of human codes, the same throughout the world, the same in all times ; it is the law written by the finger of God on the hearts of men ; and by that law, unchangeable and eternal, while men despise fraud, and loathe rapine, and abhor blood, they shall reject with indignation the wild and guilty phantasy that man can hold property in man."

THE VOICE OF IRELAND.

BURKE says :—

" Slavery is a state so improper, so degrading, and so ruinous to the feelings and capacities of human nature, that it ought not to be suffered to exist."

CURRAN says :—

"I speak in the spirit of British law, which makes liberty commensurate with and inseparable from British soil ; which proclaims even to the stranger and the sojourner, the moment he sets his foot upon British earth, that the ground on which he treads is holy and consecrated by the genius of Universal Emancipation. No matter in what language his doom may have been pronounced ; no matter what complexion, incompatible with freedom, an Indian or African sun may have burnt upon him ; no matter in what disastrous battle his liberty may have been cloven down ; no matter with what solemnities he may have been devoted upon the altar of slavery, the moment he touches the sacred soil of Britain, the altar and the god sink together in the dust ; his soul walks abroad in her own majesty ; and he stands redeemed, regenerated and disenthralled by the irresistible genius of Universa Emancipation,'

The Dublin University Magazine for December, 1856, says :—

"The United States must learn, from the example of Rome, that Christianity and the pagan institution of slavery cannot co-exist together. The Republic must take her side and choose her favorite child ; for if she love the one, she must hate the other."

THE VOICE OF SCOTLAND.

BEATTIE says :—

"Slavery is inconsistent with the dearest and most essential rights of man's nature; it is detrimental to virtue and industry ; it hardens the heart to those tender sympathies which form the most lovely part of human character; it involves the inno-cent in hopeless misery, in order to procure wealth and pleasure for the authors of that misery; it seeks to degrade into brutes beings whom the Lord of Heaven and Earth endowed with ra-tional souls, and created for immortality; in short, it is utterly repugnant to every principle of reason, religion, humanity, and conscience. It is impossible for a considerate and unprejudiced mind, to think of slavery without horror."

MILLER says :—

"The human mind revolts at a serious discussion of the sub-ject of slavery. Every individual, whatever be his country or complexion, is entitled to freedom."

MACKNIGHT says :—

"Men-stealers are inserted among the daring criminals against whom the law of God directed its awful curses. These were persons who kidnapped men to sell them for slaves ; and this practice seems inseparable from the other iniquities and oppres-sions of slavery; nor can a slave dealer easily keep free from this criminality, if indeed the receiver is as bad as the thief."

THE VOICE OF FRANCE.

LAFAYETTE says :—

"I would never have drawn my sword in the cause o America, if I could have conceived that thereby I was founding a land of slavery."

Again, while in the prison of Magdeburg, he says :—

"I know not what disposition has been made of my plantation at Cayenne ; but I hope Madame de Lafayette will take care that the negroes who cultivate it shall preserve their liberty."

O. LAFAYETTE, grandson of General Lafayette, in a letter under date of April 26th, 1851, says :—

"This great question of the Abolition of Negro Slavery, which has my entire sympathy, appears to me to have established its importance throughout the world. At the present time, the States of the Peninsula, if I do not deceive myself, are the only European powers who still continue to possess slaves ; and America, while continuing to uphold slavery, feels daily, more and more how heavily it weighs upon her destinies."

MONTESQUIEU asks :—

"What civil law can restrain a slave from running away, since he is not a member of society ?"

Again, he says :—

"Slavery is contrary to the fundamental principles of all societies."

Again :—

"In democracies, where they are all upon an equality, slavery is contrary to the principles of the Constitution."

Again :—

" Nothing puts one nearer the condition of a brute than a ways to see freemen and not be free."

Again :—

" Even the earth itself, which teems with profusion under the cultivating hand of the free born laborer, shrinks into barrenness from the contaminating sweat of a slave."

LOUIS X. issued the following edict :—

" As all men are by nature free born, and as this Kingdom is called the Kingdom of Franks, (freemen) it shall be so in reality. It is therefore decreed that enfranchisement shall be granted throughout the whole Kingdom upon just and reasonable terms."

BUFFON says :—

" It is apparent that the unfortunate negroes are endowed with excellent hearts, and possess the seeds of every human virtue.   I cannot write their history without lamenting their miserable condition."   " Humanity revolts at those odious oppressions that result from avarice."

ROUSSEAU says :—

" The terms *slavery* and *right*, contradict and exclude each other."

BRISSOT says :—

" Slavery, in all its forms, in all its degrees, is a violation of divine law, and a degradation of human nature."

THE VOICE OF GERMANY.

GROTIUS says :—

" Those are men-stealers who abduct, keep, sell or buy slaves or free men.   To steal a man is the highest kind of theft."

GOETHE says :—

Such busy multitudes I fain would see
Stand upon free soil with a people free."

LUTHER says :—

"Unjust violence is, by no means, the ordinance of God, and therefore can bind no one in conscience and right, to obey, whether the command comes from pope, emperor, king or master."

An able German writer of the present day, says, in a recent letter to his friends in this country :—

"Consider that the cause of American liberty is the cause of universal liberty; its failure, a triumph of despotism everywhere. Remember that while American liberty is the great argument of European Democracy, American slavery is the greater argument of its despotism. Remember that all our actions should be governed by the golden rule, whether individual, social, or political; and no government, and, above all, no republican government, is safe in the hands of men that practically deny that rule. Will you support by your vote a system that recognizes property of man in man? A system which sanctions the sale of the child by its own father, regardless of the purpose of the buyer? What need is there to present to you the unmitigated wrong of slavery? It is the shame of our age that argument is needed against slavery.

"Liberty is no exclusive property; it is the property of mankind of all ages. She is immortal, though crushed, can never die; though banished, she will return; though fettered, she will yet be free."

THE VOICE OF ITALY.

CICERO says :—

"By the grand laws of nature, all men are born free, and this law is universally binding upon all men."

Again, he says :—

"Eternal justice is the basis of all human laws."

Again :—

"Law is not something wrought out by man's ingenuity, nor is it a decree of the people, but it is something eternal, governing the world by the wisdom of its commands and prohibitions."

Again :—

"Whatever is just is also the true law, nor can this true law be abrogated by any written enactments."

Again :—

"If there be such a power in the decrees and commands of fools, that the nature of things is changed by their votes, why do they not decree that what is bad and pernicious shall be regarded as good and wholesome, or why, if the law can make wrong right, can it not make bad good ?"

Again :—

"Those who have made pernicious and unjust decrees, have made anything rather than laws."

Again :—

"The law of all nations forbids one man to pursue his advantage at the expense of another."

LACTANTIUS says :—

"Justice teaches men to know God and to love men, to love and assist one another, being all equally the children of God."

LEO X. says :—

"Not only does the Christian religion, but nature herself cry out against the state of slavery."

THE VOICE OF GREECE.

SOCRATES says :—

" Slavery is a system of outrage and robbery."

ARISTOTLE says :—

" It is neither for the good, nor is it just, seeing all men are by nature alike, and equal, that one should be lord and master over others."

POLYBIUS says :—

'None but unprincipled and beastly men in society assume the mastery over their fellows, as it is among bulls, bears, and cocks."

PLATO says :—

" Slavery is a system of the most complete injustice."

From each of the above, and from other nations, additional testimony is at hand ; but, for reasons already assigned, we forbear to introduce it. Corroborative of the correctness of the position which we have assumed, even Persia has a voice, which may be easily recognized in the tones of her immortal Cyrus, who says :

" To fight, in order not to be made a slave, is noble."

Than Great Britain no nation has more heartily or honorably repented of the crime of slavery—no nation, on the perception of its error, has ever acted with more prompt magnanimity to its outraged and unhappy bondsmen. Entered to her credit, many precious jewels of liberty remain in our possession, ready to be delivered when called for ; of their value some idea may be formed, when we state that they are filigreed with such names as Wilberforce, Buxton, Granville, Grattan, Camden, Clarkson, Sharp, Sheridan, Sidney, Martin, and Macaulay.

Virginia, the Carolinas, and other Southern States, which are provided with *republican (!)* forms of government, and which have abolished freedom, should learn, from the history of the monarchal governments of the Old World, if not from the example of the more liberal and enlightened portions of the New, how to abolish slavery. The lesson is before them in a variety of exceedingly interesting forms, and, sooner or later, they must learn it, either voluntarily or by compulsion. Virginia, in particular, is a spoilt child, having been the pet of the General Government for the last sixty-eight years; and like most other spoilt children, she has become froward, peevish, perverse, sulky and irreverent—not caring to know her duties, and failing to perform even those which she does know. Her superiors perceive that the abolition of slavery would be a blessing to her; she is, however, either too ignorant to understand the truth, or else, as is the more probable, her false pride and obstinacy restrain her from acknowledging it. What is to be done? Shall ignorance, or prejudice, or obduracy, or willful meanness, triumph over knowledge, and liberality, and guilelessness, and laudable enterprise? No, never! Assured that Virginia and all the other slaveholding States are doing wrong every day, it is our duty to make them do right, if we have the power; and we believe we have the power now resident within their own borders. What are the opinions, generally, of the non-slaveholding whites? Let them speak.

CHAPTER VI.

TESTIMONY OF THE CHURCHES.

"Run hence, proclaim, cry it about the streets,
Some to the common pulpits, and cry out,
Liberty, freedom, and enfranchisement!"

IN quest of arguments against slavery, we have perused
the works of several eminent Christian writers of different
denominations, and we now proceed to lay before the reader
the result of a portion of our labor. As it is the special
object of this chapter to operate on, to correct and cleanse
the consciences of slaveholding professors of religion, we
shall adduce testimony only from the five churches to
which they, in their satanic piety, mostly belong — the
Presbyterian, the Episcopal, the Baptist, the Methodist,
and the Roman Catholic—all of which, thank Heaven, are
destined, at no distant day, to become thoroughly aboli-
tionized. With few exceptions, all the other Christian
sects are, as they should be, avowedly and inflexibly opposed to the inhuman institution of slavery. The Con-
gregational, the Quaker, the Lutheran, the Dutch and
German Reformed, the Unitarian, and the Universalist,
especially, are all honorable, able, and eloquent defenders

of the natural rights of man. We will begin by introducing a mass of

PRESBYTERIAN TESTIMONY.

The Rev. Albert Barnes, of Philadelphia, one of the most learned Presbyterian preachers and commentators of the day, says :-

"There is a deep and growing conviction in the minds of the mass of mankind, that slavery violates the great laws of our nature; that it is contrary to the dictates of humanity ; that it is essentially unjust, oppressive, and cruel ; that it invades the rights of liberty with which the Author of our being has endowed all human beings ; and that, in all the forms in which it has ever existed, it has been impossible to guard it from what its friends and advocates would call '*abuses* of the system.' It is a violation of the first sentiments expressed in our Declaration of Independence, and on which our fathers founded the vindication of their own conduct in an appeal to arms. It is at war with all that a man claims for himself and for his own children ; and it is opposed to all the struggles of mankind, in all ages, for freedom. The claims of humanity plead against it. The struggles for freedom everywhere in our world condemn it. The instinctive feeling in every man's own bosom in regard to himself is a condemnation of it. The noblest deeds of valor, and of patriotism in our own land, and in all lands where men have struggled for freedom, are a condemnation of the system. All that is noble in man is opposed to it; all that is base, oppressive, and cruel, pleads for it.

"The spirit of the New Testament is against slavery, and the principles of the New Testament, if fairly applied, would abolish it. In the New Testament no man is commanded to purchase and own a slave ; no man is commended as adding anything to the evidences of his Christian character, or as performing the appropriate duty of a Christian, for owning one. No where in the New Testament is the institution referred to as a good one, or as a desirable one. It is commonly—indeed, it is almost universally—conceded that the proper application of the principles of the New Testament would abolish slavery everywhere, or that. the state of things which will exist when the Gospel shall be fairly applied to all the relations of life, slavery will not be found among those relations.

"Let slavery be removed from the church, and let the voice of the church, with one accord, be lifted up in favor of freedom ; let the church be wholly detached from the institution, and let there be adopted by all its ministers and members an interpretation of the Bible—as I believe there may be and ought to be—that shall be in accordance with the deep-seated principles of our nature in favor of freedom, and with our own aspirations for liberty, and with the sentiments of the world in its onward progress in regard to human rights, and not only would a very material objection against the Bible be taken away—and one which would be fatal if it were well founded—but the establishment of a very strong argument *in favor* of the Bible, as a revelation from God, would be the direct result of such a position."

Thomas Scott, the celebrated English Presbyterian Commentator, says :—

" To number the persons of men with beasts, sheep, and horses, as the stock of a farm, or with bales of goods, as the cargo of a ship, is, no doubt, a most detestable and anti-Christian practice."

From a resolution denunciatory of slavery, unanimously adopted by the General Assembly of the Presbyterian Church, in 1818, we make the following extract :—

" We consider the voluntary enslaving of one part of the human race by another as a gross violation of the most precious and sacred rights of human nature, as utterly inconsistent with the law of God, which requires us to love our neighbor as ourselves, and as totally irreconcilable with the spirit and principles of the Gospel of Christ, which enjoins that ' all things whatsoever ye would that men should do to you, do ye even so to them.' * * * We rejoice that the church to which we belong commenced, as early as any other in this country, the good work of endeavoring to put an end to slavery, and that in the same work many of its members have ever since been, and now are, among the most active, vigorous, and efficient laborers. * * * We earnestly exhort them to continue, and, if possible, to increase, their exertions to effect a total abolition of slavery."

A Committee of the Synod of Kentucky, in an address to the Presbyterians of that State, says :—

"That our negroes will be worse off, if emancipated, is, we feel, but a specious pretext for lulling our own pangs of conscience, and answering the argument of the philanthropist. None of us believe that God has so created a whole race that it is better for them to remain in perpetual bondage."

EPISCOPAL TESTIMONY.

BISHOP HORSLEY says :—

"Slavery is injustice, which no consideration of policy can extenuate."

BISHOP BUTLER says :—

"Despicable as the negroes may appear in our eyes, they are the creatures of God, and of the race of mankind, for whom Christ died, and it is inexcusable to keep them in ignorance of the end for which they were made, and of the means whereby they may become partakers of the general redemption."

BISHOP PORTEUS says :—

"The Bible classes men-stealers or slave-traders among the murderers of fathers and mothers, and the most profane criminals on earth."

John Jay, Esq., of the City of New-York—a most exemplary Episcopalian—in a pamphlet entitled, "Thoughts on

the Duty of the Episcopal Church, in Relation to Slavery,"
says :—

" Alas ! for the expectation that she would conform to the spirit
of her ancient mother ! She has not merely remained a mute and
careless spectator of this great conflict of truth and justice with
hypocrisy and cruelty, but her very priests and deacons may be
seen ministering at the altar of slavery, offering their talents and
influence at its unholy shrine, and openly repeating the awful
blasphemy, that the precepts of our Saviour sanction the system
of American slavery. Her Northern clergy, with rare exceptions,
whatever they may feel on the subject, rebuke it neither in public nor in private, and her periodicals, far from advancing the
progress of abolition, at times oppose our societies, impliedly defending slavery, as not incompatible with Christianity, and occasionally withholding information useful to the cause of freedom."

A writer in a late number of " The Anti-Slavery Church
man," published in Geneva, Wisconsin, speaking of a cer
tain portion of the New Testament, says :—

" This passage of Paul places necessary work in the hands of
Gospel ministers. If they preach the whole Gospel, they must
preach what this passage enjoins—and if they do this, they must
preach against American slavery. Its being connected with politics does not shield them. Political connections cannot place
sin under protection. They cannot throw around it guards that
the public teachers of morals may not pass. Sin is a violation
of God's law—and God's law must be proclaimed and enforced
at all hazards. This is the business of the messenger of God,
and if anything stands in its way, it is his right, rather it is his
solemn commission, to go forward—straightway to overpass the
lines that would shut him out, and utter his warnings. Many
sins there are, that, in like manner, might be shielded. Fashion,
and rank, and business, are doing their part to keep much sin in
respectability, and excuse it from the attacks of God's ministers.
But what are these, that they should seal a minister's lips—what
more are the wishes of politicians ?"

For further testimony from this branch of the Christian system, if desired, we refer the reader to the Rev. Dudley A. Tyng, the Rev. Evan M. Johnson, and the Rev. J. McNamara,—a l Broad Church Episcopalians, whose magic eloquence and irresistible arguments bid fair, at an early day, to win over to the paths of progressive freedom, truth, justice and humanity, the greater number of their High and Low Church brethren.

BAPTIST TESTIMONY.

Concerning a certain text, the Rev. Mr. Brisbane, once a slaveholding Baptist in South Carolina, says :—

"Paul was speaking of the law as having been made for men-stealers. Where is the record of that law? It is in Exodus xxi. 16, and in these words: 'He that stealeth a man, and selleth him, or if he be found in his possession, he shall surely be put to death.' Here it will be perceived that it was a crime to sell the man, for which the seller must suffer death. But it was no less a crime to hold him as a slave, for this also was punishable with death. A man may be kidnapped out of slavery into freedom. There was no law against that. And why? Because kidnapping a slave and placing him in a condition of freedom, was only to restore him to his lost rights. But if the man who takes him becomes a slaveholder, or a slave seller, then he is a criminal, liable to the penalty of death, because he robs the man of liberty. Perhaps some will say this law was only applicable to the first holder of the slave, that is, the original kidnapper, but not to his successors who might have purchased or inherited him. But what is kidnapping? Suppose I propose to a neighbor to give him a certain sum of money if he will steal a white child in Carolina and deliver him to me. He steals him; I pay him the money upon his delivering the child to me. Is it not my act as fully as his? Am I not also the thief? But does it alter the case whether I agree before hand or not, to pay him for the child? He steals him, and then sells him to me. He is found by his parents in my hands. Will it avail me to say I purchased him and paid my money for him? Will it not be asked, Do you not know that a white person is not merchantable? And shall I not have to pay the damage for detaining that child in my service as a slave? Assuredly, not only in the eyes of the law, but in the judgment of the whole community, I would be regarded a criminal. So when one man steals another and offers him for sale, no one, in view of the Divine law, can buy him, for the reason that the Divine law forbids that man shall in the first place be made a merchantable article. The inquiry must be, if I buy, I buy in violation of the Divine law, and it will not do for me to plead that I bought him. I have him in possession, and that is enough, God condemns me for it as a man-stealer. My having him in possession is evidence against me, and the Mosaic law says, if he be found in my hands, I must die. Now, when Paul said the law was made for men-stealers, was it not also saying the law was made for slaveholders? I am not intending to apply this term in harsh spirit. But I am bound, as I fear God to speak what I am satisfied is the true meaning of the apostle."

In his "Elements of Moral Science," the Rev. Francis Wayland, D.D., one of the most erudite and distinguished Baptists now living, says :—

"Domestic slavery proceeds upon the principle that the master has a right to control the actions, physical and intellectual, of the slave, for his own, that is, the master's individual benefit; and, of course, that the happiness of the master, when it comes in competition with the happiness of the slave, extinguishes in the latter the right to pursue it. It supposes, at best, that the relation between master and slave, is not that which exists between man and man, but is a modification, at least, of that which exists between man and the brutes.

"Now, this manifestly supposes that the two classes of beings are created with dissimilar rights: that the master posseses rights which have never been conceded by the slave; and that the slave has no rights at all over the means of happiness which God has given him, whenever these means of happiness can be rendered available to the service of his master. It supposes that the Creator intended one human being to govern the physical, intellectual and moral actions of as many other human beings as by purchase he can bring within his physical power; and that one human being may thus acquire a right to sacrifice the happiness of any number of other human beings, for the purpose of promoting his own. Slavery thus violates the personal liberty of man as a physical, intellectual, and moral being.

"It purports to give to the master a right to control the physical labor of the slave, not for the sake of the happiness of the slave, but for the sake of the happiness of the master. It subjects the amount of labor, and the kind of labor, and the remuneration for labor, entirely to the will of the one party, to the entire exclusion of the will of the other party.

"But if this right in the master over the slave be conceded, there are of course conceded all other rights necessary to insure its possession. Hence, inasmuch as the slave can be held in this condition only while he remains in the lowest state of mental imbecility, it supposes the master to have the right to control his intellectual development, just as far as may be necessary to secure entire subjection. Thus, it supposes the slave to have no right to use his intellect for the production of his own happiness; but, only to use it in such manner as may conduce to his master's profit.

And, moreover, inasmuch as the acquisition of the knowledge of his duty to God could not be freely made without the acquisition of other knowledge, which might, if universally diffused, endanger the control of the master, slavery supposes the master to have the right to determine how much knowledge of his duty a slave shall obtain, the manner in which he shall obtain it, and the manner in which he shall discharge that duty after he shall have obtained a knowledge of it. It thus subjects the duty of man to God entirely to the will of man; and this for the sake of pecuniary profit. It renders the eternal happiness of the one party subservient to the temporal happiness of the other. And

12

this principle is commonly carried into effect in slaveL.>lding countries.

If argument were necessary to show that such a system as this must be at variance with the ordinance of God, it might be easily drawn from the effects which it produces both upon *morals* and *national wealth.*

Its effects must be disastrous upon the *morals* of both parties. By presenting objects on whom passion may be satiated without resistance and without redress, it cultivates in the master, pride, anger, cruelty, selfishness and licentiousness. By accustoming the slave to subject his moral principles to the will of another, it tends to abolish in him all moral distinction ; and thus fosters in him lying, deceit, hypocrisy, dishonesty, and a willingness to yield himself up to minister to the appetites of his master.

The effects of slavery on *national wealth,* may be easily seen from the following considerations :—

Instead of imposing upon all the necessity of labor, it restricts the number of laborers, that is of producers, within the smallest possible limit, by rendering labor disgraceful.

It takes from the laborers the natural stimulus to labor, namely, the desire in the individual of improving his condition ; and sub- stitutes, in the place of it, that motive which is the least opera- tive and the least constant, namely, the fear of punishment with- out the consciousness of moral delinquency.

It removes, as far as possible, from both parties, the disposition and the motives to frugality. Neither the master learns frugality from the necessity of labor, nor the slave from the benefits which it confers. And here, while the one party wastes from ignorance of the laws of acquisition, and the other because he can have no motive to economy, capital must accumulate but slowly, if indeed it accumulate at all.

No country, not of great fertility, can long sustain a large slave population. Soils of more than ordinary fertility can not sustain it long, after the richness of the soil has been exhausted. Hence, slavery in this country is acknowledged to have impoverished many of our most valuable districts ; and, hence, it is continually migrating from the older settlements, to those new and untilled regions, where the accumulated manure of centuries of vegetation has formed a soil, whose productiveness may, for a while, sustain a system at variance with the laws of nature. Many of our free and of our slaveholding States were peopled at about the same time. The slaveholding States had every advantage, both in soil and climate, over their neighbors. And yet the accumulation of capital has been greatly in favor of the latter. If any one doubts whether this difference be owing to the use of slave labor, let him ask himself what would have been the condition of the slaveholding States, at this moment, if they had been inhabited, from the beginning, by an industrious yeomanry; each one holding his own land, and each one tilling it with the labor of his own hands.

The moral precepts of the Bible are diametrically opposed to slavery. They are, Thou shalt love thy *neighbor* as *thyself*, and *all things whatsoever* ye would that men should do unto you, do ye even so unto them.

The application of these precepts is universal. Our neighbor is *every one whom we may benefit*. The obligation respects *all things whatsoever*. The precept, then, manifestly, extends to *men, as men*, or *men in every condition;* and if to all things whatsoever, certainly to a thing so important as the right to personal liberty.

Again. By this precept, it is made our duty to cherish as tender and delicate a respect for the right which the meanest individual posseses over the means of happiness bestowed upon him by God, as we cherish for our own right over our own means of happiness, or as we desire any other individual to cherish for it. Now, were this precept obeyed, it is manifest that slavery could not in fact exist for a single instant. The principle of the precept is absolutely subversive of the principle of slavery. That of the one is the entire equality of right; that of the other, the entire absorption of the rights of one in the rights of the other.

If any one doubts respecting the bearing of the Scripture precept upon this case, a few plain questions may throw additional light upon the subject. For instance,—

" Do the precepts and the spirit of the Gospel allow me to derive my support from a system which extorts labor from my fellow-men, without allowing them any voice in the equivalent which they shall receive; and which can only be sustained by keeping them in a state of mental degradation, and by shutting them out, in a great degree, from the means of salvation?

"Would the master be willing that another person should subject him to slavery, for the same reasons, and on the same grounds, that he holds his slave in bondage?

"Would the Gospel allow us, if it were in our power, to reduce our fellow-citizens of our own color to slavery? If the gospel be diametrically opposed to the *principle* of slavery, it must be opposed to the *practice* of slavery; and therefore, were the principles of the gospel fully adopted, slavery could not exist.

"The very course which the gospel takes on this subject, seems to have been the only one that could have been taken, in order to effect the universal abolition of slavery. The gospel was designed, not for one race, or for one time, but for all races, and for all times. It looked not at the abolition of this form of evil for that age alone, but for its universal abolition. Hence, the important object of its Author was, to gain it a lodgment in every part of the known world; so that, by its universal diffusion among all classes of society, it might quietly and peacefully modify and subdue the evil passions of men; and thus, without violence, work a revolution in the whole mass of mankind.

"If the system be wrong, as we have endeavored to show, if it be at variance with our duty both to God and to man, it must be abandoned. If it be asked when, I ask again, when shall a man begin to cease doing wrong? Is not the answer, *immediately*? If a man is injuring *us*, do we ever doubt as to the time when *he* ought to cease? There is then no doubt in respect to the time when we ought to cease inflicting injury upon others."

Abraham Booth, an eminent theological writer of the Baptist persuasion, says :—

"I have not a stronger conviction of scarcely anything, than that slaveholding (except when the slave has forfeited his liberty by crimes against society) is wicked and inconsistent with Christian character. To me it is evident, that whoever would purchase an innocent black man to make him a slave, would with equal readiness purchase a white one for the same purpose, could he do it with equal impunity, and no more disgrace."

At a meeting of the General Committee of the Baptists of Virginia, in 1789, the following resolution was offered by Eld. John Leland, and adopted :—

" *Resolved*, That slavery is a violent deprivation of the rights of nature, and inconsistent with republican government, and therefore we recommend it to our brethren to make use of every measure to extirpate this horrid evil from the land ; and pray Almighty God that our honorable legislature may have it in their power to proclaim the great jubilee, consistent with the principles of good policy."

METHODIST TESTIMONY.

John Wesley, the celebrated founder of Methodism, says :—

" Men buyers are exactly on a level with men stealers."

Again, he says :—

" American Slavery is the vilest that ever saw the sun ; it constitutes the sum of all villanies."

The learned Dr. Adam Clarke, author of a voluminous commentary on the Scriptures, says :—

" Slave-dealers, whether those who carry on the traffic in human flesh and blood ; or those who steal a person in order to sell him into bondage ; or those who buy such stolen men or women, no matter of what color, or what country ; or the nations who legalize or connive at such traffic ; all these are men-stealers, and God classes them with the most flagitious of mortals."

One of the rules laid down in the Methodist Discipline, as amended in 1784, was as follows :—

"Every member of our Society who has slaves in his possession, shall, within twelve months after notice given to him by the assistant, legally execute and record an instrument, whereby he emancipates and sets free every slave in his possession."

Another rule was in these words :—

"No person holding slaves shall in future be admitted into Society, or to the Lord's Supper, till he previously complies with these rules concerning slavery."

The answer to the question—"What shall be done with those who buy or sell slaves, or give them away"—is couched in the following language :—

"They are immediately to be expelled, unless they buy them on purpose to free them."

In 1785, the voice of this church was heard as follows :—

"We do hold in the deepest abhorrence the practice of slavery, and shall not cease to seek its destruction, by all wise and prudent means."

In 1797, the Discipline contained the following wholesome paragraph :—

"The preachers and other members of our Society are re quested to consider the subject of negro slavery, with deep attention, and that they impart to the General Conference, through the medium of the Yearly Conferences, or otherwise, any important thoughts on the subject, that the Conference may have full light, in order to take further steps towards eradicating this enormous evil from that part of the Church of God with which they are connected. The Annual Conferences are directed to draw up addresses for the gradual emancipation of the slaves, to the legislatures of those States in which no general laws have been passed for that purpose. These addresses shall urge, in the most respectful but pointed manner, the necessity of a law for the gradual emancipation of slaves. Proper committees shall be appointed by the Annual Conferences, out of the most respectable of our friends, for conducting the business ; and presiding elders, elders, deacons, and traveling preachers, shall procure as many proper signatures as possible to the addresses, and give all the assistance in their power, in every respect, to aid the committees, and to forward the blessed undertaking. Let this be continued from year to year, till the desired end be accomplished."

CATHOLIC TESTIMONY.

It has been only about twenty years since Pope Gregory XVI. immortalized himself by issuing the famous Bull against slavery, from which the following is an extract :—

"Placed as we are on the Supreme seat of the apostles, and acting, though by no merits of our own, as the vicegerent of Jesus Christ, the Son of God, who, through his great mercy, condescended to make himself man, and to die for the redemption of the world, we regard as a duty devolving on our pastoral functions, that we endeavor to turn aside our faithful flocks entirely from the inhuman traffic in negroes, or any other human beings whatever. * * * In progress of time, as the clouds of heathen superstition became gradually dispersed, circumstances reached that point, that during several centuries there were no slaves allowed amongst the great majority of the Christian nations ; but with grief we are compelled to add, that there afterwards arose, even among the faithful, a race of men, who, basely blinded by the appetite and desire of sordid 'ucr' did not hesitate to reduce, in remote regions of the earth, Indians, negroes, and other wretched beings, to the misery of slavery ; or, finding the trade established and augmented, to assist the shameful crime of others. Nor did many of the most glorious of the Roman Pontiffs omit severely to reprove their conduct, as injurious to their souls' health, and disgraceful to the Christian name. Among these may be especially quoted the bull of Paul III., which bears the date of the 29th of May, 1537, addressed to the Cardinal Archbishop of Toledo, and another still more comprehensive, by Urban VIII., dated the 22d of April, 1636, to the collector Jurius of the Apostolic chamber in Portugal, most severely castigating by name those who presumed to subject either East or West Indians to slavery, to sell, buy, exchange, or give them away, to separate them from their wives and children, despoil them of their goods and property, to bring or transmit them to other places, or by any means to deprive them of liberty, or retain them in slavery; also most severely castigating those who should presume or dare to afford council, aid, favor or assistance, under any pretext, or borrowed color, to those doing the aforesaid; or should preach or teach that it is lawful, or should otherwise presume or dare to co-operate, by any possible means, with the aforesaid. *   *   * Wherefore, we, desiring to divert this disgrace from the whole confines of Christianity, having summoned several of our venerable brothers, their Eminences the Cardinals, of the H. R. Church, to our council, and, having maturely deliberated on the whole matter, pursuing the footsteps of our predecessors, admonished by our apostolical authority, and urgently invoke in the Lord, all Christians, of whatever condition, that none henceforth dare to subject to slavery, unjustly persecute, or despoil of their goods, Indians, negroes, or other classes of men, or be accessories to others, or furnish them aid or assistance in so doing; and on no account henceforth to exercise that inhuman traffic by which negroes are reduced to slavery, as if they were not men, but automata or chattels, and are sold in defiance of all the laws of justice and humanity, and devoted to severe and intolerable labors. We further reprobate, by our apostolical authority, all the above-described offences as utterly unworthy of the Christian name; and by the same authority we rigidly prohibit and interdict all and every individual, whether ecclesiastical or laical, from presuming to defend that commerce in negro slaves under pretence or borrowed color, or to teach or publish in any manner, publicly or privately, things contrary to the admonitions which we have given in these letters.

"And, finally, that these, our letters, may be rendered more apparent to all, and that no person may allege any ignorance

thereof, we decree and order that it shall be published according
to custom, and copies thereof be properly affixed to the gates of
St. Peter and of the Apostolic Chancel, every and in like manner
to the General Court of Mount Citatorio, and in the field of the
Campus Florae and also through the city, by one of our heralds,
according to aforesaid custom.

"Given at Rome, at the Palace of Santa Maria Major, under
the seal of the fisherman, on the 3d day of December, 1837, and
in the ninth year of our pontificate.

"Countersigned by Cardinal A. Lambruschini."

We have already quoted the language of Pope Leo X.,
who says :—

"Not only does the Christian religion, but nature herself cry
out against the State of slavery."

The Abbe Raynal says :—

"He who supports slavery is the enemy of the human race.
He divides it into two societies of legal assassins, the oppressors
and the oppressed. I shall not be afraid to cite to the tribunal
of reason and justice those governments which tolerate this
cruelty, or which even are not ashamed to make it the basis of
their power."

From the proceedings of a Massachusetts Anti-slavery
Convention in 1855, we make the following extract :—

"Henry Kemp, a Roman Catholic, came forward to defend the
Romish Church in reply to Mr. Foster. He claimed that the
Catholic Church is thoroughly anti-slavery—as thoroughly as
even his friend Foster."

Thus manfully do men of pure hearts and noble minds,
whether in Church or State, and without regard to sect or
party, lift up their voices against the wicked and pernicious
institution of human slavery. Thus they speak, and thus
12*

they are obliged to speak, if they speak at all ; it is only the voice of Nature, Justice, Truth, and Love, that issues from them. The divine principle in man prompts him to speak and strike for Freedom ; the diabolical principle within him prompts him to speak and strike for slavery.

From those churches which are now—as all churches ought to be, and will be, ere the world becomes Christianized—thoroughly imbued with the principles of freedom, we do not, as already intimated, deem it particularly necessary to bring forward new arguments in opposition to slavery. If, however, the reader would be pleased to hear from the churches to which we chiefly allude—and, by the bye, he might hear from them with much profit to himself —we respectfully refer him to Henry Ward Beecher, George B. Cheever, Joseph P. Thompson, Theodore Parker, E. H. Chapin, and H. W. Bellows, of the North, and to M. D. Conway, John G. Fee, James S. Davis, Daniel Wilson, and W. E. Lincoln, of the South. All these reverend gentlemen, ministers of different denominations, feel it their duty to preach against slavery, and, to their honor be it said, they do preach against it with unabated zeal and success. Our earnest prayer is, that Heaven may enable them, their cotemporaries and successors, to preach against it with such energy and effect, as will cause it to disappear forever from the soil of our Republic.

CHAPTER VII.

BIBLE TESTIMONY.

EVERY person who has read the Bible, and who has a proper understanding of its leading moral precepts, feels, in his own conscience, that it is the only original and complete anti-slavery text-book. In a crude state of society— in a barbarous age—when men were in a manner destitute of wholesome laws, either human or divine, it is possible that a mild form of slavery may have been tolerated, and even regulated, as an institution clothed with the importance of temporary recognition ; but the Deity never approved it, and, for the very reason that it is impossible for him to do wrong, he never will, never can approve it. The worst system of servitude of which we have any account in the Bible—and, by the way, it furnishes no account of anything so bad as slavery (the evil-one and his hot home alone excepted)—was far less rigorous and atrocious than that now established in the Southern States of this Confederacy. Even that system, however, the worst, which seems to have been practiced to a considerable extent by those venerable old fogies, Abraham, Isaac, and Jacob, was one of the monstrous inventions of Satan that God "winked" at; and, to the mind of the biblical scholar, nothing can be more evident than that He determined of old, that it should, in due time, be abolished. To say that the Bible sanctions slavery is to say that the sun loves darkness; to say that one man was created to domineer over another is to call in question the justice, mercy, and goodness of God.

We will now listen to a limited number of the

PRECEPTS AND SAYINGS OF THE OLD TESTAMENT.

"Proclaim liberty throughout all the land, unto all the inhabitants thereof."

"Let the oppressed go free."

"Thou shalt love thy neighbor as thyself."

"Thou shalt not respect the person of the poor, nor honor the person of the mighty; but in righteousness shalt thou judge thy neighbor."

"The wages of him that is hired shall not abide with thee all night until the morning."

"Envy thou not the oppressor, and choose none of his ways."

"Do justice to the afflicted and needy; rid them out of the hand of the wicked."

"Execute judgment and justice; take away your exactions from my people, saith the Lord God."

"Therefore thus saith the Lord; ye have not hearkened unto me, in proclaiming liberty, every one to his brother, and every man to his neighbor: behold, I proclaim a liberty for you, saith the Lord, to the sword, to the pestilence, and to the famine; and I will make you to be removed into all the kingdoms of the earth."

" He that stealeth a man, and selleth him, or if he be found in his hand, he shall surely be put to death."

" Whoso stoppeth his ears at the cry of the poor, he also shall cry, but shall not be heard."

" He that oppresseth the poor reproacheth his Maker."

" I will be a swift witness against the sorcerers, and against the adulterers, and against false swearers, and against those that oppress the hireling in his wages, the widow, and the fatherless, and that turn aside the stranger from his right, and fear not me, saith the Lord of Hosts."

" As the partridge setteth on eggs, and hatcheth them not ; so he that getteth riches, and not by right, shall leave them in the midst of his days, and at his end shall be a fool."

And now we will listen to a few selected

PRECEPTS AND SAYINGS OF THE NEW TESTAMENT.

" Call no man master, neither be ye called masters."

" All things whatsoever ye would that men should do to you do ye even so to them."

" Be kindly affectionate one to another with brotherly love ; in honor preferring one another."

" Do good to all men, as ye have opportunity."

" Stand fast therefore in the liberty wherewith Christ hath made you free, and be not entangled again with the yoke of bondage."

" If thou mayest be made free, use it rather."

" The laborer is worthy of his hire."

" Where the Spirit of the Lord is, there is liberty."

Some years ago a clerical lickspittle of the slave power

had the temerity to publish a book or pamphlet entitled "Bible Defence of Slavery,"[27] which the Baltimore *Sun*, in the course of a caustic criticism, handled in the following manner :—

"Bible defence of slavery! There is no such thing as a Bible defence of slavery at the present day. Slavery in the United States is a social institution, originating in the convenience and cupidity of our ancestors, existing by State laws, and recognized to a certain extent—for the recovery of slave property—by the Constitution. And nobody would pretend that, if it were inexpedient and unprofitable for any man or any State to continue to hold slaves, they would be bound to do so on the ground of a "Bible defence" of it. Slavery is recorded in the Bible, and approved, with many degrading characteristics. War is recorded in the Bible, and approved, under what seems to us the extreme of cruelty. But are slavery and war to *endure* for ever because we find them in the Bible? or are they to *cease* at once and for ever because the Bible inculcates peace and brotherhood?"

Thus, in the last five chapters inclusive, have we introduced a mass of anti-slavery arguments, human and divine, that will stand, irrefutable and convincing, as long as the earth itself shall continue to revolve in its orbit. Aside from unaffected truthfulness and candor, no merit is claimed for anything we have said on our own account. With the best of motives, and in the language of nature more than that of art, we have simply given utterance to the honest convictions of our heart—being impelled to it by a long-harbored and unmistakable sense of duty which grew stronger and deeper as the days passed away.

If half the time which has been spent in collecting and arranging these testimonies had been occupied in the composition of original matter, the weight of paper and binding and the number of pages would have been much greater, but the value and the effect of the contents would have been far less. From the first, our leading motive has been to convince our fellow-citizens of the South, non-slaveholders and slaveholders, that slavery, whether considered in all its bearings, or, setting aside the moral aspect of the question, and looking at it in only a pecuniary point of view, is impolitic, unprofitable, and degrading; how well, thus far, we have succeeded in our undertaking, time will, perhaps, fully disclose.

In the words of a contemporaneous German writer, whose language we readily and heartily endorse, "It is the shame of our age that argument is needed against slavery." Taking things as they are, however, argument being needed, we have offered it; and we have offered it from such sources as will, in our honest opinion, confound the devil and his incarnate confederates.

These testimonies, culled from the accumulated wisdom of nearly six thousand centuries, beginning with the great and good men of our own time, and running back through distant ages to Saint Paul, Saint John, and Saint Luke, to Cicero, Plato, and Socrates, to Solomon, David, and Moses, and even to the Deity himself, are the pillars of strength and beauty upon which the popularity of our work will, in all probability, be principally based. If the ablest writers of the Old Testament; if the eloquent prophets of old; if the renowned philosophers of Greece and Rome; if the heavenly-minded authors and compilers of the New Testament; if the illustrious poets and prose-writers, heroes, statesmen, sages of all nations, ancient

and modern ; if God himself and the hosts of learned
ministers whom he has commissioned to proclaim his
word—if all these are wrong, then we are wrong ; on the
other hand, however, if they are right, we are right ; for,
in effect, we only repeat and endeavor to enforce their
precepts.

If we are in error, we desire to be corrected ; and, if it
is not asking too much, we respectfully request the advocates of slavery to favor us with an *exposé* of what they,
in their one-sided view of things, conceive to be the advantages of their favorite and peculiar institution. Such
an *exposé*, if skillfully executed, would doubtless be regarded as the funniest novel of the times—a fit production, if not too immoral in its tendencies, to be incorporated into the next edition of D'Israeli's curiosities of
literature.

CHAPTER VIII.

FREE FIGURES AND SLAVE.

UNDER this heading we propose to introduce the remainder of the more important statistics of the Free and of the Slave States ;—especially those that relate to Commerce, Manufactures, Internal Improvements, Education and Religion.   Originally it was our intention to devote a separate chapter to each of the industrial and moral interests above-named : but other considerations have so greatly encroached on our space, that we are compelled to modify our design.   To the thoughtful and discriminating reader, however, the chief statistics which follow will be none the less interesting for not being the subjects of annotations.

At present, all we ask of pro-slavery men, no matter in what part of the world they may reside, is to look these figures fairly in the face.   We wish them to do it, in the first instance, not on the platforms of public debate, where the exercise of eloquence is too often characterized by violent passion and subterfuge, but in their own private apartments, where no eye save that of the All-seeing One will rest upon them, and where, in considering the relations which they sustain to the past, the present, and the future, an opportunity will be afforded them of securing that most valuable of all possessions attainable on earth, a conscience void of offence toward God and man.

Each separate table or particular compilation of statistics will afford food for at least an hour's profitable reflection ; indeed, the more these figures are studied, and the better they are understood, the sooner will the author's object be accomplished,—the sooner will the genius of Universal Liberty dispel the dark clouds of slavery.

TABLE NO. XXVI.

TONNAGE, EXPORTS AND IMPORTS OF THE FREE STATES—1855.

States.	Tonnage.	Exports.	Imports.
California	92,623	$8,224,066	$5,951,379
Connecticut..	137,170	878,874	636,826
Illinois..	53,797	547,053	54,509
Indiana.	3,698		
Iowa....			
Maine..............	806,587	4,851,207	2,927,443
Massachusetts.......	970,727	28,190,925	45,113,774
Michigan............	69,490	568,091	281,379
New Hampshire......	30,330	1,523	17,786
New Jersey..	121,020	687	1,473
New York...........	1,404,221	113,731,238	164,776,511
Ohio.....	91,607	847,143	600,656
Pennsylvania.....	397,768	6,274,338	15,300,935
Rhode Island....	51,038	336,023	536,387
Vermont............	6,915	2,895,468	591,593
Wisconsin..........	15,624	174,057	48,159
	4,252,615	$167,520,693	$236,847,810

TABLE NO. XXVII.

TONNAGE, EXPORTS AND IMPORTS OF THE SLAVE STATES—1855.

States.	Tonnage.	Exports.	Imports.
Alabama....	36,274	$14,270,585	$619,964
Arkansas..... ....,			
Delaware..	19,186	68,087	5,821
Florida.....	14,835	1,403,594	45,998
Georgia.	29,505	7,543,519	273,716
Kentucky....	22,680		
Louisiana	204,149	55,367,962	12,900,821
Maryland....	234,805	10,395,984	7,788,949
Mississippi..	2,475		1,661
Missouri...	60,592		
North Carolina...	60,077	433,818	243,083
South Carolina...	60,935	12,700,250	1,588,542
Tennessee.........	8,404		
Texas.	8,812	916,961	262,568
Virginia...	92,788	4,379,928	855,405
	855,517	$107,480,688	$24,586,528

TABLE NO. XXVIII.

PRODUCT OF MANUFACTURES IN THE FREE STATES—1850.

States.	Val. of Annual products.	Capital invested.	Hands employed.
California	$12,862,522	$1,006,197	3,964
Connecticut...........	45,110,102	23,890,348	47,770
Illinois...............	17,236,073	6,385,387	12,065
Indiana...............	18,922,651	7,941,602	14,342
Iowa................	3,551,783	1,292,875	1,707
Maine...............	24,664,135	14,700,452	28,078
Massachusetts........	151,137,145	83,357,642	165,938
Michigan............	10,976,894	6,534,250	9,290
New Hampshire......	23,164,503	18,242,114	27,092
New Jersey..........	39,713,586	22,184,730	37,311
New York...........	237,597,249	99,904,405	199,349
Ohio...............	62,647,259	29,019,538	51,489
Pennsylvania........	155,044,910	94,473,810	146,766
Rhode Island........	22,093,258	12,923,176	20,881
Vermont............	8,570,920	5,001,377	8,445
Wisconsin........ .	9,293,068	3,382,148	6,089
	$842,586,058	$430,240,051	780,576

TABLE NO. XXIX.

PRODUCT OF MANUFACTURES IN THE SLAVE STATES—1850.

States.	Val. of Annual products.	Capital invested.	Hands employed.
Alabama............	$4,538,878	$3,450,606	4,936
Arkansas	607,436	324,065	903
Delaware............	4,649,296	2,978,945	3,888
Florida	668,338	547,060	991
Georgia.............	7,086,525	5,460,483	8,378
Kentucky...........	24,588,483	12,350,734	24,385
Louisiana.	7,320,948	5,318,074	6,437
Maryland	32,477,702	14,753,143	30,124
Mississippi..........	2,972,038	1,833,420	3,173
Missouri.	23,749,265	9,079,695	16,850
North Carolina.......	9,111,245	7,252,225	12,444
South Carolina.......	7,063,513	6,056,865	7,009
Tennesse............	9,728,438	6,975,279	12,032
Texas.,.............	1,165,538	539,290	1,066
Virginia........	29,705,387	18,109,993	29,109
	$165,413,027	$95,029,879	161,733

TABLE NO. XXX.

MILES OF CANALS AND RAILROADS IN THE FREE STATES—
1854–1857.

States.	Canals, miles, 1854.	Railroads, miles, 1857.	Cost of Railroads, 1855.
California		22	
Connecticut..	61	600	$25,224,191
Illinois.....	100	2,524	55,663,656
Indiana.	367	1,806	29,585,923
Iowa........		253	2,300,000
Maine...	50	442	13,749,021
Massachusetts...	100	1,285	59,167,781
Michigan........		600	22,370,397
New Hampshire..	11	645	15,860,949
New Jersey..	147	472	13,840,030
New York........	989	2,700	111,882,503
Ohio....	921	2,869	67,798,202
Pennsylvania...	936	2,407	94,657,675
Rhode Island........ ..		85	2,614,484
Vermont.....		515	17,998,835
Wisconsin.		629	5,600,000
	3,682	17,855	$538,313,647

TABLE NO. XXXI.

MILES OF CANALS AND RAILROADS IN THE SLAVE STATES—
1854–1857.

States.	Canals, miles, 1854.	Railroads, miles, 1857.	Cost of Railroads, 1855.
Alabama....	51	484	$3,986,208
Arkansas..			
Delaware...	14	120	600,000
Florida.....		86	250,000
Georgia....	28	1,062	17,034,802
Kentucky...........	486	306	6,179,072
Louisiana......	101	263	1,731,000
Maryland...........	184	597	12,654,333
Mississippi....		410	4,520,000
Missouri....		189	1,000,000
North Carolina..	13	612	6,847,213
South Carolina..	50	706	13,547,093
Tennessee.		508	10,436,610
Texas.....		57	16,466,250
Virginia.....	184	1,479	
	1,116	6,859	$95,252,581

TABLE NO. XXXII.

BANK CAPITAL IN THE FREE AND IN THE SLAVE STATES— 1855.

Free States.		Slave States.	
California		Alabama........	$2,296,400
Connecticut......	$15,597,891	Arkansas....	
Illinois....	2,513,790	Delaware....	1,393,175
Indiana.	7,281,934	Florida.....	
Iowa....		Georgia.	13,413,100
Maine..........	7,301,252	Kentucky....	10,369,717
Massachusetts...	54,492,660	Louisiana	20,179,107
Michigan........	980,416	Maryland.......	10,411,874
New Hampshire..	3,626,000	Mississippi......	240,165
New Jersey..	5,314,885	Missouri...	1,215,398
New York.......	83,773,288	North Carolina...	5,205,073
Ohio.....	7,166,581	South Carolina...	16,603,253
Pennsylvania....	19,864,825	Tennessee........	6,717,848
Rhode Island....	17,511,162	Texas.	
Vermont.......	3,275,656	Virginia........	14,033,838
Wisconsin.......	1,400,000		
Total.....	$230,100,340	Total.	$102,078,940

TABLE NO. XXXIII.

MILITIA FORCE OF THE FREE AND THE SLAVE STATES—1852.

Free States.		Slave States.	
California		Alabama........	76,662
Connecticut......	51,649	Arkansas	17,137
Illinois.........	170,359	Delaware........	9,229
Indiana.........	53,918	Florida	12,122
Iowa......... ..		Georgia.........	57,312
Maine..	62,588	Kentucky.......	81,840
Massachusetts....	119,690	Louisiana.	43,823
Michigan........	63,938	Maryland	46,864
New Hampshire..	32,151	Mississippi......	36,084
New Jersey......	39,171	Missouri.	61,000
New York........	265,293	North Carolina...	79,448
Ohio........	176,455	South Carolina...	55,209
Pennsylvania.....	276,070	Tennessee.......	71,252
Rhode Island....	14,443	Texas.,.........	19,766
Vermont...... ...	23,915	Virginia...	125,128
Wisconsin...	32,203		
Total.....	1,381,843	Total...	792,876

TABLE NO. XXXIV.

POST OFFICE OPERATIONS IN THE FREE STATES—1855.

States.	Stamps sold.	Total Postage collected.	Cost of Trans. the mails.
California...............	$81,437	$234,591	$135,386
Connecticut.............	79,284	179,230	81,462
Illinois.................	105,252	279,887	280,038
Indiana.................	60,578	180,405	190,480
Iowa....................	28,198	82,420	84,428
Maine...................	60,165	151,358	82,218
Massachusetts..........	259,062	532,184	153,091
Michigan................	49,763	142,188	148,204
New-Hampshire.........	38,387	95,609	46,631
New-Jersey.............	31,495	109,697	80,084
New-York..............	542,498	1,383,157	481,410
Ohio....................	167,958	452,643	421,870
Pennsylvania...........	217,293	583,013	251,833
Rhode Island...........	30,291	58,624	13,891
Vermont.	36,314	92,816	64,437
Wisconsin..............	33,538	112,903	92,842
	$1,719,513	$4,670,725	$2,608,295

TABLE NO. XXXV.

POST OFFICE OPERATIONS IN THE SLAVE STATES—1855.

States.	Stamps sold.	Total Postage collected.	Cost of Trans. the mails.
Alabama...............	$44,514	$104,514	226.816
Arkansas..............	8,941	30,664	117,659
Delaware..............	7,298	19,644	9,243
Florida................	8,764	19,275	77,553
Georgia...............	73,880	149,063	216,003
Kentucky.............	55,694	130,067	144,161
Louisiana.............	50,778	133,753	133,810
Maryland..............	77,743	191,485	192.743
Mississippi............	31,182	78,739	170,785
Missouri..............	53,742	139,652	185,096
North Carolina........	34,235	72,759	148,249
South Carolina........	47,368	91,600	192.216
Tennessee.............	48,377	103,686	116,091
Texas.................	24,530	70,436	209,936
Virginia..............	96,799	217,861	245,592
	$666,845	$1,553,198	$2,385,953

TABLE NO. XXXVI.

PUBLIC SCHOOLS OF THE FREE STATES—1850.

States.	Number.	Teachers.	Pupils.
California.	2	2	49
Connecticut..	1,656	1,787	71,269
Illinois..	4,052	4,248	125,725
Indiana.	4,822	4,860	161,500
Iowa....	740	828	29,556
Maine....	4,042	5,540	192,815
Massachusetts.	3,679	4,443	176,475
Michigan......	2,714	3,231	110,455
New Hampshire..	2,381	3,013	75,643
New Jersey............	1,473	1,674	77,930
New York.	11,580	13,965	675,221
Ohio....	11,661	12,886	484,153
Pennsylvania......	9,061	10,024	413,706
Rhode Island	416	518	23,130
Vermont	2,731	4,173	93,457
Wisconsin.	1,423	1,529	58,817
	62,433	72,621	2,769,901

TABLE NO. XXXVII.

PUBLIC SCHOOLS IN THE SLAVE STATES—1850.

States.	Number.	Teachers.	Pupils.
Alabama...............	1,152	1,195	28,380
Arkansas...............	353	355	8,493
Delaware	194	214	8,970
Florida...............	69	73	1,878
Georgia	1,251	1,265	32,705
Kentucky	2,234	2,306	71,429
Louisiana	664	822	25,046
Maryland	898	986	33,111
Mississippi	782	826	18,746
Missouri...............	1,570	1,620	51,754
North Carolina....	2,657	2,730	104,095
South Carolina...........	724	739	17,838
Tennessee...............	2,680	2,819	104,117
Texas	349	360	7,946
Virginia...............	2,930	2,997	67,353
	18,507	19,307	581,861

TABLE NO. XXXVIII.

LIBRARIES OTHER THAN PRIVATE IN THE FREE STATES—1850.

States.	Number.	Volumes.
California		
Connecticut................	164	165,318
Illinois...................	152	62,486
Indiana...................	151	68,403
Iowa......................	32	5,790
Maine.....................	236	121,969
Massachusetts.............	1,462	684,015
Michigan..................	417	107,943
New Hampshire.............	129	85,759
New Jersey................	128	80,885
New York..................	11,013	1,760,820
Ohio......................	352	186,826
Pennsylvania..............	393	363,400
Rhode Island..............	96	104,342
Vermont...................	96	64,641
Wisconsin.................	72	21,020
	14,911	3,888,234

TABLE NO. XXXIX.

LIBRARIES OTHER THAN PRIVATE IN THE SLAVE STATES—1850.

States.	Number.	Volumes.
Alabama...................	56	20,623
Arkansas..................	3	420
Delaware..................	17	17,950
Florida...................	7	2,660
Georgia...................	38	31,788
Kentucky..................	80	79,466
Louisiana.................	10	26,800
Maryland..................	124	125,042
Mississippi...............	117	21,737
Missouri..................	97	75,056
North Carolina...........	38	29,592
South Carolina...........	26	107,472
Tennessee.................	34	22,896
Texas.....................	12	4,230
Virginia..................	54	88,462
	695	649,577

TABLE NO. XL.

NEWSPAPERS AND PERIODICALS PUBLISHED IN THE
FREE STATES—1850.

States.	Number.	Copies Printed annually.
California	7	761,200
Connecticut.	46	4,267,932
Illinois...	107	5,102,276
Indiana...	107	4,316,828
Iowa....	29	1,512,800
Maine....	49	4,203,064
Massachusetts...	202	64,820,564
Michigan....	58	3,247,736
New Hampshire..	38	3,067,552
New Jersey....	51	4,098,678
New York....	428	115,385,473
Ohio...	261	30,473,407
Pennsylvania..	309	84,898,672
Rhode Island....	19	2,756,950
Vermont....	35	2,567,662
Wisconsin...	46	2,665,487
	1,790	334,146,281

TABLE NO. XLI.

NEWSPAPERS AND PERIODICALS PUBLISHED IN THE
SLAVE STATES—1850.

States.	Number.	Copies Printed annually.
Alabama...	60	2,662,741
Arkansas...	9	377,000
Delaware	10	421,200
Florida....	10	319,800
Georgia	51	4,070,868
Kentucky	62	6,582,838
Louisiana	55	12,416,224
Maryland	68	19,612,724
Mississippi...	50	1,752,504
Missouri....	61	6,195,560
North Carolina....	51	2,020,564
South Carolina	46	7,145,930
Tennessee	50	6,940,750
Texas	34	1,296,924
Virginia..	87	9,223,068
	704	81,038,693

TABLE NO. XLII.

ILLITERATE WHITE ADULTS IN THE FREE STATES—1850.

States.	Native.	Foreign.	Total.
California.	2,201	2,917	5,118
Connecticut..	826	4,013	4,739
Illinois..	34,107	5,947	40,054
Indiana.	67,275	3,265	70,540
Iowa....	7,043	1,077	8,120
Maine.....	1,999	4,148	6,147
Massachusetts.	1,055	26,484	27,539
Michigan.....	4,903	3,009	7,912
New Hampshire..	893	2,064	2,957
New Jersey.....	8,370	5,878	14,248
New York.	23,241	68,052	91,293
Ohio....	51,968	9,062	61,030
Pennsylvania....	41,944	24,989	66,928
Rhode Island....	981	2,359	3,340
Vermont	565	5,624	6,189
Wisconsin.	1,459	4,902	6,361
	248,725	173,790	422,515

TABLE NO. XLIII.

ILLITERATE WHITE ADULTS IN THE SLAVE STATES—1850.

States.	Native.	Foreign.	Total.
Alabama....	33,618	139	33,757
Arkansas......	16,792	27	16,819
Delaware......	4,132	404	4,536
Florida......	3,564	295	3,859
Georgia.	40,794	406	41,200
Kentucky.....	64,340	2,347	66,687
Louisiana.	14,950	6,271	21,221
Maryland..	17,364	3,451	20,815
Mississippi....	13,324	81	13,405
Missouri....	34,420	1,861	36,281
North Carolina....	73,226	340	73,566
South Carolina....	15,580	104	15,684
Tennessee.	77,017	505	77,522
Texas....	8,037	2,488	10,525
Virginia.....	75,868	1,137	77,005
	493,026	19,856	512,882

TABLE NO. XLIV.

NATIONAL POLITICAL POWER OF THE FREE STATES—1857.

States.	Senators.	Rep. in lower House Cong.	Electoral votes.
California	2	2	4
Connecticut..	2	4	6
Illinois.................	2	9	11
Indiana.	2	11	13
Iowa...................	2	2	4
Maine...	2	6	8
Massachusetts..	2	11	13
Michigan.......	2	4	6
New Hampshire..	2	3	5
New Jersey..............	2	5	7
New York..	2	33	35
Ohio.....	2	21	23
Pennsylvania............	2	25	27
Rhode Island............	2	2	4
Vermont.....	2	3	5
Wisconsin.	2	3	5
	32	144	176

TABLE NO. XLV.

NATIONAL POLITICAL POWER OF THE SLAVE STATES—1857.

States.	Senators.	Rep. in lower House Cong.	Electoral votes.
Alabama....	2	7	9
Arkansas..	2	2	4
Delaware................	2	1	3
Florida.................	2	1	3
Georgia....	2	8	10
Kentucky...............	2	10	12
Louisiana....	2	4	6
Maryland................	2	6	8
Mississippi..............	2	5	7
Missouri....	2	7	9
North Carolina..	2	8	10
South Carolina..........	2	6	8
Tennessee.	2	10	12
Texas.....	2	2	4
Virginia....	2	13	15
	30	90	120

TABLE NO. XLVI.

POPULAR VOTE FOR PRESIDENT BY THE FREE STATES—1856.

States.	Republican. Fremont.	American. Fillmore.	Democratic. Buchanan.	Total.
California	20,339	35,113	51,925	107,377
Connecticut......	42,715	2,615	34,995	80,325
Illinois..	96,189	37,444	105,348	238,981
Indiana.	94,375	22,386	118,670	235,431
Iowa....	43,954	9,180	36,170	89,304
Maine...........	67,379	3,325	39,080	109,784
Massachusetts...	108,190	19,626	39,240	167,056
Michigan........	71,762	1,660	52,136	125,558
New Hampshire..	38,345	422	32,789	71,556
New Jersey......	28,338	24,115	46,943	99,396
New York.......	276,907	124,604	195,878	597,389
Ohio.....	187,497	28,126	170,874	386,497
Pennsylvania....	147,510	82,175	230,710	460,395
Rhode Island....	11,467	1,675	6,580	19,722
Vermont........	39,561	545	10,569	50,675
Wisconsin.......	66,090	579	52,843	119,512
	1,340,618	393,590	1,224,750	2,958,958

TABLE NO. XLVII.

POPULAR VOTE FOR PRESIDENT BY THE SLAVE STATES—1856.

States.	Republican. Fremont.	American. Fillmore.	Democratic. Buchanan.	Total.
Alabama........		28,552	46,739	75,291
Arkansas		10,787	21,910	32,697
Delaware........	308	6,175	8,004	14,487
Florida..........		4,833	6,358	11,191
Georgia.........		42,228	56,578	98,806
Kentucky.......	314	67,416	74,642	142,372
Louisiana.		20,709	22,164	42,873
Maryland	281	47,460	39,115	86,856
Mississippi......		24,195	35,446	59,641
Missouri.		48,524	58,164	106,688
North Carolina...		36,886	48,246	85,132
South Carolina*..				
Tennessee.......		66,178	73,638	139,816
Texas..........		15,244	28,757	44,001
Virginia...	291	60,278	89,826	150,395
	. 1,194	479,465	609,587	1,090,246

* No popular vote.

TABLE NO. XLVIII.

VALUE OF CHURCHES IN THE FREE AND IN THE SLAVE STATES—
1850.

Free States.		Slave States.	
California	$288,400	Alabama	
Connecticut........	3,599,330	Arkansas....	$1,244,741
Illinois...	1,532,305	Delaware..	149,686
Indiana...	1,568,906	Florida.....	340,345
Iowa.....	235,412	Georgia.	192,600
Maine........	1,794,209	Kentucky...	1,827,112
Massachusetts.....	10,504,888	Louisiana	2,295,353
Michigan.........	793,180	Maryland.........	1,940,495
New Hampshire...	1,483,266	Mississippi.......	3,974,116
New Jersey...... ..	3,712,863	Missouri...	832,622
New York........	21,539,561	North Carolina....	1,730,135
Ohio.............	5,860,059	South Carolina....	907,785
Pennsylvania......	11,853,291	Tennessee.........	2,181,476
Rhode Island......	1,293,600	Texas.	1,246,951
Vermont......	1,251,655	Virginia..	408,944
Wisconsin...	512,552		2,902,220
Total......	$67,773,477	Total.	$21,674,581

TABLE NO. XLIX

PATENTS ISSUED ON NEW INVENTIONS IN THE FREE AND IN
THE SLAVE STATES—1856.

Free States.		Slave States.	
California.	13	Alabama	11
Connecticut........	142	Arkansas.........	
Illinois..	93	Delaware.........	8
Indiana.	67	Florida	3
Iowa.....	14	Georgia	13
Maine.....	42	Kentucky	26
Massachusetts....	331	Louisiana..	30
Michigan.........	22	Maryland........	49
New Hampshire...	43	Mississippi	8
New Jersey.......	78	Missouri	32
New York........	592	North Carolina....	9
Ohio....	139	South Carolina....	10
Pennsylvania.....	267	Tennessee...	23
Rhode Island.....	18	Texas	4
Vermont	35	Virginia.	42
Wisconsin........	33		
Total......	1,929	Total.....	268

TABLE NO. L.

BIBLE CAUSE AND TRACT CAUSE IN THE FREE STATES—1855.

States.	Contribu. for the Bible Cause.	Contribu. for the Tract Cause.
California...	$1,900	$ 5
Connecticut...	24,528	15,872
Illinois....	28,403	3,786
Indiana....	6,755	1,491
Iowa.......	4,216	2,005
Maine....	5,449	2,981
Massachusetts....	43,444	11,492
Michigan....	5,554	1,114
New-Hampshire...	6,271	1,288
New-Jersey....	15,475	8,546
New-York....	123,386	61,233
Ohio....	25,758	9,576
Pennsylvania...	25,360	12,121
Rhode Island....	2,669	2,121
Vermont..	5,709	2,867
Wisconsin....	4,790	474
	$319,667	$131,972

TABLE NO. LI.

BIBLE CAUSE AND TRACT CAUSE IN THE SLAVE STATES—1855.

States.	Contribu. for the Bible Cause.	Contribu. for the Tract Cause.
Alabama....	$3,351	4,77
Arkansas.....	2,950	110
Delaware....	1,037	163
Florida....	1,957	5
Georgia....	4,532	1,468
Kentucky	5,956	1,366
Louisiana....	1,810	1,099
Maryland....	8,909	5,365
Mississippi....	1,067	267
Missouri....	4,711	936
North Carolina.....	6,197	1,419
South Carolina.....	3,984	3,222
Tennessee....	8,383	1,807
Texas....	3,985	127
Virginia.	9,296	6,894
	$68,125	$24,725

TABLE NO. LII.

MISSIONARY CAUSE AND COLONIZATION* CAUSE IN THE
FREE STATES—1855-1856.

States.	Contributions for Miss'y purposes, 1855.	Contributions for Coloniza. pur., 1856.
California.	$ 192	$ 1
Connecticut	48,044	9,233
Illinois	10,040	543
Indiana	4,705	34
Iowa	1,750	3
Maine	13,929	1,719
Massachusetts.	128,505	1,422
Michigan	4,935	4
New Hampshire	11,963	1,130
New Jersey	19,946	3,261
New York	172,115	24,371
Ohio	19,890	2,687
Pennsylvania	43,412	4,287
Rhode Island	9,440	2,125
Vermont	11,094	304
Wisconsin.	2,216	806
	$502,174	$51,930

TABLE NO. LIII.

MISSIONARY CAUSE AND COLONIZATION* CAUSE IN THE
SLAVE STATES—1855-1856.

States.	Contributions for Miss'y purposes, 1855.	Contributions for Coloniza. pur., 1856.
Alabama	$5,963	$1,113
Arkansas	455	1
Delaware	1,003	250
Florida	340	13
Georgia.	9,846	5,323
Kentucky	6,953	4,436
Louisiana.	334	871
Maryland	20,677	406
Mississippi	4,957	2,177
Missouri	2,712	313
North Carolina	6,010	969
South Carolina	15,248	129
Tennessee.	4,971	1,611
Texas	349	6
Virginia	22,106	10,000
	$101,934	$27,618

* For colonizing free blacks in Liberia.

TABLE NO. LIV.
DEATHS IN THE FREE STATES—1850.*

States.	Number of deaths.	Ratio to the Number living.
California		
Connecticut..............	5,781	64.13
Illinois.................	11,619	73.28
Indiana.	12,728	77.65
Iowa...................	2,044	94.03
Maine...	7,545	77.29
Massachusetts...........	19,414	51.23
Michigan...............	4,520	88.19
New Hampshire.........	4,268	74.49
New Jersey.............	6,467	75.70
New York..............	44,339	69.85
Ohio..................	28,949	68.41
Pennsylvania...........	28,318	81.63
Rhode Island...........	2,241	65.83
Vermont...............	3,132	100.13
Wisconsin..............	2,884	105.82
	184,249	72.91

TABLE NO. LV.
DEATHS IN THE SLAVE STATES—1850.*

States.	Number of deaths.	Ratio to the Number living.
Alabama....	9,084	84.94
Arkansas...............	2,987	70.18
Delaware...............	1,209	75.71
Florida.................	933	93.67
Georgia	9,920	91.93
Kentucky	15,206	64.60
Louisiana......	11,948	42.85
Maryland...............	9,594	60.77
Mississippi	8,711	69.93
Missouri...............	12,211	55.81
North Carolina..........	10,207	85.12
South Carolina..........	7,997	83.59
Tennessee.	11,759	85.34
Texas..................	3,046	69.79
Virginia...............	19,053	74.61
	133,865	71.82

* For an explanation of this Table see the next six pages.

TABLE NO. LVI.

FREE WHITE MALE PERSONS OVER FIFTEEN YEARS OF AGE

ENGAGED IN AGRICULTURAL AND OTHER OUT-DOOR LABOR IN THE
SLAVE-STATES—1850.

States.	No. engaged in Agriculture.	No. engaged in other out-door labor.	Total.
Alabama.................	67,742	7,229	74,971
Arkansas................	28,436	5,596	34,032
Delaware	6,225	4,184	10,409
Florida..................	5,472	2,598	8,070
Georgia	82,107	11,054	93,161
Kentucky	110,119	26,308	136,427
Louisiana...............	11,524	13,827	25,351
Maryland	24,672	17,146	41,818
Mississippi.............	50,028	5,823	55,851
Missouri................	64,292	19,900	84,192
North Carolina..........	76,338	21,876	98,214
South Carolina..........	37,612	6,991	44,603
Tennessee...............	115,844	16,795	132,639
Texas	24,987	22,713	47,700
Virginia................	97,654	33,928	131,582
	803,052	215,968	1,019,020

Too hot in the South, and too unhealthy there—white
men "can't stand it"—negroes only can endure the heat
of Southern climes ! How often are our ears insulted
with such wickedly false assertions as these ! In what
degree of latitude—pray tell us—in what degree of latitude do the rays of the sun become too calorific for white
men ? Certainly in no part of the United States, for in
the extreme South we find a very large number of non-
slaveholding whites over the age of fifteen, who derive
their entire support from manual labor in the open fields.
The sun, that bugbear of slaveholding demagogues, shone
on more than one million of free white laborers—mostly
agriculturists—in the slave States in 1850, exclusive of

those engaged in commerce, trade, manufactures, the mechanic arts, and mining. Yet, notwithstanding all these instances of exposure to his wrath, we have had no intelligence whatever of a single case of *coup de so-leil*. Alabama is not too hot; sixty-seven thousand white sons of toil till her soil. Mississippi is not too hot; fifty-five thousand free white laborers are hopeful devotees of her out-door pursuits. Texas is not too hot; forty-seven thousand free white persons, males, over the age of fifteen, daily perform their rural vocations amidst her unsheltered air.

It is stated on good authority that, in January, 1856, native ice, three inches thick, was found in Galveston Bay; we have seen it ten inches thick in North Carolina, with the mercury in the thermometer at two degrees below zero. In January, 1857, while the snow was from three to five feet deep in many parts of North Carolina, the thermometer indicated a degree of coldness seldom exceeded in any State in the Union—thirteen degrees below zero. The truth is, instead of its being too hot in the South for white men, it is too cold for negroes; and we long to see the day arrive when the latter shall have entirely receded from their uncongenial homes in America, and given full and undivided place to the former.

Too hot in the South for white men! It is not too hot for white women. Time and again, in different counties in North Carolina, have we seen the poor white wife of the poor white husband, following him in the harvest-field from morning till night, binding up the grain as it fell from his cradle. In the immediate neighborhood from which we hail, there are not less than thirty young women, non-slaveholding whites, between the ages of fifteen and twenty-five—some of whom are so well known to us that we could call them by name—who labor in the fields every summer ; two of them in particular, near neighbors to our mother, are in the habit of hiring themselves out during harvest-time, the very hottest season of the year, to bind wheat and oats—each of them keeping up with the reaper ; and this for the paltry consideration of twenty-five cents per day.

That any respectable man—any man with a heart or a soul in his composition—can look upon these poor toiling white women without feeling indignant at that accursed system of slavery which has entailed on them the miseries of poverty, ignorance, and degradation, we shall not do ourself the violence to believe. If they and their husbands, and their sons and daughters, and brothers and sisters, are not righted in some of the more important particulars in which they have been wronged, the fault shall lie at other doors than our own. In their behalf, chiefly, have we written and compiled this work ; and until our object shall have been accomplished, or until life shall have been extinguished, there shall be no abatement in our efforts to aid them in regaining the natural and inalienable prerogatives out of which they have been so infamously swindled. We want to see no more plowing, or hoeing, or raking, or grain-binding, by white women in the Southern States ; employment in cotton-mills and other factories would be far more profitable and congenial to them, and this they shall have within a short period after slavery shall have been abolished,

Too hot in the South for white men! What is the testimony of reliable Southrons themselves? Says Cassius M. Clay, of Kentucky :—

"In the extreme South, at New Orleans, the laboring men—the stevedores and hackmen on the levee, where the heat is intensified by the proximity of the red brick buildings, are all white men, and they are in the full enjoyment of health. But how about Cotton? I am informed by a friend of mine—himself a slaveholder, and therefore good authority—that in Northwestern Texas, among the German settlements, who true to their national instincts, will not employ the labor of a slave—they produce more cotton to the acre, and of a better quality, and selling at prices from a cent to a cent and a half a pound higher than that produced by slave labor."

Says Gov. Hammond, of South Carolina:—

"The steady heat of our summers is not so prostrating as the short, but frequent and sudden, bursts of Northern summers."

In an extract which may be found in our second chapter, and to which we respectfully refer the reader, it will be seen that this same South Carolinian, speaking of "not less than fifty thousand" non-slaveholding whites, says— "most of these now follow agricultural pursuits."

Says Dr. Cartwright of New Orleans :—

"Here in New Orleans, the larger part of the drudgery—work requiring exposure to the sun, as railroad-making, street-paving, dray-driving, ditching and building, is performed by white people."

To the statistical tables which show the number of deaths in the free and in the slave States in 1850, we would direct special attention. Those persons, particularly the propogandists of negro slavery, who, heretofore, have been so dreadfully exercised on account of what they have been pleased to term " the insalubrity of Southern climes," will there find something to allay their fearful apprehensions. A critical examination of said tables will disclose the fact that, in proportion to population, deaths occur more frequently in Massachusetts than in any Southern State except Louisiana ; more frequently in New York than in any of the Southern States, except Maryland, Missouri, Kentucky, Louisiana, and Texas ; more frequently in New Jersey, in Pennsylvania, and in Ohio, than in either Georgia, Florida, or Alabama. Leaving Wisconsin and Louisiana out of the account, and then comparing the bills of mortality in the remaining Northern States, with those in the remaining Southern States, we find the difference decidedly in favor of the latter ; for, according to this calculation, while the ratio of deaths is as only one to 74.60 of the living population in the Southern States, it is as one to 72.39 in the Northern.

Says Dr. J. C. Nott, of Mobile :—

" Heat, moisture, animal and vegetable matter are said to be the elements which produce the diseases of the South, and yet the testimony in proof of the health of the banks of the lower portion of the Mississippi River, is too strong to be doubted,— not only the river itself but also the numerous bayous which meander through Louisiana. Here is a perfectly flat alluvial country, covering several hundred miles, interspersed with interminable lakes, lagunes and jungles, and still we are informed by Dr. Cartwright, one of the most acute observers of the day, that this country is exempt from miasmatic disorders, and is extremely healthy. His assertion has been confirmed to me by hundreds of witnesses, and we know from our own observation, that the population present a robust and healthy appearance."

But the best part is yet to come. In spite of all the blatant assertions of the oligarchy, that the climate of the South was arranged expressly for the negroes, and that the negroes were created expressly to inhabit it as the healthful servitors of other men, a carefully kept register of all the deaths that occurred in Charleston, South Carolina, for the space of six years, shows that, even in that locality which is generally regarded as so unhealthy, the annual mortality was much greater among the blacks, in proportion to population, than among the whites. Dr. Nott himself shall state the facts. He says :—

"The average mortality for the last six years in Charleston for all ages is 1 in 51, including all classes. Blacks alone 1 in 44; whites alone, 1 in 58—a very remarkable result, certainly. This mortality is perhaps not an unfair test, as the population during the last six years has been undisturbed by emigration and acclimated in a greater proportion than at any former period."

Numerous other authorities might be cited in proof of the general healthiness of the climate south of Mason and Dixon's line. Of 127 remarkable cases of American longevity, published in a recent edition of Blake's Biographical Dictionary, 68 deceased centenarians are credited to the Southern States, and 59 to the Northern—the list being headed with Betsey Trantham, of Tennessee—a white woman, who died in 1834, at the extraordinarily advanced age of 154 years

TABLE NO. LVII.

NATIVES OF THE SLAVE STATES IN THE FREE STATES, AND NATIVES
OF THE FREE STATES IN THE SLAVE STATES.—1850.

States.	Natives of the Slave States.	States.	Natives of the Free States.
California................	24,055	Alabama............	4,947
Connecticut...........	1,390	Arkansas...........	7,965
Illinois..............	144,809	Delaware...........	6,996
Indiana............	176,581	Florida............	1,718
Iowa............	31,392	Georgia............	4,249
Maine............	458	Kentucky............	31,840
Massachusetts.....	2,980	Louisiana..........	14,567
Michigan...........	3,634	Maryland...........	23,815
New-Hampshire.......	215	Mississippi........	4,517
New-Jersey........	4,110	Missouri............	55,664
New-York....	12,625	North Carolina.....	2,167
Ohio.....	152,319	South Carolina.....	2,427
Pennsylvania........	47,180	Tennesee..........	6,571
Rhode Island......	982	Texas....	9,982
Vermont............	140	Virginia............	28,999
Wisconsin.........	6,353		
	609,223		205,924

This last table, compiled from the 116th page of the
Compendium of the Seventh Census, shows, in a most lucid
and startling manner, how negroes, slavery and slaveholders are driving the native non-slaveholding whites
away from their homes, and keeping at a distance other
decent people. From the South the tide of emigration still
flows in a westerly and north-westerly direction, and it
will continue to do so until slavery is abolished. The following remarks, which we extract from an editorial article
that appeared in the Memphis (Tenn.) *Bulletin* near the
close of the year 1856, are worth considering in this connection :—

" We have never before observed so large a number of immigrants going westward as are crossing the river at this point daily, the two ferry boats—sometimes three—going crowded from early morn until the boats cease making their trips at night. It is no uncommon sight to see from twenty to forty wagons encamped on the bluff for the night, notwithstanding there has been a steady stream going across the river all day, and yet the cry is, still they come."

About the same time the Cassville (Geo.) *Standard* spoke with surprise of the multitude of emigrants crowding the streets of that town bound for the far West.

Prof. B. S. Hedrick, late of Chapel Hill, North Carolina, says :—

"Of my neighbors, friends and kindred, nearly one-half have left the State since I was old enough to remember. Many is the time I have stood by the loaded emigrant wagon, and given the parting hand to those whose faces I was never to look upon again. They were going to seek homes in the free West, knowing, as they did, that free and slave labor could not both exist and prosper in the same community. If any one thinks that I speak without knowledge, let him refer to the last census. He will there find that in 1850 there were fifty-eight thousand native North Carolinians living in the free States of the West—thirty-three-thousand in Indiana alone. There were, at the same time, one hundred and eighty thousand Virginians living in the free States. Now, if these people were so much in love with the 'institution,' why did they not remain where they could enjoy its blessings?

"From my knowledge of the people of North Carolina, I believe that the majority of them who will go to Kansas during the next five years, would prefer that it should be a free State. I am sure that if I were to go there I should vote to exclude slavery."

For daring to have political opinions of his own, and because he did not deem it his duty to conceal the fact

that he loved liberty better than slavery, the gallant author of the extract above quoted was peremptorily dismissed from his post of analytical and agricultural chem-
ist in the University of North Carolina, ignominiously
subjected to the indignities of a mob, and then savagely
driven beyond the borders of his native State. His villainous persecutors, if not called to settle their accounts
in another world within the next ten years, will probably
survive to repent of the enormity of their pro-slavery
folly.[28]

TABLE NO. LVIII.

VALUE OF THE SLAVES AT $400 PER HEAD.—1850.*

States.	Value of the Slaves at $400 per head.	Val. of Real and Per. Estate, less the val. of slaves at $400 p. head.
Alabama....	$137,137,600	$81,066,732
Arkansas.....	18,840,000	21,001,025
Delaware.....	916,000	17,939,863
Florida.....	15,724,000	7,474,734
Georgia.	152,672,800	182,752,914
Kentucky....	84,392,400	217,236,056
Louisiana....	97,923,600	136,075,164
Maryland..	36,147,200	183,070,164
Mississippi....	123,951,200	105,000,000
Missouri....	34,968,800	102,278,907
North Carolina....	115,419,200	111,381,272
South Carolina....	153,993,600	134,264,094
Tennessee.	95,783,600	111,671,104
Texas.....	23,264,400	32,097,940
Virginia.....	189,011,200	202,634,638
	$1,280,145,600	$1,655,945,137

TABLES 34 and 35 show that, on account of the pitiable
poverty and ignorance of slavery, the mails were transported throughout the Southern States, during the year

* It is intended that this Table shall be considered in connection with Tables
XX and XXI, on page 80.

1855, at an extra cost to the General Government of more than six hundred thousand dollars ! In the free States, postages were received to the amount of more than two millions of dollars over and above the cost of transportation.

To Dr. G. Bailey, editor of the *National Era*, Washington city, D. C., we are indebted for the following useful and interesting statistics, to which some of our readers will doubtless have frequent occasion to refer :–

PRESIDENTS OF THE UNITED STATES.

Appointed.

Appointed	President
March 4, 1789 " 3, 1797	George Washington, *Virginia*.
March 4, 1797 " 3, 1801	John Adams, *Massachusetts*.
March 4, 1801 " 3, 1809	Thomas Jefferson, *Virginia*.
March 4, 1809 " 3, 1817	James Madison, *Virginia*.
March 4, 1817 " 3, 1825	James Monroe, *Virginia*.
March 4, 1825 " 3, 1829	John Q. Adams, *Massachusetts*.
March 4, 1829 " 3, 1837	Andrew Jackson, *Tennessee*.
March 4, 1837 " 3, 1841	Martin Van Buren, *New York*.
March 4, 1841 " 3, 1845	William H. Harrison, *Ohio*.
March 4, 1845 " 3, 1849	James K. Polk, *Tennessee*.
March 4, 1849 " 3, 1853	Zachary Taylor, *Louisiana*.
March 4, 1853 " 3, 1857	Franklin Pierce, *New Hampshire*.
March 4, 1857 " 3, 1861	James Buchanan, *Pennsylvania*.

At the close of the term for which Mr. Buchanan is elected.

it will have been seventy-two years since the organization of the present Government.

In that period, there have been eighteen elections for President, the candidates chosen in twelve of them being Southern men and slaveholders, in six of them Northern men and non-slaveholders.

No Northern man has ever been re-elected, but five Southern men have been thus honored.

Gen. Harrison, of Ohio, died one month after his inauguration, Gen. Taylor, of Louisiana, about four months after his inauguration. In the former case, John Tyler, of Virginia, became acting President, in the latter, Millard Fillmore, of New York.

Of the seventy-two years, closing with Mr. Buchanan's term, should he live it out, Southern men and slaveholders have occupied the Presidential chair forty-eight years and three months, or a little more than two-thirds of the time.

THE SUPREME COURT.

The judicial districts are organized so as to give five judges to the slave States, and four to the free, although the population, wealth, and business of the latter are far in advance of those of the former. The arrangement affords, however, an excuse for constituting the Supreme Court, with a majority of judges from the slaveholding States.

MEMBERS.

Chief Justice—R. B. Taney, *Maryland.*
Associate Justice—J. M. Wayne, *Georgia.*
" " John Catron, *Tennessee.*
" " P. V. Daniel, *Virginia.*
" " John A. Campbell, *Alabama.*
" " John McLean, *Ohio.*
" " S. Nelson, *New York.*
" " R. C. Grier, *Pennsylvania.*
" " B. R. Curtis, *Massachusetts.*
Reporter—B. C. Howard, *Maryland.*
Clerk—W T. Carroll, *D. C.*

SECRETARIES OF STATE.

The highest office in the Cabinet is that of Secretary of State, who has under his charge the foreign relations of the country. Since the year 1789, there have been twenty-two appointments to the office—fourteen from slave States, eight from free. Or, counting by years, the post has been filled by Southern men and slaveholders very nearly forty years out of sixty-seven, as follows :

Appointed.

Sept. 26, 1789, Thomas Jefferson, *Virginia.*

Jan. 2, 1794, E. Randolph, *Virginia.*

Dec. 10, 1795, T. Pickering, *Massachusetts.*

May 13, 1800, J. Marshall, *Virginia.*

March 5, 1801, James Madison, *Virginia.*

March 6, 1809, R. Smith, *Maryland.*

April 2, 1811, James Monroe, *Virginia.*

Feb. 28, 1815,   "   "   "

March 5, 1815, J. Q. Adams, *Massachusetts.*

March 7, 1825, Henry Clay, *Kentucky.*

March 6, 1829, Martin Van Buren, *New York.*

May 24, 1831, E. Livingston, *Louisiana.*

May 29, 1833, Louis McLane, *Delaware.*

June 27, 1834, J. Forsyth, *Georgia.*

March 5, 1841, Daniel Webster, *Massachusetts.*

July 24, 1843, A. P. Upshur, *Virginia.*

March 6, 1844, J. C. Calhoun, *South Carolina.*

March 5, 1845, James Buchanan, *Pennsylvania.*

March 7, 1849, J. M. Clayton, *Delaware.*

July 20, 1850, Daniel Webster, *Massachusetts.*

Dec. 9, 1851, E. Everett, *Massachusetts.*

March 5, 1853, W. L. Marcy, *New York.*

PRESIDENTS PRO TEM. OF THE SENATE.

Since the year 1809, every President *pro tem.* of the Senate of the United States has been a Southern man and slaveholder, with the exception of Samuel L. Southard, of New Jersey, who held the office for a very short time, and Mr. Bright, of Indiana, who has held it for one or two sessions, we believe, having been elected, however, as a known adherent of the slave interest, believed to be interested in slave " property."

Date	Speaker
April, 1789 / March 3, 1791	F. A. Muhlenberg, *Penn.*
Oct. 24, 1791 / March 2, 1793	J. Trumbull, *Connecticut.*
Dec. 2, 1793 / March 3, 1795	F. A. Muhlenberg, *Penn.*
Dec. 7, 1795 / March 3, 1797	Jonathan Dayton, *New Jersey.*
May 15, 1797 / March 3, 1799	" " "
Dec. 2, 1799 / March 3, 1801	Theodore Sedgwick, *Mass.*
Dec. 7, 1801 / March 3, 1807	Nathaniel Macon, *N. Car.*
Oct. 26, 1807 / March 3, 1811	J. B. Varnum, *Massachusetts.*
March 4, 1811 / Jan. 19, 1814	Henry Clay, *Kentucky.*
Jan. 19, 1814 / March 2, 1815	Langdon Cheves, *S. Car.*
Dec. 4, 1815 / Nov. 13, 1820	Henry Clay, *Kentucky.*
Nov. 15, 1820 / March 3, 1821	J. W. Taylor, *New-York.*
Dec. 3, 1821 / March 3, 1823	P. B. Barbour, *Virginia.*
Dec. 1, 1823 / March 3, 1825	Henry Clay, *Kentucky.*
Dec. 5, 1825 / March 3, 1827	J. W. Taylor, *New-York.*
Dec. 3, 1827 / June 2, 1834	A. Stevenson, *Virginia.*
June 2, 1834 / March 3, 1835	John Bell, *Tennessee.*
Dec. 7, 1835 / March 3, 1839	James K. Polk, *Tennessee.*
Dec. 16, 1839 / March 3, 1841	R. M. T. Hunter, *Virginia.*
May 31, 1841 / March 3, 1843	John White, *Tennessee.*

Dec. 4, 1843 March 3, 1845	J. W. Jones, *Virginia.*
Dec. 1, 1845 March 3, 1847	J. W. Davis, *Indiana.*
Dec. 6, 1847 March 3, 1849	R. C. Winthrop, *Mass.*
Dec. 22, 1849 March 3, 1851	Howell Cobb, *Georgia.*
Dec. 1, 1851 March 3, 1853	Linn Boyd, *Kentucky.*
Dec. 1, 1853 March 3, 1855	" " "
Feb. 28, 1856 March 3, 1857	Nathaniel P. Banks, *Mass.*

POSTMASTERS-GENERAL.

Appointed—

Sept. 26, 1789, S. Osgood, *Massachusetts.*
Aug. 12, 1791, T. Pickering, *Massachusetts.*
Feb. 25, 1795, J. Habersham, *Georgia.*
Nov. 28, 1801, G. Granger, *Connecticut.*
March 17, 1814, R. J. Meigs, *Ohio.*
June 25, 1823, John McLean, *Ohio.*
March 9, 1829, W. T. Barry, *Kentucky.*
May 1, 1835, A. Kendall, *Kentucky.*
May 18, 1840, J. M. Niles, *Connecticut.*
March 6, 1841, F. Granger, *New York.*
Sept. 13, 1841, C. A. Wickliffe, *Kentucky.*
March 5, 1845, C. Johnson, *Tennessee.*
March 7, 1849, J. Collamer, *Vermont.*
July 20, 1850, N. K. Hall, *New York.*
Aug. 31, 1852, S. D. Hubbard, *Connecticut.*
March 5, 1853, J. Campbell, *Pennsylvania.*

Sectionalism does not seem to have had much to do with this Department or with that of the Interior, created in 1848–'49.

SECRETARIES OF THE INTERIOR.

Appointed—

March 7, 1849, T. Ewing, *Ohio.*
July 20, 1850, J. A. Pearce, *Maryland.*
Aug. 15, 1850, T. M. T. McKennon, *Pennsylvania.*
Sept. 12, 1850, A. H. H. Stuart, *Virginia.*
March 5, 1853, R. McClelland, *Michigan.*

ATTORNEYS-GENERAL.

Appointed—

Sept. 26, 1789, E. Randolph, *Virginia.*
June 27, 1794, W. Bradford, *Pennsylvania.*
Dec. 10, 1795, C. Lee, *Virginia.*
Feb. 20, 1801, T. Parsons, *Massachusetts.*
March 5, 1800, L. Lincoln, *Massachusetts.*
March 2, 1805, R. Smith, *Maryland.*
Dec. 23, 1805, J. Breckinridge, *Kentucky.*
Jan. 20, 1807, C. A. Rodney, *Pennsylvania.*
Dec. 11, 1811, W. Pinkney, *Maryland.*
Feb. 10, 1814, R. Rush, *Pennsylvania.*
Nov. 13, 1817, W. Wirt, *Virginia.*
March 9, 1829, J. McPherson Berrien, *Georgia.*
July 20, 1831, Roger B. Taney, *Maryland.*
Nov. 15, 1833, B. F. Butler, *New York.*
July 7, 1838, F. Grundy, *Tennessee.*
Jan. 10, 1840, H. D. Gilpin, *Pennsylvania.*
March 5, 1841, J. J. Crittenden, *Kentucky.*
Sept. 13, 1841, H. S. Legare, *South Carolina.*
July 1, 1843, John Nelson, *Maryland.*
March 5, 1845, J. Y. Mason, *Virginia.*
Oct. 17, 1846, N. Clifford, *Maine.*
June 21, 1848, Isaac Toucey, *Connecticut.*
March 7, 1849, R. Johnson, *Maryland.*
July 20, 1850, J. J. Crittenden, *Kentucky.*
March 5, 1853, C. Cushing, *Massachusetts.*

SECRETARIES OF THE TREASURY.

*T*he post of Secretary of the Treasury, although one ot great 𝚒ᴍportance, requires financial abilities of a high order, which are more frequently found in the North than in the South, and affords little opportunity for influencing general politics, or the questions springing out of Slavery. We need not therefore be surprised to learn that Northern men have been allowed to discharge its duties some forty-eight years out of sixty-seven, as follows:

`' .ppointed—

Sept. 11, 1789, A. Hamilton, *New York*.
Feb. 3, 1795, O. Wolcott, *Connecticut*.
Dec. 31, 1800, S. Dexter, *Massachusetts*.
May 14, 1801, A. Gallatin, *Pennsylvania*.
Feb. 9, 1814, G. W. Campbell, *Tennessee*.
Oct. 6, 1814, A. J. Dallas, *Pennsylvvania*.
Oct. 22, 1816, W. H. Crawford, *Georgia*.
March 7, 1825, R. Rush, *Pennsylvania*.
March 6, 1829, S. D. Ingham, *Pennsylvania*.
Aug. 8, 1831, L. McLane, *Delaware*.,
May 29, 1833, W. J. Duane, *Pennsylvania*.
Sept. 23, 1833, Roger B. Taney, *Maryland*.
June 27, 1834, L. Woodbury, *New Hampshire*.
March 5, 1841, Thomas Ewing, *Ohio*.
Sept. 13, 1841, W. Forward, *Pennsylvania*.
March 3, 1843, J. C. Spencer, *New York*.
June 15, 1844, G. M. Bibb, *Kentucky*.
March 5, 1845, R. J. Walker, *Mississippi*.
March 7, 1849, W. M. Meredith, *Pennsylvania*.
June 20, 1850, Thomas Corwin, *Ohio*.
March 5, 1843, James Guthrie, *Kentucky*.

SECRETARIES OF WAR AND THE NAVY.

The Slaveholders, since March 8th, 1841, a period of nearly sixteen years, have taken almost exclusive supervision of the Navy, Northern men having occupied the Secretaryship only two

14

years. Nor has any Northern man been Secretary of War since 1849. Considering that nearly all the shipping belongs to the free States, which also supply the seamen, it does seem remarkable that Slaveholders should have monopolized for the last sixteen years the control of the Navy.

SECRETARIES OF WAR.

Appointed—

Sept. 12, 1789, Henry Knox, *Massachusetts.*
Jan. 2, 1795, T. Pickering, *Massachusetts.*
Jan. 27, 1796, J. McHenry, *Maryland.*
May 7, 1800, J. Marshall, *Virginia.*
May 13, 1800, S. Dexter, *Massachusetts.*
Feb. 3, 1801, R. Griswold, *Connecticut.*
March 5, 1801, H. Dearborn, *Massachusetts.*
March 7, 1802, W. Eustis, *Massachusetts.*
Jan. 13, 1813, J. Armstrong, *New York.*
Sept. 27, 1814, James Monroe, *Virginia.*
March 3, 1815, W. H. Crawford, *Georgia.*
April 7, 1817, G. Graham, *Virginia.*
March 5, 1817, J. Shelby, *Kentucky.*
Oct. 8, 1817, J. C. Calhoun, *South Carolina.*
March 7, 1825, J. Barbour, *Virginia.*
May 26, 1828, P. B. Porter, *Pennsylvania.*
March 9, 1829, J. H. Eaton, *Tennessee.*
Aug. 1, 1831, Lewis Cass, *Ohio.*
March 3, 1837, B. F. Butler, *New York.*
March 7, 1837, J. R. Poinsett, *South Carolina.*
March 5, 1841, James Bell, *Tennessee.*
Sept. 13, 1841, John McLean, *Ohio.*
Oct. 12, 1841, J. C. Spencer, *New York.*
March 8, 1843, J. W. Porter, *Pennsylvania.*
Feb. 15, 1844, W. Wilkins, *Pennsylvania.*
March 5, 1845, William L. Marcy, *New York.*
March 7, 1849, G. W. Crawford, *Georgia.*
July 20, 1850, E. Bates, *Missouri.*
Aug. 15, 1850, C. M. Conrad, *Louisiana.*
March 5, 1853, Jefferson Davis *Mississippi.*

SECRETARIES OF THE NAVY.

Appointed—

May   3, 1798, G. Cabot, *Massachusetts.*
May 21, 1798, B. Stoddart, *Massachusetts.*
July 15, 1801, R. Smith, *Maryland.*
May   3, 1805, J. Crowninshield, *Massachusetts.*
March 7, 1809, P. Hamilton, *South Carolina.*
Jan. 12, 1813, W. Jones, *Pennsylvania.*
Dec. 17, 1814, B. W. Crowninshield, *Massachusetts.*
Nov. 9, 1818, Smith Thompson, *New York.*
Sept. 1, 1823, John Rogers, *Massachusetts.*
Sept. 16, 1823, S. L. Southard, *New Jersey.*
March 9, 1819, John Branch, *North Carolina.*
May 23, 1831, L. Woodbury, *New Hampshire.*
June 30, 1834, M. Dickerson, *New Jersey.*
June 20, 1838, J. K. Paulding, *New York.*
March 5, 1841, G. F. Badger, *North Carolina.*
Sept. 13, 1841, A. P. Upshur, *Virginia.*
July 24, 1843, D. Henshaw, *Massachusetts.*
Feb. 12, 1844, T. W. Gilmer, *Virginia.*
March 14, 1844, James Y. Mason, *Virginia.*
March 10, 1845, G. Bancroft, *Massachusetts.*
Sept. 9, 1846, James Y. Mason, *Virginia.*
March 7, 1849, W. B. Preston, *Virginia.*
July 20, 1850, W. A. Graham, *N. Carolina.*
July 22, 1852, J. P. Kennedy, *Maryland.*
March 3, 1853, J. C. Dobbin, *N. Carolina.*

RECAPITULATION.

Presidency.—Southern men and Slaveholders, 48 **years 3** months ; Northern men, 23 years 9 months.

Pro. Tem. Presidency of the Senate.—Since 1809, held by Southern men and Slaveholders, except for three or four sessions by Northern men.

Speakership of the House.—Filled by Southern men and Slaveholders forty-three years, Northern men, twenty-five.

Supreme Court.—A majority of the Judges, including Chief Justice, Southern men and Slaveholders.

Secretaryship of State.—Filled by Southern men and Slave-holders forty years, Northern, twenty-seven.

Attorney Generalship.—Filled by Southern men and Slave-holders forty-two years, Northern men, twenty-five.

War and Navy.—Secretaryship of the Navy, Southern men and Slaveholders, the last sixteen years, with an interval of two years.

WILLIAM HENRY HURLBUT, of South Carolina, a gentle-man of enviable literary attainments, and one from whom we may expect a continuation of good service in the emi-nently holy crusade now going on against slavery and the devil, furnished not long since, to the *Edinburgh Re-view,* in the course of a long and highly interesting article, the following summary of oligarchal usurpations—show-ing that shaveholders have occupied the principal posts of the Government nearly two-thirds of the time :—

Presidents - - - - -	11 out of 16
Judges of the Supreme Court - -	17 out of 28
Attorneys-General - - - -	14 out of 19
Presidents of the Senate - - -	61 out of 77
Speakers of the House - - -	21 out of 33
Foreign Ministers - - - -	80 out of 134

As a matter of general interest, and as showing that, while there have been but 11 non-slaveholders directly be-fore the people as candidates for the Presidency, there have been *at least* 16 slaveholders who were willing to serve their country in the capacity of chief magistrate, the following tabl may be here introduced :—

RESULT OF THE PRESIDENTIAL ELECTIONS IN THE UNITED STATES
FROM 7796 TO 1856.

Year.	Name of Candidate.	Elect'l vote.
1796	John Adams	71
	Thomas Jefferson	68
1800	Thomas Jefferson	73
	John Adams	64
1804	Thomas Jefferson	162
	Charles C. Pinckney	14
1808	James Madison	128
	Charles C. Pinckney	45
1812	James Madison	122
	De Witt Clinton	89
1816	James Monroe -	183
	Rufus King -	34
1820	James Monroe -	218
	No opposition but one vote -	
1824	Andrew Jackson*	99
	John Q. Adams	84
	W. H. Crawford	41
	Henry Clay	37
1828	Andrew Jackson	178
	John Q. Adams	83
1832	Andrew Jackson	219
	Henry Clay	49
	John Floyd	11
	William Wirt	7
1836	Martin Van Buren	170
	William H. Harrison	73
	Hugh L. White	26
	Willie P. Mangum -	11
	Daniel Webster	14
1840	William H. Harrison	234
	Martin Van Buren	60
1844	James K. Polk	170
	Henry Clay	105
1848	Zachary Taylor	163
	Lewis Cass	127
1852	Franklin Pierce	254
	General Winfield Scott	42
1856	James Buchanan	174
	John C. Fremont	114
	Millard Fillmore	8

* No choice by the people; John Q. Adams elected by the House of Representatives.

AID FOR KANSAS.

As a sort of accompaniment to tables, 50, 51, 52 and 53, we will here introduce a few items which will more fully illustrate the liberality of Freedom and the niggardliness of Slavery.

From an editorial article that appeared in the Richmond (Va.,) *Dispatch*, in July, 1856, bewailing the close-fistedness of slavery, we make the following extract :—

"Gerrit Smith, the Abolitionist, has just pledged himself to give $1,500 a month for the next twelve months to aid in establishing Freedom in Kansas. He gave, but a short time since, at the Kansas relief meeting in Albany, $3,000. Prior to that, he had sent about $1,000 to the Boston Emigrant Committee. Out of his own funds, he subsequently equipped a Madison county company, of one hundred picked men, and paid their expenses to Kansas. At Syracuse he subscribed $10,000 for Abolition purposes, so that his entire contributions amount to at least $40,000."

An Eastern paper says :—

"The sum of $500 was contributed at a meeting at New Bedford on Monday evening, to make Kansas free. The following sums have been contributed for the same purpose: $2,000 in Taunton : $600 in Raynham : $800 in Clinton: $300 in Danbury, Ct. In Wisconsin, $2,500 at Janesville : $500 at Dalton: $500 at the Women's Aid Meeting in Chicago : $2,000 in Rockford, Ill."

A telegraphic dispatch, dated Boston, January 2, 1857, informs us that—

"The Secretary of the Kansas Aid Committee acknowledges the receipt of $42,678."

Exclusive of the amounts above, the readers of the New-

York *Tribune* have contributed about $30,000 for the purpose of securing Kansas to Freedom ; and, with the same object in view, other individuals and societies have, from time to time, made large contributions, of which we have failed to keep a memorandum. The legislature of Vermont has appropriated $20,000 ; and other free State legislatures are prepared to appropriate millions, if necessary. Free men have determined that Kansas shall be free, and free it soon shall be, and ever so remain. Harmoniously the work proceeds.

Now let us see how slavery has rewarded the poor, ignorant, deluded, and degraded mortals—swaggering lickspittles—who have labored so hard to gain for it " a local habitation and a name" in the disputed territory. One D. B. Atchison, Chairman of the Executive Committee of Border Ruffians, shall tell us all about it. Over date of October 13th, 1856, he says :

"Up to this moment, from all the States except Missouri, we have only received the following sums, and through the following persons :—

A. W. Jones, Houston, Miss., ...	$152
H. D. Clayton, Eufala, Ala., ...	500
Capt. Deedrick, South Carolina, . . .	500
	$1,152."

On this subject, further comment is unnecessary.

Numerous other contrasts, equally disproportionate, might be drawn between the vigor and munificence of freedom and the impotence and stinginess of slavery. We will, however, in addition to the above, advert to only a single instance. During the latter part of the summer of

1855, the citizens of the niggervilles of Norfolk and Portsmouth, in Virginia, were sorely plagued with yellow fever. Many of them fell victims to the disease, and most of those who survived, and who were not too unwell to travel, left their homes, horror-stricken and dejected. To the horror of mankind in general, and to the glory of freemen in particular, contributions in money, provisions, clothing, and other valuable supplies, poured in from all parts of the country, for the relief of the sufferers. Portsmouth alone, according to the report of her relief association, received $42,547 in cash from the free States, and only $12,182 in cash from all the slave States, exclusive of Virginia, within whose borders the malady prevailed. Including Virginia, the sum total of all the slave State contributions amounted to only $33,398. Well did the Richmond *Examiner* remark at the time—" we fear that generosity of Virginians is but a figure of speech." Slavery ! thy name is shame !

IN CONNECTION with tables 44 and 45 on page 292, it will be well to examine the following statistics of Congressional representation, which we transcribe from Reynold's Political Map of the United States :—

UNITED STATES SENATE.

16 free States, with a white population of 13,238,670, have 32 Senators.

15 slave States, with a white population of 6,186,477, have 30 Senators.

So that 413,708 free men of the North enjoy but the same political privileges in the U. S. Senate as is given to 206,215 slave propagandists.

HOUSE OF REPRESENTATIVES.

The free States have a total of 144 members.

The slave States have a total of 90 members.

One free State Representative represents 91,935 white men and women.

One slave State Representative represents 68,725 white men and women.

Slave Representation gives to slavery an advantage over free dom of 30 votes in the House of Representatives.

CUSTOM-HOUSE RECEIPTS.—1854.

Free States,....................................	$60,010,489
Slave States,................................	5,136,969
Balance in favor of the Free States,.............	$54,873,520

A contrast quite distinguishable !

THAT THE apologists of slavery cannot excuse the shame and the shabbiness of themselves and their country, as we have frequently heard them attempt to do, by falsely as-serting that the North has enjoyed over the South the ad-vantages of priority of settlement, will fully appear from the following table :—

FREE STATES.

1614. New-York first settled by the Dutch.

1620. Massachusetts settled by the Puritans.

1623. New-Hampshire settled by the Puritans.

1624. New-Jersey settled by the Dutch.

1635. Connecticut settled by the Puritans.

1636. Rhode Island settled by Roger Williams.

1682. Pennsylvania settled by William Penn.

1791. Vermont admitted into the Union.

1802. Ohio admitted into the Union.

1816. Indiana admitted into the Union.

14*

1818. Illinois admitted into the Union.
1820. Maine admitted into the Union.
1836. Michigan admitted into the Union.
1846. Iowa admitted into the Union.
1848. Wisconsin admitted into the Union.
1850. California admitted into the Union.

SLAVE STATES.

1607. Virginia first settled by the English.
1627. Delaware settled by the Swedes and Fins.
1635. Maryland settled by Irish Catholics.
1650. North Carolina settled by the English.
1670. South Carolina settled by the Huguenots.
1733. Georgia settled by Gen. Oglethorpe.
1782. Kentucky admitted into the Union.
1796. Tennessee admitted into the Union.
1811. Louisiana admitted into the Union.
1817. Mississippi admitted into the Union.
1819. Alabama admitted into the Union.
1821. Missouri admitted into the Union.
1836. Arkansas admitted into the Union.
1845. Florida admitted into the Union.
1846. Texas admitted into the Union.

In the course of an exceedingly interesting article on the early settlements in America, R. K. Browne, formerly editor and proprietor of the San Francisco *Evening Journal*, says :—

"Many people seem to think that the Pilgrim Fathers were the first who settled upon our shores, and therefore that they ought to be entitled, in a particular manner, to our remembrance and esteem.

This is not the case, and we herewith present to our readers a list of settlements made in the present United States, prior to that of Plymouth

1564. A Colony of French Protestants under Ribault settled in Florida.

1565. St. Augustine* founded by Pedro Melendez.

1584. Sir Walter Raleigh obtains a patent and sends two vessels to the American coast, which receives the name of Virginia.

1607. The first effectual settlement made at Jamestown, Va., by the London Company.

1614. A fort erected by the Dutch upon the site of New-York.

1615. Fort Orange built near the site of Albany, N. Y.

1619. The first General Assembly called in Virginia.

1620. The Pilgrims land on Plymouth Rock."

FREEDOM AND SLAVERY AT THE FAIR.

WHAT FREEDOM DID.

At an Agricultural Fair held at Watertown, in the State of New-York, on the 2d day of October, 1856, two hundred and twenty premiums, ranging from three to fifty dollars each, were awarded to successful competitors—the aggregate amount of said premiums being $2,396, or an average of $10.89 each. From the proceedings of the Awarding Committee we make the following extracts :—

Best Horse Colt,	George Parish, -	$25.00
Best Filly,	J. Staplin, - - -	20.00
Best Brood Mare,	A. Blunt, - - -	25.00
Best Bull,	Wm. Johnson, -	25.00
Best Heifer,	A. M. Rogers, -	20.00
Best Cow,	C. Baker, - - -	25.00
Best Stall-fed Beef,	J. W. Taylor, -	10.00
Best sample Wheat,	Wm. Ottley, - -	5.00
Best sample Flaxseed,	H. Weir, - - -	3.00
Best sample Timothy Seed,	E. S. Hayward, -	3.00
(Highest) Best Team of Oxen,	Hiram Converse,	50.00
(Lowest) Best sample Sweet Corn,	L. Marshall, - -	3.00

Aggregate amount of twelve premiums, - - - $214.00
An average of $17.83 each.

* The oldest town in the United States.

WHAT SLAVERY DID.

At the Rowan County Agricultural Fair, held at Mineral Springs, in North Carolina, on the 13th day of November, 1856, thirty premiums, ranging from twenty-five cents to two dollars each, were awarded to successful competitors —the aggregate amount of said premiums being $42, or an average of $1.40 each. From the proceedings of the Awarding Committee we make the following extracts :—

	Best Horse Colt,	T. A. Burke, - -	$2.0C
	Best Filly,	James Cowan, - -	2.00
	Best Brood Mare,	M. W. Goodman, -	2.00
	Best Bull,	J. F. McCorkle, - -	2.0C
	Best Heifer,	J. F. McCorkle, -	2.00
	Best Cow,	T. A. Burke, - - -	2.00
	Best Stall-fed Beef,	S. D. Rankin, - -	1.00
	Best Sample Wheat,	M. W. Goodman, -	50
	Best lot Beets,	J. J. Summerell, -	25
	Best lot Turnips,	Thomas Barber, - -	25
(Highest)	Best pair Match Horses,	R. W. Griffith, - -	2.00
(Lowest)	Best lot Cabbage,	Thomas Hyde, - -	25

Aggregate amount of twelve premiums, $16.25
An average of $1.36 each.

Besides the two hundred and twenty premiums, amounting in the aggregate to $2,396, freedom granted several diplomas and silver medals ; besides the thirty premiums amounting in the aggregate to $42, slavery granted none —nothing. While examining these figures, it should be recollected that agriculture is the peculiar province of the slave States. If commerce or manufactures had been the subject of the fair, the result might have shown even a greater disproportion in favor of freedom, and yet there would have been some excuse for slavery, for it makes no pretensions to either the one or the other ; but as agriculture was the subject, slavery can have no excuse whatever, but must bear all the shame of its niggardly and revolting impotence ; this it must do for the reason that agriculture is its special and almost only pursuit.

THE REPORTS of the Comptrollers of the States of New York and North Carolina, for the year 1856, are now before us. From each report we have gleaned a single item, which, when compared, the one with the other, speaks volumes in favor of freedom and against slavery. We refer to the average value per acre of lands in the two States ; let slavocrats read, reflect, and repent.

In 1856, there were assessed for taxation in the State of

NEW YORK,

Acres of land	30,080,000
Valued at	$1,112,133,136
Average value per acre . .	$36.97

In 1856, there were assessed for taxation in the State of

NORTH CAROLINA,

Acres of land	32,450,560
Valued at	$98,800,636
Average value per acre . .	$3.06

It is difficult for us to make any remarks on the official facts above. Our indignation is struck almost dumb at this astounding and revolting display of the awful wreck that slavery is leaving behind it in the South. We will, however, go into a calculation for the purpose of ascertaining as nearly as possible, in this one particular, how much North Carolina has lost by the retention of slavery. As we have already seen, the average value per acre of land in the State of New York is $36.97 ; in North Carolina it is only $3.06 ; why is it so much less, or even any less, in the latter than in the former ? The answer is, *slavery*. In soil, in climate, in minerals, in water-power for manufactural purposes, and in area of territory, North Carolina has the advantage of New York, and, with the exception of slavery, no plausible reason can possibly be assigned why land should not be *at least* as valuable in the valley of the Yadkin as it is along the banks of the Genesee.

The difference between $36.97 and $3.06 is $33.91, which, multiplied by the whole number of acres of land in North Carolina, will show, in this one particular, the enormous loss that Freedom has sustained on account of Slavery in the Old North State. Thus :—

32,450,560 acres *a* $33,91. . . . $1,100,398,489.

Let it be indelibly impressed on the mind, however, that this amount, large as it is, is only a moity of the sum that it has cost to maintain slavery in North Carolina. From time to time, hundreds upon hundreds of millions of dollars have left the State, either in search of profitable, permanent investment abroad, or in the shape of profits to Northern merchants and manufactures, who have become the moneyed aristocracy of the country by supplying to the South such articles of necessity, utility, and adornment, as would have been produced at home but for the pernicious presence of the peculiar institution.

A reward of Eleven Hundred Millions of Dollars is offered for the conversion of the lands of North Carolina into free soil. The lands themselves, desolate and impoverished under the fatal foot of slavery, offer the reward. How, then, can it be made to appear that the abolition of slavery in North Carolina, and, indeed, throughout all the Southern States—for slavery is exceedingly inimical to them all—is not demanded by every consideration of justice, prudence, and good sense? In 1850, the total value of all the slaves of the State, at the rate of four hundred dollars per head, amounted to less than one hundred and sixteen millions of dollars. Is the sum of one hundred and sixteen millions of dollars more desirable than the sum of eleven hundred millions of dollars? When a man has land for sale, does he reject thirty-six dollars per acre and take three? Non-slaveholding whites! look well to your interests! Many of you have lands; comparatively speaking, you have nothing else. Abolish slavery, and you will enhance the value of every league, your own and your neighbors', from three to thirty-six dollars per acre. Your little tract containing two hundred acres, now valued at the pitiful sum of only six hundred dollars, will then be worth seven thousand. Your children, now deprived of even the meagre advantages of common schools, will then reap the benefits of a collegiate education. Your rivers and smaller streams, now wasting their waters in idleness, will then turn the wheels of multitudinous mills. Your bays and harbors, now unknown to commerce, will then swarm with ships from every enlightened quarter of the globe. Non-slavehold-ing whites! look well to your interests!

Would the slaveholders of North Carolina lose anything by the abolition of slavery? Let us see. According to their own estimate, their slaves are worth, in round num-bers, say, one hundred and twenty millions of dollars. There are in the State twenty-eight thousand slaveholders, owning, it may be safely assumed, an average of at least five hundred acres of land each—fourteen millions of acres in all. This number of acres, multiplied by thirty-three dol-lars and ninety-one cents, the difference in value between free soil and slave soil, makes the enormous sum of four hundred and seventy-four millions of dollars—showing that, by the abolition of slavery, the slaveholders them-selves would realize a net profit of not less than three hundred and fifty-four millions of dollars!

Compensation to slaveholders for the negroes now in their possession! The idea is preposterous. The suggestion is criminal. The demand is unjust, wicked, monstrous, damn-able. Shall we pat the bloodhounds of slavery for the sake of doing them a favor? Shall we fee the curs of slavery in order to make them rich at our expense? Shall we pay the whelps of slavery for the privilege of converting them into decent, honest, upright men? No, never! The non-slavehol-ders expect to gain, and will gain, something by the abolition of slavery; but slaveholders themselves will, by far, be the greater gainers; for, in proportion to population, they own much larger and more fertile tracts of land, and will, as a matter of course, receive the lion's share of the increase in the value of not only real estate, but also of other gen-

uine property, of which they are likewise the principal
owners. How ridiculously absurd, therefore, is the objection, that, if we liberate the slaves, we ruin the masters !
Not long since, a gentleman in Baltimore, a native of Maryland, remarked in our presence that he was an abolitionist because he felt that it was right and proper to be
one ; " but," inquired he, " are there not, in some of the
States, many widows and orphans who would be left
in destitute circumstances, if their negroes were taken
from them ?" In answer to the question, we replied that
slavery had already reduced thousands and tens of thousands of non-slaveholding widows and orphans to the lowest depths of poverty and ignorance, and that we did not
believe one slaveholding widow and three orphans were
of more, or even of as much consequence as five non-
slaveholding widows and fifteen orphans.   " You are
right," exclaimed the gentleman, " I had not viewed the
subject in that light before ; I perceive you go in for the
greatest good to the greatest number."   Emancipate the
negroes, and the ex-slaveholding widow would still retain
her lands and tenements, which, in consequence of being
surroundnd by the magic influences of liberty, would soon
render her far more wealthy and infinitely more respectable, than she could possibly ever become while trafficking
in human flesh.

The fact is, every slave in the South costs the State in
which he resides at least three times as much as he, in the
whole course of his life, is worth to his master.   Slavery
benefits no one but its immediate, individual owners, and
them only in a pecuniary point of view, and at the sacri-

fice of the dearest rights and interests of the whole mass
of non-slaveholders, white and black. Even the masters
themselves, as we have already shown, would be far better off without it than with it. To all classes of society
the institution is a curse ; an especial curse is it to those
who own it not. Non-slaveholding whites ! look well to
your interests !

CHAPTER IX.

COMMERCIAL CITIES—SOUTHERN COMMERCE.

OUR theme is a city—a great Southern importing, ex·
porting, and manufacturing city, to be located at some
point or port on the coast of the Carolinas, Georgia or Virginia, where we can carry on active commerce, buy, sell,
fabricate, receive the profits which accrue from the exchange of our own commodities, open facilities for direct
communication with foreign countries, and establish all
those collateral sources of wealth, utility, and adornment,
which are the usual concomitants of a metropolis, and
which add so very materially to the interest and importance of a nation.   Without a city of this kind, the South
can never develop her commercial resources nor attain to
that eminent position to which those vast resources would
otherwise exalt her.   According to calculations based upon
reasonable estimates, it is owing to the lack of a great
commercial city in the South, that we are now *annually*
drained of more than One Hundred and Twenty Millions
of Dollars !   We should, however, take into consideration
the negative loss as well as the positive.   Especially
should we think of the influx of emigrants, of the visits of
strangers and cosmopolites, of the patronage to hotels and

public halls, of the profits of travel and transportation, of
the emoluments of foreign and domestic trade, and of numerous other advantages which have their origin exclusively in wealthy, enterprising, and densely populated
cities.

Nothing is more evident than the fact, that our people
have never entertained a proper opinion of the importance
of home cities. Blindly, and greatly to our own injury,
we have contributed hundreds of millions of dollars towards
the erection of mammoth cities at the North, while our
own magnificent bays and harbors have been most shame-
fully disregarded and neglected. Now, instead of carrying all our money to New-York, Philadelphia, Boston, and
Cincinnati, suppose we had kept it on the south side of
Mason and Dixon's line—as we would have done, had it
not been for slavery—and had disbursed it in the upbuilding of Norfolk, Beaufort, Charleston, or Savannah, how
much richer, better, greater, would the South have been
to-day ! How much larger and more intelligent would
have been our population. How many hundred thousand
natives of the South would now be thriving at home, instead of adding to the wealth and political power of other
parts of the Union. How much greater would be the number and length of our railroads, canals, turnpikes, and telegraphs. How much greater would be the extent and
diversity of our manufactures. How much greater would
be the grandeur, and how much larger would be the number of our churches, theatres, schools, colleges, lyceums,
banks, hotels, stores, and private dwellings. How many
more clippers and steamships would we have sailing on

the ocean, how vastly more reputable would we be abroad, how infinitely more respectable, progressive, and happy, would we be at home.

That we may learn something of the importance of cities in general, let us look for a moment at the great capitals of the world. What would England be without London? What would France be without Paris? What would Turkey be without Constantinople? Or, to come nearer home, what would Maryland be without Baltimore? What would Louisiana be without New Orleans? What would South Carolina be without Charleston? Do we ever think of these countries or States without thinking of their cities also? If we want to learn the news of the country, do we not go to the city, or to the city papers? Every metropolis may be regarded as the nucleus or epitome of the country in which it is situated; and the more prominent features and characteristics of a country, particularly of the people of a country, are almost always to be seen within the limits of its capital city. Almost invariably do we find the bulk of the floating funds, the best talent, and the most vigorous energies of a nation concentrated in its chief cities; and does not this concentration of wealth, energy, and talent, conduce, in an extraordinary degree, to the growth and prosperity of the nation? Unquestionably. Wealth develops wealth, energy develops energy, talent develops talent. What, then, must be the condition of those countries which do not possess the means or facilities of centralizing their material forces, their energies, and their talents? Are they not destined to occupy an inferior rank among the nations of the earth ? Let the South answer.

And now let us ask, and we would put the question particularly to Southern merchants, what do we so much need as a great Southern metropolis ? Merchants of the South, slaveholders ! you are the avaricious assassinators of your country ! You are the channels through which more than one hundred and twenty millions of dollars— $120,000,000—are annually drained from the South and conveyed to the North. You are daily engaged in the unmanly and unpatriotic work of impoverishing the land of your birth. You are constantly enfeebling our resources and rendering us more and more tributary to distant parts of the nation. Your conduct is reprehensible, base, criminal.

Whether Southern merchants ever think of the numerous ways in which they contribute to the aggrandizement of the North, while, at the same time, they enervate and dishonor the South, has, for many years, with us, been a matter of more than ordinary conjecture. If, as it would seem, they have never yet thought of the subject, it is certainly desirable that they should exercise their minds upon it at once. Let them scrutinize the workings of Southern money after it passes north of Mason and Dixon's line. Let them consider how much they pay to Northern railroads and hotels, how much to Northern merchants and shop-keepers, how much to Northern shippers and insurers, how much to Northern theatres, newspapers, and periodicals. Let them also consider what disposition is made of it after it is lodged in the hands of the North.

Is not the greater part of it paid out to Northern manufacturers, mechanics, and laborers, for the very articles
which are purchased at the North—and to the extent that
this is done, are not Northern manufacturers, mechanics,
and laborers directly countenanced and encouraged, while,
at the same time, Southern manufacturers, mechanics,
and laborers, are indirectly abased, depressed, and dis-
abled? It is, however, a matter of impossibility, on
these small pages, to notice or enumerate all the methods in which the money we deposit in the North
is made to operate against us; suffice it to say that
it is circulated and expended there, among all classes of
the people, to the injury and impoverishment of almost
every individual in the South. And yet, our cousins of
the North are not, by any means, blameworthy for availing
themselves of the advantages which we have voluntarily
yielded to them. They have shown their wisdom in growing great at our expense, and we have shown our folly in
allowing them to do so. Southern merchants, slaveholders,
and slave-breeders, should be the objects of our censure;
they have desolated and impoverished the South; they
are now making merchandize of the vitals of their country; patriotism is a word nowhere recorded in their vocabulary; town, city, country—they care for neither;
with them, self is always paramount to every other consideration.

Having already compared slavery with freedom in the
States, we will now compare it with freedom in the cities.
From every person as yet unconvinced of the despicable-

ness of slavery, we respectfully ask attention to the following letters, which fully explain themselves :—

FINANCE DEPARTMENT COMPTROLLER'S OFFICE,
New-York, February 17th, 1857.

H. R. HELPER, ESQ.,
    Dear Sir:—

Your letter to Mayor Wood has been handed to me for an answer, which I take pleasure in giving as follows:

The last assessment of property in this city was made in August, 1856.

The value of all the real and personal property in the city, according to that assessment, is $511,740,492.

A census of the city was taken in 1855, and the number of inhabitants at that time can be obtained only from the Secretary of State.
           Very truly yours,
           A. S. CADY.

————

STATE OF NEW-YORK, SECRETARY'S OFFICE,
Albany, February 24, 1857.

H. R. HELPER, ESQ.,
    Dear Sir :—

Yours of the 17th February, in regard to the population of the city of New York, is before me. According to the census of

1855 the population was	- - - - - -	629,810
1850 "	"	" - - - - - -	515,547
1845 "	"	" - - - - - -	371,223
1840 "	"	" - - - - - -	312,710
1835 "	"	" - - - - - -	268,089
1830 "	"	" - - - - - -	197,112

As to the population now, you have the same facilities of judging that we have from the above table.
           Very truly yours,
           A. N. WAKEFIELD, *Chief Clerk.*

————

MAYOR'S OFFICE, CITY HALL, }
Baltimore, December 26, 1856. }

H. R. HELPER, ESQ.,
   Dear Sir:—

His Honor the Mayor of this City has requested me to reply to your communication of the 24th inst., addressed to him, requesting answers to certain questions.

In answer to your first interrogatory, I would state that the amount of direct taxation assessed January 1st, 1856, was $102,053,839; the amount of exempt taxation (i. e. property out of the limits of direct tax) assessed at that date was $6,054,733.

In reply to your second inquiry, I would state that no census of the city has been taken since 1850. The estimated population at this time is about 250,000. Respectfully Yours, &c., &c.,

D. H. BLANCHARD, *Secretary.*

OFFICE OF THE MAYOR OF THE CITY OF PHILADELPHIA, }
December 30, 1856. }

H. R. HELPER, ESQ.,
   Dear Sir:

In reply to your note of the 25th inst., received to-day, I hasten to give you the estimates you ask.

Real Estate, 150 millions; it is about one-half the real value. Its market price is at least 300 million dollars.

The Personal Estate is returned at 20 millions; it is over 110 millions. There has been no census since 1850. The population now is 500,000.   Yours truly,

G. VAUX.

STATE OF LOUISIANA, MAYORALTY OF NEW ORLEANS, }
City Hall, 3d day of Jan'y, 1857. }

Mr. H. R. HELPER,
   New-York:
   Dear Sir:—

In answer to your note of the 24th December, I beg to refer you to the enclosed abstract for the value of real estate and slaves according to the last assessment.

15

There has heretofore been no assessment of personal property —there having been no tax authorized until this year. The assessment is now being made and will probably add about $5,000,000 to the assessment as stated in the abstract.

There has been no census since the U. S. census of 1850, except an informal census, made in 1852, for the purpose of dividing the city into wards anew.

The estimated population now is about 150 to 175,000 inhabitants—permanent population—including the floating population at this season, it would probably reach not less than 210,000 inhabitants. The U. S. census was taken in the summer months, and is very incorrect as to the absolute population of New Orleans.   Very respectfully,

Your obed't serv't,

J. B. WALTON,

Secretary.

By reference to the abstract of which Mr. Walton speaks, we find that the value of real and personal property is summed up as follows :—

Real Estate, - - -	$67,460,115
Slaves, - - - -	5,183,580
Capital, - - - -	18,544,300
Total, - - -	$91,188,195

CITY HALL, BOSTON, ⎰
Dec. 31, 1856. ⎱

Dear Sir:—Yours of the 25th inst., addressed to the Mayor, has been handed to me for a reply—and I would accordingly state that the value of real and personal estate in this city, on the first day of May, A.D. 1856, was $249,162,500.

The census of the city of Boston, on the first day of May, A.D. 1855, was 162,748 persons.

The estimated population of the city of Boston at this date—
say January 1st, 1857—is 165,000.

Yours, very respectfully,
SAML. T. McCLEARY,
City Clerk.

ST. LOUIS, }
Feb. 27, 1857. }

H. R. HELPER, ESQ.,

New-York :

Dear Sir :—

In reply to yours of the 9th inst., I beg leave to state, that a
census of our population was taken in the spring of 1856 by the
Sheriff, and although it was inaccurate, yet the population as returned by him was then 125,500. That his census is too low
there is no doubt. Our population at this time is at least
140,000.

Our last assessment was made in February, 1856. Value of
real and personal estate, is, in round numbers, $63,000,000.

Trusting this information will be sufficient for your purpose,
I remain,   Yours, &c.,

JOHN HOW,
Mayor.

MAYOR'S OFFICE, CITY HALL, BROOKLYN, }
January 24th, 1857. }

H. R. HELPER, ESQ.,

Sir :—

The answers to your inquiries are as follows :

The last assessment of property in this city was made in
August, 1856.

The value of all the real and personal property in the city, according to that assessment, is $95,800,440.

A census of the city was taken in 1855, and the number of inhabitants, according to it, was 205,250.

The estimated population now is 225,000.

The last annual report of the Comptroller, together with a

communication of the Mayor to the Common Council, made on the 5th of Jan., 1857, have been transmitted by mail to your address, and from them you may be able to obtain any further information you may desire. Yours, respectfully,

S. S. POWELL,
Mayor.
By C. S. BRAINERD.

MAYOR'S OFFICE,
Charleston, Feb. 16, 1857.

H. R. HELPER, ESQ.,
(New York,)
Dear Sir:—

Yours of the 9th has just been received, I sent you, through the Clerk of Council, some time ago, the Annual Fiscal Statement of the Committee on Accounts made to the City Council, which would give some of the information which you desire. I will have another copy sent you.

No census has been taken since 1848. The population at present must be between fifty and sixty thousand.

Any information which it may be in my power to furnish you with, will always give me pleasure to supply.

Very respectfully,
WM. PORCHER MILES,
Mayor.

From a report of the " Annual accounts of the city of Charleston, for the fiscal year ending the 31st of August, 1856," it appears that the total value of real and personal property, including slaves—nearly half the population— was $36,127,751.

MAYOR'S OFFICE,
Cincinnati, Jan'y 2, 1857.

Dear Sir:—In reply to your note of the 25th ult., I beg leave to say that the value of all the real and personal property in this city, as assessed for taxation, amounts to $88,810,734. The realty being $60,701,267 ; the personalty $20,795,203, and the bank and brokers' capital $7,314,264. The assessment of the realty was made in 1853 ; that of the personalty is made in March of each year.

Our present population is estimated at 210,000. No complete census has been taken since 1850.

The total of taxes levied on the above assessment of $88,810,-734, for city purposes, was $529,727,05.

Very respectfully,
Your ob'dt. serv't,

H. R. HELPER, ESQ.,   JAS. J. FARAN,
   New-York.   *Mayor.*

———

MAYOR'S OFFICE,
Louisville, Ky., January 1st, 1857. }

H. R. HELPER, ESQ.,
      New-York City,
         Dear Sir :—

Your favor 24th ult. is received—contents noted. I will remark in reply, that the taxes of this city are levied only on real estate, slaves, and merchandise, (exclusive of home manufactures,) which are taken at what is supposed to be their cash value, but is much less than the real value. Our last assessment was made the 10th January, 1856, and amounted to $31,500,000.

There has been no census of this city taken since 1850, our charter requiring that it shall be taken this year. I am now preparing to have it done. It is supposed Louisville at this time has a population of 65 or 70 thousand.

I send with this my last annual message to the Gen. Council and accompanying documents.

Respectfully yours,
JOHN BARBEE, *Mayor.*

———

H. R. HELPER, ESQ.

    Sir :—

In the May No. of Hunt's Merchants' Magazine you will find some of your questions answered. The actual cash value of property is not taken by the assessors. Citizens are not sworn as to the value of their personal effects, nor is real estate given in at twenty per cent. of its selling cash price. An elaborate estimate of the real value, in cash, of Chicago, which we have seen,

puts the real estate at - - - - -	$125,000,000
Improvements on the same, - - - -	$24,000,000
Personal property, - - - - - -	$22,000,000
In 1857 total value, - - - - -	$171,000,000

On half a dozen streets in this city lots sell readily at $1,000 to $1,200 per foot front, exclusive of improvements.

A census of the population of Chicago was taken in October, 1853, and in June, 1855, the latter by State authority. That of October '53 found 60,652; that of June '55 found 80,509. The best estimate at present makes the number, on May 1st, 1857, to be 112,000, which is rather under than over the truth. The amount of building, in the city, is immense, but as quickly as a tenement can be spiked together, it is taken at a high rent; and at no former period has there seemed so rapid an augmentation of population.   Very truly yours,

        RAY & MEDILL,
          Eds. Ch. Trib.

H. R. HELPER, ESQ.,

    Dear Sir :—

Yours of the 14th inst. has been received, and should have been answered sooner, but it was impossible to get the information you desired earlier. The value of the real estate in the city of Richmond is $18,000,000. The value of the personal is $191,920. Total value $18,201,920. This does not include slaves, of whom there are 6,472 in the city. The State values each slave at $300 each—making $1,941,600, which, added to the total above, makes $20,143,520. The number of inhabitants—white and black, is 34,612 within the corporation limits. The assessment was made in 1855 throughout the whole State.

Yours, very respectfully,

B. W. STARKE.

———

MAYOR'S OFFICE,
Providence, Dec. 31st, 1856.

H. R. HELPER, ESQ.,
New York,
Dear Sir :—

Yours of 25th is this moment received. You will receive with this a communication from the Chairman of the Board of Assessors, giving the requisite information from that department. I send you this day a census report, taken 1855, which will give you the information asked. Our population at this time is between 50 and 60,000. Respectfully,

JAMES Y. SMITH,
Mayor.

———

ASSESSOR'S OFFICE,
Providence, Dec. 31st, 1856.

H. R. HELPER, ESQ.,
Dear Sir :—

His Honor, the Mayor of this City, has requested me to answer your communication of the 25th inst., addressed to him, so far as relates to the valuation of this city, &c., which is herewith presented.

The valuation of this City in 1856 is as follows :

Real Estate,	$36,487,116
Personal Estate,	21,577,400
Total,	$58,064,516

Our last assessment was ordered in June last, and completed on the 1st day of September last.

Rates of taxation $7 75 per $1000.
Amount of tax raised $450,000.

> Respectfully yours,
> JOSEPH MARTIN,
> *Chairman of the Board of Assessors.*

HERALD OFFICE,
Norfolk, Va., 28th April, 1857.

H. R. HELPER, ESQ.,
    New-York,
       Dear Sir :—

The value of all the real estate, as re-assessed about two months ago, is set down, say, in round numbers, at five and a half millions. The actual value would bring it somewhat above that mark. The assessment of the personal property will be completed in three or four weeks hence ; but its *exact* value cannot be arrived at from the fact that a large portion of this description of property—including slaves—is taxed specifically without regard to its value. It is estimated by the assessors, however, that the *personal* exceeds the *real estate*, and may be safely set down at six and a half millions.

There has been no census taken since 1850. The State authorities assume the population to be 16,000, but I am informed by the assessors that 17,000 is a fairer estimate.

Hoping that the information given may answer the purpose for which you require it, I am,   Respectfully yours,

> R. G. BROUGHTON.

MAYOR'S OFFICE,
Buffalo, March 10, 1857.

Dear Sir :—Yours, of the 9th inst., was received this morning. The answers to your questions are as follows :

The last valuation of the property of our city was made in April, 1856.

Valuation of real estate,	. . .	$38,114,040
" personal estate,	. .	7,360,436
	Total real and personal,	$45,474,476

The last census was the State census, taken in the summer of 1855. That showed a population of 74,214 ; a fair estimate now is 90,000.   Respectfully,

Your ob't serv't,

F. P. STEVENS.

MAYOR'S OFFICE,

Savannah, 9th January, 1856. }

H. R. HELPER, ESQ.,

New-York,

Dear Sir :—

In reply to your first interrogatory, I send you the last Mayor's report, in which you will find the information you seek.

No census has been taken of the city since 1850.

The estimated population is 25,000.

Very respectfully yours,

J. P. SCREVEN,

Mayor.

From the Mayor's annual report, we learn that the " assessments or value of lands and improvements," for the year ending October 31st, 1856, amounted to $8,999,015. The value of the personal property is, perhaps, about $3,000,000—total value of real and personal estate $11,999,015.

CITY OF NEW-BEDFORD,

Mayor's Room, 1 mo., 6th, 1857. }

H. R. HELPER :—

Yours of the 4th inst. came to hand this morning.

In reply to your inquiries, I will say that the amount assessed on the 1st day of May, 1856, was as follows :—

Real Estate, - - - - -	$9,311,500
Personal, - - - - - -	17,735,500
Total, - - - - - -	$27.047,000

15*

The returns of a census taken the previous autumn gave 20,391 persons, from which there is not probably much change.

Respectfully,

GEO. HOWLAND, JR.

Mayor.

————

MAYOR'S OFFICE,
Wilmington, N. C., May 23d, 1857.

H. R. HELPER, ESQ.,

New-York,

Dear Sir :—

I am in receipt of yours of 19th inst.   The value of real estate as per last assessment, 1st April, 1856, was $3,350,000

We have no system by which to arrive at the value of personal property : I estimate the amount, however, exclusive of merchandize, at $4,509,000

There has been no census taken since 1850—the present number of inhabitants is estimated at 10,000.

I regret my inability to afford you more definite information.

Very respectfully, &c.,

O. G. PARSLEY,

Mayor.

From the foregoing communications, we make up the following summary of the more important particulars :—

NINE FREE CITIES.

Name.	Population.	Wealth.	Wealth per capita.
New York............	700,000	$511,740,492	$731
Philadelphia	500,000	325,000,000	650
Boston	165,000	249,162,500	1,510
Brooklyn..	225,000	95,800,440	425
Cincinnati.	210,000	88,810,734	422
Chicago.............	112,000	171,000,000	1,527
Providence..........	60,000	58,064,516	967
Buffalo.............	90,000	45,474,476	505
New Bedford........	21,000	27,047,000	1,288
	2,083,000	$1,572,100,158	$754

NINE SLAVE CITIES.

Name.	Population.	Wealth.	Wealth per capita.
Baltimore...	250,000	$102,053,839	$408
New Orleans.........	175,000	91,188,195	521
St. Louis............	140,000	63,000,000	450
Charleston...	60,000	36,127,751	602
Louisville...........	70,000	31,500,000	450
Richmond.	40,000	20,143,520	503
Norfolk.............	17,000	12,000,000	705
Savannah...........	25,000	11,999,015	480
Wilmington..	10,000	7,850,000	785
	787,000	$375,862,320	$477

Let it not be forgotten that the slaves themselves are valued at so much per head, and counted as part of the wealth of slave cities ; and yet, though we assent, as we have done, to the inclusion of all this fictitious wealth, it will be observed that the residents of free cities are far wealthier, *per capita*, than the residents of slave cities. We trust the reader will not fa'l to examine the figures with great care

In this age of the world, commerce is an indispensable element of national greatness. Without commerce we can have no great cities, and without great cities we can have no reliable tenure of distinct nationality. Commerce is the forerunner of wealth and population; and it is mainly these that make invincible the power of undying States.

Speaking in general terms of the commerce of this country, and of the great cities through which that commerce is chiefly carried on, the Boston *Traveler* says :—

"The wealth concentrated at the great commercial points of the United States is truly astonishing. For instance, one-eighth part of the entire property of this country is owned by the cities of New-York and Boston. Boston alone, in its corporate limits, owns one-twentieth of the property of this entire Union, being an amount equal to the wealth of any three of the New-England States, except Massachusetts. In this city is found the richest community, *per capita*, of any in the United States. The next city in point of wealth, according to its population, is Providence, (R. I.,) which city is one of the richest in the Union, having a valuation of fifty-six millions, with a population of fifty thousand."

The same paper, in the course of an editorial article on the "Wealth of Boston and its Business," says :—

"The assessors' return of the wealth of Boston will probably show this year an aggregate property of nearly three hundred millions. This sum, divided among 160,000 people, would give nearly $2,000 to each inhabitant, and will show Boston to be much the wealthiest community in the United States, save New York alone, with four times its population. The value of the real estate in this city is increasing now with great rapidity, as at least four millions of dollars' worth of new houses and stores will be built this year. The personal estate in ships, cargoes, stocks, &c., is greatly increasing with each succeeding year, not-withstanding the many disasters and losses constantly occurring in such kinds of property.

" It is impossible to get the exact earnings of the nearly six hundred thousand tons of shipping owned in this city. But per-haps it would not be much out of the way to set the total amount for 1855 at from fifteen to twenty millions of dollars. This sum has probably been earned by our fleet engaged in the domestic trade, and in commercial transactions with the East and West Indies, South America, the Pacific, Europe and Africa. The three sources from which the population of Boston is maintained, and its prosperity continued, are these : Commerce, trade, and manu-factures. Its annual trade and sales of merchandise are said now, by competent judges, to amount to three hundred millions of goods per annum, and will soon greatly exceed that vast sum. The annual manufactures of this city are much more in amount than in many entire States in this Union. They amount, accord-ing to recent statistics, to nearly seventy-five millions of dollars."

Freeman Hunt, the accomplished editor of *Hunt's Mer-chants' Magazine*, writing on the " Progressive Growth of Cities," says :—

" London is now the greatest concentration of human power the world has ever known. Will its supremacy be permanent ? or will it, like its predecessors, be eclipsed by western rivals ? New-Yorkers do not doubt, and indeed have no reason to doubt, that their city, now numbering little more than one-third of the population of London, will, within the next fifty years, be greater than the metropolis of the British empire.

" New York, with her immediate dependencies, numbers about 900,000. Since 1790 she has established a law of growth which doubles her population once in fifteen years. If this law con-tinues to operate, she may be expected to possess 1,800,000 in 1871, 3,600,000 in 1886, and 7,200,000 in 1901. If twenty years be allowed New York as her future period of duplication, she would overtake London by the end of fifty years ; London *may* then have five millions; New-York will almost certainly have more than that number.

Will the star of empire become stationary at New-York? The interior plain of North America has within itself more means to sustain a dense population in civilized comfort than any other region of the world. The star of empire cannot be arrested in its western course before it reaches this plain. Its most promising city at present is Chicago. The law of its growth since 1840 seems to be a duplication within four years. In 1840 it numbered 4,379. In June of this year it will contain 88,000. At the same rate of increase carried forward, it would overtake New-York within twenty years. If six years be allowed for each future duplication, Chicago would overtake New-York in thirty-three years. If the growth of Chicago should in future be measured by a duplication of every seven years, it would contain 5,622,000 in forty-two years.

"In 1901, forty-five years from this time, the central plain, including the Canadas, will contain about eighty millions of people. Its chief city may be reasonably expected to contain about one-tenth of this population. Before the end of this century the towns and cities of the central plain will contain, with their suburbs, not less than half the entire population; that is to say, forty millions. How these millions shall be apportioned among the cities of that day, is a subject for curious speculation."

A FLEET OF MERCHANTMEN.

The Boston *Journal*, of a late date, says :—

"About one hundred sail of vessels, of various descriptions, entered this port yesterday, consisting of traders from Europe, South America, the West Indies, and from coastwise ports. The waters of the bay and harbor presented a beautiful appearance from the surrounding shores, as this fleet of white-winged messengers made their way towards the city, and crowds of people must have witnessed their advent with great delight. A more magnificent sight is seldom seen in our harbor."

Would to God that such sights could sometimes be seen

in Southern harbors ! When slavery shall cease to para-
lyse the energies of our people, then ships, coming to us
from the four quarters of the globe, will, with majestic
grandeur, begin to loom in the distance ; our bays will
rejoice in the presence of "the white-winged messengers,"
and our levees resound as never before with the varied
din of commerce.

COMMERCE OF NORFOLK.

The *Southern Argus* thus speaks of the ruined commerce
of a most despicable niggerville :—

"We question if any other community, certainly no other in
the United States of America, have made greater exertions to
resuscitate the trade of Norfolk than the mercantile portion of
the inhabitants ; in proof of which nineteen-twentieths of those
engaged in foreign commerce have terminated in their insolvency,
the principal cause of which has been in the unrelenting hostility,
to this day, from the commencement of the present century, of
the Virginia Legislature, with the co-operation of at least the
commercial portions of the citizens of Richmond, Petersburg and
Portsmouth."

How it is, in this enlightened age, that men of ordinary
intelligence can be so far led into error as to suppose that
commerce, or any other noble enterprise, can be established
and successfully prosecuted under the dominion of slavery,
is, to us, one of the most inexplicable of mysteries.   "Commercial" Conventions, composed of the self-titled lordlings
of slavery—Generals, Colonels, Majors, Captains, etcætera
—may act out their annual programmes of farcical nonsense from now until doomsday ; but they will never add
one iota to the material, moral, or mental interests of the

South,—never can, until their ebony idol shall have been utterly demolished.

BALTIMORE—PAST, PRESENT, AND FUTURE.

We are indebted to the Baltimore *Patriot* for the following interesting sketch of the Monumental City as it was, and as it is, and as it may be :—

"The population of Baltimore in 1790 was 13,503 ; in 1800, 15,514; in 1810, 35,583; in 1820, 62,738; in 1830, 80,625; in 1840, 110,313; in 1850, 169,054. The increase of inhabitants within two particular decades, will be found, by reference to the above table, to be remarkable. Between 1800 and 1810, the population nearly doubled itself; between 1840 and 1850, the increase was two-thirds ; and for the past five years, the numerical extension of our population has been even more rapid than during the previous decade. We may safely assume that Baltimore contains at the present time not less than 250,000 inhabitants. But the increase in the manufactured products of the State, as shown by the report of the Secretary of the Treasury, is a matter of even greater astonishment. The statistical tables of 1840 estimate the aggregate value of the manufactures of Maryland at $13,509,636—*thirteen million five hundred and nine thousand six hundred and thirty-six dollars.* In 1850, the value of the articles manufactured within the limits of the State amounted to $32,593,635—*thirty-two million five hundred and ninety-three thousand six hundred and thirty-five dollars !* A signal proof that the wealth of the State has increased with even far greater rapidity than its population. A quarter of a century ago, the sum of our manufactures did not much exceed five millions of dollars per annum. At this day it may be set down as falling but little short of fifty millions. These are facts taken from official sources, and therefore understated rather than exceeded. They are easily verified by any one who will take the necessary trouble to examine the reports for himself; and they justify us in the assertion that we are but fifteen years behind Philadelphia in population, and are only at the same relative distance from her in point of wealth.

A change has been going on for some time past in our commercial and industrial affairs which all may have noticed, but the extent of which is known to but few, and we hazard nothing in saying that this enormous progression must continue, because it is based upon a solid foundation, and therefore subject to no ordinary contingencies.

Occupying geographically the most central position on this Continent, with vast mines of coal lying within easy distance to the North and West of us, with a harbor easy of access, and with railroads penetrating by the shortest routes the most fertile sections of the Union, we need nothing but the judicious fostering of a proper spirit among our citizens to make Baltimore not only the commercial emporium of the South and West, but also the great coal mart of the Union. Our flour market is already the most extensive in the known world—we speak without exaggeration, for this also is proven by unquestionable facts. There is more guano annually brought into our port than into all the other ports of the United States put together, and the demand for this important article of commerce is steadily increasing. Our shipments of tobacco are immense, and as the improvement in the depth of the channel of the Patapsco increases, must inevitably become much greater.

Such, then, is our present condition as a commercial community, and when we add that our prosperity is as much owing to our admirable geographical position as to the energy of our merchants and manufacturers, we design to cast no imputation on these excellent citizens, but rather to stimulate them to renewed efforts in a field where enterprise cannot fail of reaping its due reward.

Take any common map of the United States and rule an air line across it from Baltimore to St. Louis, and midway between the two it will strike Cincinnati—the great inland centre of trade—traversing at the same time those wonderfully fertile valleys which lie between the latter point and the Mississippi river. Now let it be remembered that since the introduction of railways fluvial naviga 'on has been, to a considerable extent, superseded by inland transport, because of the greater speed and cer tainty of the latter. Let it be remembered also that the migra- tion westward is incessantly going on, and that with every farm opened within striking distance of a great arterial railway, or its anastomosing branches, a certain amount of freight must find its way to the seaboard markets, while the demand for manufactured products, and for domestic or foreign commodities, in exchange for breadstuffs or raw material, must necessarily increase; thereby adding greatly to the prosperity of the commercial cen- tre towards which articles of export tend, and from which im- ports in return are drawn. It would be difficult to estimate the value of what this trade will be fifty years hence, or what the population of Baltimore, situated as she is, will by that time have become.

Reasoning from causes to effects, and presuming that ordinary perseverance will be used in promoting the interests of our city, industrially and commercially, we are justified in believing that its progress must be in an accelerated ratio, and that there are those now living who will look back with surprise and wonder at its growth and magnitude, as we have done while comparing its present aspect with that which it exhibited within our own memory."

It is a remarkable fact, but one not at all surprising to those whose philosophy leads them to think aright, that Baltimore and St. Louis, the two most prosperous cities in the slave States, have fewer slaves in proportion to the aggregate population than any other city or cities in the South. While the entire population of the former is now estimated at 250,000, and that of the latter at 140,000— making a grand total of 390,000 in the two cities, less than 6,000 of this latter number are slaves; indeed, neither city is cursed with half the number of 6,000.

In 1850, there were only 2,946 slaves in Baltimore, and 2,656 in St. Louis—total in the two cities 5,602; and in both places, thank Heaven, this heathenish class of the population was rapidly decreasing. The census of 1860 will, in all probability, show that the two cities are entirely exempt from slaves and slavery ; and that of 1870 will, we prayerfully hope, show that the United States at large, at that time, will have been wholly redeemed from the unspeakable curse of human bondage.

What about Southern Commerce ? Is it not almost entirely tributary to the commerce of the North ? Are we not dependent on New-York, Philadelphia, Boston, and Cincinnati, for nearly every article of merchandise, whether foreign or domestic ? Where are our ships, our mariners, our naval architects ? Alas ! echo answers, where ?

Reader ! would you understand how abjectly slaveholders themselves are enslaved to the products of Northern industry ? If you would, fix your mind on a Southern "gentleman"—a slave-breeder and human-flesh monger, who professes to be a Christian ! Observe the routine of his daily life. See him rise in the morning from a Northern bed, and clothe himself in Northern apparel ; see him walk across the floor on a Northern carpet, and perform his ablutions out of a Northern ewer and basin. See him uncover a box of Northern powders, and cleanse his teeth with a Northern brush ; see him reflecting his physiognomy in a Northern mirror, and arranging his hair with a Northern comb See him dosing himself with the medicaments of Northern quacks, and perfuming his handkerchief with Northern cologne. See him referring to the time in a Northern watch, and glancing at the news in a Northern gazette. See him and his family sitting in

Northern chairs, and singing and praying out of Northern books. See him at the breakfast table, saying grace over a Northern plate, eating with Northern cutlery, and drinking from Northern utensils. See him charmed with the melody of a Northern piano, or musing over the pages of a Northern novel. See him riding to his neighbor's in a Northern carriage, or furrowing his lands with a Northern plow. See him lighting his segar with a Northern match, and flogging his negroes with a Northern lash. See him with Northern pen and ink, writing letters on Northern paper, and sending them away in Northern envelopes, sealed with Northern wax, and impressed with a Northern stamp. Perhaps our Southern "gentleman" is a merchant; if so, see him at his store, making an unpatriotic use of his time in the miserable traffic of Northern gimcracks and haberdashery; see him when you will, where you will, he is ever surrounded with the industrial products of those whom, in the criminal inconsistency of his heart, he execrates as enemies, yet treats as friends. His labors, his talents, his influence, are all for the North, and not for the South; for the stability of slavery, and for the sake of his own personal aggrandizement, he is willing to sacrifice the dearest interests of his country.

As we see our ruinous system of commerce exemplified in the family of our Southern "gentleman," so we may see it exemplified, to a greater or less degree, in almost every other family throughout the length and breadth of the slaveholding States. We are all constantly buying, and selling, and wearing, and using Northern merchandise, at a double expense to both ourselves and our neighbors. If we but look at ourselves attentively, we shall find that we are all clothed *cap a pie* in Northern habilaments. Our hats, our caps, our cravats, our coats, our vests, our pants, our gloves, our boots, our shoes, our under-garments—all come from the North; whence, too, Southern ladies procure all their bonnets, plumes, and flowers; dresses, shawls, and scarfs; frills, ribbons, and ruffles; cuffs, capes, and collars.

True it is that the South has wonderful powers of endurance and recuperation; but she cannot forever support the reckless prodigality of her sons. We are all spendthrifts; some of us should become financiers. We must learn to take care of our money; we should withhold it from the North, and open avenues for its circulation at home. We should not run to New-York, to Philadelphia, to Boston, to Cincinnati, or to any other Northern city, every time we want a shoe-string or a bedstead, a fish-hook or a handsaw, a tooth-pick or a cotton-gin. In ease and luxury we have been lolling long enough; we should now bestir ourselves, and keep pace with the progress of the age. We must expand our energies, and acquire habits of enterprise and industry; we should arouse ourselves from the couch of lassitude, and inure our minds to thought and our bodies to action. We must begin to feed on a more substantial diet than that of pro-slavery politics; we should leave off our siestas and post-meridian naps, and employ our time in profitable vocations. Before us there is a vast work to be accomplished—a work which has been accumulating on our hands for many years. It is no less a work than that of infusing the spirit of liberty into all our systems of commerce, agriculture, manufactures, government, literature, and religion.   Oligarchal despotism must be overthrown ; slavery must be abolished.

For the purpose of showing how absolutely Southern "gentlemen," particularly slaveholding merchants, are lost to all sense of true honor and patriotism, we will here introduce an extract from an article which appeared more than three years ago in one of the editorial columns of the leading daily newspaper of the city of New-York. It is in these words :—

"Southern merchants do indeed keep away from New-York for the reason that they can't pay their debts ; there is no doubt that if the jobbers of this city had not trusted Southern traders for the past three years, they would be a great deal better off than they are. * * * Already our trade with Canada is becoming as promising, sure, and profitable, as our trade with the South is uncertain, riskful, and annoying."

Now, by any body of men not utterly debased by the influences of slavery, this language would have been construed into an invitation to stay at home.   But do Southern merchants stay at home ?   Do they build up Southern commerce ?   No ! off they post to the North as regularly as the seasons, spring and fall, come round, and there, like cringing sycophants, flatter, beg, and scheme, for favors which they have no money to command.

The better classes of merchants, and indeed of all other people, at the North, as elsewhere, have too much genuine respect for themselves to wish to have any dealings whatever with those who make merchandise of human beings. Limited as is our acquaintance in the city of New-York, we know one firm there, a large wholesale house, that makes it an invariable rule never to sell goods to a merchant from the slave States except for cash. Being well acquainted with the partners, we asked one of them, on one occasion, why he refused to trust slave-driving merchants. "Because," said he, "they are too long-winded and uncertain; when we credit them, they occasion us more loss and bother than their trade is worth." Non-slaveholders of the South! recollect that slavery is the only impediment to your progress and prosperity, that it stands diametrically opposed to all needful reforms, that it seeks to sacrifice you entirely for the benefit of others, and that it is the one great and only cause of dishonor to your country. Will you not abolish it? May Heaven help you to do your duty!

CHAPTER X.

FACTS AND ARGUMENTS BY THE WAYSIDE.

FINDING that we shall have to leave unsaid a great many things which we intended to say, and that we shall have to omit much valuable matter, the product of other pens than our own, but which, having collected at considerable expense, we had hoped to be able to introduce, we have concluded to present, under the above heading, only a few of the more important particulars.

In the first place, we will give an explanation of the reason

WHY THIS WORK WAS NOT PUBLISHED IN BALTIMORE.

A considerable portion of this work was written in Baltimore ; and the whole of it would have been written and published there, but for the following odious clause, which we extract from the Statutes of Maryland :—

"Be it enacted by the General Assembly of Maryland, That after the passage of this act, it shall not be lawful for any citizen of this State, knowingly to make, print or engrave, or aid in the making, printing or engraving, within this State, any pictorial representation, or to write or print, or to aid in the writing or printing any pamphlet, newspaper, handbill or other paper of an inflammatory character, and having a tendency to excite discontent, or stir up insurrection amongst the people of color of this State, or of either of the other States or Territories of the United States, or knowingly to carry or send, or to aid in the carrying or sending the same for circulation amongst the inhabitants of either of the other States or Territories of the United States, and any person so offending shall be guilty of a felony, and shall on conviction be sentenced to confinement in the penitentiary of this State, for a period not less than ten nor more than twenty years, from the time of sentence pronounced on such person."—*Act passed Dec.* 1831. *See 2nd Dorsey, page* 1218.

Now so long as slaveholders are clothed with the mantle of office, so long will they continue to make laws, like the above, expressly calculated to bring the non-slaveholding whites under a system of vassalage little less onerous and debasing than that to which the negroes themselves are accustomed. What wonder is it that there is no native literature in the South? The South can never have a literature of her own until after slavery shall have been abolished. Slaveholders are too lazy and ignorant to write it, and the non-slaveholders—even the few whose minds are cultivated at all—are not permitted even to make the attempt. Down with the oligarchy! Ineligibility of slaveholders—never another vote to the trafficker in human flesh!

LEGISLATIVE ACTS AGAINST SLAVERY.

In his Compendium of the Seventh Census, Mr. DeBow has compiled the following useful and highly interesting facts :—

"The Continental Congress of 1774 resolved to discontinue the slave trade, in which resolution they were anticipated by the Conventions of Delegates of Virginia and North Carolina. In 1789 the Convention to frame the federal Constitution, looked to the abolition of the traffic in 1808. On the 2nd of March, 1807, Congress passed an act against importations of Africans into the United States after January 1st, 1808. An act in Great Britain in 1807 also made the slave trade unlawful. Denmark forbid the introduction of African slaves into her colonies after 1804. The Congress of Vienna, in 1815, pronounced for the abolition of the trade. France abolished it in 1817, and also Spain, but the acts were to take effect after 1820. Portugal abolished it in 1818.

"In Pennsylvania slavery was abolished in 1780. In New Jersey it was provisionally abolished in 1784 ; all children born of a slave after 1804 are made free in 1820. In Massachusetts, it was declared after the revolution, that slavery was virtually abolished by their Constitution, (1780). In 1784 and 1797, Connecticut provided for a gradual extinction of slavery. In Rhode Island, after 1784, no person could be *born* a slave. The Constitutions of Vermont and New Hampshire, respectively, abolished slavery. In New York it was provisionally abolished in 1799, twenty-eight years' ownership being allowed in slaves born after that date, and in 1817 it was enacted that slavery was not to exist after ten years, or 1827. The ordinance of 1787 forbid slavery in the territory northwest of the Ohio."

Besides the instances enumerated above, slavery has been abolished in more than forty different parts of the world within the last half century, and with good results everywhere, except two or three West India islands, where the negro population was greatly in excess of the whites ; and even in these, the evils, if any, that have followed, are not justly attributable to abolition, but to the previous demoralization produced by slavery.

In this connection we may very properly introduce the testimony of a West India planter to the relative advantages of Free over Slave Labor. Listen to Charles Petty-john, of Barbadoes, who, addressing himself to a citizen of our own country, says :—

"In 1834, I came in possession of 257 slaves, under the laws of England, which required the owner to feed, clothe, and furnish them with medical attendance. With this number I cultivated my sugar plantation until the Emancipation Act of August 1st, 1838, when they all became free. I now hire a portion of those slaves, the best and cheapest of course, as you hire men in the United States. The average number which I employ is 100, with which I cultivate more land at a cheaper rate, and make more produce than I did with 257 slaves. With my slaves I made from 100 to 180 tons of sugar yearly. With 100 free negroes I think I do badly if I do not annually produce 250 tons.

If, in the forty and more instances to which we have alluded, the abolition of slavery had proved injurious in a majority of cases, the attempt to abolish it elsewhere might, perhaps, be regarded as an ill-advised effort ; but, seeing that its abolition has worked well in at least four-teen-fifteenths of all the cases on record, the fact becomes obvious that it is our duty and our interest to continue to abolish it until the whole world shall be freed, or until we shall begin to see more evil than good result from our acts of emancipation.

THE TRUE FRIENDS OF THE SOUTH.

Freesoilers and abolitionists are the only true friends of the South ; slaveholders and slave-breeders are downright enemies of their own section. Anti-slavery men are working for the Union and for the good of the whole world ; proslavery men are working for the disunion of the States, and for the good of nothing except themselves. Than such men as Greeley, Seward, Sumner, Clay, and Birney, the South can have no truer friends—nor can slavery have more implacable foes.

For the purpose of showing that Horace Greeley is not, as he is generally represented by the oligarchy, an invete-rate hater of the South, we will here introduce an extract from one of his editorial articles in a late number of the New York *Tribune*—a faithful advocate of freedom, whose circulation, we are happy to say, is greater than the aggregate circulation of more than twenty of the principal proslavery sheets published at the South :—

"Is it in vain that we pile fact upon fact, proof on proof, show-ing that slavery is a blight and a curse to the States which cher-ish it ? These facts are multitudinous as the leaves of the forest ; conclusive as the demonstrations of geometry. Nobody attempts to refute them, but the champions of slavery extension seem de-termined to persist in ignoring them. Let it be understood. then, once for all, that we do not hate the South, war on the South, nor seek to ruin the South, in resisting the extension of slavery. We most earnestly believe human bondage a curse to the South, and to all whom it affects ; but we do not labor for its overthrow otherwise than through the conviction of the South of its injustice and mischief. Its extension into new Territories we determinedly resist, not by any means from ill will to the South, but under the impulse of good will to all mankind. We believe the establishment of slavery in Kansas or any other Western Territory would prolong its existence in Virginia and Maryland, by widening the market and increasing the price of slaves, and thereby increasing the profits of slave-breeding, and the conse-quent incitement thereto. Those who urge that slavery would not go into Kansas if permitted, wilfully shut their eyes to the fact that it *has gone* into Missouri, lying in exactly the same lati-tude, and is now strongest in that north-western angle of said State, which was covertly filched from what is now Kansas, within the last twenty years. Even if the growth of hemp, corn and tobacco were not so profitable in Eastern Kansas, as it evidently must be, the growth of slaves for more Southern consumption would inevitably prove as lucrative there as in Virginia and Maryland, which lie in corresponding latitudes, and whose chief staple export to-day consists of negro bondmen destined for the plantations of Louisiana and Mississippi, which could be supplied more conveniently and cheaply from Kansas than from their present breeding-places this side of the Alleghanies.

Whenever we draw a parallel between Northern and Southern production, industry, thrift, wealth, the few who seek to parry the facts at all complain that the instances are unfairly selected— that the commercial ascendancy of the North, with the profits and facilities thence accruing, accounts for the striking preponderance of the North. In vain we insist that slavery is the cause of this very commercial ascendancy—that Norfolk and Richmond and Charleston might have been to this country what Boston, New-York and Philadelphia now are, had not slavery spread its pall over and paralyzed the energies of the South."

This may be regarded as a fair expression of the sentiments of a great majority of the people north of Mason and Dixon's line. Our Northern cousins " do not hate the South, war on the South, nor seek to ruin the South ;" on the contrary, they love our particular part of the nation, and, like dutiful, sensible, upright men, they would promote its interests by facilitating the abolition of slavery. Success to their efforts !

SLAVERY THOUGHTFUL—SIGNS OF CONTRITION.

The real condition of the South is most graphically described in the following doleful admissions from the Charleston *Standard* :—

"In its every aspect our present condition is provincial. We have within our limits no solitary metropolis of interest or ideas

-no marts of exchange—no radiating centres of opinion. Whatever we have of genius and productive energy, goes freely in to swell the importance of the North. Possessing the material which constitutes two-thirds of the commerce of the whole country, it might have been supposed that we could have influence upon the councils of foreign States ; but we are never taken into contemplation. It might have been supposed that England, bound to us by the cords upon which depend the existence of four millions of her subjects, would be considerate of our feelings ; but receiving her cotton from the North. it is for them she has concern, and it is her interest and her pleasure to reproach us. It might have been supposed, that, producing the material which is sent abroad, to us would come the articles that are taken in exchange for it ; but to the North they go for distribution, and to us are parcelled out the fabrics that are suited to so remote a section.

Instead, therefore, of New-York being tributary to Norfolk, Charleston, Savannah or New Orleans, these cities are tributary to New-York. Instead of the merchants of New-York standing cap in hand to the merchants of Charleston, the merchants of Charleston stand cap in hand to the merchants of New-York.— Instead of receiving foreign ships in Southern waters, and calling up the merchants of the country to a distribution of the cargo, the merchants of the South are hurried off to make a distribution elsewhere. In virtue of our relations to a greater system, we have little development of internal interests ; receiving supplies from the great centre, we have made little effort to supply ourselves. We support the makers of boots, shoes, hats, coats, shirts, flannels, blankets, carpets, chairs, tables, mantels, mats, carriages, jewelry, cradles, couches, coffins, by the thousand and hundreds of thousands ; but they scorn to live amongst us. They must have the gaieties and splendors of a great metropolis, and are not content to vegetate upon the dim verge of this remote frontier.

As it is in material interests, so it is in arts and letters—our pictures are painted at the North, our books are published at the North, our periodicals and papers are printed at the North. We are even fed on police reports and villany from the North. The papers published at the South which ignore the questions at issue between the sections are generally well sustained; the books which expose the evils of our institution are even read with avidity beyond our limits, but the ideas that are turned to the condition of the South are intensely provincial. If, as things now are, a man should rise with all the genius of Shakspeare, or Dickens, or Fielding, or of all the three combined, and speak from the South, he would not receive enough to pay the costs of publication. If published at the South, his book would never be seen or heard of, and published at the North it would not be read.— So perfect is our provincialism, therefore, that enterprise is forced to the North for a sphere—talent for a market—genius for the ideas upon which to work—indolence for ease, and the tourist for attractions."

This extract exhibits in bold relief, and in small space, a large number of the present evils of past errors. It is charmingly frank and truthful. DeQuincey's Confessions of an opium eater are nothing to it. A distinguished writer on medical jurisprudence informs us that "the knowledge of the disease is half the cure;" and if it be true, as perhaps it is, we think the *Standard* is in a fair way to be reclaimed from the enormous vices of proslavery statism.

PROGRESS OF FREEDOM IN THE SOUTH.

" Now, by St. Paul, the work goes bravely on."

As well might the oligarchy attempt to stay the flux and reflux of the tides, as to attempt to stay the progress of Freedom in the South. Approved of God, the edict of the genius of Universal Emancipation has been proclaimed to the world, and nothing, save Deity himself, can possibly reverse it. To connive at the perpetuation of slavery is to disobey the commands of Heaven. Not to be an abolitionist is to be a wilful and diabolical instrument of the devil. The South needs to be free, the South wants to be free, the South *shall* be free !

The following extracts from Southern journals will show that the glorious light of a better era has already begun to penetrate and dispel the portentous clouds of slavery. The Wellsburg (Va.) *Herald*, an independent paper, referring to the vote of thirteen Democrats from that section, refusing, in the Virginia Legislature, in 1856, " to appropriate money from the general treasury for the recapture of runaway slaves," says :—

" We presume these delegates in some degree represent their constituents, and we are thereby encouraged and built up in the confidence that there are other interests in Virginia to be seen to besides those pertaining to slavery."

A non-slaveholding Southron, in the course of a communication in a more recent number of the same journal, says :—

" We are taxed to support slavery. The clean cash goes out of our own pockets into the pockets of the slaveholder, and this in many ways. I will now allude to but two. If a slave, for crime, is put to death or transported, the owner is paid for him out of the public treasury, and under this law thousands are paid out every year. Again, a standing army is kept up in the city of Richmond for no other purpose than to be ready to quell insurrection among the slaves ; this is paid for out of the public treasury annually. This standing army is called the public guard, but it is no less a standing army always kept up. We will quote from the acts of 1856 the expense of these two items to the State, on the 23d and 24th pages of the acts :—' To pay for slaves executed and transported, $22,000 ;' ' to the public guard at Richmond, $24,000.' This, be it noticed, is only for one year, making near $50,000 for these two objects in one year; but it can be shown by the present unequal plan of taxation between slave property and other property, that this is but a small item of our cash pocketed by the slaveholders; and yet some will say we have no reason to complain."

The editor of the Wheeling *Gazette* publishes the following as his platform on the slavery question :—

" Allying ourself to neither North nor South, on our own hook we adopt the following platform as our platform on this question, from which we never have and never will recede. *We may* FALL *on it, but* WILL NEVER LEAVE IT.

The severance of the General Government from slavery.

The REPEAL *of the fugitive slave law.*

The REPEAL *of the Nebraska Kansas Bill.*

No more slave territories.

THE PURCHASE AND MANUMISSION OF SLAVES IN THE DISTRICT OF COLUMBIA, OR THE REMOVAL OF THE SEAT OF GOVERNMENT TO FREE TERRITORY."

Says the Baltimore *Clipper:—*

'The South is contending for, and the North against, the extension of slavery into the territories; but we do not think that either side would consent to dissolve the Union about the negro population—a population which we look upon as a curse to the nation, and should rejoice to see removed to their native clime of Africa."

The *National Era*, one of the best papers in the country, published in Washington City, D. C., says :—

" The tendency of slavery to diffuse itself, and to crowd out free labor, was early observed by American patriots, North and South; and Mr. Jefferson, the great apostle of Republicanism, made an effort, in 1784, to cut short the encroaching tide of barbaric despotism, by prohibiting slavery in all the territories of

16*

the Union, down to thirty-one degrees of latitude, which was
then our Southern boundary. His beneficent purpose failed, not
for want of a decisive majority of votes present in the Congress
of the Confederation, but in consequence of the absence of the
delegates from one or two States, which were necessary to the
constitutional majority. When the subject again came up, in
1787, Mr. Jefferson was Minister to France, and the famous ordinance of that year was adopted, prohibiting slavery North and
West of the Ohio river. Between 1784 and 1787, the strides of
slavery westward, into Tennessee and Kentucky, had become too
considerable to admit of the policy of exclusion; and besides
those regions were then integral parts of Virginia and North
Carolina, and of course they could not be touched without the
consent of those States. In 1820, another effort was made to ar-
rest the progress of slavery, which threatened to monopolize the
whole territory west of the Mississippi. In the meantime the
South had apostatized from the faith of Jefferson. It had ceased
to love universal liberty, and the growing importance of the cotton culture had caused the people to look with indifference upon
the moral deformity of slavery; and, as a matter of course, the politicians became its apologists and defenders. After a severe struggle a compromise was agreed upon, by which Missouri was to be
admitted with slavery, which was the immediate point in controversy; and slavery was to be excluded from all the territory
North and West of that State.

"We have shown, from the most incontestable evidence, that
there is in slave society a much greater tendency to diffuse itself
into new regions, than belongs to freedom, for the reason that it
has no internal vitality. It cannot live if circumscribed, and
must, like a consumptive, be continually roving for a change of
air to recuperate its wasting energies."

In the Missouri Legislature, in January, 1857, Mr. Brown,
of St. Louis, proved himself a hero, a patriot, and a statesman, in the following words :—

"I am a Free-Soiler and I don't deny it. No word or vote of
mine shall ever inure to the benefit of such a monstrous doctrine

as the extension of Slavery over the patrimony of the free white laborers of the country. I am for the greatest good of the greatest number, and against the system which monopolizes the free and fertile territory of our country for a few slaveholders, to the exclusion of thousands upon thousands of the sinewy sons of toil. The time will come, and perhaps very soon, when the people will rule for their own benefit *and not for that of a class which, numerically speaking, is insignificant.* I stand here in the midst of the assembled Legislature of Missouri to avow myself a Free-Soiler. Let those who are scared at names shrink from the position if they will. I shall take my stand in favor of the white man. Here in Missouri I shall support the rights, the dignity and the welfare of the 800,000 non-slaveholders in preference to upholding and perpetuating the dominancy of the 30,000 slaveholders who inhabit our State."

The St. Louis *Democrat,* in an editorial article, under date of January 28, 1857, entitled itself to the favorable regard of every true lover of liberty, by talking thus boldly on the subject of the "Emancipation of Slavery in Missouri" :—

"Viewing the question as a subject of State policy, we will venture to say that it is the grandest ever propounded to the people. If it were affirmed in a constitutional convention, and thoroughly carried out without any violation of vested rights, Missouri, in a few years subsequent to its consummation, would be the foremost State on the American continent. Population would flow in from all sides were the barrier of negro slavery once removed, and in place of 80,000 slaves, we should have 800,000 white men, which, in addition to the population we would have at that time, would give us at once an aggregate of two millions.

Is Missouri ambitious of political power?—a power which is slipping away from the South. The mode of acquiring it is found. We are not rash enough to attempt a description of our condition if the element of free labor were introduced. The earth would give up its hidden treasures at its bidding as the sea will give up its dead; and the soil would bloom more luxuriantly than if it drank the dews of Hermon nightly; ten thousand keels would vex our rivers, towns along their banks would grow into cities, and St. Louis would soon unite in itself the attributes of the greatest commercial manufacturing and literary metropolis in the world. Let it be remembered that we have every inanimate element of wealth and power within our limits, and that we require only labor—free labor—for we need not say that servile labor is inadequate.   *   *   *

There need be no pernicious agitation, and even if there should, it is the penalty which we cannot avoid paying at some time; and it is easier to pay it now, than in the future. Who that watches passing events and indications, is not sensible of the fact that great internal convulsions await the slave States? Better to grapple with the danger in time, if danger there be, and avert it, than wait until it becomes formidable. One thing is certain, or history is no guide: that is, that slavery cannot be perpetuated anywhere. An agitation now would be the effort of the social system to throw off a disease which had not touched its vitals; hereafter it would be the struggle for life with a mortal sickness. But we do not apprehend any agitation more violent than has been forced upon us for years by the pro-slavery politicians. Agitating the slavery question, has been their constant business, and nothing worse has resulted from it than their elevation to office—no very trifling evil, by the way—and the temporary subjugation of Kansas.

Besides, we know that all the free States emancipated their slaves, and England and France theirs suddenly; and we have yet to learn that a dangerous agitation arose in any instance."

In addition to all this, it is well known, and we thank Heaven for the fact and for the indication, that, at the election held for Mayor of St. Louis, in April, 1857, the Abolition candidate, himself a native of Virginia, was triumphantly elevated to the chief magistracy of the city. Three cheers for St. Louis! nine for Missouri! thirteen for the South!

In reference to the late election in St. Louis, in which the Emancipation party triumphed, the Wheeling (Va.) *Intelligencer* says :—

"These elections do demonstrate this fact, beyond a cavil, that the sentiment of the great majority of the people of this Union is irrevocably opposed to the extension of slavery ; that they are determined, if overwhelming public sentiment can avail anything, another slave State shall not be admitted into the confederacy. And why are they so determined? Because they believe, and not only believe, but see and know, that slavery is an unmitigated curse to the soil that sustains it. They know this, because they see every free State outstripping every slave State in all the elements that make a people powerful and prosperous ; because they see the people in the one educated and thrifty, and in the other ignorant and thriftless ; because they have before their eyes a State like our own, once the very Union itself almost in importance, to-day taking her rank as a fifth rate power."

Non-slaveholders of the South ! fail not to support the papers—the Southern papers—that support your interests. Chief amongst those papers are the St. Louis (Mo.) *Democrat*, the *National Era*, published in Washington City, D. C., the Baltimore *Clipper*, the Wheeling (Va.) *Intelligencer*, and the Wellsburg (Va.) *Herald*.

A RIGHT FEELING IN THE RIGHT QUARTER.

There is but one way for the oligarchy to perpetuate slavery in the Southern States, and that is by perpetuating absolute ignorance among the non-slaveholding whites. This it is quite impossible for them to do. God has scattered the seeds of knowledge throughout every portion of the South, and they are, as might have been expected, beginning to take roo in her fertile soil. The following extracts from letters which have been received since we commenced writing this work, will show how powerfully the spirit of freedom is operating upon the minds of intelligent, thinking men in the slave States.

A Baltimorean, writing to us awhile previous to the last Presidential election, says :—

"I see that the Trustees of the University of North Carolina have dismissed Prof. Hedrick for writing a letter in favor of Republican principles. Oh, what an inglorious source of reflection for an American citizen! To think, to know that our boasted liberty of speech is a myth, an abstraction. To see a poor professor crushed under the feet of the tyrannical magnates of slavery, for daring to speak the honest sentiments of his heart. Where is fanaticism now, North or South? Oh, my country, my country, whither art thou tending? Truly we have fallen upon degenerate days. God grant that they may not be like those of ancient Greece and Rome, the forerunners of our country's ruin."

In a letter under date of November 1, 1856, a friend who resides in the eastern. part of North Carolina, says :—

"In the papers which reached me last week I notice that our own State has been disgraced by a junto of pro-slavery hot-spurs, who had the audacity to meet in Raleigh for the express purpose of concocting measures for a dissolution of the Union. It appears that the three leading spirits of this cabal were the present governors of three neighboring States—three treasonable disturbers of the public peace, who, under the circumstances, should, in my opinion, have been shot dead upon the spot! I have each of their names noted down in my memorandum, and I shall certainly die unsatisfied, if I do not live to hear of their being thoroughly tarred and feathered, and ridden on a rail, by the non-slaveholding whites, against whose welfare their machinations have been chiefly leveled. Rely upon it, that, if they do not soon sneak away into their graves, a day of retributive justice will most assuredly overtake them."

A native and resident of one of the towns in western North Carolina, under date of March 19, 1857, writes to us as follows :—

" While patrolling a few nights ago I was forcibly struck with the truthfulness of the remarks contained in your last letter.— Here I am, a poor but sober and industrious man, with a family dependent on me for support, and after I have finished my day's labor, I am compelled to walk the streets from nine in the evening till three in the morning, to restrain the roving propensities of other people's 'property'—niggers. Why should I thus be deprived of sleep that the slaveholder may slumber? I frankly acknowledge my indebtedness to you for opening my eyes upon this subject. The more I think and see of slavery the more I detest it. * * * I am becoming restless, and have been debating within my own mind whether I had not better emigrate to a free State. * * * If I live, I am determined to oppose slavery somewhere—here or elsewhere. It will be impossible for me to keep my lips sealed much longer. Indeed, I sometimes feel that I have been remiss in my duty in not having opened them ere now. But for the unfathomable ignorance that pervades the mass of the poor, deluded, slavery saddled whites around me, I would not suppress my sentiments another hour."

Again, under date of April 7, 1857, he says :—

"I thank God that slavery will, in my opinion, soon be abolished. I wish to Heaven I had the ability to raise my voice successfully in favor of a just system to abolish it. I would indeed be rejoiced to have an opportunity to do something to relieve the South of the awful curse. Fear not that you will meet with no sympathizers in the South. You will have hosts of friends on every side—even in this town, if I am not greatly mistaken, a large majority of the citizens will add an enthusiastic *Amen!* to your work."

We might furnish similar extracts from other letters, but these, we think, are quite sufficient to show that the millennium of freedom is rapidly dawning throughout the benighted regions of slavery. Coveted events are happening in charming succession. All we have to do is to wait and work a little longer.

THE ILLITERATE POOR WHITES OF THE SOUTH.

Had we the power to sketch a true picture of life among the non-slaveholding whites of the South, every intelligent man who has a spark of philanthropy in his breast, and who should happen to gaze upon the picture, would burn with unquenchable indignation at that system of African slavery which entails unutterable miseries on the superior race. It is quite impossible, however, to describe accurately the deplorable ignorance and squalid poverty of the class to which we refer. The serfs of Russia have reason to congratulate themselves that they are neither the negroes nor the non-slaveholding whites of the South. Than the latter there can be no people in Christendom more unhappily situated. Below will be found a few extracts which will throw some light on the subject now under consideration.

Says William Gregg,[29] in an address delivered before the South Carolina Institute, in 1851 :—

" From the best estimates that I have been able to make, I put down the white people who ought to work, and who do not, or who are so employed as to be wholly unproductive to the State, at one hundred and twenty-five thousand. Any man who is an observer of things could hardly pass through our country, without being struck with the fact that all the capital, enterprise, and intelligence, is employed in directing slave labor; and the consequence is, that a large portion of our poor white people are wholly neglected, and are suffered to while away an existence in a state but one step in advance of the Indian of the forest. It is an evil of vast magnitude, and nothing but a change in public sentiment will effect its cure. These people must be brought into daily contact with the rich and intelligent—they must be stimulated to mental action, and taught to appreciate education and the comforts of civilized life; and this, we believe, may be effected only by the introduction of manufactures. My experience at Graniteville has satisfied me that unless our poor people can be brought together in villages, and some means of employment afforded them, it will be an utterly hopeless effort to undertake to educate them. We have collected at that place about eight hundred people, and as likely looking a set of country girls as may be found—industrious and orderly people, but deplorably ignorant, three-fourths of the adults not being able to read or to write their own names.

"It is only necessary to build a manufacturing village of shanties, in a healthy location, in any part of the State, to have crowds of these people around you, seeking employment at half the compensation given to operatives at the North. It is indeed painful to be brought in contact with such ignorance and degradation."

Again he asks :—

"Shall we pass unnoticed the thousands of poor, ignorant, degraded white people among us, who, in this land of plenty, live in comparative nakedness and starvation? Many a one is reared in *proud* South Carolina, from birth to manhood, who has never passed a month in which he has not, some part of the time, been stinted for meat. Many a mother is there who will tell you that her children are but scantily provided with bread, and much more scantily with meat; and, if they be clad with comfortable raiment, it is at the expense of these scanty allowances of food. These may be startling statements, but they are nevertheless true; and if not believed in Charleston, the members of our legislature who have traversed the State in electioneering campaigns can attest the truth."

In an article on " *Manufactures in South Carolina*," published some time ago in *DeBow's Review*, J. H. Taylor, of Charleston (S. C.) says :—

" There is in some quarters, a natural jealousy of the slightest innovation upon established habits, and because an effort has been made to collect the poor and unemployed white population into our new factories, fears have arisen that some evil would grow out of the introduction of such establishments among us. * * * The poor man has a vote as well as the rich man, and in our State the number of the former will largely overbalance the latter. So long as these poor but industrious people can see no mode of living except by a degrading operation of work with the negro upon the plantation, they will be content to endure life in its most discouraging forms, satisfied that they are *above* the slave, though faring often worse than he."

Speaking in favor of manufactures, the Hon. J. H. Lumpkin, of Georgia, said in 1852 :—

" It is objected that these manufacturing establishments will become the hot-beds of crime. But I am by no means ready to concede that our poor, degraded, half-fed, half-clothed, and ignorant population—without Sabbath Schools, or any other kind of instruction, mental or moral, or without any just appreciation of character—will be injured by giving them employment, which will bring them under the oversight of employers, who will inspire them with self-respect by taking an interest in their welfare."

In a paper on the "*Extension of Cotton and Wool Factories at the South*," Mr. Steadman, of Tennessee, says :—

"In Lowell, labor is paid the fair compensation of 80 cents a day for men, and $2 a week for women, beside board, while in Tennessee the average compensation for labor does not exceed 50 cents per day for men, and $1,25 per week for women."

In the course of a speech which he delivered in Congress several years ago, Mr. T. L. Clingman, of North Carolina, said :—

"Our manufacturing establishments can obtain the raw material (cotton) at nearly two cents on the pound cheaper than the New-England establishments. Labor is likewise one hundred per cent. cheaper. In the upper parts of the State, the labor of either a free man or a slave, including board, clothing, &c., can be obtained for from $110 to $120 per annum. It will cost at least twice that sum in New-England. The difference in the cost of female labor, whether free or slave, is even greater."

The Richmond (Va.) *Dispatch* says :—

"We will only suppose that the ready-made shoes imported into this city from the North, and sold here, were manufactured in Richmond. What a great addition it would be to the means of employment! How many boys and females would find the means of earning their bread, who are now suffering for a regular supply of the necessaries of life."

A citizen of New-Orleans, writing in *DeBow's Review*, says :—

"At present the sources of employment open to females (save in menial offices) are very limited ; and an inability to procure suitable occupation is an evil much to be deplored, as tending in its consequences to produce demoralization. The superior grades of female labor may be considered such as imply a necessity for education on the part of the employee, while the menial class is generally regarded as of the lowest ; and in a slave State, this standard is 'in the lowest depths, a lower deep,' from the fact, that, by association, it is a reduction of the white servant to the level of their colored fellow-menials."

Black slave labor, though far less valuable, is almost invariably better paid than free white labor. The reason is this : The fiat of the oligarchy has made it *fashionable* to "have negroes around," and there are, we are grieved to say, many non-slaveholding whites, (lickspittles,) who, in order to retain on their premises a hired slave whom they falsely imagine secures to them not only the appearance of wealth, but also a position of high social standing in the community, keep themselves in a perpetual strait.

Last Spring we made it our special business to ascertain the ruling rates of wages paid for labor, free and slave, in North Carolina. We found sober, energetic white men, between twenty and forty years of age, engaged in agricultural pursuits at a salary of $84 per annum—including board only ; negro men, slaves, who performed little more than half the amount of labor, and who were exceedingly sluggish, awkward, and careless in all their movements, were hired out on adjoining farms at an average of about $115 per annum, including board, clothing, and medical attendance. Free white men and slaves were in the employ of the North Carolina Railroad Company ; the former, whose services, in our opinion, were at least twice as valuable as the services of the latter, received only $12 per month each ; the masters of the latter received $16 per month for every slave so employed. Industrious, tidy white girls, from sixteen to twenty years of age, had much difficulty in hiring themselves out as domestics in private families for $40 per annum—board only included ; negro wenches, slaves, of corresponding ages, so ungraceful, stupid and filthy that no decent man would ever permit one of them to cross the threshold of his dwelling, were in brisk demand at from $65 to $70 per annum, including victuals, clothes, and medical attendance.   These are facts, and in considering them, the students of political and social economy will not fail to arrive at conclusions of their own.

Notwithstanding the greater density of population in the free States, labor of every kind is, on an average, about one hundred per cent. higher there than it is in the slave States.   This is another important fact, and one that every non-slaveholding white should keep registered in his mind.

Poverty, ignorance, and superstition, are the three leading characteristics of the non-slaveholding whites of the South.   Many of them grow up to the age of maturity, and pass through life without ever owning as much as five dollars at any one time.   Thousands of them die at an advanced age, as ignorant of the common alphabet as if it had never been invented.   All are more or less impressed with a belief in witches, ghosts, and supernatural signs. Few are exempt from habits of sensuality and intemperance. None have anything like adequate ideas of the duties which they owe either to their God, to themselves, or to their fellow-men.   Pitiable, indeed, in the fullest sense of the term, is their condition.

It is the almost utter lack of an education that has reduced them to their present unenviable situation. In the whole South there is scarcely a publication of any kind devoted to their interests. They are now completely under the domination of the oligarchy, and it is madness to suppose that they will ever be able to rise to a position of true manhood, until after the slave power shall have been utterly overthrown.

CHAPTER XI.

SOUTHERN LITERATURE.

IT is with some degree of hesitation that we add a chapter on Southern Literature—not that the theme is inappropriate to this work ; still less, that it is an unfruitful one ; but our hesitation results from our conscious inability, in the limited time and space at our command, to do the subject justice. Few, except those whose experience has taught them, have any adequate idea of the amount of preparatory labor requisite to the production of a work into which the statistical element largely enters ; especially is this so, when the statistics desired are not readily accessible through public and official documents. The author who honestly aims at entire accuracy in his statements, may find himself baffled for weeks in his pursuit of a single item of information, not of much importance in itself perhaps, when separately considered, but necessary in its connection with others, to the completion of a harmonious whole. Not unfrequently, during the preparation of the preceding pages, have we been subjected to this delay and annoyance.

The following brief references to the protracted preparatory labors and inevitable delays to which authors are subjected, may interest our readers, and induce them to regard with charity any deficiencies, either in detail or in general arrangement, which, owing to the necessary haste of preparation, these concluding pages of our work may exhibit :

Goldsmith was engaged nine years in the preparation of "*The Traveller*," and five years in gathering and arranging the incidents of his "*Deserted Village*," and two years in their versification.

Bancroft, the American Historian, has been more than thirty years engaged upon his History of the United States, from his projection of the work to the present date ; and that History is not yet completed.

Hildreth, a no less eminent historian, from the time he began to collect materials for his History of the United States to the date of its completion, devoted no less than twenty-five years to the work.

Webster, our great lexicographer, gave thirty-five years of his life in bringing his Unabridged Dictionary of the English Language to the degree of accuracy and completeness in which we now find it.

Dr. John W. Mason, after ten years' labor in the accumulation of materials for a Life of Alexander Hamilton, was compelled to relinquish the work on account of impaired health.

Mr. James Banks, of Fayetteville, North Carolina, who recently delivered a lecture upon the Life and Character of Flora McDonald, was eighteen years in the collection of his materials.

Oulibicheff, a distinguished Russian author, spent twenty-five years in writing the Life of Mozart.

Examples of this kind might be multiplied to an almost indefinite extent. Indeed, almost all the poets, prose-writers, painters, sculptors, composers, and other devotees of Art, who have won undying fame for themselves, have done so through long years of earnest and almost unre-mitted toil.

We are quite conscious that the fullness and accuracy of statement which are desirable in this chapter cannot be attained in the brief time allowed us for its completion ; but, though much will necessarily be omitted that ought to be said, we shall endeavor to make no statement of facts which are not well authenticated, and no inferences from the same which are not logically true. We can only promise to do the best in our power, with the materials at our command, to exhibit the inevitable influence of slavery upon Southern Literature, and to demonstrate that the ac-cursed institution so cherished by the oligarchy, is no less prejudicial to our advancement in letters, than it is destruc-tive of our material prosperity.

What is the actual condition of Literature at the South ? Our question includes more than simple authorship in the various departments of letters, from the compilation of a primary reader to the production of a Scientific or Theo-logical Treatise. We comprehend in it all the activities engaged in the creation, publication, and sale of books and periodicals, from the penny primer to the heavy folio, and from the dingy, coarse-typed weekly paper, to the large, well-filled daily.

17

It were unjust to deny a degree of intellectual activity to the South. It has produced a few good authors—a few competent editors, and a moderately large number of clever magazinists, paragraphists, essayists and critics. Absolutely, then, it must be conceded that the South has something that may be called a literature ; it is only when we speak of her in comparison with the North, that we say, with a pardonably strong expression, "The South has no literature." This was virtually admitted by more than one speaker at the late "Southern Convention" at Savannah. Said a South Carolina orator on that occasion : " It is important that the South *should have* a literature of her own, to defend her principles and her rights ;" a sufficiently plain concession that she has not, now, such a literature. But *facts* speak more significantly than the rounded periods of Convention orators. Let us look at facts, then.

First, turning our attention to the periodical literature of the South, we obtain these results : By the census of 1850, we ascertain that the entire number of periodicals, daily, semi-weekly, weekly, semi-monthly, monthly and quarterly, published in the slave States, including the District of Columbia, were seven hundred and twenty-two. These had an aggregate *yearly* circulation of ninety-two million one hundred and sixty-seven thousand one hundred and twenty-nine. (92,167,129). The number of periodicals, of every class, published in the non-slaveholding States (exclusive of California) was one thousand eight hundred and ninety-three, with an aggregate yearly circulation of three hundred and thirty-three million three hundred and eighty-six thousand and eighty-one. (333,386,081).

We are aware that there may be inaccuracies in the fore-going estimates ; but the compilers of the census, not we, are responsible for them. Besides, the figures are unquestionably as fair for the South as for the North ; we accept them, therefore, as a just basis of our comparisons. Nearly seven years have elapsed since these statistics were taken, and these seven years have wrought an immense change in the journalism of the North, without any corresponding change in that of the South. It is noteworthy that, as a general thing, the principal journals of the free States are more comprehensive in their scope, more complete in every department, and enlist, if not a higher order of talent, at least *more* talent, than they did seven years ago. This improvement extends not only to the metropolitan, but to the country papers also. In fact, the very highest literary ability, in finance, in political economy, in science, in statism, in law, in theology, in medicine, in the belles-lettres, is laid under contribution by the journals of the non-slave-holding States. This is true only to a very limited degree of Southern journals. Their position, with but few exceptions, is substantially the same that it was ten years ago. They are neither worse nor better—the imbecility and inertia which attaches to everything which slavery touches, clings to them now as tenaciously as it did when Henry A. Wise thanked God for the paucity of newspapers in the Old Dominion, and the platitudes of "Father" Ritchie were recognized as the political gospel of the South. They have not, so far as we can learn, increased materially in number, nor in the aggregate of their yearly circulation. In the free States, no week passes that does not add to the number of their journals, and extend the circle of their readers and their influence. Since the census tables to which we have referred were prepared, two of the many excellent weekly journals of which the city of New-York can boast, have sprung into being, and attained an aggregate circulation more than twice as large as that of the entire newspaper press of Virginia in 1850—and exceeding, by some thousands, the aggregate circulation of the two hundred and fifty journals of which Alabama, Arkansas, Kentucky, Georgia, North Carolina and Florida, could boast at the time above-mentioned.

In this connection, we beg leave to introduce the following letter, kindly furnished us by the proprietors of the N. Y. Tribune, in answer to enquiries which we addressed to them :—

TRIBUNE OFFICE, NEW YORK,
30th May, 1857.

MR. H. R. HELPER,
            Sir :—

In answer to your inquiry we inform you that we employ in our building one hundred and seventy-six persons regularly : this does not include our carriers and cartmen, nor does it include the men employed in the Job Office in our building. During the past year we have used in printing *The Tribune*, Forty-four thousand nine hundred and seventy nine (44,979) reams of paper, weighing two million three hundred and ten thousand one hundred and thirty (2,310,130) pounds. We publish one hundred and seventy-six thousand copies of our weekly edition, which goes to press, the second form, at 7 1-2 o'clock, A. M. and is finished at 2 A. M. the next morning. Our mailers require eighteen to nineteen hours to mail our Weekly, which makes from thirty to thirty-two cart loads.

            Very respectfully,
                GREELEY & McELRATH.

Throughout the non-slaveholding States, the newspaper or magazine that has *not* improved during the last decade of years, is an exception to the general rule. Throughout the entire slaveholding States, the newspaper or magazine that *has* improved during that time, is no less an exception to the general rule that there obtains. Outside of the larger cities of the South, there are not, probably, half a dozen newspapers in the whole slaveholding region that can safely challenge a comparison with the country-press of the North. What that country-press was twenty years ago, the country-press of the South is now.

We do not deny that the South has produced able journalists ; and that some of the newspapers of her principal cities exhibit a degree of enterprise and talent that cannot fail to command for them the respect of all intelligent men. But these journals, we regret to say, are marked exceptions to the general condition of the Southern press ; and even the best of these fall far below the standard of excellence attained by the leading journals of the North. In fact, whether our comparison embraces quantity only, or extends to both quantity and quality, it is found to be immeasurably in favor of the non-slaveholding States, which in journalism, as in all other industrial pursuits, leave their slavery-cursed competitors at an infinite distance behind them, and thus vindicate the superiority of free institutions, which, recognizing labor as honorable, secure its rewards for all.

The literary vassalage of the South to the North constitutes in itself a most significant commentary upon the diatribes of the former concerning " a purely Southern literature." To begin at the beginning—the Alphabetical Blocks and Educational tables from which our Southern abecedarian takes his initial lesson, were projected and manufactured in the North. Going forward a step, we find the youngling intent in spelling short sentences, or gratifying his juvenile fondness for the fine arts by copying the wood-cuts from his Northern primer. Yet another step, and we discover him with his Sanders' Reader, his Mitchell's Geography, his Emerson's Arithmetic, all produced by Northern mind and Northern enterprise. There is nothing *wrong* in this ; it is only a little ridiculous in view of the fulminations of the Southern proslavery press against the North. Occasionally however we are amused by the efforts of the oligarchs to make their own school-books, or to root out of all educational text-books every reference to the pestilential heresy of freedom. A " gentleman" in Charleston, S. C. is devoting his energies to the preparation of a series of pro-slavery elementary works, consisting of primers, readers, &c.—and lo ! they are all printed, stitched and bound north of Mason and Dixon's line ! A single *fact* like this is sufficient to overturn whole folios of *theory* concerning the divinity of slavery. The truth is, that, not school-books alone, but works of almost every class produced by the South, depend upon Northern enterprise and skill for their introduction to the public. Mr. DeBow, the eminent Statistician, publishes a Southern Review, purporting to be issued from New Orleans. It is printed and bound in the city of New York. We clip the following paragraph from a recent number of the Vicksburgh (Miss.) *Whig :*—

" SOUTHERN ENTERPRIZE.—Even the Mississippi Legislature, at its late session allowed its laws to go to Boston to be printed, and made an appropriation of $3,000 to pay one of its members to go there and read the proof sheets instead of having it done in the State, and thereby assisting in building up a Southern publishing house. What a commentary on the Yankee-haters !"

The Greensboro (N. C.) *Patriot* thus records a similar contribution, on the part of that State, to " the creation of a purely Southern Literature :"

" We have heard it said, that those who had the control of the printing of the revised Statutes of North Carolina, in order to save a few dimes, had the work executed in Boston, in preference to giving the job to a citizen of this State. We impugn not the motives of the agents in this matter ; but it is a little humiliating that no work except the commonest labor, can be done in North Carolina ; that everything which requires a little skill, capital, or ingenuity, must be sent North. In the case under consideration, we have heard it remarked, that when the whole bill of expenses connected with the printing of the Revised Statutes in Boston was footed up, it only amounted to a few thousand dollars more than the job would have cost in this State. But then we have the consolation of knowing that the book *came from the North*, and that it was printed among the *abolitionists* of Boston ; the *peculiar friends* of North Carolina and the South generally.—Of course we ought to be willing to pay a few extra thousands in consideration of these important facts !"

Southern divines give us elaborate " Bible Arguments ;" Southern statists heap treatise upon treatise through which the Federal Constitution is tortured into all monstrous shapes ; Southern novelists bore us *ad infinitum* with pictures of the beatitudes of plantation life and the negro-quarters ; Southern verse-wrights drone out their drowsy dactyls or grow ventricous with their turgid heroics all in defence of slavery,—priest, politician, novelist, bardling, severally ringing the changes upon "the Biblical institution," "the conservative institution," "the humanizing institution," "the patriarchal institution"—and then—have their books printed on Northern paper, with Northern types, by Northern artizans, stitched, bound and made ready for the market by Northern industry; and yet fail to see in all this, as a true philosophical mind *must* see, an overwhelming refutation of their miserable sophisms in behalf of a system against which humanity in all its impulses and aspirations, and civilization in all its activities and triumphs, utter their perpetual protest.

From a curious article in the "American Publishers' Circular" on "Book Making in America," we give the following extracts:

"It is somewhat alarming to know that the number of houses now actually engaged in the publishing of books, not including periodicals, amounts to more than three hundred. About three-fourths of these are engaged in Boston, New-York, Philadelphia, and Baltimore—the balance being divided between Cincinnati, Buffalo, Auburn, Albany, Louisville, Chicago, St. Louis, and a few other places. There are more than three thousand book-sellers who dispense the publications of these three hundred, besides six or seven thousand apothecaries, grocers, and hardware dealers, who connect literature with drugs, molasses, and nails.

"The best printing in America is probably now done in Cambridge; the best cloth binding in Boston, and the best calf and morocco in New-York and Philadelphia. In these two latter styles we are, as yet, a long distance from Heyday, the pride of London. His finish is supreme. There is nothing between it and perfection.

"Books have multiplied to such an extent in our country, that it now takes 750 paper mills, with 2,000 engines in constant operation, to supply the printers, who work day and night, endeavoring to keep their engagements with publishers. These tireless mills produced 270,000,000 pounds of paper the past year, which immense supply has sold for about $27,000,000. A pound and a quarter of rags were required for a pound of paper, and 400,000.000 pounds were therefore consumed in this way last year. The cost of manufacturing a twelve months' supply of paper for the United States, aside from labor and rags, is computed at $4,000,000. * * *

"The Harper establishment, the largest of our publishing houses, covers half an acre of ground. If old Mr. Caxton, who printed those stories of the Trojan war so long ago, could follow the Ex-Mayor of New-York in one of his morning rounds in Franklin Square, he would be, to say the least, a little surprised. He would see in one room the floor loaded with the weight of 150 tons of presses. The electrotyping process would puzzle him somewhat; the drying and pressing process would startle him; the bustle would make his head ache; and the stock-room would quite finish him. An edition of Harpers' Monthly Magazine alone consists of 175,000. Few persons have any idea how large a number this is as applied to the edition of a book. It is computed that if these magazines were to rain down, and one man should attempt to pick them up like chips, it would take him a fortnight to pick up the copies of one single number, supposing him to pick up one every second, and to work ten hours a day."

"The rapidity with which books are now manufactured is almost incredible. A complete copy of one of Bulwer's novels, published across the water in three volumes, and reproduced here in one, was swept through the press in New-York in fifty hours, and offered for sale smoking hot in the streets. The fabulous edifice proposed by a Yankee from Vermont, no longer seems an impossibility. 'Build the establishment according to my plan,' said he; 'drive a sheep in at one end, and he shall immediately come out at the other, four quarters of lamb, a felt hat, a leather apron, and a quarto Bible.'"

17*

The business of the Messrs. Harper, whose establishment is referred to in the foregoing extract, is probably
more generally diffused over every section of this country
than that of any other publishing house. From enquiries
recently made of them we learn that they issue, on an
average, 3,000 bound volumes per day, throughout the year,
and that each volume will average 500 pages—making a
total of about one million of volumes, and not less than
five hundred millions of pages per annum. This does not
include the Magazine and books in pamphlet form, each
of which contains as much matter as a bound volume.—
Their bills for paper exceed $300,000 annually, and as the
average cost is fifteen cents per pound, they consume
more than two millions of pounds—say one thousand tons
of white paper.

There are regularly employed in their own premises
about 550 persons, including printers, binders, engravers,
and clerks. These are all paid in full once a fortnight in
bankable money. Besides these, there are numerous authors and artists in every section of the country, who furnish manuscripts and illustrations, on terms generally
satisfactory to all the parties interested.

The Magazine has a monthly circulation of between
175,000 and 200,000, or about two millions of copies annually. Each number of the Magazine is closed up about
the fifth of the month previous to its date. Three or four
days thereafter the mailing begins, commencing with
more distant subscribers, all of whom are supplied before
any copies are sold for delivery in New-York. The intention of the publishers is, that it shall be delivered as nearly

as possible on the same day in St. Louis, New-Orleans, Cincinnati, Philadelphia, Boston, and New-York. It takes from ten to twelve days to dispatch the whole edition, (which weighs between four and five tons,) by mail and express.

Their new periodical, "Harpers' Weekly," has, in a little more than four months, reached a sale of nearly 70,000 copies. The mailing of this commences on Tuesday night, and occupies about three days.

Ex-Mayor Harper, whom we have found to be one of the most affable and estimable gentlemen in the city of New-York, informed us, sometime ago, that, though he had no means of knowing positively, he was of the opinion that about eighty per cent. of all their publications find final purchasers in the free States—the remainder, about twenty per cent., in the slave States. Yet it is probable that, with one or two exceptions, no other publishing house in the country has so large a per centage of Southern trade.

Of the "more than three hundred houses engaged in the publication of books," to which the writer in the "American Publishers' Circular" refers, upwards of nine-tenths of the number are in the non-slaveholding States, and these represent not less than ninety-nine hundredths of the whole capital invested in the business. Baltimore has twice as many publishers as any other Southern city; and nearly as many as the whole South beside. The census returns of 1850 give but twenty-four publishers for the entire South, and ten of these were in Maryland. The relative disproportion which then existed in this branch of enterprise, between the North and the South, still exists ; or, if it has been changed at all, that change is in favor of the North. So of all the capital, enterprise and industry involved in the manufacture of the *material* that enters into the composition of books. All the paper manufactories of the South do not produce enough to supply a single publishing house in the city of New-York.— Perhaps "a Southern Literature" does not necessarily involve the enterprises requisite to the *manufacture* of books ; but experience has shown that there is a somewhat intimate relation between the author, printer, paper-maker and publisher ; in other words, that the intellectual activity which expresses itself in books, is measurable by the mechanical activities engaged in their manufacture.— Thus a State that is fruitful in authors will almost necessarily be fruitful in publishers ; and the number of both classes will be proportioned to the *reading* population. The poverty of Southern literature is legitimately shown, therefore, in the paucity of Southern publishers. We do not deny a high degree of cultivated talent to the South ; we are familiar with the names of her sons whose genius has made them eminent ; all that we insist upon is, that the same accursed influence which has smitten her industrial enterprises with paralysis, and retarded indefinitely her material advancement, has exerted a corresponding influence upon her literature. How it has done this we shall more fully indicate before we close the chapter.

At the " Southern Convention" held some months since at Savannah, a good deal was said about " Southern literature," and many suggestions made in reference to the best means for its promotion. One speaker thought that

" they could get text-books at home without going to either Old England or New England for them." Well—they can try. The effort will not harm them ; nor the North either. The orator was confident " that the South had talent enough to do anything that needs to be done, and independence enough to do it." The *talent* we shall not deny ; the *independence* we are ready to believe in when we see it. When she throws off the incubus of slavery under which she goes staggering like the Sailor of Bagdad under the weight of the Old Man of the Sea, she will prove her independence, and demonstrate her ability " to do anything that needs to be done." Till then she is but a fettered giant, whose vitals are torn by the dogs which her own folly has engendered.

Another speaker, on the occasion referred to, half-unconsciously it would seem, threw a gleam of light upon the subject under discussion, which, had not himself and his hearers been bat-blind, would have revealed the clue that conducts from the darkness in which they burrow to the day of redemption for the South. Said he :—

" Northern publishers employ the talent of the South and of the whole country to write for them, and pour out thousands annually for it ; but Southern men expect to get talent without paying for it. The *Southern Quarterly Review* and the *Literary Messenger* are literally struggling for existence, for want of material aid. * * * It is not the South that builds up Northern literature—*they do it themselves*. There is talent and mind and poetic genius enough in the South to build up a literature of a high order ; but Southern publishers cannot get money enough to assist them in their enterprises, and, therefore, the South has no literature."

Here are truths. " Southern men expect to get talent without paying for it." A very natural expectation, considering that they have been accustomed to have all their material wants supplied by the uncompensated toil of their slaves. In this instance it may seem an absurd one, but it results legitimately from the system of slavery. That system, in fact, operates in a two-fold way against the Southern publisher : first, by its practical repudiation of the scriptural axiom that the laborer is worthy of his hire ; and secondly, by restricting the circle of readers through the ignorance which it inevitably engenders. How is it that the people of the North build up their literature ?— Two words reveal the secret : *intelligence—compensation.* They are *a reading people*—the poorest artizan or day-laborer has his shelf of books, or his daily or weekly paper, whose contents he seldom fails to master before retiring at night ; and *they are accustomed to pay for all the books and papers which they peruse.* Readers and payers—these are the men who insure the prosperity of publishers. Where a system of enforced servitude prevails, it is very apt to beget loose notions about the obligation of paying for anything ; and many minds fail to see the distinction, morally, between compelling Sambo to pick cotton without paying him wages, or compelling Lippincott & Co. to manufacture books for the planter's pleasure or edification upon the same liberal terms. But more than this—where a system of enforced servitude prevails, a fearful degree of ignorance prevails also, as its necessary accompaniment. The enslaved masses are, of course, thrust back from the fountains of knowledge by the strong arm of law, while the poor non-slaveholding classes are almost as effectually excluded from the institutions of learning by their poverty—the sparse population of slaveholding districts being unfavorable to the maintenance of free schools, and the exigencies of their condition forbidding them to avail themselves of any more costly educational privileges.

Northern publishers can " employ the talent of the South and of the whole country to write for them, and pour out thousands annually for it," simply because a *reading* population, accustomed to *pay* for the service which it receives, enables them to do so. A similar population at the South would enable Southern publishers to do the same. Substitute free labor for slave labor, the institutions of freedom for those of slavery, and it would not long remain true that " Southern publishers cannot get money enough to assist them in their enterprises, and therefore the South has no literature." This is the discovery which the South Carolina orator from whom we quote, but narrowly escaped making, when he stood upon its very edge, and rounded his periods with the truths in whose unapprehended meanings was hidden this germ of redemption for a nation.

The self-stultification of folly, however, was never more evident than it is in the current gabble of the oligarchs about a " Southern literature." They do not mean by it a healthy, manly, normal utterance of unfettered minds, without which there can be no proper literature ; but an emasculated substitute therefor, from which the element of freedom is eliminated ; husks, from which the kernel has escaped—a body, from which the vitalizing spirit has fled—a literature which ignores manhood by confounding it with brutehood ; or, at best, deals with all similes of freedom as treason against the "peculiar institution." There is not a single great name in the literary annals of the old or new world that could drawf itself to the stature requisite to gain admission into the Pantheon erected by these devotees of the Inane for their Lilliputian deities. Thank God, a "Southern literature," in the sense intended by the champions of slavery, is a simple impossibility, rendered such by that exility of mind which they demand in its producers as a prerequisite to admission into the guild of Southern authorship. The tenuous thoughts of such authorlings could not survive a single breath of manly criticism. The history of the rise, progress, and decline of their literature could be easily written on a child's smooth palm, and leave space enough for its funeral oration and epitaph. The latter might appropriately be that which, in one of our rural districts, marks the grave of a still-born infant :—

> "If so early I am done for,
> I wonder what I was begun for !"

We desire to see the South bear its just proportion in the literary activities and achievements of our common country. It has never yet done so, and it never will until its own manhood is vindicated in the abolition of slavery. The impulse which such a measure would give to all in-dustrial pursuits that deal with the elements of material prosperity, would be imparted also to the no less valuable but more intangible creations of the mind. Take from the intellect of the South the incubus which now oppresses it, and its rebound would be glorious ; the era of its diviner inspirations would begin ; and its triumphs would be a perpetual vindication of the superiority of free institutions over those of slavery.

To Duyckinck's " Cyclopedia of American Literature—a sort of *Omnium-gatherum* that reminds one of Jeremiah's figs—we are indebted for the following facts : The whole number of " American authors" whose place of nativity is given, is five hundred and sixty-nine. Of these seventy-nine were foreign born, eighty-seven were natives of the South, and four hundred and three—a vast majority of the whole, first breathed the vital air in the free North. Many of those who were born in the South, received their education in the North, quite a number of whom became permanent residents thereof. Still, for the purposes of this computation, we count them on the side of the South. Yet how significant the comparison which this computation furnishes i Throwing the foreign born (adopted citizens, mostly residents of the North) out of the reckoning, and the record stands,—Northern authors *four hundred and three;* Southern, *eighty-seven*—a difference of three hundred and sixteen in favor of the North ! And this, probably, indicates very fairly the relative intellectual activity of the two sections.

We accept the facts gleaned from Duyckinck's work as a basis, simply, of our estimate : not as being absolutely accurate in themselves, though they are doubtless reliable in the main, and certainly as fair for the South as they are for the North. We might dissent from the judgment of the compiler in reference to the propriety of applying the term "literature" to much that his compilation contains ; but as tastes have proverbially differed from the days of the venerable dame who kissed her cow —not to extend our researches into the condition of things anterior to that interesting event—we will not insist upon *our* view of the matter, but take it for granted that he has disentombed from forgotten reviews, newspapers, pamphlets, and posters, a fair relative proportion of "authors" for both North and South, for which "American Literature" is unquestionably under infinite obligations to him !

Griswold's "Poets and Poetry of America" and Thomas Buchanan Read's "Female Poets of America" furnish evidence, equally conclusive, of the benumbing influence of slavery upon the intellect of a country. Of course, these compilers say nothing about Slavery, and probably never thought of it in connection with their respective works, but none the less significant on that account is the testimony of the *facts* which they give. From the last edition of Griswold's compilation, (which contains the names of none of our female writers, he having included them in a separate volume) we find the names of one hundred and forty-one writers of verse : of these *one* was foreign-born, *seventeen* natives of the slaveholding, and *one hundred and twenty-three* of the non-slaveholding States. Of our female poets, whose nativity is given by Mr. Read, *eleven* are natives of the South ; and *seventy-three* of the North ! These simple arithmetical figures are God's eternal Scripture against the folly and madness of Slavery, and need no aid of rhetoric to give emphasis to the startling eloquence of their revelations.

But, after all, literature is not to be estimated by cubic

feet or pounds averdupois, nor measured by the bushel or
the yardstick. Quality, rather than quantity, is the true
standard of estimation. The fact, however, matters little
for our present purpose ; for the South, we are sorry to
say, is as much behind the North in the former as in the
latter. We do not forget the names of Gayarre, Benton,
Simms, and other eminent citizens of the Slave States,
who have by their contributions to American letters conferred honor upon themselves and upon our common country, when we affirm, that those among our authors who
enjoy a cosmopolitan reputation, are, with a few honorable exceptions, natives of the Free North ; and that the
names which most brilliantly illustrate our literature, in
its every department, are those which have grown into
greatness under the nurturing influence of free institutions. " Comparisons are odious," it is said ; and we will
not, unnecessarily, render them more so, in the present
instance, by contrasting, name by name, the literary men
of the South with the literary men of the North. We do
not depreciate the former, nor overestimate the latter.
But let us ask, whence come our geographers, our astron-
omers, our chemists, our meteorologists, our ethnologists,
and others, who have made their names illustrious in the
domain of the Natural Sciences ? Not from the Slave
States, certainly. In the Literature of Law, the South
can furnish no name that can claim peership with those of
Story and of Kent ; in History, none that tower up to the
altitude of Bancroft, Prescott, Hildreth, Motley and Washington Irving ; in Theology, none that can challenge
favorable comparison with those of Edwards, Dwight,

Channing, Taylor, Bushnell, Tyler and Wayland : in Fiction, none that take rank with Cooper, and Mrs. Stowe ; and but few that may do so with even the second class novelists of the North ;* in Poetry, none that can command position with Bryant, Halleck, and Percival, with Whittier, Longfellow, and Lowell, with Willis, Stoddard and Taylor, with Holmes, Saxe, and Burleigh ; and—we might add twenty other Northern names before we found their Southern peer, with the exception of poor Poe, who, within a narrow range of subjects, showed himself a poet of consummate art, and occupies a sort of debatable ground between our first and second-class writers.

We might extend this comparison to our writers in every department of letters, from the compiler of school-books to the author of the most profound ethical treatise, and with precisely the same result. But we forbear. The task is distasteful to our State pride, and would have been entirely avoided had not a higher principle urged us to its performance. It remains for us now to enquire,

WHAT HAS PRODUCED THIS LITERARY PAUPERISM OF THE SOUTH ? One single word, most pregnant in its terrible meanings, answers the question. That word is—SLAVERY ! But we have been so long accustomed to the ugly thing itself, and have become so familiar with its no less ugly fruits, that the common mind fails to apprehend the connection between the one, as cause, and the other as effect ; and

---

* We Southrons all glory in the literary reputation of Mr. Simms; yet we must confess his inferiority to Cooper, and prejudice alone will refuse to admit, that, while in the *art* of the novelist he is the superior of Mrs. Stowe 'n genius he must take position below her.

it therefore becomes necessary to give a more detailed answer to our interrogatory.

Obviously, then, the conditions requisite to a flourishing literature are wanting at the South. These are—

I. Readers. The people of the South are not a reading people. Many of the adult population never learned to read ; still more, do not care to read. We have been impressed, during a temporary sojourn in the North, with the difference between the middle and laboring classes in the Free States, and the same classes in the Slave States, in this respect. Passing along the great routes of travel in the former, or taking our seat in the comfortable cars that pass up and down the avenues of our great commercial metropolis, we have not failed to contrast the employment of our fellow-passengers with that which occupies the attention of the corresponding classes on our various Southern routes of travel. In the one case, a large proportion of the passengers seem intent upon mastering the contents of the newspaper, or some recently published book. The merchant, the mechanic, the artizan, the professional man, and even the common laborer, going to or returning from their daily avocations, are busy with their morning or evening paper, or engaged in an intelligent discussion of some topic of public interest. This is their leisure hour, and it is given to the acquisition of such information as may be of immediate or ultimate use, or to the cultivation of a taste for elegant literature. In the other case, newspapers and books seem generally ignored, and noisy discussions of village and State politics, the tobacco and cotton-crops, filibusterism in Cuba, Nicaragua, or Sonora, the price of negroes generally, and especially of "fine-looking wenches," the beauties of lynch-law, the delights of horse-racing, the excitement of street fights with bowie-knives and revolvers, the "manifest destiny" theory that justifies the stealing of all territory contiguous to our own, and kindred topics, constitute the warp and woof of conversation. All this is on a level with the general intelligence of the Slave States. It is true, these States have their educated men,—the majority of whom owe their literary culture to the colleges of the North. Not that there are no Southern colleges—for there are institutions, so called, in a majority of the Slave States.— Some of them, too, are not deficient in the appointments requisite to our higher educational institutions ; but as a general thing, Southern colleges are colleges only in *name*, and will scarcely take rank with a third-rate Northern academy, while our academies, with a few exceptions, are immeasurably inferior to the public schools of New-York, Philadelphia, and Boston. The truth is, there is a vast inert mass of stupidity and ignorance, too dense for individual effort to enlighten or remove, in all communities cursed with the institution of slavery. Disguise the unwelcome truth as we may, slavery is the parent of ignorance, and ignorance begets a whole brood of follies and of vices, and every one of these is inevitably hostile to literary culture. The masses, if they think of literature at all, think of it only as a costly luxury, to be monopolized by the few.

The proportion of white adults over twenty years of age,

in each State, who cannot read and write, to the *whole* white population, is as follows :

Connecticut,	1 to every	568	Louisiana,	1 to every	38½
Vermont,	1 "	473	Maryland	1 "	27
N. Hampshire,	1 "	310	Mississippi,	1 "	20
Massachusetts,	1 "	166	Delaware,	1 "	18
Maine,	1 "	108	South Carolina,	1 "	17
Michigan,	1 "	97	Missouri,	1 "	16
Rhode Island,	1 "	67	Alabama,	1 "	15
New Jersey,	1 "	58	Kentucky,	1 "	13½
New York,	1 "	56	Georgia,	1 "	13
Pennsylvania,	1 "	50	Virginia,	1 "	12½
Ohio,	1 "	43	Arkansas,	1 "	11½
Indiana,	1 "	18	Tennessee,	1 "	11
Illinois,	1 "	17	North Carolina,	1 "	7

In this table, Illinois and Indiana are the only Free States which, in point of education, are surpassed by any of the Slave States ; and this disgraceful fact is owing, principally, to the influx of foreigners, and to immigrants from the Slave States. New-York, Rhode Island, and Pennsylvania have also a large foreign element in their population, that swells very considerably this percentage of ignorance. For instance, New-York shows, by the last census, a population of 98,722 who cannot read and write, and of this number 68,052 are foreigners ; Rhode Island, 3,607, of whom 2,359 are foreigners ; Pennsylvania, 76,272, of whom 24,989 are foreigners. On the other hand, the ignorance of the Slave States is principally *native* ignorance, but comparatively few emigrants from Europe seeking a home upon a soil cursed with "the peculiar institution." North Carolina has a foreign population of only 340, South Carolina only 104, Arkansas only 27, Tennessee only 505, and Virginia only 1,137, who cannot read and write ; while the aggregate of *native* ignorance in these five States (exclusive of the *slaves*, who are debarred all education by *law*) is 278,948 ! No longer ago than 1837, Governor Clarke, of Kentucky, in his message to the Legislature of that State, declared that "by the computation of those most familiar with the subject, *one-third of the adult population of the State are unable to write their names ;*" and Governor Campbell, of Virginia, reported to the Legislature, that "from the returns of ninety-eight clerks, it appeared that of 4,614 applications for marriage licenses in 1837, no less than 1,047 were made by men unable to write."

In the Slave States the proportion of free white children between the ages of five and twenty, who are found at any school or college, is not quite *one-fifth* of the whole ; in the Free States, the proportion is more than *three-fifths*.

We could fill our pages with facts like these to an almost indefinite extent, but it cannot be necessary. No truth is more demonstrable, nay, no truth has been more abundantly demonstrated, than this : that Slavery is hostile to general education ; its strength, its very life, is in the ignorance and stolidity of the masses ; it naturally and necessarily represses general literary culture. To talk, therefore, of the " creation of a purely Southern Literature," without *readers* to demand, or *writers* to produce it, is the mere babble of idiocy.

II. Another thing essential to the creation of a literature is MENTAL FREEDOM. How much of *that* is to be found in the region of Slavery ? We will not say that there is *none;* but if it exists, it exists as the outlawed antagonist of human chattelhood. He who believes that the despotism of the accursed institution expends its malignant forces upon the *slave,* leaving intact the white and (so called) free population, is the victim of a most monstrous delusion. One end of the yoke that bows the African to the dust, presses heavily upon the neck of his Anglo-Saxon master. The entire mind of the South either stultifies itself into acquiescence with Slavery, succumbs to its authority, or chafes in indignant protest against its monstrous pretensions and outrageous usurpations. A free press is an institution almost unknown at the South. Free speech is considered as treason against slavery : and when people dare neither speak nor print their thoughts, free thought itself is well nigh extinguished. All that can be said in *defence* of human bondage, may be spoken freely ; but question either its morality or its policy, and the terrors of lynch law are at once invoked to put down the pestilent heresy. The legislation of the Slave States for the suppression of the freedom of speech and the press, is disgraceful and cowardly to the last degree, and can find its parallel only in the meanest and bloodiest despotisms of the Old World. No institution that could bear the light would thus sneakingly seek to burrow itself in utter darkness. Look, too, at the mobbings, lynchings, robberies, social and political proscriptions, and all manner of nameless outrages, to which men in the South have been subjected, simply upon the suspicion that they were the enemies of Slavery. We could fill **page**

18

after page of this volume with the record of such atrocities. But a simple reference to them is enough. Our
countrymen have not yet forgotten why John C. Under-
wood was, but a few months since, banished from his
home in Virginia, and the accomplished Hedreck driven
from his College professorship in North Carolina. They
believed Slavery inimical to the best interest of the South,
and for daring to give expression to this belief in moderate yet manly language, they were ostracised by the
despotic Slave Power, and compelled to seek a refuge
from its vengeance in States where the principles of freedom are better understood. Pending the last Presidential election, there were thousands, nay, tens of thousands
of voters in the Slave States, who desired to give their
suffrages for the Republican nominee, John C. Fremont,
himself a Southron, but a non-slaveholder. The Constitution of the United States guaranteed to these men an
expression of their preference at the ballot-box. But were
they permitted such an expression? Not at all. They
were denounced, threatened, overawed, by the Slave
Power—and it is not too much to say that there was
really no *Constitutional election,*—that is, no such free expression of political preferences as the Constitution aims
to secure—in a majority of the Slave States.

From a multiplicity of facts like these, the inference is
unavoidable, that Slavery tolerates no freedom of the
press—no freedom of speech—no freedom of opinion. To
expect that a whole-souled, manly literature can flourish
under such conditions, is as absurd as it would be to look
for health amid the pestilential vapors of a dungeon, or

for the continuance of animal life without the aid of oxygen.

III. Mental activity—force—enterprise—are requisite to the creation of literature. Slavery tends to sluggishness—imbecility—inertia. Where free thought is treason, the masses will not long take the trouble of thinking at all. Desuetude begets incompetence—the *dare-not* soon becomes the *cannot*. The mind thus enslaved, necessarily loses its interest in the processes of other minds ; and its tendency is to sink down into absolute stolidity or sottishness. Our remarks find melancholy confirmation in the abject servilism in which multitudes of the non-slaveholding whites of the South are involved. In them, ambition, pride, self-respect, hope, seem alike extinct. Their slaveholding fellows are, in some respects, in a still more unhappy condition—helpless, nerveless, ignorant, selfish ; yet vain-glorious, self-sufficient and brutal. Are these the chosen architects who are expected to build up " a purely Southern literature ?"

The truth is, slavery destroys, or vitiates, or pollutes, whatever it touches. No interest of society escapes the influence of its clinging curse. It makes Southern religion a stench in the nostrils of Christendom—it makes Southern politics a libel upon all the principles of Republicanism— it makes Southern literature a travesty upon the honorable profession of letters. Than the better class of Southern authors themselves, none will feel more keenly the truth of our remarks. They write books, but can find for them neither publishers nor remunerative sales at the South The executors of Calhoun seek, for his works, a

Northern publisher. Benton writes history and prepares voluminous compilations, which are given to the world through a Northern publisher. Simms writes novels and poems, and they are scattered abroad from the presses of a Northern publisher. Eighty per cent. of all the copies sold are probably bought by Northern readers.

When will Southern authors understand their own interests? When will the South, as a whole, abandoning its present suicidal policy, enter upon that career of prosperity, greatness, and true renown, to which God by his word and his providences, is calling it? " If thou take away from the midst of thee the yoke, the putting forth of the finger and speaking vanity ; and if thou draw out thy soul to the hungry and satisfy the afflicted soul ; then shall thy light rise in obscurity and thy darkness be as the noonday : And the Lord shall guide thee continually and satisfy thy soul in drought, and make fat thy bones ; and thou shalt be like a watered garden, and like a spring of water, whose waters fail not. And they that shall be of thee shall build the old waste places ; thou shalt raise up the foundations of many generations ; and thou shalt be called, The repairer of the breach, The restorer of paths to dwell in."

Our limits, not our materials, are exhausted. We would gladly say more, but can only, in conclusion, add as the result of our investigations in this department of our subject, that *Literature and Liberty are inseparable ; the one can never have a vigorous existence without being wedded to the other.*

Our work is done. It is the voice of the non-slaveholding whites of the South, through one identified with them by interest, by feeling, by position. That voice, by whomsoever spoken, must yet be heard and heeded. The time hastens—the doom of slavery is written—the redemption of the South draws nigh.

In taking leave of our readers, we know not how we can give more forcible expression to our thoughts and intentions than by saying that, in concert with the intelligent free voters of the North, we, the non-slaveholding whites of the South, expect to elevate JOHN C. FREMONT, CASSIUS M. CLAY, JAMES G. BIRNEY, or some other Southern non-slaveholder, to the Presidency in 1860 ; and that the patriot thus elevated to that dignified station will, through our cordial co-operation, be succeeded by WILLIAM H. SEWARD, CHARLES SUMNER, JOHN McLEAN, or some other non-slaveholder of the North ;—and furthermore, that if, in these or in any other similar cases, the oligarchs do not quietly submit to the will of a constitutional majority of the people, as expressed at the ballot-box, the first battle between freedom and slavery will be fought at home—and may God defend the right !

THE END.

NOTES
INDEX

NOTES

1. All of this paragraph, except the first sentence, was left out of the *Compendium*, presumably to make less obvious the contradiction between Helper's abolitionism and the "free soil" doctrines of the Republican Party.

2. William Cooke Taylor, born in Dublin in 1800, was a British historian, biographer, and economist. As the passage quoted by Helper would indicate, he was an early statistician and proponent of statistical studies. In 1847 he was appointed a statistical writer for the British government. Helper may have been influenced, not only by Taylor's appeal for statistics as determining the course of "the science of political economy," but also by the promotional uses to which he put his statistical knowledge. Taylor was a Whig and a strong proponent of British industrialization.

3. James Dunwoody Brownson De Bow (1820–1867) was a leading promoter of Southern economic development. As the editor of *De Bow's Review*, he called for investment in Southern manufactures and improved agricultural methods. He was also a fervent defender of slavery and increasingly, as the sectional conflict grew in intensity in the 1840's and '50s, he opened his magazine to militant proslavery opinions. He maintained—and here is where Helper disagreed violently— that Negro slavery was compatible with a diversified economy and a rapid growth of manufacturing.

4. Thomas Ritchie, Sr. (1778–1854), editor of the *Richmond Enquirer* (originally called the *Examiner*) from 1804 to

1845, was, as subsequent passages reveal, Helper's major symbol for Virginia's apostasy from the antislavery views of the founding fathers and a man whose reputation Helper sought to blacken in every possible way.

5. See p. 218 for Helper's full description of the Mecklenburg "Declaration of Independence."

6. Modern historians have determined that the first slaves probably arrived in August 1619 rather than 1620.

7. Recent historical studies, especially Robert McColley, *Slavery and Jeffersonian Virginia* (Urbana, Ill., 1964), would indicate that Helper overestimated the depth and extent of opposition to slavery in Virginia during the Revolutionary period.

8. No evidence has come to light which would substantiate Helper's charge that bribery was involved in the outcome of the Virginia slavery debate of 1831–1832. The most careful study of these debates, Joseph Clarke Robert, *The Road From Monticello: A Study of the Virginia Slavery Debate of 1832* (Durham, N.C., 1941), describes the defeat of antislavery resolutions as a natural consequence of the dominance of slaveholding interests in the Virginia legislature.

9. These charges of personal malfeasance against Thomas Ritchie, Sr., are of doubtful validity, a fact which may have influenced Helper in his decision to leave them out of the *Compendium*. Ritchie, of course, is the ——— ———, referred to on p. 104. The cabinet officer who is implicated in what Helper describes as the corrupt transaction which led to the founding of the *Washington Union* is Robert John Walker of Mississippi, who was Polk's secretary of the treasury. Ritchie's biographer, C. H. Ambler (*Thomas Ritchie: A Study in Virginia Politics*, Richmond, 1913), claims on good evidence that Ritchie was very reluctant to assume the editorship of the *Union* as an organ for the Polk administration and was more-or-less drafted for the position. He claims further that Ritchie had no knowledge whatever of the transactions and arrangements that led to the founding of the *Union*.

Helper is on firmer ground when he suggests that the purchase of the *Globe* and the founding of the *Union* indicated that the national leadership of the Democratic Party was assuming a more openly proslavery position.

10. It is doubtful that Lawrence actually made the trip described by Helper. Hamilton Andrews Hill in his *Memoir of Abbott Lawrence* (Boston, 1883) explicitly denies Helper's story, claiming that the overtures came from Virginia and that Lawrence failed to respond simply because "vast interests were at stake nearer home." (pp. 34–35)

11. This is another attack on Thomas Ritchie, Sr., who died in 1854 and was buried in Hollywood Cemetery. This paragraph was not included in the *Compendium*.

12. Daniel R. Goodloe (1814–1902) was Helper's principal precursor as an economic critic of slavery in North Carolina (see my Introduction, p. xlii). After publishing his *Inquiry into the Causes Which Have Retarded the Accumulation of Wealth and Increase of Population in the Southern States* in 1841, Goodloe found himself unpopular in North Carolina and went to Washington, D.C., where he was first a government clerk and then an editor of the moderate antislavery paper, *The National Era*. In 1858, he published another pamphlet, *The Southern Platform* (Boston, 1858), which resembles Chapter III of *The Impending Crisis* in that it is essentially a compilation of Southern antislavery opinion of a previous era. After the Civil War, Goodloe played a minor role in North Carolina Reconstruction, first supporting the Radical regime and then turning against it.

13. The passage beginning, "Do you aspire to become the victims of white non-slave-holding vengeance by day, and of barbarous massacre by negroes at night," (p. 128), and ending with " 'the mother of harlots,' " was left out of the *Compendium*. But it was nevertheless the section most frequently cited by Southerners to support their claim that the Re-

publicans, by endorsing Helper's book, had revealed their design to foster insurrection in the South.

14. The section beginning, "As a striking illustration of the selfish and debasing influences . . ." (p. 138) and ending "the idle zephyr of summer" was left out of the *Compendium*.

15. This paragraph was not included in the *Compendium*.

16. This paragraph was not included in the *Compendium*.

17. In the *Compendium* the date for the abolition of slavery in the South was changed to 1870.

18. This section beginning "From the eleventh year previous to the close of the eighteenth century," and ending, ". . . never before was there such an appropriate period to strike for freedom in the South" was left out of the *Compendium*.

19. Proposals 5, 8, 9, 10, 11 were not included in the *Compendium*.

20. Most of the names in this list are of Southern Whig politicians who at some point in their careers had either taken a moderate antislavery stand or had at least refused to endorse the militant proslavery position. John Minor Botts (1802–1869) was a notable renegade, who, as a Whig Congressman from Virginia, supported the efforts of John Quincy Adams to repeal the Gag resolutions, voted for the Compromise of 1850, and voted against the Kansas-Nebraska act. Bott's guiding principles were free speech, sectional harmony, and non-extension of slavery. Alexander H. H. Stuart (1807–1891) was a prominent Virginia Whig and supporter of Henry Clay who served one term in Congress and was secretary of the interior during the Taylor-Fillmore administration. In 1860, he was a vigorous opponent of secession. "Raynor" is undoubtedly Kenneth Rayner (1810–1884), a North Carolina Whig Congressman who continued to argue that slavery was at best a necessary evil long after this approach had ceased to be fashionable in the South. In general Rayner took the Whig

position that any agitation of the slavery issue should be discouraged, and he was equally opposed to abolitionists and Southern "fire-eaters." John Motley Moorehead (1796–1866) was the Whig governor of North Carolina from 1841 to 1845. William A. Graham (1804–1875) was another prominent North Carolina Whig who succeeded Moorehead as governor after serving three years in U.S. Senate. In 1852 he ran for vice president of the United States as the Whig nominee. Edward Stanly (1810–1872) was a North Carolina Whig Congressman from 1837 to 1843 and an outspoken Unionist. Henry Winter Davis (1817–1865) was a prominent Maryland politician who was successively a Whig, a Know-nothing, and a Republican. Francis P. Blair, Jr. (1821–1875) and Thomas Hart Benton (1782–1858) of Missouri were leading free soil Democrats at the time of the writing of *The Impending Crisis*. Blair, however, was soon to become a Republican. Benton, a Democratic Senator for thirty years, had recently been retired from public office largely because his free soil views were unpopular in Missouri. "The Marshalls of Kentucky" are probably Humphrey Marshall (1812–1872), a Whig Congressman from 1849 to 1852, and T. A. Marshall, also a Whig, who served in the House of Representatives from 1831 to 1835 and was a justice of the Kentucky Court of Appeals from 1835 to 1856. Emerson Etheridge of Tennessee served in Congress from 1847 to 1857, first as a Whig and then as a Know-nothing. The other names in Helper's list of potential Southern opponents of slavery are not readily identifiable.

21. This paragraph was not included in the *Compendium*.

22. This paragraph was not included in the *Compendium*.

23. See my Introduction, pp. xlii and xliii, for a discussion of Cassius M. Clay as a Southern critic of slavery.

24. Helper is referring to Judge William Gaston who was associate justice of the North Carolina Supreme Court from 1833 to 1844. The speech which Helper claims was suppressed was a commencement address delivered at the University of North

422

Carolina in 1832 and entitled "The Duties of Citizenship." In this address Gaston made the following statement: "Disguise the truth as we may and throw the blame where we will, it is slavery which, more than any other cause, keeps us back in the career of improvement. It stifles industry and suppresses enterprise; it is fatal to economy and prudence; it discourages skill, impairs our strength as a community, and poisons morals at the fountain head." (Quoted in John Herman Schauinger, "William Gaston and the Supreme Court of North Carolina," *North Carolina Historical Review*, 21 [April 1944] 107.) As a justice of the North Carolina Supreme Court Gaston was noted for his acknowledgement of the slave's right "to defend himself against the unlawful attempt of his master to deprive him of life." (Quoted from one of Gaston's decisions, *ibid.*, p. 109).

25. Helper is quoting William Henry Hurlbert (1827–1895) who was born William Henry Hurlbut but changed his name early in his career. Hurlbert was born in Charleston, the son of a Unitarian Minister from Massachusetts. He graduated from Harvard College in 1847 and subsequently attended both the Harvard Divinity School and the Harvard Law School. After a short period as a Unitarian minister, he began a career as a Northern journalist and in 1855 became a staff writer for *Putnam's Magazine*. In 1857 he joined the staff of the *New York Times*. In only the most attenuated sense was he, as Helper would have us believe, a South Carolina critic of slavery. Hurlbert was a South Carolinian only by accident of birth. By family tradition and personal inclination, he was a Northerner and his sympathies were to be with the Union during the Civil War. The high point of his later career was his editorship of the *New York World* from 1876 to 1883.

26. Benjamin F. Perry (1805–1886) was an important figure in South Carolina politics in the ante-bellum period. Along with James L. Orr, he spoke for the under-represented uplands and vigorously opposed the policies of the dominant low-country aristocracy. He was a Unionist, favored affiliation with the

national Democratic party, and advocated democratic reforms in state institutions—a program which was anathema to the ruling group in state politics. After the Civil War, Perry served as provisional Governor of South Carolina under Presidential Reconstruction and later became known as a bitter opponent of Radical Reconstruction.

27. Helper is probably referring to Josiah Priest, *Bible Defense of Slavery; and Origin, Fortunes, and History of the Negro Race* (Glasgow, Ky., 1852).

28. Benjamin Sherwood Hedrick was dismissed as professor of chemistry at the University of North Carolina for admitting in 1856 that he would vote for Frémont, the Republican candidate for President, if Frémont's name were placed on the ballot.

29. William Gregg of South Carolina was the most significant promoter of textile manufacturing in the Old South. He was one of the earliest to argue that employment in industry was the path of social and economic salvation for the South's "poor whites."

INDEX

THE JOHN HARVARD LIBRARY

*The intent of
Waldron Phoenix Belknap, Jr.,
as expressed in an early will, was for
Harvard College to use the income from a
permanent trust fund he set up, for "editing and
publishing rare, inaccessible, or hitherto unpublished
source material of interest in connection with the
history, literature, art (including minor and useful
art), commerce, customs, and manners or way of
life of the Colonial and Federal Periods of the United
States . . . In all cases the emphasis shall be on the
presentation of the basic material." A later testament
broadened this statement, but Mr. Belknap's interests remained constant until his death.*

*In linking the name of the first benefactor of
Harvard College with the purpose of this later,
generous-minded believer in American culture the
John Harvard Library seeks to emphasize the importance of Mr. Belknap's purpose. The John Harvard
Library of the Belknap Press of Harvard University
Press exists to make books and documents
about the American past more readily
available to scholars and the
general reader.*